LOUISBOURG

FROM ITS FOUNDATION TO ITS FALL

1713–1758

Canadian Cataloguing in Publication Data

McLennan, J. S. (John Stewart), 1853-1939
  Louisbourg from its foundation to its fall, 1713-1758

Originally publ.: London: Macmillan, 1918.
ISBN 0-9690177-5-8

  1. Louisbourg (N.S.) – History.   2. Louisbourg
(N.S.) – History – Siege, 1745.   3. Louisbourg
(N.S.) – History – Siege, 1758.   I. Title.
II. Book Room Limited.

FC2349.L6M34 1990   971.6'95501   C90-090312-0
F1039.5.L8M34 1990

FIRST PUBLISHED 1918 BY
MACMILLAN & CO. LTD., LONDON

THIRD EDITION 1969 BY
FORTRESS PRESS

FOURTH EDITION 1979 BY
THE BOOK ROOM LIMITED
HALIFAX, NOVA SCOTIA B3J 2N7

REPRINTED 1983
(with additional foreword pp. iv and v)

TO THE MEMORY

OF MY SON

HUGH McLENNAN

BORN IN CAPE BRETON, JANUARY 27, 1886

WHO, A STUDENT AT THE BEAUX-ARTS, PARIS, ENLISTED

IN AUGUST 1914 IN THE CANADIAN FIELD ARTILLERY,

AND WAS KILLED IN ACTION NEAR YPRES, APRIL 27, 1915

I DEDICATE THIS BOOK

PRINTED AND BOUND IN CANADA BY
GAGNE PRINTING LTD.
LOUISEVILLE

PART OF THE ISLAND OF CAPE BRETON

THE HARBOUR

A survey of the City and Fortress of Louisbourg at the Second Siege, 1758

(author: William Bontain — photo courtesy William L. Clements Library, University of Michigan.)

LOUISBOURG

FROM ITS FOUNDATION
TO ITS FALL

1713–1758

BY

J. S. McLENNAN

WITH ILLUSTRATIONS

THE BOOK ROOM LIMITED
HALIFAX, NOVA SCOTIA, CANADA
B3J 2N7
1979

FOREWORD

JOHN STEWART McLENNAN, 1853-1939

J. S. McLennan's *Louisbourg From Its Foundation To Its Fall* is in several ways a remarkable book. To begin with, it is because of its continuing popularity. Though it was first published over six decades ago, it remains the standard work on the 45 year history of the French settlement at Louisbourg. Dozens, perhaps hundreds, of detailed studies have been done on Louisbourg since McLennan's appeared, each one illuminating some theme or aspect of life there, but none has replaced it as the authoritative chronicle of the town's history. First published in 1918, re-editions have appeared in 1957, 1969, 1979, and now in 1983.

McLennan's achievement in writing such a lasting book is all the more remarkable when one realizes that he undertook the project largely as an avocation. He had first come to Cape Breton from Montreal in 1882 to look into a difficulty at one of the coal mines. He ended up making his home in the area, becoming an important industrialist, first in coal and then in iron and steel. Following a brief retirement at the turn of the century McLennan embarked on a new career in 1904, as a newspaper publisher, when he purchased the Sydney *Post* (which later merged with another paper to become the *Post-Record*). A dozen years later he was named to the Canadian Senate.

J. S. McLennan's interest in Louisbourg was kindled in 1882, when he first toured the ruins. During the 1890s McLennan and his family spent their summers at Louisbourg (and the rest of the time in Boston where he was the agent for a coal company), where he came into close contact with local Anglican Archdeacon T. F. Draper. It was Draper who aroused the industrialist's interest in writing a book on the French period. McLennan was unable to do any serious research on the 18th century history of the town until his "retirement" in 1900; thereafter he devoted what time he could to the project and made annual visits to archives in Paris, London and Boston. His first historical paper on Louisbourg was presented to the Nova Scotia Historical Society in 1908, and published the following year. In 1914 he contributed an article, "Louisbourg: an outpost of empire", to the well-known series on Canadian history, *Canada and Its Provinces*. Later that same year he completed the manuscript of his major study, *Louisbourg From Its Foundation To Its Fall*, and submitted it as requested to the Champlain Society. However, the manuscript was rejected because it was not simply a collection of documents, so McLennan turned instead to the publishing house of Macmillan, which brought it out in 1918. Over the next few years favourable reviews of the book appeared in the *Canadian Historical Review*, *English Historical Review*, *Transactions of the Royal Society of Canada*, *Dalhousie Review*, and many more journals and newspapers.

That someone who had spent much of his adult life dealing with matters pertaining to the marketing and production of coal and steel could turn out a first-rate study of a vanished 18th century French town is not too surprising, when one considers J. S. McLennan's background. He was one of those cultured gentleman of the late Victorian and Edwardian eras who had wide-ranging interests in art, business, history, social progress, the development of a national identity, and many more areas. In 1923-24 he lectured at Mount Allison

University on history and present problems; in subsequent years he gave lectures in Montreal, Halifax and Sydney on Italian art and Louisbourg. The *Montreal Standard* described him as "the most polished and cosmopolitan type of Canadian". Following his death on the eve of World War II his fellow Senators paid tribute to his "gentlemanly instincts", "wide reading" and "devotion to public business".

J. S. McLennan came by his cosmopolitan background easily. He was born in Montreal, then raised in Chicago where his father was involved in the grain trade, and then spent his adolescence back in Montreal. He graduated from McGill in 1874 with first-rank honours in Mental and Moral Philosophy and went on to Cambridge, where he took a second B.A., this time in Moral Sciences. Although academic life held definite attractions for McLennan, he decided to join his father's grain trade business in Montreal. He remained there until the early 1880s when he relocated to Cape Breton. Long periods of residence in Boston and later Ottawa, combined with frequent trips to Great Britain, France and Italy, gave him the broadest possible perspective on his life and work. After 1900 McLennan's home, when in Cape Breton, was at his Petersfield estate, across the harbour from Sydney.

One of the areas that remained important to J. S. McLennan during his later years was Louisbourg. Throughout the 1920s and 1930s the Senator urged the federal government to acquire the historic site and develop it into a major outdoor museum and tourist attraction. From his years of research on the fortress town he knew that "there is abundant material for an almost complete reconstruction of the town and its fortifications". Little did he dream, however, that in the 1960s such a reconstruction would actually take place, if only for one quarter of the original town. The most that he had advocated was a partial rebuilding of selected buildings and parts of the fortifications.

J. S. McLennan's daughter Katherine carried on at Louisbourg after his death. For a quarter of a century Katherine McLennan was the Honorary Curator of the Louisbourg Museum, constructed in 1935-36. During that period she wrote the Park brochure, catalogued the artifact collection, organized the displays, made a large model of the 18th century town, and handled the many day-to-day problems which arose. Like her father, all such efforts were undertaken with a commitment to excellence and without any remuneration.

The closing comment belongs to John Stewart McLennan's friend and fellow historical enthusiast, Dr. J. C. Webster of Shebac. It was Dr. Webster's heartfelt opinion that J. S. McLennan stood apart from most of his contemporaries. As he put it: "Few men in Canadian business life have equalled Senator McLennan in combining business acumen and enterprise with long-continued cultivation of mind and absorption in the arts, literature, or other spheres of interest not concerned with material considerations."

A. J. B. Johnston
Historian, Fortress of Louisbourg.

FOREWORD

JOHN STEWART McLENNAN, 1853-1939

John McLennan's grandfather came to Canada from Ross in Scotland in 1802. After some changes of abode in Canada, his father settled in Montreal and engaged in the grain trade. The family was large, John being the eldest son. He was educated at the Montreal High School and McGill University, graduating in 1875 with Honours in Philosophy, and the Governor General's Gold Medal. The Governor General at that date was Lord Dufferin. He then went on to Cambridge University, England, to Trinity Hall, one of the smallest and oldest of the colleges, and graduated with Honours in Moral Science in 1879. Returning home he went into his father's office to learn the intricacies of the grain trade. Seven years passed and his routine was broken, temporarily it was thought, by a trip to Cape Breton to look into, and possibly straighten out, some difficulty in one of the mines of the International Coal Co., of which his father was a founder and director. One decision he made was to live in Cape Breton, in Sydney, with his wife and young family. He became manager of the Old International Mine, Lingan, until, in the nineties, he was made agent for the company in Boston. During the Boston period of some nine years the family spent the summers at Louisbourg, occupying a house, in Victorian Gothic style, standing on rising ground overlooking the harbour entrance, and beyond to the low peninsula where the French fortress had once stood, known as "The Old Town". The new town was two and a half miles around the harbour with a population of a few hundred; its industry fishing. A coal pier for loading ships in winter as the harbour stays unfrozen, provided some work. Among the clergy in the town was Archdeacon Draper, an exceptionally well educated Englishman; he it was who aroused John McLennan's interest in Louisbourg's history. *Louisbourg From Its Foundation To Its Fall* was written at the request of the Champlain Society which, at intervals, issues volumes on Canadian history. Shortly before the First World War the book was finished, but given the Society's policy of publishing only contemporary annotated documents, *Louisbourg* was not acceptable. McLennan had it brought out by Macmillan & Co. Ltd. of London in 1918.

It was dedicated to his only son, Hugh, student in Architecture at the Beaux, Paris, killed at the Second Battle of Ypres, 1916, Sergeant, 5th Battery, R.C.A.

In 1928 the "Old Town" was set aside as a National Historic Site, and in 1935 a museum was built. In 1960 the Royal Commission on Coal recommended that the Federal Government, to give employment and to attract tourists, should re-construct certain buildings.

Let us glance at the famous historian Francis Parkman's description of the site as he saw it in the early 1880s; he describes the stormy sea, the calm little harbour, the green mounds, the grazing sheep, the two small farmhouses of the Old Town's only inhabitants. If he could return today he would stand in the shadow of the re-erected Chateau St. Louis and could not but be impressed as we are by it and the massive walls of the King's Bastion.

Katherine McLennan

Sydney, N.S.

vi

The reconstruction of the Fortress of Louisbourg was begun in 1961 under the auspices of the Department of Indian Affairs and Northern Development, National and Historic Parks Branch. By 1968 the Chateau St. Louis and King's Bastion had been rebuilt, and work is continuing on the Dauphin Gate and other buildings

LIST OF ILLUSTRATIONS

The cover illustration shows Louisbourg reconstructed,
as seen from Louisbourg Harbour

CHAPTER I

THE foundation of Louisbourg was the result of a crisis in French colonial development. Before the readjustment of territory arranged by the Treaty of Utrecht, April 1713,[1] France possessed the fairest colonial empire the world had seen. India knew her fleets and her factories. She held, on the seaboard of America, from the Arctic to what is now the State of Maine. Her influence was paramount from the St. Lawrence to the mouth of the Mississippi, in the vast backlands of the continent, to the westward of the Alleghanies. The West Indian islands belonging to her were the most prosperous of European settlements in those seas. At Placentia in Newfoundland she had an establishment, founded about 1660, which served as a base for her fisheries, and although weak as a place of arms, it was yet strong enough to resist English attacks and to send out expeditions which captured St. John's, the principal seat of the rival power.

Wars between England and France had gone on with brief intermissions from 1689 to 1713. The War of the Spanish Succession, in which Europe formed a coalition to resist the pretensions of the Great Louis, had left France exhausted. Many treaties, signed at Utrecht, settled the terms of the peace, but certain clauses in the one between France and England alone concern this narrative. It was agreed that the French should evacuate Placentia, retaining certain fishing rights on the coasts of Newfoundland; that Acadia, unhappily with indeterminate limits, should be yielded to England, but that France should hold with full sovereignty the islands lying in the Gulf of the St. Lawrence and its outlets. The most important of these was Cape Breton.

The first position taken by the English negotiators was that France should not be allowed to fortify the island. This was, however, yielded. Although England, by previous ownership, or this Treaty, thereafter held the littoral of North America from Hudson's Bay to the Spanish territory of Florida, the belief survived in New England

---

[1] Cf. *Les Grands Traités de Louis XIV*, Vast, Paris, Picard, 1893.

for a generation that these terms were the result of the purchase of the English plenipotentiaries by French gold.[1]

Acadia was the earliest of European settlements on the northern coast of America. Its history had been an extraordinary one, made up of neglect at home, internal strife by rival proprietaries in its forests, and frequent harryings of its struggling settlements by English colonists. These began with the foray of the Virginian Argal in 1613, and only ceased in 1710, when it was captured by New England forces, supported by an English fleet. So pitiful is its story that it is a cause for wonder that its chief place, Port Royal, survived, and that there, and at other settlements, lived about 2400 Acadians on lands so fertile that they excited the cupidity of the invaders.

The pastoral prosperity of these people made them self-supporting. They contributed little to the trade of France ; therefore the relinquishment of Acadia, which so inadequately fulfilled the purpose for which colonies were established, the enrichment of the mother-country, would not justify describing the consequence in America of the Treaty of Utrecht as making a crisis in French colonial affairs. That expression is made accurate by two conditions which were of vital importance : for one affected her retention of Canada, the most extensive of her dependencies ; the other, the prosecution of a trade, not only important from its own profits, but indirectly from the commerce of which it was the source, and the military[2] advantages of its permanent prosperity.

Newfoundland and Nova Scotia being in the hands of England, Cape Breton was a sentinel in the gateway of the St. Lawrence,[3] through which passed the traffic of Canada—through which, in event of new hostilities, attack on that colony would be made. The value of Cape Breton, as a naval base to protect Canada and French commerce in the Western Ocean, is so obvious that it need not be more than mentioned.

The trade of such importance was that of the North Atlantic fisheries. It had been vigorously followed, at all events, from the beginning of the sixteenth century ; Portuguese, Basques from the Spanish side of the Bidassoa, those of their French ports, Bayonne and St. Jean de Luz, the fishermen of Bordeaux, of Normandy, as well as West Country English, visited the teeming waters of the western coasts of the North Atlantic. New England, too, about the mid-seventeenth century, turned, with far-reaching effects on her people, from the demoralizing fur trade.

---

[1] *Douglass Summary*, London, 1760, vol. i. p. 3.

[2] The distinction between naval and military forces was of later date than this time. Macaulay, with his usual brilliancy and wealth of illustration, states the relation of the sea and land forces which continued in France until later than the fall of Louisbourg (Macaulay's *Hist. Eng.* vol. i. chap. iii.).

[3] The Strait of Belle Isle was not used at this time.

"The two pursuits had very little in common. One partook of the departing barbarism, the other was a sure harbinger of the incoming civilisation. The one, lusty in its occasional prosperity, lean in its certain periods of scarcity, bred the lazy lounger of the trading-post, half-savage, half-pinchbeck citizen. The other, an uncertain chance combined with industry, made the hardy fisherman and bold sailor of the New England coast." [1]

The thrift of her people saved from the harvest of the sea the beginnings of that wealth which the enterprise of their descendants has made so potent in developing the resources of this continent. In early times, after providing for sustenance, they exploited the land as subsidiary to the fisheries, and the traffic over seas of which they were the origin. First fishing, then coasting, then deep-sea voyages, the building of vessels for these trades, the providing cargo for them from their other industries, mark the course of New England's early economic development. It is fitting that a golden codfish hangs in the legislative chamber of Massachusetts, to remind the representatives of her people of the origin of their prosperity.

The importance of the fisheries was of more than colonial significance. The direct returns of the enterprise were large, and at the beginning of the eighteenth century were mostly the fruits of voyages made from Europe. "While many finny fellows have finer tissues and more exquisite flavours, few survive time, endure salt, and serve daily use as well as the Cod." These qualities opened for it large markets among the Catholic countries of Europe, as well as the Mahometan people of the Levant. Trade in other commodities followed that in fish, with proportional benefits to the nation, so that all interested in its prosperity set a high value on an industry the indirect advantages of which were so widespread and conspicuous. [2]

The industry was fostered, also, by statesmen as a "nursery of seamen." France, but a few years before, owned a navy which, under Tourville, had withstood the combined fleets of England and Holland. [3] Her naval decline was still incipient, so the reserve of seamen employed in her fisheries was a prime factor in its encouragement. [4] "As these cost the King nothing in time of peace, and are immediately available for his ships in time of war, and are no less skilled in handling a vessel on dangerous coasts than intrepid in combat," the commercial value of this industry was enhanced by its military importance.

---

[1] Weeden's *Economic and Social History of New England*, vol. i. p. 129.

[2] As the fisheries of the French increased, English writers expressed alarm over this aspect of the situation. Weeden has a score of allusions to the importance of this trade.

[3] "Of Maritime powers France was not the first. But though she had rivals on the sea, she had not yet a superior. Such was her strength during the last forty years of the seventeenth century, that no enemy could singly withstand her, and that two great coalitions, in which half Christendom was united against her, failed of success" (Macaulay, vol. i. chap. ii.).   [4] Shirley about 1745 estimated the number as 27,000.

The experience of a century had shown that an establishment near the fishing grounds was essential. Boat as well as bank fishing was important. Vessels required a port in which they could refit in security. The taste of certain markets demanded a fish which had to be dried on shore. The necessity of selecting a site for this establishment, and removing to it the people of Placentia, required by the Treaty to be evacuated, so that no delay should imperil one of the most productive industries of the kingdom, was the crisis with which Pontchartrain, Minister of Marine, was confronted.

Before going on to recount in outline the progress of the colony which was carried on under his administration and that of his successors, for colonial affairs were in charge of this Ministry, it is fair to caution the reader that a narrative dealing only with the affairs of one colony is quite untrustworthy as a ground for condemning men or systems. The basis for such a comparison is only sound when it embraces knowledge of what was happening in other establishments where conditions were not essentially different.

The perusal of the scores of volumes of documents dealing with the affairs of Louisbourg leaves an impression that the administrators of that colony must have been corrupt and inefficient beyond all men then in similar positions ; that the Minister was indifferent to its fortunes; that its soldiers were ill-fed and clothed, its fortifications ineffective, its people drunken, its growth trifling, the establishment more likely to perish from its own corruption than to require formidable armaments for its capture.

Corruption was also charged against officials in the English colonies. Ill-clothed soldiers in Nova Scotian winters kept watch wrapped in their blankets. On the eve of a war foreseen for years, one writes of an English outpost, " Canso lyes naked and defenceless " ; another, of Annapolis, the chief seat of English power in the province, as so weak, that even the cow of the neutral Acadian found its moat and ramparts practicable for assault. The consumption of spirits during the colonial occupation of Louisbourg shows that drunkenness was a vice the ravages of which were not confined to the French ; while the failure of the English colony of Georgia, founded not long after Louisbourg, proves that disappointing results followed enterprises under other flags than the white standard of the Bourbons. This introduction is not the place for these illuminating comparisons. It must, however, touch on some general considerations which will make more intelligible the narrative of the events which took place in Louisbourg.

France applied to her colonies the same paternal system of administration as at home. Colbert thus stated in one of his letters the principles on which a sound colonial administration was founded :

"Apply your industry and knowledge of affairs to these three points, the complete expulsion of foreigners, liberty to all French, and cultivate with care, justice, and good order."[1]

Such was the standard Colbert set. Unmodified as an ideal, it guided the policy of successive ministers.[2]

But, while they wished the colonies to develop along these lines, other considerations modified this desire. No foreigner should live in them, nor were French heretics welcome. One of the advantages of the colony was that to it might be sent those whose presence in France was a disgrace to their families or a danger to the community.[3] It was in the sands of Louisiana that the frail grace of Manon ceased from troubling her generation. In its commercial development passion for working to a plan, often conceived with foresight and elaborated with intelligence, imposed on its people regulations which checked their enterprise. Its authorities were ordered to undertake elaborate schemes for development, beyond their ability and their resources to carry out.

Trades and occupations were regulated ; the wages paid, and the prices of commodities produced, were determined by enactments, which, in one form or another, had the force of Royal authority. France with this system had reached, in the years immediately preceding this period, a commanding position, not only in military affairs, but in arts, manufactures, and ship-building.[4] Her industries still retain the direction, and in instances the eminence, they attained in the earlier years of Louis's reign before Louvois became more powerful in his councils than Colbert. A system which produced such results, one akin to that under which modern nations are making great progress, had unquestioned merits. These are, however, most conspicuous in a country of settled conditions, of regular economic development. Among the ever-changing circumstances of a new settlement, regulations made by the best intentioned of bureaucrats were hampering to the settlers. The system accounts, in part at least, for the centrifugal tendency of the people of the French colonies. The energetic and the enterprising went to the confines of colonial civilization to escape rules which fettered their activities. This tendency is most marked among the *coureurs du bois* of Canada. It is also seen in Isle Royale, for Ingonish soon became, after Louisbourg, the principal place in the colony. This was attributed by the authorities to the absence there of any settled administration. Distance, the lack of supervision, the personal interest of

---

[1] Colbert, *Deschamps*, p. 161.

[2] Cf. Mims, *Colbert's West Indian Policy*, Yale Historical Press, 1912.

[3] Instances were not uncommon in Louisbourg.

[4] Even when, at a later time, England was destroying her naval power, supremacy in shipbuilding had not passed from France. It was acknowledged in the saying current in the rival service, "The French to build ships, the English to fight 'em."

officials, however, made it easy to ignore instructions from the home authorities, of which the rigid observance was unpopular, inconvenient, or unprofitable.[1]

These regulations have sometimes been described as if the intention of the authorities was to gratuitously vex and annoy the colonist. There is abundant evidence that the intention was to help him. The dependence of English ministers on parliamentary majorities, of which the members of trading constituencies were a part, made a care of the commercial interests of the country indispensable. Their French contemporaries were also zealous in doing all they could to promote trade. Suggestions were made of means by which the volume of business could be increased or more effectively carried on. The early history of Cape Breton furnishes these examples. In 1687 coal was taken from the island to France and tried in the royal forges; a little earlier (1681) trade with the West Indian colonies was considered; while a scheme for establishing an entrepôt at which seagoing ships would exchange cargoes with lighter vessels, the former, thus relieved from the tedious voyage to Quebec, to have time for two voyages a year instead of one, was favourably looked on by Colbert.[2] Coal from Cape Breton was made free of duty, as at a later date were its other principal products.

The Council of Commerce founded by Colbert in 1664, the scope of which was greatly extended in 1700, did much to promote French trade and to relieve it from regulations which fettered it. Many volumes of its deliberations are extant.[3] In these it is rare to find a case in which the decision is not in favour of the trader. An English writer in 1745 ascribes to its fostering "the Steps by which the French Commerce and Colonies, from being inferior to ours, have risen to a dangerous Superiority over us, in less than half a Century."[4]

The decisions of this body and the enactments of all contemporary authorities were dominated by a theory which has had some influence to within memory of the living, namely, the conception that colonies were entirely for the benefit of the mother-country. It was stated as follows by the writer of a memorial on the settlement of Cape Breton : "Colonies are necessary only as they are useful to the states from which they take their origin ; they are useful only in as much as they procure for these states new advantages and solid means of extending their commerce." When the interests of the French merchant clashed with those of the colonist, the latter had to give way.[5] There does not seem to be any evidence that the French had, as had in a misty

---

[1] "A des distances aussi grandes, quelle peut être l'énergie des loix de la métropole sur les sujets, l'obéïssance des sujets à ces loix ?" (Raynal, *Isles Françoises*, p. 3). The same disregard was shown in the English colonies. Cf. Channing, *History of the U.S.* vol. ii. chap. viii.

[2] Ar. Col. B, vol. 1, p. 137. Other references are B, vol. 13, pp. 59 and 67, and MSS. Que. vol. 1, pp. 243, 276.

[3] Ar. Nat. F. 12.

[4] *State of the British and French Trade Compared*, London, 1745, quoted in "Two Letters on Cape Breton," London, 1746.   [5] Instances of this occur in the history of Louisbourg. Cf. p. 49.

instinctive way the English, the foreshadowing of the Imperial idea of mother-country and colony, sharing burdens and mutually adapting production to a common profit. We do not find in their administration anything to correspond to the permitted competition on equal terms of the cheaply built colonial ship with English vessels,[1] nor the prohibition of growing tobacco at home, for the advantage of the southern colonies.

There followed from this theory the prohibition of trade with foreigners. In this regard the system broke down. Communities in which trade was of paramount importance evaded and defied those enactments, which interfered with profits. A course of illicit trade which could scarcely be called smuggling, so open and well known it was, contributed to the prosperity of every European establishment over seas. Louisbourg did much trade with New England. The condition in these British colonies is thus described :

" The existing records of original transactions are few and scattered, yet enough remains to show clearly that the commercial business of New England went forward under different forms in the several governments, but always towards one end. That end was money and profit, parliamentary law and Crown administration to the contrary notwithstanding. The interesting letter cited from Gilbert Deblois, a Boston official, to Samuel Curwin, a prominent merchant of Salem, reveals the practice of Boston and Salem in handling imported merchandise which had escaped the King's duties :

" Bos. *Aug.* 6, 1759.

" Sam. Curwin, Esq.,

" Sir : I shall Esteem it a fav. you'l take an Opp^y to Inform all your Merchts. & Others, Concerned in Shipping up Wine, Oyl, Olives, Figs, Raisins, &c., that I am Determined Publickly to Inform the Collector of this Port, of any those Articles I can find out, are on board any Vessell Commanded by or under the Care of Captain Ober, in order they may be Seized. I shall not Concern myself ab^t any other Coaster, let 'em bring up what they will, but this Capt. Ober has Cheated me in such a manner (tho to no great Value), that I'm determined to keep a good look out on him, therefore would have all those Concern'd in that Trade, Regulate themselves accordingly, & if they will Risque any such Prohibetted Goods in s^d Ober^s Vessell, they must not (after such notice of my Design) think hard of me, as what I may do will be to punish s^d Ober and not them —I have just told s^d Ober that I would send this notification to Salem and w^d Certainly get his Vessell & Cargo Seized sooner or Later.

I am S^r

Your hble Servt

Gilbr. Deblois.

" P.S. I'm a lover of Honest Men, therefore dont be Surprised at the above, as I look upon Ober to be a great Cheat.

" Pray destroy this when done with."

" Answered Augt 13th."

[1] In 1724 sixteen shipbuilders of the Thames complained to the King that their trade was injured and their workmen emigrating on account of the New England competition (Weeden, vol. ii. p. 573). (For a brief, lucid statement of the English position, the reader is referred to *Cambridge Modern History*, vol. vi. ch. ii.)

"The honest candour of the energetic Deblois in visiting vengeance on Captain Ober —who had offended the official—is as astonishing as it is naive. Here a public officer deliberately warns a community of respectable law-breakers that they will suffer the penalty due any and all transgression, if they presume to ship their goods by a particular and prescribed captain. 'They must not (after such notice of my Design) think hard of me, as what I may do will be to punish s^d Ober and not them.' Debauched public sentiment and corrupt official practice was never more plainly manifest in an individual action. If we had Ober's counter idea of honesty and cheating, then eighteenth-century public morality would stand out in full relief." [1]

These practical and effective modifications of a parental system of administration, and the exploitation of colonies for the benefit of the merchant of the home ports, fitted in with the practice of others than the trading classes. Offices were bought, and the fees attached to them made their salaries comparatively unimportant. The command of a British regiment which long served in Nova Scotia was computed to be worth £4000 a year. Prize money stimulated the commanders of King's ships, as booty the privateersman, nor did the commanders in the French navy disdain the profits of trade for which they carried a store of goods.

Nevertheless the splendid spirit of the seventeenth century which rings out in Lescarbot's address to France [2] was not entirely dead. The letter of instructions to each new Governor of Isle Royale brings to his notice that the sole purpose of the King in colonization was the promotion of religion. This purpose so far held good, that, notwithstanding the enormous disadvantages at which the prohibition of the sale of drink placed the French trader competing for the trade of the natives, that prohibition was enforced. It also finds an expression, for example, in the letter of the Minister Pontchartrain to the officials of Isle Royale in which he says : "Nothing can contribute more to the success of the establishment, nor draw down on it more effectively the blessings of Heaven, than good order and the repression of license." [3] Nevertheless, it was in the main true of France, as of her rivals, that "the period is one of peace, uneventful, almost undisturbed ; its chief crisis due to stock-jobbing ; its chief disputes about currency ; its chief victories those of commerce ; its type, if not its hero, the business man." [4]

Such was the general spirit of the times, the general principles on which the new colony was to be governed.

The island had long been known. It was possibly a land-fall of the first explorers. The Basques, who were among its earliest fishermen, claimed that

---

[1] Weeden, p. 660.   [2] Lescarbot, *Champlain Society*, vol. i. p. 12.   [3] June 4, 1715, B, 37, f. 226.
[4] *Cambridge Modern History*, vol. vi. p. 40.

long before Columbus their ancestors had visited its ports. It seems to owe its name to the town which stands at the place where the Adour once flowed into the Bay of Biscay.[1] Traders visited it for traffic with the Indians, and during each season the fishermen carried on their industry on the adjacent banks. Each nationality kept to its own ports for mutual help and protection, and the names of the principal harbours show this usage. Until 1713 Louisbourg was known as English Harbour (Havre à l'Anglois) ; as late as the last generation deeds described lots as situated on the shores of " Sydney or Spanish Bay " (Baie des Espagnols), and a favourite patroness of the French gave her name, St. Anne, to the port frequented by the fishermen of that nation. Certain it is that during the sixteenth and seventeenth centuries it was constantly visited by European fishermen. In 1629 rival and ephemeral settlements were made on it by Lord Ochiltree for England, and Captain Daniel for France. About twenty years later Nicholas Denys of Tours had settlements at two places on Cape Breton, St. Peter's and St. Anne's, so well established that traces of them had not in a half-century of abandonment been obliterated by the wilderness.

Little was known of it ; even its shape, that of a closed hand, with the index finger pointing to the north-east, is inaccurately given in all the earlier maps. Its strategic and commercial possibilities drew attention to it long before its resources were known. In 1613 it was proposed as the seat of a Viceroy controlling French interests in it and Newfoundland.[2] Under Colbert, in addition to the efforts to develop its trade already cited, a project was submitted which looked towards using the coal of the shores of Sydney harbour, the refining there of West India sugars, and the building of ships with the oak which grew to the water's edge.

With the beginning of the eighteenth century interest in it was heightened. The Ste. Maries officers in the colonial troops asked for a grant of the island in 1700.[3] Memorials flowed in to the Minister. He asked a report from Raudot, Intendant of Canada, on its settlement, which Raudot sent on in 1706,[4] and followed by other papers on the subject. About simultaneously with his first report, an anonymous memoir was sent to Pontchartrain. Raudot shows in his dealing with the question not only the capacity of the experienced administrator, but also of the political thinker. His estimate of the required outlay of the proposed establishment was not materially exceeded for many years after the foundation of the colony. Long before Adam Smith published his book, he recognized the advantages of freer trade. He thus concluded his first memoir :

---

[1] Duceré, *Les Corsaires.*

[2] Bn. Nat. MSS., Moreau, 781.

[3] Arch. de la Fn., Carton 3, No. 130.

[4] This paper contains so much that is valuable about Cape Breton, as it was then thought to be more important than later acquired knowledge of its resources, that a précis is given later, p. 23.

"If it is desired to establish this Island so that its commerce shall flourish, it is necessary to open to it intercourse with all the ports of France, of Spain, of the Levant, of the French West Indies and of New England."[1]

One is inclined to ascribe the difficulties of the establishment on Cape Breton to the incapacity of Pontchartrain, as his defects have been kept alive for readers of memoirs in the scathing pages of St. Simon. For five or six years no project concerned with the American colonies had been placed before him more fully. He was apparently not only interested, but convinced of the advantages to France of the colony, and deferred action only until the end of the war. Before the Treaty was concluded he was aware that Placentia was to be ceded, and therefore that the establishment on Cape Breton was essential. He had warned his colonial subordinates to prepare for the change.

When the time for action came, Pontchartrain took the ground that he was inadequately informed, and secured the sanction of the Council for his scheme. It passed an order that a vessel should be sent with certain officers from the garrison of Placentia, who with L'Hermitte, major and engineer of that place, should select the most suitable port. This, the Minister states in his letter of instructions, must be good, easy for ingress, exit, and defence; that the fisheries shall be abundant and near; that there shall be plenty of beaches and space for curing; that there shall be good lands near; but that the excellence of the port and the fishing is of prime importance.[2]

This policy was carried out; Placentia was handed over to the English, the inhabitants and the movable property transferred to Cape Breton, but as the English were not ready to take possession,[3] Costebelle[4] the Governor and part of the garrison had to remain there until the transaction was completed, and until preparations were made for receiving the inhabitants in their new homes.

This disturbing of their organizations for the prosecution of the fisheries led to appeals from the people of the fishing ports of France to have an arrangement made with England by which they could carry on in Newfoundland that industry during 1714. Pontchartrain, however, informed, among others, the Bayle and Jurats of Siboure and of St. Jean de Luz that this was impossible, and described to them Isle Royale in attractive colours. St. Ovide de Brouillant[5] was in France in the spring of 1713 and received instructions to go at once to

---

[1] Raudot's paper is summarized by Charlevoix and in Brown's *History of Cape Breton*.

[2] B, vol. 35.　　　　　　　　　　[3] English Documents in C.O., Grants and Warrants, vol. 15.

[4] Philippe Pasteur de Costebelle, Lieut. at Placentia, 1692; Capt. 1694; Lieut. de Roi, 1695; Governor Placentia, 1706; Chev. de St. Louis, 1708; Governor Isle Royale, 1714; died Nov. 16, 1717.

[5] Ste. Ovide de Brouillant, nephew of de Brouillant, Governor of Newfoundland and Acadia, entered the naval service as Garde-Marine in 1689. He went to Newfoundland in 1691 and took part in the defences and attacks of the local war until 1710, in which year he served on the frigate *La Valeur*, received two wounds, and spent some time in prison in England. Passing to Isle Royale in 1713 as King's Lieutenant, he succeeded Costebelle as Governor in 1717, and retired with a pension of 3100 livres in 1738.

La Rochelle and embark on the *Semslack*,[1] commanded by Lieut. Meschin,[2] then a young officer whose service in the navy was to extend in all over sixty years. Ste. Ovide was to command the expedition. On her also were to embark the officers and men of the Acadian Companies who had been at Oleron near Rochelle since their surrender in 1710 at Port Royal.

In his course Pontchartrain gave some weight to the representations of Villien, an officer of long experience in garrison at Port Royal in Acadia, who represented that the troops from this place, familiar with local conditions, should form part of the garrison ; that some Acadians, for the same reason, should be sent, and that great care in choosing a site should be exercised, as mistakes had been made both in Canada and in Louisiana which had proved costly to the King and discouraging to the inhabitants ; a frank criticism which is not unique in correspondence of the Navy Department.

The officers who embarked in France were four in number, with two cadets, two servants, and fifteen soldiers. At Placentia the *Semslack* took on board L'Hermitte, de la Ronde Denys, de la Vallière, and twenty-five soldiers, some officials, women, and children, the meagre stores which the Minister had ordered to be sent, and sailed from Placentia on July 23. Pontchartrain ordered her to proceed after Placentia to Quebec. Vaudreuil the Governor, and d'Alogny, commander of the troops in Canada, had been ordered to select from the troops under their charge forty or fifty men, some of them skilled axemen, but all steady, strong, handy, and industrious. These men, under command of two officers who were serving in Canada, De Rouville and Péan, were to form part of the new garrison. The *Semslack* could not get to Quebec in time ; Begon the Intendant therefore chartered from Boularderie—a name we shall continually meet—a vessel in which he, a retired naval officer, was trading, on which these troops and some provisions were carried to Cape Breton.

The ordinary sources do not give any account of the voyage of the *Semslack*, but the declaration of taking possession indicated generally their course, and that the Quebec detachment had joined them before they arrived. This declaration runs as follows :—

In the year 1713 and the 2nd day of September, we, Joseph Ovide de Brouillant, King's Lieutenant at Plaisance, Knight of the Military Order of St. Louis, commanding His Majesty's ship *Semslack* with M. L'Hermitte, Major and Engineer, La Ronde and

---

[1] The *Semslack* was a vessel of 270 tons, captured from the Dutch in 1703, and used by the French as a freighter and fire-ship. Her crew and armament on a peace footing was 100 men and 14 guns, in war 140 men and 28 guns, half of which were six and the others four pounders. She was described as an ordinary sailer, and disappears from the Navy Lists in 1718 (Arch. Nat. Marine, 11, and B 5, Marine 3).

[2] Jérémie de Meschin, born in 1674, entered as Garde-Marine at Rochefort in 1687, promoted Enseigne in 1700, commanded a fire-ship in 1711, but did not reach the full grade of Capitaine de Vasseau until 1738. He saw much service. He died in 1757 (*Dictionnaire de la Noblesse*, La Chenaye-Debois, vol. x., Paris, 1775).

Rouville, Captains, and other officers named below, have seized and taken possession of the Island of Cape Breton, situated in the entrance to the Gulf of St. Lawrence, following the orders which we have thereon from His Most Christian Majesty, dated the 20th day of March of the present year, to place there the inhabitants of Plaisance, St. Pierre, and other places which have been ceded by the treaty of peace to the Queen of Great Britain.

We declare and testify to all whom it may concern, to have found on the said island but one French inhabitant and twenty-five or thirty families of Indians, and that the said Island of Cape Breton was ceded about eighty years ago to Messieurs Denis of Tours, who established there two forts, one in the Bay of Ste. Anne's and the other at Port St. Peter near the Strait of Canceau, of which we have still found traces, and after having visited all the ports in the said Island of Cape Breton which have been indicated to us, we believed and decided that we could not make a better choice for the present than that of Port St. Louis, formerly known as English Harbour, in which port we have this day landed the troops, the munitions of war and provisions which we have left under the orders of Sr. L'Hermitte. Signed by Decouagne, De Lavalliere, De Laperrelle, Péan Delivandiere, de Pensens, La Ronde Denys, de Rouville, Duvivier, f. Dominique De Lamarche (Recollet), L'Hermitte, St. Ovide de Brouillant.

The *Semslack* sailed back to France with St. Ovide on board, and arrived in the first part of December at the Isle d'Aix.[1] He made his report to the Minister, and the tentative name of Port St. Louis, which they gave to Havre à l'Anglois, was changed to Louisbourg.[2] Ste. Anne's was to be called Port Dauphin ; St. Peter's, Port Toulouse ; and the whole island, Isle Royale.[3]

The little band of 116 men, 10 women, and 23 children, the founders of Louisbourg, were left on the thickly wooded shores of that harbour with an inadequate equipment and an unknown wilderness before them.

The supplies were four fishing boats and their gear, four herring nets and a seine ; six cannons from St. John's, balls, masons' tools and picks, two hundredweight of resin, a forge and bellows, and the King's mules and the horses from St. John's ; from Quebec three hundredweight of flour, ten barrels of peas, one barrel of Indian corn, forty pairs of snow-shoes, 150 pairs of mocassins, one deerskin, 1000 planks, thirty shovels, eighty little axes, 300 pounds of tobacco, three barrels of tar, and six cows. Costebelle added to this a few pounds of steel and sixty axes, all he could obtain in Placentia. An ample list had been made out for supplies from France, but were apparently only partly shipped. The Minister ordered specially 100 axes from a maker, one Bidard, near Bayonne, as he had the reputation of being a specially good workman.[4]

They made their encampment at the Barachois, formed by a little brook, directly across the south-west arm of Louisbourg harbour from the site on which the town was afterwards built.[5] They made some rough preparations for shelter, and began thereafter the task which lay before them. The first thing which

---

[1] Marine, B², f. 235.   [2] Arch. Col. B, vol. 36.
[3] The importance of the illegitimate children of the King is shown in the honour done to the Comte de Toulouse, the son of Madame de Montespan.   [4] Arch. Col. B, 35, f. 230.
[5] The advantages of the beaches on the latter side caused some of the people to settle there at once.

was done was to cut through the woods a road to the Miré, along the banks of which was the most available supply of timber.   At this they were working early in October, and later the detachments were sent into the woods to cut timber for the proposed buildings, in particular the barracks, which L'Hermitte had at once designed.   A detachment of troops under Duvivier was placed at the head of the river, and that of Rouville about twelve miles lower down.   Duvivier was in a poor district, and a month was wasted before L'Hermitte visited the encampment and moved him to a more favourable place.   The inexperience of most of the officers told against their effectiveness.   L'Hermitte wished for four or five like Rouville, and while he considered all the soldiers good, the Canadians proved particularly valuable.   On the other hand, he says that only five men in Duvivier's detachment knew how to saw, and that had it not been for a small quantity of steel sent by Costebelle, they would have been without axes ; but in spite of all these disadvantages they got out more timber than they were able to transport in the next season to Louisbourg.

The season was a bad one ; winter set in early, the men suffered from scurvy, and as early as December they had to kill the cattle sent from Quebec. Three of their horses, the spoils of the capture of St. John's, succumbed ; and out of twenty-one head of cattle with which they began, only two were alive in the spring, which this year reached almost the extreme limit of the island's climatic unsatisfactoriness.   Snow was on the ground, and drift-ice off the coast, as late as the end of May.   The first vessel to arrive, the *Hercule*, was in the icefields for twenty days, and a small vessel laden with provisions for the troops at Miré was wrecked on her voyage.

La Ronde Denys, Couagne, who was an engineer, and Rouville had been sent to examine Port Dauphin and to explore the country.   They came back with a good report, having examined the fertile lands on the Bras d'Or about Baddeck, and found them suitable for settlement.

In the interval L'Hermitte worked over his plans for fortifications, and submitted them to Vaudreuil and Begon, the Governor-General and Intendant of Canada, who arrived at Louisbourg on the 20th of May and remained there until the 7th of June.   He discussed with them on the ground the simple system of isolated forts which he proposed to build.   He received from the Minister instructions that the works should be built solidly, and, in his trouble, bitterness of heart showed through the respectful phrases of his reply.   There was neither building stone nor lime, and as the vessels had brought no supplies, his many workmen were ineffective, for he had neither nails nor iron, and only eighteen bad axes and twelve picks.   He also was without funds, and found that the Indians would not work without pay.

While this work was going on steps were taken towards the removal of the Acadians to Isle Royale. By Article XIV. of the Treaty of Utrecht, they were entitled to remove from Acadia with their personal effects within one year. Queen Anne, to mark her recognition of Louis XIV. having released, at her request, French Protestants from the galleys, gave special permission to those who left the country to sell their lands.[1]

The twenty-four hundred Acadians affected by these provisions were the descendants of about sixty families brought from Western France in 1633–38, and of one hundred and twenty or thirty men who settled in the colony between that time and its cession to England.[2] The earliest settlers were familiar with the reclamation of marsh lands by dyking as practised in their native districts. They found conditions favourable to this system on the shores of the Bay of Fundy, " the Coasts whereof and the banks of the adjacent Rivers abound with Salt Marshes, which by the Force of a Rich Soil, constantly recruited with marine Salts, and so, not to be impoverished, by constant Tillage, produce large crops of English grain, with little labour to the Husbandman."[3]

The waters of this bay are indeed a fountain of perpetual youth, for some of these lands, never fertilized but by the deposits of its tides, still bear most abundant crops within dykes built by the French, and in the work of bringing in the marshes which is now going on about the Isthmus of Chignecto no change has been made from the methods of the Acadian pioneers. As land of this extraordinary fertility could be obtained for the most part by co-operative dyking, and yielded its crops with a minimum of labour, the Acadian was indisposed to attack the adjoining forest to obtain land relatively poor. Their settlements, except as determined by the seat of Government, were therefore at points where these advantages could be obtained. Vetch, who governed Annapolis for three years, says they had five thousand black cattle "and a great number of Sheep and Hoggs," indicative of a fair degree of prosperity. The name of Port Royal had been changed to Annapolis Royal, and there, Francis Nicholson, who had seen a varied service in all the colonies from Virginia northwards, had charge of Acadia as Governor-General and Commander-in-Chief of all the forces in that province and in Newfoundland. His Lieutenant-Governor was Thomas Caulfield, and these two, with a very small military and civil establishment, administered a British colony, none of the people of which were British subjects. The French Court was extremely anxious to accomplish the removal of its former subjects to French territory. The Ministerial correspondence contains many letters to Vaudreuil, to the other Canadian officials, and to the priests of Acadia, asking for their help to incite the Acadians

---

[1] N.S. Arch. vol. 1, p. 15.   [2] Hannay, *History of Acadia*, p. 290.
[3] *Shirley Memoirs*, 1747, p. 3.

to take advantage of their treaty rights.[1] The efforts made went further. Baron de St. Castin received much praise for not having availed himself of a leave of absence, but instead spent the winter among the Acadian Indians with whom he was allied by ties of companionship and blood, in an effort to induce them to move to Isle Royale. In this he was not successful, but he received praise for having kept alive their unfriendly feelings against the English, and these good offices doubtless led the authorities to condone his behaviour in the previous winter by which he had scandalized the nuns in Quebec.[2]

L'Hermitte, on the 23rd of July 1714, addressed a letter to Nicholson, quoting the terms of the treaty by which the Acadians might withdraw. His orders were that should he learn that the Acadians were hindered in taking advantage of these privileges he should send an officer to confer with Nicholson, to whom was addressed the Queen's letter[3] granting the additional concessions. He goes on to say that several Acadians had informed him that Caulfield had refused permission to certain who wished to leave, and in consequence he sends to him Captain La Ronde Denys, bearing the orders of the King, to discuss the matter with him, and trusts that Nicholson has no other views than carrying out the wishes of his Sovereign, concluding with a request that they should mutually return deserters for the benefit of each colony. A few days later St. Ovide also writes that he is sending Captain de Pensens with L'Hermitte's letter, and asks Nicholson to discuss these questions with the two officers.

They set out from Louisbourg on two vessels, both of which had arrived at Annapolis before July 23, for on that day they write to Nicholson beginning, "We de la Ronde Denys and de Pensens, Captains of Companies Franches de la Marine, which His Christian Majesty maintains at Isle Royale, sent by Monsieur St. Ovide de Brouillan, Lieutenant du Roy of the said Island to represent to Monsieur de Nicholson General de la Nouvelle Ecosse et Isle de Terre Neuve" the rights which Her British Majesty has been pleased to accord to the inhabitants of the said country, and as the intention of His Most Christian Majesty is to maintain them, we beg the General to give attention to the following articles. These were : a request that he would cause to be assembled, first the inhabitants of Port Royal, thereafter those of the other settlements, and appoint a British officer who with one of them would hear and register the decisions of the inhabitants as to remaining in Acadia or leaving ; that those who decide to go shall have a year from the time permission is given, during which time they may live without molestation from the authorities, carry away all their personal property ; build vessels for this purpose ; that there shall be no obstacles to bringing in French rigging for such vessels ; that the General

---

[1] I.R. Series B, vols. 35 and 36.   [2] A.N. C", (Canada), vol. 33, f. 265.

[3] June 13, 1713.

should publish in all inhabited places permission for them to sell their lands, for the English to buy them, and that if within the year they cannot sell, they shall have the right to give a power of attorney to some one to act for them until buyers are found ; and finally, that justice shall be done to those who have suffered at the hands of Vetch and Colonel Hobby in the time between the capitulation and the treaty of peace. To this they add a postscript, saying that as one of them must return at once to give a report, they beg that he will assemble the inhabitants no later than Sunday the 25th.

This was immediately taken into consideration by the Council, and, as an answer, a copy of the minutes was returned. The assembly of the inhabitants was granted, Major Mascarene and Lieut. Bennett were appointed to go with the French envoys to the other settlements and carry out the negotiations in the same way as at Annapolis, and to arrange with Denys their time of leaving and the means of transport ; the Governor would not fix the time when the year of grace was to begin, but would submit the matter to the decision of Her Majesty, as well as all the other points raised, except the last, on which he asked for all available information, and promised full justice.

The proclamation calling together the inhabitants was issued and the meeting held on the feast-day of St. Louis at the fort of Annapolis. The Governor, Lieutenant-Governor, and the principal officers of the garrison were present, as were two missionaries, the Fathers Justinien and Bonaventure, and Father Gaulin the priest. La Ronde Denys alone represented France as De Pensens was unwell. A list was made of the inhabitants present, they numbered nine hundred and sixteen, represented by one hundred and sixty-nine heads of families.[1] They encircled the officers in the square, and heard read to them Nicholson's order for the meeting and the Queen's letter, both of which were translated for them, and the latter formally compared with La Ronde's copy. Then, invited by Nicholson, La Ronde made his propositions. If his letters indicate his oratorical style he was a fervid speaker, careless of grammar, and not altogether accurate as to facts.[2] He, on this occasion, went beyond his instructions in the promises he made to the Acadians. He spoke of the goodwill of the King who would furnish to them vessels for their transport, provisions for a year to those who needed them, freedom from duties on all their trade for ten years, and added a promise which was of great importance to them, for the Acadians disliked the land system of Canada, that there would be no seignories, but that they would hold their lands direct from the King. Nicholson added that he was ready to receive any complaints of bad treatment. La Ronde thanked

---

[1] 151 men, 165 women, 325 boys, 275 girls.

[2] L'Hermitte said of him that his flatteries and lies would trouble the universe. The Minister wrote to Beauharnois May 18, 1728 about La Ronde Denys then serving in Canada, "Of all the officers in the colony he is the least deserving of consideration" (B, vol. 53).

him in the name of all the inhabitants for "the civil, upright and frank manner" in which he had acted with them, and then by his permission they went to La Ronde's lodgings and there one hundred and forty-six of them signed "avec toute la joie et le contentment dont nous sommes capables" the document by which they pledged themselves to live and die faithful subjects of Louis and to migrate to Isle Royale.

Fifteen embarked immediately on the *Marie Joseph* and went to Cape Breton with De Pensens. Of these only one of those whose age is given was under forty, and as regards social status they were about equally divided between those who had a trunk and those who had their property in bags.[1] Charles D'Entremont, Sieur de Pobomicou, his wife, son, and daughter, went on their own vessel with a crew of two, and four passengers. The details bear out Vetch's statement that these first emigrants were of no very great substance.

The transaction at Annapolis being thus concluded, La Ronde Denys and the two British officers went to Minas, where the inhabitants met them, were numbered, and one hundred and thirty-nine agreed to go to Isle Royale. [Population : 139 men, 140 women, 306 boys, 289 girls ; total, 874 ; heads of families, 145.] At Cobequid seventeen signed. [Population : 20 men, 20 women, 52 boys, 44 girls ; total, 136 ; 21 heads of families.] La Ronde Denys then told the English officers that everything had been done to his satisfaction. They set sail together and the vessels parted company in the basin of Minas on September 8, La Ronde on the *St. Louis*, having with him several inhabitants, one of them with a substantial quantity of grain.

These transactions were carried out with great formality, certified copies of all documents were interchanged, and there was no disagreement between the parties. Nicholson wrote civilly to L'Hermitte and St. Ovide, and both Governors sent a report of these events to the home authorities. In the accounts of the meetings at Cobequid and Minas, there is no mention of the priests having been present. The proportion of signers at these two meetings was even greater than at Annapolis, so that the inhabitants did not require the direct presence of their leaders to make them follow wishes, which, however, these leaders had previously many opportunities of making known to them. In any community so simply organized that it contains no great landed proprietors and few, if any, lawyers or professional men, whether the religion of that community be Roman Catholic or Protestant, the influence of the clergymen in all matters is great. It seems to have been so in New England at that time ; those who knew Cape Breton a generation ago, know its force then, and that in civil affairs the dictum of a Presbyterian divine was as potent as that of a priest. It

[1] The live stock they took with them was twelve sheep, three bullocks, a cow and a calf.

is inevitable that such power should exist ; its justification is in the results which follow its exercise.

The mission of La Ronde was highly successful. With a few exceptions all the people he saw agreed to go to Isle Royale. No obstacle was put in their way, and the outcome would seem to have depended entirely on the French authorities carrying out the promises which had been made on their behalf. The population of Beaubassin and the other settlements about the isthmus of Chignecto were not visited by La Ronde and Mascarene.[1]

While but a score or so of Acadians accompanied the Envoys on their return to Isle Royale, certain others more enterprising had previously gone there. Two brothers from the head of the river at Annapolis, anxious about their destiny, " which they could not ascertain in that country," [2] started in a Biscay shallop towards the end of May, and coasted along the shores of Nova Scotia to Isle Royale. On the eighth day they arrived at St. Peter's and Isle Madame, then they spent a day at Louisbourg, another at Mordienne (Port Morien), the following at St. Anne's, where a Canadian had already settled and the fisheries were being successfully prosecuted. Returning, they called at L'Indienne (Lingan), abounding in coal and oysters, with one inhabitant ; at Menadou (Mainadieu), and came back to Louisbourg on June 15. There they remained, building a house for M. Rodrigue, lately King's pilot at Annapolis, until August 12, and then proceeded along the coast, through Canso, home by Baie Verte. They give a fair picture of Louisbourg, with what they describe as a large fort which was being built, many cannons landed on the shore, ninety-three from Placentia, vessels making a good catch of cod, two King's ships about to sail for Placentia. Reports were abroad that the *Charente* would shortly arrive with supplies, and also the *Affriquain* from Quebec with

---

[1] The authorities for this episode are to be found at Ottawa (M. $\frac{395}{3}$), and Record Office ; B.T.N.S. vol. 1, has the English version. The population is based on a table prepared for me at the Canadian Archives, which may be condensed thus :

Men.	Women.	Boys.	Girls.	Total.	Heads of Families.
		ANNAPOLIS.			
151	165	325	275	916	169
		MINAS.			
139	140	306	289	874	145
		COBEQUID.			
20	20	52	44	157	21
		BEAUBASSIN.			
55	58	136	102	351	56
365	383	819	710	2277	391

A total population of 2277, which with 123 at outlying points makes 2400. One third of the signers of the declarations were able to sign their names ; out of 302 heads of families all but 100 signed with a mark.

[2] B.T.N.S. vol. 2, 66.

Vaudreuil on board. They saw there a Boston trader with boards, salt, and general merchandise ; and on their way home passed another from Cascoe Bay, with the same cargo. All these facts they swore to in a declaration made before Nicholson on their return, but this document is silent as to their destinies.

Another Acadian, one Arceneau, adventurous enough to voyage in a canoe from Baie Verte to the Baie de Chaleurs, and then in a shallop to Louisbourg, makes the same report of good fishing not only on the Cape Breton coast but among the many Basque vessels in the Gulf of St. Lawrence.[1] L'Hermitte, authorized to place people on the land at the King's pleasure, gave, up to the end of August, permission to twenty-four Acadians to settle on a little river near St. Peter's. Another party was also sent there, but without any definite promise of land, as L'Hermitte wished to have them as settlers at Port Dauphin. After Vaudreuil's second visit in October a party of Acadians was sent under the leadership of De Couagne to inspect the lands on the Bras d'Or, but they did not approve of them, and the officials thought that their secret desire was to go to the Isle St. Jean (Prince Edward Island). The comparison from a farming standpoint of the best lands in well-wooded Isle Royale, and the meadows which they had reclaimed, or which lay ready for reclamation, along the Bay of Fundy, was so obviously to the disadvantage of the former, that it demanded a genuine loyalty to consider emigration. A council was held at Louisbourg on October 16, at which Vaudreuil and the Recollect Missionary, Felix Pain, were present, with Costebelle and the new Commissaire-Ordonnateur, Soubras. Regret was expressed that the promises made to the Acadians had not been kept, and they were specifically renewed for another year.

Costebelle had remained at Placentia. He was advised in the autumn of 1713, that to avoid the hardship of moving in the inclement season the evacuation was off until the spring, and at the close of the year issued a proclamation to the people announcing the cession of the island and the necessity for removal to Cape Breton. The English expedition to take possession of Newfoundland, two regiments under the command of Colonel Moody, had been driven into Vigo and had spent the winter at Lisbon, and only arrived in Newfoundland the next year. During the season the guns and stores were transported to Cape Breton. On July 23, 1714, Costebelle himself left on the *Heros*, and in the autumn the inhabitants straggled over in their own boats. The weather was bad, some were lost, and all suffered in this difficult voyage.

Thus the year ended. Some building was done, but L'Hermitte was in despair about the ineffectiveness of the troops, the lack of care of the King's stores, the use by private individuals of the building material he had gathered,

---

[1] These voyages in small boats may stand to the credit of the Acadians against the many bad reports given of them by the French authorities.

and the evils of divided authority. Soubras, the newly appointed Commissaire-Ordonnateur, complained of the bad effects of drink ; of the gambling and mutinous soldiery, who, nevertheless, were better paid, fed, and clothed than any troops he had ever seen ; and of the ineffectiveness of L'Hermitte. The soldiers had not received the bonus for their work which had been promised. This had not only made it exceedingly ineffective, but had aggravated them to the point of mutiny, and they had begun that excessive indulgence in drink with which the authorities were powerless to cope.

It had been intended that the troops should winter in Baie des Espagnols, but the necessary arrangements were not made, and in December it was decided to place them at Miré, where the cabins left standing from last year could be utilized. Sickness prevailed, and the first death noted at Louisbourg is that of M. Du Vivier. On the other hand the fishing had been excellent, fourteen or fifteen vessels had engaged in it, fewer than would have been the case had there not been a scarcity of salt in France. As it had been bad in Newfoundland, it gave the newcomers a favourable impression of the country, arduous as had been the struggle with the elements by which they reached it.

The population in January 1715 numbered about 720, exclusive of unmarried soldiers, but including military and civil officers. It was arranged by habitations, and with few exceptions they were the people from Placentia (men, 118 ; women, 80 ; children, 170 ; servants, 39 ; fishermen, 300). Incidentally this document throws light on the way of life in the colony. The Governor, Costebelle, whose salary was 4000 livres, lived alone. His establishment consisted of a secretary, one woman and two men servants, and seventeen fishermen. St. Ovide had with him his wife, three children, and three men servants, a gardener, cook and valet, and he employed thirteen fishermen. Soubras kept a bachelor establishment with two young officers, Fontenay and Péan, and had ten fishers. L'Hermitte had a clerk and eight fishers, and his household arrangements were looked after by his wife and one servant. St. Marie had twelve fishers and seven men on his boat (batteau), but La Ronde, Rouville, Legondez, and other officers did not fish.[1]

The merchants who flourished at Louisbourg, and whose names reappear from time to time in the scanty records of its commerce, for the most part came this year, and already had formed establishments, the largest of which were those of Berrichon, Rodrigue, and Daccarette, respectively of twenty-nine, twelve, and nineteen men. There were among the women five widows of the official class, the most recent being Madame Du Vivier, who had arrived with her children from France only a short time before her husband's death, and eight others, of whom three had fishing establishments, two of them of importance, one with twelve and the other with thirteen men. The widow Onfroy of St. Malo claimed that she was the first to send vessels to Cape

[1] I.R.G. 466.

Breton, and with such satisfactory results that the fleets of St. Malo and Grandville imitated her.[1] This much is certain at this early time, that the fishing was largely done by Basques. The Acadian explorers of this year mention only Basque vessels on their voyages in the gulf and on the coasts of Cape Breton.

The new establishment was amid surroundings which might appear unfavourable, and while it was inadequately supported by the home authorities, its personnel could not have found Louisbourg relatively unsatisfactory. Most of the officers had been a long time in Placentia, and although Costebelle places both towns "in the most sterile deserts of America," in climate and other conditions the comparison is not against Isle Royale. Rouville and his Canadians were now in a less severe climate than Quebec, and the nucleus of the population were fisher-folk from Newfoundland, skilled in an art which they began at once to practise under conditions which they found, allowance being made for the unsettled condition and high prices of a new colony, not unfavourable. With an Acadian population drawn to Isle Royale, as seemed probable, its position would be strong. Colonel Vetch, unlikely to overvalue the Acadians, thus expresses the advantage to France of the conditions which they expected to find the next year (1715) in Cape Breton :

"And as the accession of such a number of Inhabitants to Cape Breton will make it at once a very populous Colony ; (in which the strength of all the Country's consists) So it is to be considered that one hundred of the French, who were born upon that continent, and are perfectly known in the woods, can march upon snowshoes, and understand the use of Birch Canoes, are of more value and service than five times their number of raw men, newly come from Europe. So their skill in the Fishery, as well as the cultivating of the soil, must inevitably make that Island, by such an accession of people, and French, at once the most powerful colony the French have in America, and of the greatest danger and damage to all the British Colony's as well as the universal trade of Great Britain." [2]

One, Jethro Furber, who declared vaguely that, being on a voyage, probably smuggling, he took refuge in Louisbourg, gives an interesting picture, closely tallying with that of the Acadians, of the new settlement, "with forty vessels loading and six sail of men-of-warr in its harbour, commodious enough for five hundred sail of shipps," its fishing so good that the boats twice daily brought in their loads, and its people elated that "ye English gave them a Wedge of Gold tor a piece of silver." [3]

These testimonies seem to justify entirely the view taken in the first appeal for funds for Louisbourg which Pontchartrain makes to the King's Treasurer :

---

[1] Arch. Col. B, 36.   [2] Nova Scotia Archives, vol. 1, p. 6.
[3] An affidavit signed at Kingston in Jamaica, April 20, 1715 (B.T.N.S. vol. 2).

"The English are well aware of the importance of this post, and are already taking umbrage in the matter. They see that it will be prejudicial to their trade, and that in time of war it will be a menace to their shipping, and on the first outbreak of trouble they will be sure to use every means to get possession of it. It is therefore necessary to fortify it thoroughly. If France were to lose this Island the loss would be an irreparable one, and it would involve the loss of all her holdings in North America."[1]

APPENDIX TO CHAPTER I

ANONYMOUS MEMOIRS OF 1706[2]

This anonymous memoir is worthy of attention, as it is written by one who had been on the ground, and sets forth what he conceived to be the advantages of the proposed colony and its resources. In passages which have not been reprinted he refers several times to the visit of the fleet of the Chevalier du Palais to Baie des Espagnols in 1692, and writes of that port as an eye-witness. It is probable that he was an officer in that squadron.

The memoir begins with a statement as to the purpose of colonies, the solid advantages of the mother-country and the extension of its commerce. On these principles the southern colonies are useful, as they produce commodities which, otherwise, France would have to buy from foreigners, and trade with them employs many ships and men who consume French products and produce revenues to the State. Even Canada is important for its furs, and the home consumption and exportation of beaver hats.

The proposed colony is important for the commerce in cod, one of the most important in the kingdom, for it uses much salt, sustains many seamen and fishers and their families, pays heavy taxes, and the new establishment would place it entirely in the hands of the French. It has, moreover, the advantage in extreme healthfulness over those of the West Indies.

Cape Breton is selected as the seat of the colony, as it has advantages in the extent of the commerce which can be carried on with all parts of the world, the excellence of its ports, the mildness of its climate and its salubrity, the fertility of its soil, and the excellence of its fisheries.

Then follows a description of the island and its ports, great importance being given and a plan attached of Baie des Espagnols (Sydney), which the writer thinks the best in the island, not only as a harbour, but from its situation, as from it roads could easily be made to all the other principal ports, and thus easy intercommunication be given to the settlers.

---

[1] Arch. Col. B, vol. 37, f. 26, 1/2.
[2] Arch. Col. C¹¹, *Amérique du Nord*, vol. 8, in which are also Raudot's Memoirs.

The land is highly praised on account of the trees it produces—elm, maple, ash, beech, and birch, the same as Canada, and therefore presumably will produce, as Canada does, good crops. Its climate, he points out, will improve as it is cleared, as it is the retention of the snows and the shading of the ground by the primæval forest which make Canada so much colder than corresponding latitudes in Europe—the prevailing view among scientists of the time.

Then follows a description, which subsequent exploration has materially modified, of the possibilities of the country, its timber, tar, pitch, its gypsum and marble and other stones, its " porphire qu'on a trouvé fort beau à la Cour où feu M. le Marquis de Louvois en fit apporter," its coal and its furs, and, above all, its advantageous position for the fisheries, thus dealt with by the writer :

Productions extérieures de l'Isle du Cap Breton

Elles se renferment toutes dans la seule pesche des molues, il ne s'agit pas icy d'en donner le détail ny la description, le Sieur Denis y a satisfait dans son histoire naturelle de l'Amérique Septentrionale avec toute l'exactitude qu'on sçauroit désirer, il n'est question que de faire voir ainsy qu'on se l'est proposé qu'on ne retirera jamais tous les avantages des pesches qu'en les rendant sédentaires, et que ce n'est que dans l'Isle du Cap Breton qu'on peut exécutter avec succez une enterprise de cette importance.

La pesche des molues se fait en deux manières, l'une avec des vaisseaux sur les bancs de terre neuve au large des costes de Canada, l'autre à terre et sur les bords de la mer, par la première, on salle dans les vaisseaux les molues comme on les tire de la mer, ce qu'on appelle les poissons verds qui n'est autre chose que la molue blanche dont il se fait une si grande consommation à Paris ; par la Seconde, on fait sécher les molues sur les côtes de la mer après les avoir sallées, et c'est ce qu'on appelle le poisson sec ou vulgairement merluche, qui se débite par tout le monde et dont on ne fait presqu'aucun usage à Paris, faute d'en connoître le mérite.

Tous ceux qui ont écrit des pêches sédentaires, ou qui ont travaillé à les établir jusques à présent n'ont pensé qu'à la pêche sèche, on se propose de faire voir icy qu'on en peut faire de mesme de la pesche verte, pourvu qu'on en fixe l'établissement dans l'Isle du Cap Breton, la préférence luy en doit appartenir par le droit de sa situation elle est comme assise au milieu des mers les plus poissonneuses, et dans le centre de tous les bancs, sur lesquels les vaisseaux de France ont accoutumé de faire la pesche, par conséquent l'on y peut faire l'une et l'autre pesche et les rendre l'une et l'autre sédentaires dans cette Isle.

L'expérience en décide, de tems immémorial, les vaisseaux ont fait la pesche sèche sur les côtes du Cap Breton, le Forillon, l'Isle plate, l'Indiane, Niganiche, Achpé Le Chadie, carceaux, le havre à l'Anglois et la Balaine qui en dépendent, ne sont jamais sans vaisseaux en temps de paix ils y font ordinairement leur pesche complette, à moins de quelqu'accident, c'est une marque certaine que la morue y est abondante, mais ce n'est pas à dire pour cela qu'il n'y en ayt précisément que dans ces endroits là quand on les désigne icy en particulier comme des lieux de pesche, c'est que de la manière que les vaisseaux ont fait la pesche jusques à présent, ils n'ont pratiqué que ces endroits là que parce qu'ils ne trouvoient pas à se mettre à l'abry ailleurs, et que la petitesse de leurs chaloupes de pesche ne permettoit pas aux pescheurs de s'en éloigner beaucoup, pour chercher la molue ailleurs ainsi on a parlé à cet égard comme s'il n'y en avoit eu qu'au Forillon, à Niganiche, au Havre à l'anglois, et coetera, et point du tout ailleurs ; mais ce seroit une erreur de le penser ainsi, la molue est aussy abondante par tout le reste des costes de l'Isle que dans ces endroits fréquentez, on en trouve également partout ailleurs.

Ainsy dès que la pesche sera devenue sédentaire, et qu'elle ne se fera plus que par les habitans de l'Isle, il ne sera plus question de s'assujettir aux endroits où les vaisseaux peuvent seulement se mettre à l'abry, pendant le temps de la pesche les habitans pouvant pêcher indifféremment sur toutes les costes, les couvriront de leurs chaloupes, et feront deux fois plus de poisson que celles de France par cette raison, et parce qu'étant sur les lieux ils commenceront plustost et finiront la pesche plus tard, si les chaloupes ordinaires ne leur suffisent pas ils auront des barques de toutes grandeurs avec lesquelles ils iront au large sur les bancs poissonneuses où ils trouveront toujours à charger ; les vaisseaux de France ne peuvent pas faire la mesme chose faute de barques qu'ils ne peuvent pas aporter aussi facilement que de petites chaloupes.

Et c'est par le moyen de ces barques que l'on se propose de faire voir icy que la pesche vert peut devenir sédentaire aussi bien que la sesche, c'est un fait constant que la plus part des vaisseaux de France viennent faire la pesche verte sur le banc à verd, sur le banc de Saint Pierre, sur ceux de l'Isle de Sable et même jusque dans le golfe de Canada. C'est un autre fait, encore plus constant, que tous ces bancs sont à portée de l'Isle du Cap Breton et qu'elle en est environnée, il seroit donc par conséquent plus facile aux habitans de l'Isle qui seroient sur les lieux de faire cette pesche avec leurs barques, qu'aux vaisseaux de France qui ont huit cent lieues, et de grands frais à faire, et de grands risques à courir pour s'y rendre.

On peut dire de mesme de la pesche verte du grand Banc, les habitans du Cap Breton qui n'en seroient qu'à quatre vingt lieues, la pourroient faire avec plus de facilité que les vaisseaux de France qui font sept cent lieues et de grands frais pour s'y rendre, ces vaisseaux qui peschent au large et hors de la vue de la terre, sont obligez de saller la molue telle que les pescheurs la tirent de la mer, ils en peschent de quatre sortes, de grandes, de moyennes, de petites, et de plus petites qu'ils appellent " Raquet," sur ce pied là lorsqu'ils retournent en France, ils emportent de quatre sortes de poissons, qui ont chacun leur prix à la vente, outre que c'est un embaras que de concilier ces différents prix, il arrive souvent que se trouvant plus de petit et de raquet, que de grand et de moyen, celuy des deux premières qualitez ne se vend pas avantageusement.

Il n'en seroit pas de mesme, si la pesche verte étoit sédentaire, quoy que les habitans du Cap Breton fussent obligez de saller dans leurs barques toutes les molues telles qu'ils les tireroient de la mer, ainsi que les pescheurs de France, ils seroient néanmoins les maîtres d'en faire le tirage dans leurs barques mêmes, de n'habiller au verd que le grand et le moyen poisson, et de réserver tout l'inférieur pour mettre au sel, par ce moyen les cargaisons de poisson verd seroient uniformes, les ventes en seroient plus faciles et plus avantageuses, et la qualité du poisson beaucoup meilleure.

La pesche sèche y trouveroit aussi son avantage, comme il n'y a que le moyen et le petit poisson qui puisse sécher, il arrive souvent qu'on pesche autant de grandes molues que de petits, on a regret de jetter les grandes à la mer, on risque de les faire sécher, on consomme beaucoup de sel à les saller, parceque étant fort époisses elles pourriroient si on y

épargnoit le sel, la moindre pluye, le moindre brouillard y met la corruption et l'on est
obligé de les jetter après avoir perdu beaucoup de sel et de tems à les soigner, cela n'ar-
riveroit plus si la pesche verte étoit sédentaire, on ne risqueroit plus de faire sécher le grand
poisson, on le salleroit au verd et rien ne seroit perdu.

On en a un exemple dans la pesche qui se fait à l'Isle Percée à l'embrochure du fleuve
de Saint Laurens, il y vient ordinairement sept ou huit vaisseaux en temps de paix, il y a des
Basques et des Normands, les Normands ne veullent point de poisson sec, les Basques n'en
veullent point de verd, ils s'accommodent ensemble, les Normands prennent le grand poisson
des Basques, et les Basques reçoivent des Normands deux petites molues pour une grande,
ainsi toute le monde est content et cela détruit en même temps l'opinion de quelques
particuliers qui prétendent que le grand poisson qui se pesche sur les côtes n'est pas aussi
bon que celuy du grand Banc, si cela estoit, les Normands qui sçavent leurs intérêts et qui
n'aportent ce poisson verd au havre que pour Paris, ne se chargeroient pas d'une marchandise
dont ils ne trouveroient pas le débit, si donc les grandes molues de l'Isle Percée sont bonnes
à mettre au verd, à plus forte raison celles qui se peschent dans toute le golfe de Canada, surtout autour des Isles de la Madelaine et de Brion, où elles sont communément d'une grandeur
prodigieuse, fort grasse et d'une meilleure qualité.

En rendant ainsy sédentaire la pesche du poisson verd et celle du poisson sec, il n'y
aurait plus à l'avenir que de grandes molues vertes et par conséquent de la meilleure qualité,
tout le poisson seroit pareillement de la qualité propre pour les différents pays où le commerce
s'en fait, on en feroit le tirage au Cap Breton, l'on y tiendroit des magazins assortis de chaque
qualité où les vaisseaux trouveroient leurs charges de grandes molues vertes pour France, de
petit poisson sec pour Marseille et pour le Levant, de grand poisson sec pour l'Espagne et le
Portugal, et de moyen poisson sec pour le Royaume, au lieu que jusques à présent, ces
vaisseaux ont été obligez de n'emporter que ce qu'ils peschoient, et comme ils le peschoient.

On jugera par ce détail de l'étendue des productions extérieures de l'Isle du Cap Breton,
quoy qu'elles ne soient que d'une espèce, on peut dire sans exagération qu'on en pourroit
faire avec le temps un commerce de plus de deux vaisseaux tous les ans, qui tiendroient en
mouvement tous les peuples de cette Isle, et leur donneroient les moyens de subsister aisé-
ment de leur travail, joint aux productions de leurs terres, il s'agit à l'heure qu'il est de
trouver dans cette grande Isle un endroit capable de recevoir un Etablissement de cette
importance et dont on en puisse faire le chef lieu, après quoy on fera voir les avantages que
le Roy, l'État et le commerce en pourront retirer. . . .

Le chef lieu de l'Etablissement

Il y a deux raisons principalles de l'établir dans la Baye aux Espagnols.

Premièrement :

La bonté de son Port et de ses Rades ;

Secondement :

Les communications qu'elle a avec tous les autres ports de l'Isle et même avec l'Acadie par
le Labrador.

On voit par le plan que le Pilote Jean Albert en a levé en 1692, et par la description qu'il en donne dans son Journal qu'il est difficile de trouver un endroit plus commode et plus avantageux pour le commerce, le Sieur de Montégu, Capitaine de frégate dit dans son journal de la même année qu'il a sondé toute cette Baye et que c'est un des plus beaux ports qu'on sçauroit voir, la description qu'on en a desja donnée en marque assés tous les avantages pour qu'on puisse convenir que cet endroit mérite la préférence de cet Etablissement.

On peut entrer et mouiller dans ses rades la nuit comme le jour, on en peut sortir de même, on est à couvert dans son port des plus mauvais tems et des ennemis, il y a partout six, sept, huit et neuf brasses d'eau dans ses rades, dans son port, et même jusque tout auprès de terre, les fonds sont de sable vazeux, il n'y a aucuns roshers qui puissent endomager les câbles et les anchres, les vaisseaux peuvent charger commodément partout, on pourroit bâtir la ville principalle entre les deux bras qui partagent la Baye à une lieue de son entrée ; la situation en seroit avantageuse et magnifique, il ne seroit nécessaire de la fortifier que du costé de la terre, on peut à peu de frais la mettre en deffense contre tous les efforts des ennemis, on pourroit encore la placer avec les mêmes avantages entre la Rivière aux cerfs et le bras gauche de cette Baye, la longue digue qui paroît dans le plan en fait un port très spacieux, très assuré et très commode, c'est sur quoy il seroit difficile de se déterminer sans être sur les lieux.

Cette ville deviendroit en peu de tems considérable et d'une grande étendue, les magazins seuls pour recevoir les poissons, les productions du pays, les sels, les appareaux de pesche, aussi bien que les marchandises de France, de Québec et d'ailleurs, occuperoient beaucoup de terrain, l'abord d'un grand nombre de vaisseaux, le mouvement continuel d'une infinité de barques et de chaloupes y atireroient beaucoup de marchands et d'artisans, la campagne surtout des environs se peupleroit de bourgs et de villages, on cultiveroit la terre avec d'autant plus de soin que les grains et les denrées y trouveroient un prompt débit par la consommation qui s'en feroit dans le lieu même et par le transport qui s'en feroit au dehors, on n'y verroit ny pauvres, ny fainéans, on y trouveroit toujours de l'occupation, jusqu'aux femmes et aux enfans qui y seroient employez à laver, à tourner, à porter et à préparer le poisson sur la grave et sur les vignaux, tout le peuple seroit pescheur, ou laboureur, ou artisan, les bourgeois et les marchands seroient occupez de leur commerce, les communications que cet endroit a d'ailleurs par terre avec les autres ports de l'Isle et mesme avec l'Acadie par le Labrador, seroient seules un motif de luy donner la préférence de l'Etablissement principal, dont il s'agit de faire voir les avantages dans les articles suivans.

LES AVANTAGES DE CET ETABLISSEMENT

Premièrement.

Il rend le commerce des pesches certain de casuel qu'il a toujours été jusques à présent.

Secondement.

Il réunit tout ce commerce dans la seule main des François à l'exclusion des Anglois qui l'usurpent depuis longtemps.

Troisièmement.

Il devient le Boulvard et le magazin des colonies de Canada, de l'Acadie et de Plaisance.

Quatrièmement.

Il sera l'entrepost et le refuge des vaisseaux qui reviennent des grandes Indes, des Indes Espagnoles, des Isles de l'Amérique et de tous ceux qui fréquentent les mers de Canada.

En parlant avec ordre de ces quatre avantages principaux, on en découvrira une infinité d'autres particulières qui font d'autant mieux juger du mérite de cet Etablissement.

Premier Avantage.

De la manière que l'on a fait la pesche du poisson sec jusques à présent, on a été obligé de faire partir les vaisseaux de France dès le mois de Mars, pour arriver aux côtes de Canada dans la saison que la molüe commence à s'en aprocher, les mers sont rudes et les vents violens dans les mois de Mars et d'Avril à cause de l'Equinoxe, souvent ils sont contraires pour sortir jusques bien avant dans le mois de May, quand ces vaisseaux partent trop tard, ils n'ont pas le temps de faire leur pesche quand ils partent assés tost, ils trouvent des tourments à la mer, ils démâtent, ils perdent une partie de leurs sels et de leurs vivres, ils relâchent, la dépense de leur équipement est perdue pour les marchands ou pour les assureurs.

Les vaisseaux qui partent pour le poisson verd, n'ont pas à la vérité les mêmes risques à courir, parce qu'ils peuvent sortir dans la belle saison, mais ils ont à essuyer sur le grand Banc les coups de vent les plus violents qui les empeschent de pescher, qui souvent les obligent de débarquer, et quelque fois de relâcher en France en quelque état que soit leur pesche.

Suposans les uns et les autres de ces vaisseaux heureusement arrivez au lieu de leur destination, si le poisson n'est pas abondant, si les grands vents les empeschent de pescher, si les pluyes empeschent de sécher le poisson, s'ils perdent leurs chaloupes par quelque tempeste, comme il arrive assés souvent, s'ils manquent de vivres, s'ils sont jettez à la coste par le mauvais temps ou incommaudez sur le grand Banc, on peut compter que dans les uns ou les autres de ces cas, leur pesche est notablement interrompue, si celle n'est pas tout à fait perdue.

En quelque saison que ces vaisseaux partent pour la pesche, ils ont une longue et rude traversée à faire avant que d'arriver aux côtes de Canada ou sur le grand Banc, personne n'ignore que les vents sont presque toujours contraires pour ces voyages, les vaisseaux qui font le poisson sec demeurent près de quatre mois à la coste et ne mettent guère moins de huit mois à tout leur voyage ; ceux qui font le poisson verd ne sont pas si longtemps dehors, mais ils sont toujours exposez, ainsi ces voyages qui sont toujours longs coûtent beaucoup aux marchands, qui souvent sont trop heureux de retirer une partie de leurs avances, bien loin d'y trouver du profit.

On n'obtient que rarement pendant la guerre des équipages pour la pesche, les vaisseaux des particuliers auxquels on en accorde sont en proye aux Corsaires Anglois de Boston, aussy bien sur le grand Banc que sur les côtes de Canada, tous les vaisseaux pris à l'Isle Percée, à Bonnaventure, à Gaspé, au Cap Breton et sur le grand Banc pendant la dernière guerre, ne le prouve que trop, mais quand le peu de vaisseaux qui sortent pendant la guerre pour la pêche des molües reviendroit à bon port, ce poisson estant rare est toujours si cher dans le Royaume, qu'on n'en sçauroit trouver la consommation entière, sans être à charge au public.

Tous ces inconvéniens cesseroit si les pesches devenoient sédentaires, ce commerce seroit aussy florissant en temps de guerre que pendant la paix, les marchands n'en feroient [*sic*] plus les avances, il n'y auroit presque plus de risques à le faire, les vaisseaux ne partiroient plus à l'équinoxe de Mars, assurez de trouver à l'Etablissement la pesche toute faite par les habitans, ils ne mettoient plus à la mer qu'en May, Juin et Juillet dans une saison si belle, ils ne risqueroient plus de perdre leurs sels, leurs vivres, leurs marchandises, ny de relâcher ; leur navigation seroit heureuse, ils ne prendroient que des Equipages ordinaires, et des vivres qu'autant qu'il leur en faudroit pour se rendre à l'Etablissement, ils ne feroient plus la dépense d'embarquer les chaloupes ny les autres appareaux de pesche, ils chargeroient entièrement de marchandises et de choses à la vérité nécessaires à la pesche, mais ce ne seroit plus pour la consommer par eux-mêmes en faisant la pesche comme autrefois, ce seroit un pur commerce, et pour revendre aux marchands de l'Etablissement qui les payeroient en poisson tout fait et en d'autres effets ; ils passeroient en quarante jours de France à l'établissement, ils n'y séjourneroient qu'autant qu'il seroit nécessaire pour décharger et recharger, ils repasseroient en France en vingt jours et pourroient faire tout le voyage en trois mois, ils pourroient en faire deux par an ; ceux qu'on destineroit pour les Isles de l'Amérique, pour le Mexique, pour l'Espagne, le Portugal, la Méditerranée ou pour le Levant feroient trois fois leur frêt dans la même année de France à l'Etablissement, de là dans les pays Etranges, et des pays étrangers en France, ils prendroient des vivres à l'Etablissement pour leur retour, en quelqu'endroit qu'ils le fissent, ils y trouveroient des mâts, des vergues, et d'autres pièces s'ils en avoient besoin, ils pourroient mesme s'en garnir entièrement sans autre dépense que de les couper quelque difficulté qu'il y eust d'obtenir des Equipages en esté, pendant la guerre ils en auroient au pis aller vers la fin d'aoust que les vaisseaux du Roy ont continué de désarmer, alors ils partiroient en flotte sous l'escorte de deux ou trois frégates de Sa Majesté qui les conduiroient à l'Etablissement et les rameneroient en France, par là le commerce de la pesche ne seroit jamais interrompu, parce qu'il se feroit par les habitans du lieu, qui comptans sur l'arrivée de la flotte prépareroient le poisson en l'attendant. Sa Majesté en recevroit toujours les droits et la molue seroit à bon marché dans le Royaume en guerre comme en paix.

Deuxième Avantage.

La pesche sédentaire que les Anglois ont établis à la coste de l'Est de l'Isle de Terre Neuve depuis quarante ans est une usurpation formelle de leur part, cette Isle apartient sans contredit à Sa Majesté suivant le partage de l'Amérique Septentrionale entre la France et l'Angleterre, le peu d'attention qu'on a eue pour une affaire de cette conséquence a donné lieu à la possession que les Anglois en ont prise, il paroît par de bons mémoires qu'ils y chargent tous les ans plus de cent vaisseaux de poisson sec.

La pesche qu'ils font encore avec les barques de la côte de Baston sur celles de l'Acadie est une autre usurpation, ils n'en peuvent pas contester la propriété à la France puis qu'ils l'ont rendue plusieurs fois par des traitez de paix, mais quoy qu'ils n'y trafiquent plus avec les habitans, ils ne discontinuent pas pour cela d'y faire la pesche des molües qu'ils portent sécher sur leurs costes, le peu d'oposition qu'ils y trouvent de la part des François n'est pas capable de les en empêcher, ils font encore par cette pesche au moins la charge de cent vaisseaux de poisson sec tous les ans.

Comme les Anglois ne consomment presque point de poisson sec en Europe, ils le portent en Espagne, en Portugal et jusques dans le Levant où ils le vendent en concurrence avec les François qui devroient estre seuls maîtres de ce commerce.

Il n'y a que l'Etablissement proposé qui puisse en donner l'exclusion aux Anglois, s'ils trouvent la côte de l'Acadie occupée par les Barques et les chaloupes des habitans du Cap Breton on peut compter que d'eux-mêmes ils ne s'y présenteroient plus, ainsy même en pleine paix, sans recommencer la guerre, sans effusion de sang, sans aucune dépense, Sa Majesté n'usant que de son droit, peut oster pour jamais aux Anglois un commerce usurpé qui a formé et qui soutient encore aujourd'huy leur Colonie de Baston, ainsy qu'ils en conviennent eux-mêmes.

Il ne seroit pas si facile de leur ôter celuy de la côte de Terre Neuve, comme les Anglois en ont pris une espèce de possession, il semble qu'on ne pourroit les en chasser qu'en tems de guerre, mais pour lors la chose seroit fort aisé, si quelques Canadiens venus de Québec à Plaisance, où il y a plus de deux cens lieues par mer, ont ruiné ces dernières années toute la côte angloise, fait le dégât de leur sel, brûli leurs chaloupes, et leurs maisons, les habitans du Cap Breton qui seroient en bien plus grand nombre, qui auroient un intérêt particulier de détruire cette côte, et qui n'auroient que trente ou trente-cinq lieues de mer à traverser pour se rendre à Plaisance, seroient en état de les harceler si souvent qu'ils les forceroient enfin d'abandonner pour jamais un pays stérile qui ne produit rien et qu'ils n'occupent que par raport à la pesche qui y est très abondante.

Suposant donc les Anglois exclus de ces pêches, comme cela seroit sans doute lorsque l'Etablissement du Cap Breton seroit formé, ce commerce doubleroit chaque année en faveur de la France aussi bien que les droits des fermes de Sa Majesté, la chose parle d'elle-même.

Troisième Avantage.

Si l'on considère avec attention la progression des Anglois dans leurs Colonies de la Nouvelle Angleterre, on aura lieu de trembler pour celle de Canada, il n'y a point d'année qu'il ne naisse parmy eux autant d'enfans qu'il y a d'hommes dans tout le Canada, en peu d'années ce peuple sera dangereux et redoutable, et le Canada ne sera guères plus peuplé qu'il n'est aujourd'huy, soit douceur de climat qui favorise la culture de leurs terres, la progression de leurs bestiaux, et qui leur permet de naviguer en tout tems, soit industrie particulière, il est certain que leurs colonies sont établies de ce côte-là comme l'Angleterre même.

Il est encore tems de prévoir et de prévenir les suites inévitables de cette supériorité des Anglois, on ne doit pas douter qu'elle ne leur inspire enfin quelque jour, le dessein de se rendre maîtres du Canada et par là de toute l'Amérique septentrionale, quoy que le Canada ne paroisse pas fort important à ceux qui ne le connoissent pas à fond, il est certain néantmoins que la France perdroit avec ce pays-là le commerce des castors qui ne laisse pas d'être nécessaire et considérable par sa circulation celuy des originaux et des pelleteries qui se débitent dans le Royaume et chez les Etrangers et de quelques autres effets qu'on en pourroit tirer, mais on doit adjouter à cela qu'il est de la gloire et de la piété du Roy de ne pas laisser tomber un si grands pays entre les mains d'une nation hérétique, jealous du commerce des François et qui commenceroit à étouffer dans les cœurs de ses sujets et des sauvages les semences de la Religion.

En perdant le Canada la France perdroit encore les pesches des molües, les Anglois pour s'en assurer se fortifieroient dans tous les endroits avantageux, ils couvriroient ces mers et le grand Banc de leurs vaisseaux, la navigation en seroit fermée aux François, les matelots diminueroient de la moitié dans le Royaume, on seroit obligé de racheter la molüe des Anglois, les François perdroient la consommation des sels et des effets propres à la pesche, et Sa Majesté les droits que luy aportoit un si grand commerce, le mal seroit trop grand pour que Sa Majesté le pût souffrir, et ce ne pourroit être que par des dépenses prodigieuses et par la guerre ouverte qu'on pourroit rentrer dans la possession de ce qu'il est aisé de ne pas perdre en occupant le Cap Breton.

Cette Isle est le clef du Canada et de toutes les côtes de la Nouvelle France, en la fortifiant les Anglois ne pourront plus rien entreprendre de ce côté-là, ils ne s'aviseront jamais d'entrer dans le profondeur du Golfe de Saint Laurens pour monter jusqu'à Québec, pendant qu'ils auront derrière eux un poste de cette importance.

L'Acadie et Plaisance ne seroient pas moins en sûreté par cet Etablissement, le nombre et la valleur de ses habitans, leur expérience au fait de la navigation et des armes dont ils feroient un exercise continuel, les mettroient en peu de tems en état de tout entreprendre, de faire trembler les Anglois jusques dans Baston, et de désoler toutes leurs côtes en temps de guerre.

Le Cap Breton seroit encore le magasin général de tous ces pays, les habitans y trouveroient les marchandises, les effets et leurs secours dont ils auroient besoin en échange des vivres, des denrées et des autres choses qu'ils y apporteroient de Québec et d'ailleurs.

Quatrième Avantage.

Tous les vaisseaux qui reviennent des Isles de l'Amérique, du Mexique, du Pérou, de la Mer du Sud et mesme des grandes Indes sont obligez par la disposition des vents de venir chercher les hauteurs de Canada, et de passer à la pointe méridionale du Grand Banc de Terre Neuve pour retourner en Europe ; il arrive assés souvent que la plus part de ces vaisseaux manquent ou de vivres ou d'eau, ou de bois, qu'ils sont démâtez, qu'ils ont des voyes d'eau ou que leurs équipages sont malades, il y a encore près de sept cens lieues de là en France, où ils ne sont pas en estat de se rendre sans estre . . .

Tous les vaisseaux pescheurs et ceux qui passent au Cap Breton en allant à Québec s'y refugieront dans la nécessité la navigation de Canada étant des plus rudes, surtout en revenant de Québec dans l'arrière saison, les équipages et les passagers des vaisseaux qui auroient le malheur de faire naufrage dans le golfe de Canada pourroient trouver leur salut dans cet Etablissement. . . .

The writer then takes up objections to his project and concludes.

CONCLUSION

L'Etablissement proposé réunit toutes les pesches dans la main des François, en donne l'exclusion absolue aux Anglois, deffend les colonies de Canada, de Terre Neuve et de l'Acadie contre tous leurs efforts, empeschent [*sic*] qu'ils ne se rendent maîtres de tous ces grands pays, et par là mesme de toutes les pesches, il ruine leur colonie de Baston en les en excluant et sans leur faire la guerre, il est le refuge des vaisseaux incommodez qui fréquentent ces mers, ou pour la pesche ou pour les voyages de Canada, il devient le rendez-vous et l'entrepost des vaisseaux des Indes, des Isles de l'Amérique, de la Nouvelle Espagne, il augmente le nombre des matelots, il facilite le commerce de Canada et favorise le débit de ses grains et de ses denrées, il fournira les arceneaux de Sa Majesté de mâts, de vergues, de bordages, de planches, de pièces de construction, de bray, de goldrons, d'huiles de poisson, de charbon de terre, de plâtre et mesme de molües pour les victuailles des équipages, les étrangers qui ont accoutumé de fournir tous ces effets n'emporteront plus l'argent du Royaume, il augmente la domination de Sa Majesté, le commerce de ses sujets, les droits de ses fermes, et la consommation de sels et des denrées du Royaume, c'en est assez pour faire voir que cet Etablissement est enfin devenu d'une nécessité indispensable, et qu'il est tems d'y mettre efficacement la main.

Il ne reste plus qu'à donner dans un mémoire particulier les moyens de former à peu de frais un Etablissement de cette importance.—A Paris le trentième Novembre 1706.

NON SIGNÉ.

Note.—This document, with the exception of some changes in punctuation, and the correction of a few mistakes obviously those of a copyist, is printed verbatim. The soundness of its views as to the importance of Cape Breton, the stability of New England, the previsions of danger to French rule from its people, merit the attention of the reader.

CHAPTER II

THE declaration of the taking possession of Isle Royale stated that the selection of Louisbourg was provisional. The reports made and the plans submitted in person by St. Ovide to the King secured his approval, which was transmitted to L'Hermitte, with orders to place the fort on the point and the town behind it. This led to complaints from the latter that his plans had been modified and his views inaccurately stated by St. Ovide.

These instructions were definite ; but a discussion arose at once as to which should be made the principal place of the three settlements which were thought of. These were Louisbourg, Port Dauphin, and Port Toulouse. Each of them had many advantages, which were dealt with in many letters and memorials. Costebelle wrote to the Minister expressing his opinion, that great attention should be given to Port Toulouse, without claiming that it should be the seat of government, and asked a hearing for Meschin, Commander of the *Semslack*, who had revisited Louisbourg. When Meschin sought an audience with Pontchartrain he was sent on by him to Raudot the younger, who had been promoted from Quebec to the position of Intendant des Classes (Service Rolls). The Minister wrote to the latter that he would discuss the matter with him after his interview with Meschin.

Other letters also were sent to Pontchartrain. Rouville and La Ronde, in thanking him for their appointments on this pioneer expedition, gave their views on the three ports. The latter was enthusiastic over Port Dauphin, where they could do more work for ten thousand livres than for two hundred thousand in Louisbourg. Trees twenty-eight to thirty-eight inches in diameter and seventy feet long abound ; there is an abundance of oak, and not an inch of ground which is not fit to cultivate. He concluded by saying that New England is not worth one-tenth part of Cape Breton, but that he has seen with his own eyes how flourishing is the British colony, where every year they build fifteen hundred vessels.[1]

Costebelle repeated his first impression that they were working uselessly at

---

[1] These are exaggerations which go far to justify L'Hermitte's opinion of La Ronde. See note, p. 16.

Louisbourg, and that Vaudreuil, St. Ovide, and Soubras agreed with him, if their thoughts corresponded to their language. L'Hermitte tried to confine his expression to a statement of the advantages of the different places, but in sending his requisitions for material and men he added an estimate that it would take eight to ten years to build the forts at Louisbourg at a cost, even without the artillery, of eight or nine hundred thousand livres.

Bourdon, an experienced officer, whose map of Cape Breton was being used, was sent out with de Saugeon, the officer in command of the *Affriquain*, who was unfamiliar with these waters. Bourdon, too, submitted a memoir on this vexed and important question.[1] The advantages of Louisbourg, in his summing up the various views, were the ease of access, the excellent fishing close at hand, and, while the beaches were less in extent than at Port Dauphin, this was compensated for by the excellent sites found at various adjacent outports. The Port Dauphin beaches were less useful, as they were shut in by the high hills, the name of which has descended from the romance of Les Quatres Fils d'Aymon to Smith's Mountain. Port Dauphin was more easily fortified, the land was fertile, but the fishing grounds were several leagues from the port, and therefore required larger boats. Port Toulouse was not then seriously considered, nor does the name of Baie des Espagnols often appear, notwithstanding the anonymous memoir of 1706. Its wide entrance would be difficult to fortify, and it was distant from the fishing grounds. Louisbourg, moreover, had the advantage of not freezing over, and of being less incommoded by the drift ice in the spring, although this was not dwelt on and was perhaps unknown to the pioneers. Bourdon points out in his memoir that the fisheries are the sole object of care, that the only grain they need to grow is for poultry and fodder, as their requirements of wheat would make a commerce with Canada. He thus disposes of the agricultural superiority of Port Dauphin, enforcing this view by the fact that the Acadians would not go there, as they were seeking for meadows. He also takes up various questions as to the forts ; says that L'Hermitte's are too costly, and proposes in their stead two fortifications, one on the island and one on the point, which, giving protection against a sudden attack, would, as peace is likely to last, be all that is required. He concludes that, for ease of living, every one would prefer Port Dauphin, but, for public interest, Louisbourg is comparably better. The weight of local authority was against him. It was supported by the merchants of France, while the Court was dismayed at the amount of money which Louisbourg would require.

Instructions were sent out to Costebelle and Soubras that Port Dauphin should be made the principal place ; that they, the staff, and the larger part of the garrison, four companies, should be established in that place ; that St. Ovide

[1] C^{11} I.R. vol. I, p. III.

should command at Louisbourg with two companies, and De Pensens, aide-major, should go to Port Toulouse. These instructions arrived in due course, but Costebelle, advised by a private letter of the decisions before they came to hand, had already taken action. In June he sent L'Hermitte to lay out the work at Port Dauphin. Rouville also went there, and again merited the praises of his superiors, by doing with his sixty men effective work in building a storehouse, bakehouse, and forge. In September they were engaged on the barracks, which were substantial, as it was proposed that they should serve afterwards as an hospital, and Costebelle, who was on the ground, hoped that these would be finished before winter.

Port Toulouse, preferred by the Acadians, was allotted a garrison of forty men under De Pensens, and a small fort for the purpose of giving confidence to the new settlers was laid out by Couagne. The value of this place had been considered small on account of the shallow entrance of its harbour, but soundings proved that there were three channels with deep water—two of four and a half, and one of three fathoms. Meschin and his pilot went with Costebelle from Port Dauphin to Port Toulouse, by the Bras d'Or Lakes, and confirmed the information. The channels were crooked, but could be made safe by buoys, which in time of war could be removed, making the harbour "easy to friends, inaccessible to enemies."

Louisbourg was so neglected that Soubras urged Costebelle to send to Port Toulouse, St. Ovide and most of the Louisbourg garrison, as no work could be done at the latter place during the winter. L'Hermitte's part of this work was tentative, for he had been superseded by Beaucour, who arrived in the autumn, and he had experienced the bitterness of receiving the Minister's strictures on his slowness before the letters arrived promoting him to the post of Major at Three Rivers. Thereafter in the more settled conditions of Canada he did good work, until, returning from France on the *Chameau* in 1725, his long career in the public service ended in her shipwreck a few miles from Louisbourg.

The Acadian situation was not easy; although Vaudreuil, Costebelle, and Soubras had signed a memoir begging the Court to do the impossible by sending a vessel, nothing more was accomplished than sending some of the gear for their boats.[1] Part of it was delivered, but very few of them had come to Isle Royale. Early in the year 1715 news came to Louisbourg that Nicholson had in the autumn told the Acadians that those of them who intended leaving must go at once and not wait until the spring. The King instructed the French ambassador to ask permission to send a ship for them, and the request having been made, time was being lost in waiting for a reply, and the action of the

[1] Vol. I, 107, October 16, 1714.

French Government was thus hampered. The solution was left to the local authorities ; they were to avail themselves of any of the three vessels which had to come out—the *Semslack*, the *Affriquain*, or the *Mutine*—and send one of them for the Acadians.

Father Dominique de la Marche, who was Grand Vicar of the Bishop of Quebec, had been sent on a mission to the Acadians at Port Toulouse, where he met representatives of prosperous families of Minas who were there, the results of which he stated in a letter, September 7. In it he recounts the position and fidelity of the Acadians, and states that promises solemnly made through the missionaries as well as the envoys, La Ronde and Pensens, had not been kept, and urges that a vessel should be sent, as he fears further delay. Although Costebelle was absent at Port Dauphin, a council was held the same day, at which Soubras, St. Ovide, Villejouin, Renon, Ste. Marie, de la Perelle, officers of the garrison, met the missionary. They decided that they must have some pretext for sending a vessel, either the disavowal of the Indian hostilities against the English or replacing a missionary. They decided that de Pensens, a favourite with the Acadians, and de la Perelle, who spoke English, should go on the *Mutine* (Captain de Courcey), which should be provisioned for bringing back the Acadians ; but that if they could not make them come, or if opposition was offered, they should return. The *Mutine* started on the voyage, but, meeting heavy weather and contrary winds, returned to Louisbourg without having reached Annapolis.

In August of the following year (1716) de la Marche left Port Dauphin, where he was established, and visited Acadia, returning in September. He says that the Acadians were not to blame for not coming, and acknowledges that they were no longer in the mood to come, while Costebelle had made up his mind that they would remain where they were. The authorities wrote to the Minister that the Acadians were to take an oath that the Anglican Church was the only true one, that the Virgin was a woman like any other, that the Pretender was a bastard, and that they would be faithful to the new King ; but this fable, possibly because it was a fable, moved neither the Acadians to leave nor the Ministry to come to their aid.[1]

These are the first of many incidents which mark the care of the French officials to avoid giving offence to the English. Their attitude was defensive ; the instructions sent out to them were to avoid quarrels and not to resent aggressions. The only firm note in many years is La Ronde's letter to Nicholson, in which he states that the King intends to maintain the rights accorded to the Acadians by Queen Anne, the outcome of his preference for the

---

[1] "Contenant que la religion Anglicanne est la seule véritable, que la Ste. Vierge est une femme comme une autre, que le Prétendu Prince de Galles est bâtard, et qu'ils promettent fidélité au nouveau Roy" (C¹¹ I.R. 2, p. 90).

grand manner rather than of the instructions given to him. The garrison of Annapolis, weaker than that of Louisbourg, was powerless to prevent the Acadians removing. They were entitled to leave ; the question of time had not been settled, and, had the policy of France been aggressive or a pacific one administered by strong men, the sending of ships for the Acadians could have been defended as entirely justifiable. But when we take up later in this chapter the conditions in France, the causes of many things which happened in Louisbourg will be made clear.

The efforts of the French to prevent the Indians of Acadia from acknowledging the sovereignty of England had been successful, and they had largely moved to Antigonish, nearer Isle Royale, without making any settlement. The relations of the New Englanders with the Indians of Acadia had not been friendly. The fishermen who frequented the adjacent fishing-grounds could not dry their catch on shore, as they were driven off by the savages, although solitary Frenchmen lived among them and traded with the English vessels. The Indian hostility was bitter. The Micmacs, finding two dead bodies of their young men, jumped to the conclusion that they had been killed by the English, and in revenge pillaged nine or ten vessels. A vessel of twelve or fourteen guns which was cast away in St. George's Bay was taken and the crew ill-treated, in spite of the efforts of Father Gaulin to protect them. The cause of this outbreak was their belief that all their tribe at Minas was dying of poison administered by the English. A similar case occurred at Beaubassin, and again the crew were protected by Father Felix. Costebelle, referring to these and similar incidents, informed the Minister that pillaging was going on which they tried to prevent. Capon, storekeeper at Annapolis, was sent to Louisbourg in 1715 to complain of the action of the allies of the French. An account of this mission is found in Meschin's answer to a charge of wasting His Majesty's stores, brought against him by the purser of his own ship, who reported that, being a godfather at Louisbourg, he had fired a salute of one hundred guns and wasted powder to the value of 1600 livres. Meschin said in reply that he had proved to the Commandant and Intendant of Rochefort, where the charge was made, that this was untrue. The facts were that Sieur Capon, Commissary-General, had come from Acadia to Isle Royale representing General Neilson (Nicholson) to ask for justice from the Indians, our allies, who had captured some English vessels in the Strait of Canso and pillaged their crews. On which matter, the heads of the Colony not being able otherwise to satisfy the envoy, we had tried to content him with many civilities and feasting ("De le contenter par beaucoup de caresses et de bonne chère"). Meschin contributed to this end by a dinner on board the *Semslack*, given the third day of Capon's stay, to which he invited the Governor, Soubras, other officers, and the principal inhabitants to the number of forty-five. Monsieur Capon desired to drink the health of King Louis, and Meschin felt bound, as a loyal servant, to fire a salute of nine guns ; courtesy demanded an equal number when they drank to King George, then five were fired for the Admiral of France, and an uncertain number for the principal French and English general officers. The hospitable officer was forgiven for having only a general knowledge that the number of guns was less than one hundred. The Navy Board did not make him pay for these *feux de joie*.[1]

The guests of Meschin gathered from miserable quarters. The houses in which they lodged, grouped about the larger dwelling of the Governor, were built of pickets upright in the ground, a meaner type of construction than a log hut. On the other side of the little stream was a temporary battery of twelve guns, and the remainder of the cannon lay on the beach immediately below the Governor's house.[2] The merchants who were bidden came for the most part from the other side of the arm, where they had already established their simple dwellings adjacent to the beaches, where their fish were cured, and the site selected for the fortifications. We have some idea of the military officers who gathered on this occasion, for Costebelle, in a long letter to the Minister treating of various subjects, gives a description of himself and his associates.[3] He himself is fifty-four, his passions weakened by years, but his zeal great. He works from daylight till noon ; at dinner they sit long and make decently merry. This is borne out by Soubras, who says that, although Costebelle is despotic, his sociable humour contributes to keep the peace between them. Besides the difficulties of his office, Costebelle is overwhelmed by private debts, and is anxious to get to France to find means to extricate himself. St. Ovide, he says, is devout, and has all the talents of a man of the sword and of a writer, but he exaggerates. Beaucour has talents, and will find plenty of room for their exercise. Ligondez is a good officer, is never too slow, sometimes too lively. La Ronde Denys is also good, independent, energetic, fine, but will be better when age has modified his temperament and he is free from the influence of doubtful relations. Villejouin is good. Rouville, a phœnix for labours. Ste. Marie, Costebelle's brother-in-law, a Provençal, is inclined to be close.

[1] Ar. Nat. Marine, C, 7, 206.   [2] Young's Map.

[3] "Pour luy deffiner le cours de ma vie présante il est temps que j'ai atteint l'aage de 54 ans, où les passions vives et turbulentes s'affoiblessent d'elle meme, il n'y a que celles de mon devoir que se soient fortfié et je n'ay jamais eu tant d'occasion de faire briller mon zelle par la situation où toutes choses se trouvent aujourd'hui, pour d'accuser juste à votre grandeur je lui diray que je suis vigilant à toutte sorte d'heure de point de jour jusque à midy m'occupe le plus, apres quoy je reste assa longtemps à table avec l'élitte des officiers mais il se commet rien dans nos plus riantes societtés qui tiennent de la Crapule, ni que derrange les fonctions militaires, non plus que les travaux projettés que mes orders ont précédés, nostre honneste gallanterie ne scandalise personne et s'il y a quelque libertinage outre dans le commun du peuple, il n'est toléré qu'autant qu'il m'est inconu.

"Monsieur de St. Ovide me ressamble assais avec 15 ans de moins, il prie dieu un peu plus longtemps sans adorer plus humblemant que moy sa divine providence" (C^{11} I.R. vol. I, p 152½).

Renon also is good, and all the junior officers satisfactory, especially Couagne, who deserves promotion. These descriptions testify to his amiability, but they have to be modified from other sources. Ligondez the Major says : "Rouville's is the only company looked after, that the other Captains think it beneath their dignity to care for their men, and that Villejouin is lazy." Ste. Marie was ordered under arrest by the Minister for allowing a girl to escape from the primitive hut which served as the town prison, and severe reproofs were administered to Villejouin.

Costebelle was overwhelmed by the condition in which they found themselves in the autumn. It was against both discipline and effective work. The *Semslack* and the *Mutine* had come out, the former with 5000 livres in money and a few stores, costing an equal amount, which were spoiled on the voyage, to meet 180,000 livres unpaid for 1714, and 450,000 livres allotted to the expenses of this year. The arrival of the *Affriquain*, which had their supplies, was expected with more and more eagerness, until, when her arrival became doubtful, famine seemed imminent. The provisioning of the outports was put off as late as possible, but as well as they could they worked on. The principal officers and troops were moved to Port Dauphin. The guns brought from Placentia, both English and French, were tested by the Aide-Artillerie of the garrison and the master gunner of the *Semslack*, and the greater part allotted to Port Dauphin, although only eighteen were taken there in this season.[1]

Civil government went on also. Soubras, new to the colonies, made ordinances regulating the beaches, hospital dues, the prices of fish and the rates of wages, and the entries and clearances of vessels. These provoked remonstrances from the outfitting merchants in France as well as the inhabitants of the town. They also disturbed the Acadians, who, from what a writer calls the republican state in which they had lived, found all regulations irksome. Neither effective work could be done nor good morals preserved with the prospect of famine before the people and the officers. Costebelle had hoped to have the barracks at Port Dauphin finished by the winter, but in the late autumn Soubras found that nothing had been done for three months, as the soldiers, even under de Rouville, the most capable of all the officers, had been building

[1] Port Dauphin.		Louisbourg.	
6 of 36 lbs.		3 of 36 lbs.	
8 „ 24 „		4 „ 24 „	
12 „ 18 „		9 „ 18 „	
12 „ 12 „		5 „ 12 „	
6 „ 8 „		8 „ 8 „	
6 „ 6 „		14 „ 6 „	
50 guns		43 guns	
26 mortars.		1 mortar.	

Not only the number but the calibre of the guns sent to Port Dauphin were greatly superior.

themselves huts in the woods. The scarcity of provisions was increased by the necessity of supplying the *Semslack* for her voyage back to France. At the end of the season the authorities, after sending back all the sick and young soldiers, two hundred and twenty in all, about half the garrison, took from the merchants of the town, the ships in the harbour, and even from private houses the provisions they could find. Laforest, the clerk who was charged with this duty, says he made many enemies by undertaking this odious task. Costebelle does not hesitate to write to the Minister that the Government plunders those whom it should protect. The condition at Louisbourg, as the declining, although the most populous place, was worst. Its inhabitants were in consternation, and had represented to Costebelle and Soubras that their port was the only one; the captains of the French vessels also confirmed this view, and held that Louisbourg must be re-established. If, instead of drawing the good men from all the companies for Port Dauphin, St. Ovide had been given a few workmen and the two companies allotted to that place, he could have made it tenable; as it was he had three captains, one lieutenant, two ensigns, three corporals, seventeen soldiers, five workmen, and one sick carpenter.

The fishing had been good on the whole, especially at Port Toulouse and Port Dauphin. Sixty-four vessels had come out from France, which had three hundred and eight boats in all. The prediction that the vicissitudes of 1715 would tell on the industry the following year was justified by the results, for in 1716 only twenty vessels came from France. The situation was so bad that St. Ovide wrote that he feared that the pirates who infested these waters, knowing the unprotected condition of the town, might attack it after the King's ships had left. Soubras said the colony by a single repetition of this state of affairs would be ruined, that the officers were as badly off as the privates, and Laperelle was sent to Court to represent personally their desperate position.

It is difficult to read the documents from which this narrative has been compiled and not to believe that the wretched state of Isle Royale was owing to incompetence and neglect on the part of the home administration. It is equally difficult to read the accounts of France in the previous score of years, while the kingly sun of the great Louis was descending behind the clouds, all of which tell of hideous poverty, of a stagnant commerce, of an almost naked peasantry suffering from severe winters, from plague and pestilence, of governmental interference which aggravated the miseries of the people, and not to wonder how the ordinary expenses were provided for, how pensions could be allotted or gratuities given to deserving officers, or a new establishment like Louisbourg carried on.

The exhaustion not only of the public treasury but of public credit was complete in the last year of Louis XIV.'s reign. The Navy Board met and made their

arrangements for the season's work.   The King had approved the appropriation of
410,000 l. for Isle Royale, a trifle of 10,000 l. had been asked for the Acadians,
but Demarêts, the Treasurer, had not sent it.   Pontchartrain put himself on
record as to the importance of Isle Royale, in a passage which has been quoted.
No reply was received to this letter.   He asks for these funds in March, as the
needs are most urgent and the time is short.   At the end of the month he
takes up the question of overdue bills of exchange for Canada.   He brings
pressure to bear on the Treasurer, through Monsieur de Nointel, to whom he
suggests a lottery, or a tax on lotteries.   Meantime, the usual administrative
details are being carried on for the officering and provisioning of the ships and
providing the cargoes.

Funds for the navy were so low in these years that it was found impossible to equip a
frigate and buy supplies without borrowing fifty to sixty thousand livres from private
sources.   (Pontchartrain to Desmarets, April 21, 1713, M. St. M. vol. 50.)

Lettre de M. des Maretz, ministre des finances, à M. le Comte de Pontchartrain
(Versailles, 31 décembre 1713), extrait :

"A l'Egard des fonds que vous demandez pour l'Evacuation de Plaisance, et
l'Establissemᵗ de l'Isle Royale, Je prendray incessamment les ordres du Roy pour destiner
à cette dépense ceux que sa Majesté jugera àpropos sur les premiers deniers qui pouront
estre ménagez. . . ."   (Arch. Nat. Marine, B3, 216.)

Three weeks later he writes again, expressing surprise and pleasure that one
of his Intendants had found means to pay the men who had been working on the
ships for Isle Royale, and by the middle of May insists that the money be found ;
otherwise, that colony will fail and England will be mistress of the cod fisheries.
He is disquieted by the news from the outfitting port of Rochefort, where the
long unpaid men refused to work on these ships.   Later in the month the
Intendant Montholon writes him that merchants will not supply goods without
prompt payment.   Early in June the *Semslack* is sent off to show the troops
and settlers that the King has not forgotten them, but the evil conditions
continue.   Other merchants will not sell, even with special assurance of payment ;
other workmen refuse to continue in the King's dockyards ; seamen engaged for
the voyages of these ships have deserted ; there was no money to be found.   His
proposal, made in March, to establish a new lottery for the benefit of the colony,
or to impose a tax, for the same purpose, of 3 per cent on existing lotteries, was
not accepted, and the end came on the 21st of August 1715, three days before
the illness of the King began, when the Minister sent orders to the Intendant of
La Rochelle to have the *Affriquain* dismantled, as it was too late to send her
to Isle Royale.   Compared with the early years of other settlements, Annapolis,
for example, Isle Royale was not badly off ; compared with great monarchies,

few of those which have survived ever found themselves more exhausted than was France at this time.

On September 1, 1715, Louis XIV. died. It is not a necessary part of this narrative to recount the disposition he made for the Regency during the minority of his great-grandson. Parliament was summoned at once; Orléans triumphed over the legitimized princes and the will of the King, and was made Regent with the power to nominate the Council of the Regency, to whose hands was committed the conduct of affairs. The dissoluteness of Philip Duke of Orléans, the extravagance, the gracefulness of the art of his epoch, Law's marvellous achievements, his stupendous breakdown, are the things which stand out in the popular conception of the Regent's history. They are just elements in that conception, but it is equally true that the Regent is perhaps the most conspicuous instance of modern times of one in a splendid position whose moral corruption made impotent, except for evil, a great capacity for affairs.

France saw with relief the ending of the epoch of Louis XIV. Her people gladly welcomed the declaration of the Regent that he intended to follow the plans of the Duke of Burgundy, that upright and intelligent grandson of the late King, the docile pupil of Fénelon, whose advent to the throne, until his premature death, had been regarded as the promise of better things. Louis XIV.'s boast that "L'État c'est moi" had been as nearly realized as possible, but it had worked out, in the view of the Regent's supporters, into there being in administrative affairs an absolute ruler in each department into which the business of the State was divided. The remedy proposed for this was the institution of Councils. The "Seven Councils" proposed by the Duke of Burgundy were established by the Regent. They gave a great subdivision of labour, and a firmer grasp of administration than under the previous system. In the division of affairs under Louis XV. a more logical view was taken by the recognition of the internal affairs of the kingdom as worthy a department, and by the institution, as an afterthought, of a Conseil de Commerce. One historian of the Regency speaks disparagingly of the composition of the Councils, but La Cour-Gayet,[1] the historian of the French Navy in the reign of Louis XV., who begins a chapter, "Banqueroute financière, banqueroute morale, banqueroute politique, c'est sous les auspices de cette triple faillite nationale que s'ouvrit le règne de l'arrière petit-fils de Louis le Grand," and therefore may fairly be assumed to have no predisposition to apologise for the acts of the Regent, says of the Navy Board that it would have been difficult to find eleven better names than those the Regent selected. His only criticism is that Duguay-Trouin was not a member.

At the head of the Council was the Comte de Toulouse, one of the

[1] La Cour-Gayet, *La Marine militaire de la France sous Louis XV*, Paris, 1902.

legitimized sons of the King, Admiral of France, owing his place to his origin, but who, nevertheless, had distinguished himself in command of the French fleet in battle with those of England and Holland at Velez Malaga. D'Estrées was President, and he too had shared in the same battle. St. Simon praises him as honourable, upright, and understanding the Navy. Tessé, Coëtlogon, d'Asfeild, and Champigny were officers of merit and brilliant services. Renau was a naval engineer of resource whose invention of the bomb ketch marked a distinct advance in naval warfare, De Vauvré an Intendant of the Navy of more than excellent reputation, Ferraud a lawyer. Bonrepaus, a collaborator of Colbert and predecessor of Raudot as Intendant des Classes, had always had a reputation as an unequalled administrator. Pontchartrain was dismissed, although to secure this result his position was promised to his son Maurepas, then a boy of fifteen. A more systematic way of carrying on the affairs of the department was instituted. The regulation for the colonial correspondence was business-like. Instructions were sent out that each letter should deal with one matter only ; [1] subordinate officers were to be no longer permitted to write to the Council as they had to the Minister ; military officers would report to the Governor, civil officers to the Intendant or Commissaire-Ordonnateur, on their private affairs ; officials could write to members of the Board, but should address it only if they were giving information of malversation.

The documents concerning Isle Royale bear out the views of La Cour-Gayet. Careful agenda for the meetings of the Board were now prepared, business was disposed of promptly, although precedent seemed slavishly followed, marginal notes indicated the reference of many questions to the best-informed officials, such as Raudot and Verville, when he was in France, and all items of importance were brought to the personal notice of the Regent, who gave immediate decisions. Whatever may have been his vices, or the soundness of his views, he attended to the business of Isle Royale.

[1] This was ignored at Louisbourg.

CHAPTER III

THE Navy Board took up the direction of affairs with vigour, although they were seriously cramped by the lack of funds; for the hope of better things, which the Regent's government inspired, had relieved, only to the slightest degree, the scarcity of money. At the earliest possible time, letters were written to the officials saying that provisions would be sent them from one of the southern ports early in the spring, and that the deplorable conditions of the winter of 1715 would not be permitted to occur again. This promise was kept, for the first merchant ships arrived on the 10th of April 1716, and in May the first provisions sent out had been received. The sufferings of the winter had not been extreme, although conditions must have been far from comfortable. At Port Toulouse they were almost without bread, many of their cattle had died from lack of fodder, and two shipwrecks on Isle Madame had added to the miseries of their situation. To relieve the distress of the inhabitants at Louisbourg, St. Ovide had to supply them from the stores of the garrison. On the other hand, the supply of intoxicants being reduced to a minimum, the garrison was never in better health.

The change of administration at home leads naturally to an account of the objects which were sought in the settlement of Isle Royale, the conditions there which affected the attainment of the end aimed at, and the administrative machinery which the Navy Board employed. The narrative of what took place at Louisbourg will show the degree of success its administration attained, as well as the effectiveness of the methods the Board employed. The object was to establish at Isle Royale a flourishing settlement based on its principal industry, the fisheries, and the development of the other resources of the Island, and an *entrepôt* at which the commerce based on these industries might be carried on with France, the West Indies, and Canada. The first encouragement given to this trade before the Board took charge was the remission of the duties on coal coming from Isle Royale (January 29, 1715). A year later fish and fish oils were also allowed free importation into France, and at a later date again, duties on products of the French West Indies, coming

43

by way of Louisbourg, were also removed.   The exemptions were each for a term of ten years, but in each case they were, as the time elapsed, renewed.[1]

The sustenance of several hundred people on an island which produced at the time no food for man except its abundant fish and game, was the object of vital importance.   Supplies were to be drawn from France and Canada, which was entirely in accordance with the economic policy of the time; also from Acadia.   This trade was on the border-land of the permitted, for although it was a British colony, the fact that its inhabitants were French, who, it was hoped, would remove to Isle Royale, made it politic to encourage this intercourse.   On account, however, of the higher state to which agriculture had been developed in New England, and the keenness for profitable trade of its inhabitants, it was not only the surest, but the cheapest source of supply for the nourishment of these French settlers.

The advantages of this commerce, foreseen by Raudot, were felt by Coste-belle, who wrote proposing that, as far as concerned the products of those colonies, it should be permitted to Isle Royale.   The Board, being advised that French merchants would cease to send their vessels to Isle Royale if his view was accepted, decided, instead, to make more stringent rules against all commercial intercourse with foreigners.

The cost of food stuffs from France was very high, the supply in Canada was uncertain, from both the voyage was difficult, and the cost of transportation therefore high; intercourse with Acadia was dependent on the inaction of its English administration, who complained at a later date that there was often scarcity in Annapolis when Louisbourg was abundantly supplied.   The local officials therefore found themselves hampered by the prohibition of commercial intercourse with its most advantageous source of supply.

The administration of the Colony was nominally part of the government of New France, but the affairs of Isle Royale were directed from the Cabinet of the Minister, and the Governor and Intendant of Canada were advised about the affairs of Isle Royale only in as far as the business of the two colonies was concerned.   The connection was kept alive, however, in the phraseology of Royal documents which were addressed to the authorities of New France as well as those of Isle Royale, although the subject-matter concerned the latter colony alone.

The chief official of the Colony was the Governor, and next to him in rank was, in Isle Royale, the Commissaire-Ordonnateur discharging the functions which, in more important colonies, as Canada, in the provinces of France, and in quasi-dependent states such as Lorraine during the reign there of Stanislas of Poland, were those of the Intendant.

[1] Moreau St. Méry, vol. 50, pp. 27, 43, 54, 576.

All military matters except the commissariat were under the exclusive control of the Governor, as well as the disposition of any vessels, which, however, he was obliged to supply to the Commissaire-Ordonnateur. Grants of lands and the maintenance of order were common to both, while the administration of justice, the supervision of the hospital, the care of the King's stores, and the providing of supplies belonged exclusively to the Commissaire-Ordonnateur. The Governor represented the military, the Commissaire-Ordonnateur the civil element. There was natural antagonism between the two, and every letter of joint instructions from the Minister inculcated the necessity of harmony. But the distinction between their departments was not easy to draw, and constant friction resulted, although the home administration did all that it could to minimize its causes. Their seats in church, the order in which the sacrament should be administered, their places in processions were regulated. While the easy-going Costebelle had no trouble with Soubras, St. Ovide constantly quarrelled with the three Commissaire-Ordonnateurs who served with him. They quarrelled about precedence, about the realities of business, about its formalities, and while probably no staff of a government or corporation is free from jealousy or rivalry, these motives are not allowed, under a strong administration, to interfere with efficiency. The conditions at Louisbourg, however, were so bad that, as an instance, the Council writes that the Governor and the Commissaire-Ordonnateur seem to agree only in one thing, that being to hamper the engineer in the work of building the fortifications. Their disagreements reached, in the same year, such a point that St. Ovide, the Governor, and de Mezy, who had replaced Soubras, were informed that if they could not agree, remedies would be proposed to the Regent which would be disagreeable to them both.[1] Even so sharp a threat as this did not make things go smoothly for long. But it would be unfair to come to the conclusion that the officials of Isle Royale were entirely occupied in such rivalries. Each in his own department was desirous of doing well, or at least of standing well with the Minister. Each was jealous of the dignity of his office, and feared to secure an immediate benefit to the common weal by making concessions which might diminish the prestige of the position he occupied.

Verville and Verrier, the engineers of the fortifications, Isabeau and Ganet, the contractors who built them, saw only the necessity of hastening on this work to which they were urged by the home Government. They complained of St. Ovide, who, as military head, was bound to protect the interest of the captains whose soldiers worked for the contractors. The Commissaire-Ordonnateur, equally with the Governor, did not care for this work, being in great part independent of them, and the latter having to submit to the outlay for the fortifications

[1] B, vol. 42, f. 480 and 490, July 9, Sept. 20, 1720.

being kept separate from the current accounts of the establishment. Zeal is not as likely to produce such friction as slackness, but in an isolated community, without a supreme head, so distant that it took months to get a decision from the highest authority, public interest suffered even from the unharmonized zeal of the officials.

The ordinary course of business was that the Commissaire-Ordonnateur and the Governor wrote joint letters to the Board, and that each addressed it separately, on subjects exclusively in his control ; and that in reply the Board, and afterwards the Minister, wrote in the same way. Sometimes it happened that the Commissaire-Ordonnateur, in another letter, withdrew statements which he had signed in the joint letter in the interests of harmony.[1] This correspondence and the accounts were taken up at headquarters, analyzed, evidently by well-informed and able subordinates of the Minister, and the replies sent out by the men of war which sailed in the early summer ; so that the normal intercourse was to have letters written in the autumn answered in the following May or June. It is obvious from Ministerial replies that other sources of information than the letters of colonial officials were available. One of these sources was the presence in France of officers of the garrison on leave, who were given the despatches and probably had an audience with the Minister.[2] Another unquestionably was correspondence which no longer is available, and a third was the presence in France of officials familiar with the conditions of the Colony. From one or all of these were gathered the statements on which the decisions of the Council and Ministers were made.[3]

A superior council was established in 1717 which consisted of the Governor, the King's Lieutenant, the Commissaire-Ordonnateur sitting as first councillor, two other councillors, a procureur-general, and a greffier. This was a Court of Justice governed by the Coutume de Paris, from which appeals were allowed to Quebec and France, and only after registration by it did patents, proclamations, regulations, and grants of land become effective. There was also established an Admiralty Court [4] which had charge of shipping, wrecks, and marine police. It was sustained by moderate fees on the shipping of the port, and being under the High Admiral of France, who had certain rights over prizes, confiscations, and wrecks, created a new source of conflict.

Of greater importance than the " men of the pen," who were officials, Treasurer, clerks, and the like, under the Commissaire-Ordonnateur, were the " men of the sword," the officers of the troops which the French administration, unlike that of England, thought it necessary to keep in an isolated colony even

---

[1] *E.g.* Soubras, I.R. vol. 3, f. 186.

[2] La Perelle, who went with dispatches in 1721, had an audience with the Regent arranged for him (I.R. 2, 378).

[3] The major of the troops, the Treasurer and officers of the Admiralty wrote annually. The rules of the Board as to correspondence were not strictly observed.   [4] Edict of Jan. 12, 1727.

in time of profound peace. These troops were neither regular regiments of the splendid armies of France nor "Compagnies Franches de la Marine," which, formed in 1690, garrisoned the naval depôts of France and served on her King's ships, although in organization and uniform the Louisbourg troops closely resembled the latter corps. They were apparently supplementary companies organized on the same basis, for the total number of the Compagnies Franches[1] is accounted for in other services than that of the Colony. There is some looseness in the way the Isle Royale troops are described. La Ronde and de Pensens announced themselves to Armstrong in 1714 as captains of "Compagnies Franches." Later these were described as "Compagnies Dé-tachées," also as "Compagnies Françaises." Each company was a separate unit, and the only purely military officer over the company commanders was a major in each garrison to supervise the discipline of the companies in the place. He had so little authority that the supervision was usually ineffective, and a status so uncertain that he had to have at Louisbourg a declaration that he took precedence of the captains of the companies.

The strength of the garrison of Louisbourg varied from six of these companies to twenty-four in the last years. Each consisted of forty-five men, raised later to sixty, and in 1742 to seventy, not counting the drummer, under command of a captain, lieutenant, enseigne (an enseigne en deux was added, and two cadets a l'aiguilette), two sergeants and two corporals.[2] The rations were somewhat better than those of Canada, following in this the custom which had obtained in Placentia, and for the lower grades of the officers the pay also was slightly higher, although Soubras states that it was inadequate.[3] The uniform was white with blue facings. At Louisbourg the soldiers were allowed to marry, and apparently it was a perquisite of the married soldiers to keep taverns.

The pay of the men was small, but they were supposed to carry on the work of the King in building fortifications and similar works, for which they received extra pay. They were also allowed to work for the inhabitants, which added to their income. The fact that they were only paid twice a year, their fondness for drink, their captains supplying them with it, and at a profit to themselves,[4] made of these troops an undisciplined and ineffective body, which punishments did not deter from evil courses nor inducements to settle, turn into good citizens.

The officers began their career early; they were entered as soldiers at the

---

[1] The only account I have found of this body, which deals only incidentally with the troops at Isle Royale, is *Les Anciennes Troupes de la Marine*, by G. Coste, Paris, 1893.

[2] B, 35, f. 786.   [3] I.R. vol. 2, p. 120.

[4] The outfit was inadequate. Soubras pointed out in 1717 that it was impossible that one pair of shoes and stockings should last for a year.

earliest age, even unweaned, "à la mamelle," says L'Hermitte, but, counting this an exaggeration, it is known that the sons, six years old, of officers served in the ranks, that is, drew rations and pay. They passed through the various grades reasonably certain of a pension, unless by gross misconduct they forfeited their positions. An early act of the Regency was to fix the age of entrance at sixteen. The commissions in these companies were not confined exclusively to those trained for them. Indeed the militant forces were rather treated as one, whether their service was on sea or land, and there were not infrequent instances of company officers taking a position on board ships, and of sea officers being translated into officers of these companies. The rank of the captain corresponded to Enseigne de Vaisseau, for practical purposes as well as precedence.[1]

The conditions at Louisbourg were bad for the officers as well as for the men, their relations, the superior making pecuniary profit out of the inferior, were demoralizing for both parties, and the permanence of residence for both officers and men added another to the many causes which worked against effectiveness. There were few changes among the officers except by death, and in the quietude of Louisbourg, man after man rose slowly through the different grades, placing his sons in the same service, and passed away without at any moment discharging the serious duties of his profession. Eight company officers signed the declaration of taking possession in 1713, the descendants of six of them were at the siege in 1745, and in addition to these, many of the earlier officers were represented by sons and grandsons at the second siege. From 1713 to 1744 not more active duty was required of these officers than garrison service in the town, in one of its outposts, or an occasional mission to Quebec or Boston. Thus, owing to the trivial distances they travelled, to that extraordinary genius of the French for dealing with the aborigines, they had neither the training in adventurous journeys nor in the diplomacy which the transforming into permanent allies of new tribes gave to the officer serving in Canada. The glimpses which they got of France in the leave which many of them enjoyed, brought them in touch from time to time with social conditions different from their own. The effect of such visits was transitory. The permanent pressure on the individual came from the standards of a small place, with its relationships of blood, marriage, and the social and official adjustments which propinquity forces on the members of an isolated community. The fishing which the officers carried on in their own names in 1717, and not improbably through other parties to a later time, brought them into touch with the bourgeois merchants, marriages took place, and in time we find children of these merchants and of civil officials serving as officers of these companies. In

[1] St. Ovide in 1732 was made a post-captain in the navy (B, vol. 57).

every respect the conditions were unfavourable to professional and social development, so that the readiness for service and the zeal we find in many instances is satisfactory evidence of the tough fibre of sound moral qualities. In one instance, that of Joseph de Catalogne, an officer spent his leisure in scientific studies to such effect that his treatise on the magnet gained for him a seat in the Académie des Sciences. Some of these officers had some training as engineers, and although the fortifications of Louisbourg were in charge of an engineer sent out from France, these officials assisted him and were in charge of the fortifications which were built at the outports. The Couange family were in this position, and the work of some other young officers was praised by the authorities, while incidentally it may be mentioned that Lartigue, the King's storekeeper, an amateur engineer, displayed skill during the first siege, and there remains to us an admirable map of the siege of 1758 which is his handiwork.[1] The garrison was further supplemented by some half companies of the Swiss regiment of Karrer, which was first formed in 1719, and included in its ranks many deserters from foreign regiments. It was in 1720 transferred to the department of the navy, and thereafter detachments were sent out, not only to Louisbourg, but to the southern colonies of France. One of the advantages of these troops was that they were a relief to those of France, and furnished a larger proportion of skilled workmen than could be found among the recruits for the French companies.

The industry for which this organization was established, the fisheries, and for the protection of which not only was the garrison maintained but fortifications were built, was carried on both by vessels filled out in France and by merchants resident in Louisbourg and its outports.[2]

A complicated trade of this kind, in which the Government undertook to regulate wages and prices of the product, gave rise to much controversy. The disposition of the local authorities was naturally to favour the merchants and fishermen of the place against their competitors who came out for the season. Regulations were passed against the traders from France remaining all winter, against their seiling at retail.[3] The French merchants as well as the natives complained of a tax, following the precedent of Placentia, of a quintal of fish from each boat for the support of the hospital. The Board gave way to the representations of the merchants, and it was not till some years later that the tax was imposed. So far did St. Ovide at a later date carry his favouring of local enterprise that the trade with Quebec received a most serious check on account of the regulations that vessels from Canada should not leave port with their cargoes unsold. This placed them at the mercy of a ring of local buyers, so that

---

[1] *Arch. de la M. Sec. Hydro.* herein reproduced.
[2] For details of this trade see Chapter XII.   [3] Those were disallowed by the Navy Board.

the Quebec vessels ceased for a time to come to Louisbourg. Regulations were also attempted to prevent larger vessels from fishing near the port, as it interfered with boat fishing, and, in short, in every one of these early years are to be found instances of flagrant violation of Colbert's maxim, that entire liberty in trade should be allowed to those whom alone the State recognized, its own citizens.

Under these conditions and with this administration proceeded the development of the Colony. It was decided, probably on account of the complaints against his regulations, that Soubras should return to Dunkerque. His career had certainly not been marked by success, but his correspondence gives the impression that he was efficient, although not forceful, for most of the steps he had taken for what he had considered the welfare of the Colony were either disallowed by superior authority or proved ineffective. A petition from the people asking that he should be retained in Cape Breton was forwarded to France, but de Mezy, who was on the retired list as Commissaire-Ordonnateur, was appointed to the position in 1718. He did not, however, come out until the following year.

In the summer of 1716 L'Hermitte returned to Cape Breton and made an expedition to Sable Island, rumours having reached the Court that its settlement might be possible. But then, as now, these shifting sand-banks were but a menace to the navigator. A vessel from Quebec, with a valuable cargo, had been lost there in 1713, only two of her crew escaping to the Island, whence they were rescued by a New England vessel.[1] L'Hermitte also made some plans of Louisbourg and Port Toulouse and in the autumn returned to Paris. Beaucours, who succeeded him, was apparently not more satisfactory as an engineer, and his estimates, like those of L'Hermitte, were considered excessive. He was moved from headquarters at Port Dauphin to Port Toulouse as major, and the Sieur Verville was sent out from France as engineer in charge of the fortifications. The instructions given to him were to examine the places, to fortify Louisbourg against a sudden attack until the works at Port Dauphin were completed, to prepare complete plans and estimates of cost for the three places, and before returning to France to leave instructions for the preparation of materials. He was advised not to forget that it is not necessary to fortify on so large a scale in the colonies as in Europe. The special grant for this year was sixty thousand livres.

Verville, to whom these instructions[2] were given in June, visited Isle Royale in the autumn and returned to France, where he made a report to the Board. His plans and estimates for the fortifications were accepted and work was begun.[3]

---

[1] Among those lost was the Marquis d'Alogny, commander of the troops in Canada.
[2] June 23, 1716, M. St. M. vol. 51.   [3] July 3, 1717.

The Board directed that the works at Louisbourg, notwithstanding the previous decisions which made Port Dauphin the seat of government, should be first gone on with. At the former place Verville took as the key of his system of fortifications the little hillock which dominates the peninsula as well as the plain of Gabarus lying to the westward, and established there a bastion-redoubt in masonry, which was to contain a barracks for at least six companies and their officers, and was to be protected from a surprise by a ditch and covered way. Other bastions were to be built at the two hills found between this point and the sea ; another on the hillock " E " on the harbour side, where a demi-bastion would protect this end of the works as well as cover by its fire the adjacent waters of the port, the whole occupying a distance of something over one thousand yards (495 toises).

A heavy battery was to be established at the point " K," which would sweep the upper part of the harbour. These, all of which were to be executed in fascines and connected by earth-works (*retranchements de campagne*), together with the Island battery, formed the basis of the elaborate system of fortifications which on the same principles and on the same site, were carried out at a very considerable expense by Verville himself and his successors. The map opposite indicates his scheme, and incidentally shows the site of the town to have at that time a considerable number of inhabitants.

Verville, owing to his character or the confidence he felt in the security of his position, did not confine himself to a narrow interpretation of the scope of his duties. He pointed out the loss of time in the troops travelling about six miles to and fro between the barracks and their work. He examined for himself the shores adjacent to the town, which he had been assured were inaccessible, and found that in five places it was possible to land without wetting his shoe, thus proving unfounded the opinion of St. Ovide and Soubras that the only attack to be feared was by the harbour. He established a battery at " K," afterwards known as the Grand or Royal Battery, which was intended to sweep both the upper part of the harbour and its entrance. It was never of any practical use, as it was exposed on the land side, and as pointed out by Chaussegros de Lery, the engineer of Quebec, a fort on the easterly side, near the site on which the lighthouse was afterwards built, would have been extremely effective in the defence of the place.[1]

In a climate like that of Louisbourg, masonry, which Verville substituted for provisional earthwork and fascines, was not only expensive to build but costly to maintain. The present condition of the earthworks erected along the coast in 1757 indicates that the latter system of construction would not only have been vastly cheaper in first cost, but much more permanent, and as the results proved, equally effective when put to the test. In minor matters his observation was not

[1] MSS. Que. vol. 3, p. 267.

always accurate. He thought, for example, that the environs of Louisbourg would supply firewood for the town and garrison for a century, and yet within a few years we find the greater part of this supply brought from places as distant as Port Toulouse. But the difficulty of ascertaining the resources of an unknown and heavily wooded country is shown by their considering the value of the discovery of limestone at Canso of sufficient importance to merit a gratuity ; by their bringing this material from Port Dauphin to Louisbourg, and by their establishing a brickyard at Port Toulouse. It is now known that limestone is abundant at Barasois de Miré (Catalone Lake), about six miles from Louisbourg, and on the Miré River, not far from its mouth, is a bed of perfect brick clay.[1]

The notes of the Navy Board frequently quote Verville's opinions, or refer matters to him, although he criticized the policy of the Board in encouraging soldiers to settle. The chief outcome of his representations on extra-professional matters was the forbidding of officers to engage in fishing, which was enacted in 1718. He urged this course on the Government on the ground that it was unprofitable to the officers, detrimental to their soldiers, and unfair to the civilians.

The first year of the settlement (1714) New England vessels came in to trade. St. Ovide bought four of their cargoes, L'Hermitte says, a fact which he deplores, as they can undersell the local merchants ; but similar transactions are not noted in the following two or three years. St. Ovide says four or five vessels came in for wood and water, but that he only allowed them to remain for twenty-four hours, and placed on each a sergeant and two men to prevent illicit trading. In September 1716 he reports that an English frigate visited Louisbourg to claim eighty deserters from Annapolis. He, mortified that his own cellar was so low that he could not make this little present, allowed the captain to buy from merchants of the town a cask of wine and a keg of brandy, for which molasses was exchanged.[2]

This was the frigate *Rose*,[3] twenty guns, cruising from Boston, seeking for deserters from Annapolis (Captain's letters, 1596). She arrived at Louisbourg on the 29th of August, and saluted the fort with eleven guns, which was properly returned, and after remaining there till the 7th of September left on a cruise to the westward. She was under the command of Lieutenant B. Young. He reports that a French vessel of forty guns, which was the *Attlante*, arrived shortly before his leaving. Lieutenant Young occupied part of his time by drawing a rough map of the port and the operations then going on, which is now preserved in the Colonial Office, London.

Legitimate trade shows its first beginnings in those years. A vessel from Martinique was wrecked at Isle Madame. Boularderie, who had saved the situation in 1713 as far as the Quebec supplies and garrison were concerned,

---

[1] These were used after 1727 (B, 50, f. 599).   [2] I.R. vol. 1, p. 455.   [3] B.T.N.S. vol. 2, p. 96.

branched out by sending a vessel for molasses for the supply of the settlements.[1] The authorities at Quebec had been urged to establish trade with Isle Royale. This was carried on from the first, an important part of it being supplies of flour, peas, etc., for the troops, which were annually sent except in years of scarcity in Canada. The frigate *Attlante* loaded coal for Rochefort, and the fishing industry was prosecuted by an increasing number of vessels, but the trade which gave the authorities the greatest concern was that with the British colonies. In addition to the New England vessels a constant trade was carried on by way of the Gulf by the French inhabitants of Nova Scotia, a development which was foreseen by Mascarene and Bennett, the officers who had accompanied La Ronde on his visit to these settlements. The profitable business of supplying Louisbourg with provisions made New England traders indifferent to regulations, and they took full advantage of this new market.[2]

The transfer of the Acadians to Cape Breton, so ardently hoped for, the advantages of which were recognized by both the French and English as of the utmost value to the new establishment, became year by year more obviously impossible. One reason, and perhaps the most important, next to the disadvantages of Cape Breton from their standpoint as compared with Nova Scotia, was that the promises of the French Government had not been carried out ; possibly many of the other reasons alleged by them for remaining, even under distressing conditions, were meant to conceal the real one. The Regent's Council was annoyed at a report to the effect that some of those who had worked for the King had not been paid, a report which Costebelle denied. Soubras described them as a people naturally froward, distrustful, and irresolute,[3] those of them who had rations too lazy to clear land even for a garden ; the first statement, in connection with Isle Royale, of that disparagement of the colonial fellow-citizen which is so difficult for the European to suppress.[4]

Barrailh, a competent officer, thought that the priests were at the bottom of their trouble, as they could more completely govern these people and live at their ease in Acadia, but that if they were moved to Isle Royale the people would follow them. Verville showed accuracy of observation in stating that he thought the Acadians were of more service to the new colony where they were than if removed, and the last time there was talk of sending a vessel for them was in the instructions given to Barrailh to go in the *Charente*. These instructions were as usual pacific, and ordered him to take every care to avoid a rupture with the English authorities. He was not sent by the Louisbourg

---

[1] I.R. vol. 1, p. 455.

[2] The traders of New England began by claiming that commerce was free to them, possibly a misapprehension as to the terms of the Commercial Treaty of Utrecht. This, however, referred only to the European territories of the contracting parties, and, moreover, never went into effect, as its ratification was refused by Parliament.

[3] " Ce peuple naturellment indociles diffiantes et irresolus."   [4] I.R. 2, p. 52.

authorities, but instead, the Acadians were informed that if they came in their own vessels they would receive a welcome. So far a fall from the promises of de la Ronde was followed by an equal abatement in their enthusiasm. De Mezy saw they would not leave a good for a poor country ; Father de la Marche, while sure of their loyalty, had to admit that they would not leave Nova Scotia. Doucette,[1] in a letter to St. Ovide, May 15, 1718, took the view that the agreement might be null and void if the inhabitants of Nova Scotia desired, if not, that speedy orders might be issued to provide for their retirement into the dominions of France. This was an adequate warrant for more effective steps than any of the authorities at Louisbourg took.[2] Had they removed to Isle Royale, or had France not sought to retain its influence over them, their subsequent history had been less tragic. The danger which Vetch feared[3] passed away, for those who did come were a few farmers, many idlers who were supported by the Government, and a certain number of carpenters, boat-builders, longshoremen, and tavern-keepers, who found in the activities of Louisbourg more profitable employment than Nova Scotia afforded them. It was not until Isle St. Jean was opened up that any considerable number of them again lived under the French Crown.

Costebelle sailed from Louisbourg on the *Attlante* on the 12th of October 1716. Her voyage was so protracted that he landed at Belle Isle no earlier than Christmas Day. A week later he was at Croisic, whence he forwarded the dispatches he had brought, as he was so ill that he could not say when his health would permit him to take horse for Paris.[4] His business was to obtain a settlement of various claims he had against the Crown for outlays at Placentia, which included supplies to the King's stores, the sending of a vessel to France and one to Boston with La Ronde in 1711,[5] in that curious attempt to play on the republican feelings of New England which they had conceived and most un-successfully carried out after it had received the approval of Pontchartrain. A more important item was that of 18,000 l. for the entertainment of the English prisoners at his table.[6] The total amount was 71,000, l. but his vouchers were inadequate, and there were outstanding claims against him respecting the spoils of St. John's which came into his possession after its capture.[7]

Costebelle obtained from the Regent a gratuity of 2000 l., and he remained in France for some months. He visited, in the following August, his birth-place, St. Alexandre, a hamlet on the borders of Languedoc, which from the highlands looks down on Pont St. Esprit and the valley of the majestic Rhone. He

---

[1] Doucette was Lieut.-Governor of Nova Scotia from 1717 to 1726.   [2] B.T.N.S. vol. 2.
[3] P. 21.   [4] I.R. 1, 457.   [5] Mass. Arch. vol. 6.
[6] The sum seems large, but the Governors apparently entertained constantly. St. Ovide, who in 1717 had not received his salary for 1714, says that at his table were always twenty to twenty-four persons.
[7] I.R. 5, p. 11.

returned to Louisbourg on the *Attlante*, and on the voyage was so ill that on September 6, 1717, in a shaky hand, he made his will leaving 500 l. to his servant, the chain on which he wore his Cross of St. Louis to his eldest daughter, and some papers to his brother. The fact that in his will he did not mention his wife, a member of the De la Tour family, a widow whom he had married in 1704, at Placentia, indicates his feebleness at the moment and the embarrassment of his affairs. He was an affectionate husband, who knew the heights of married felicity, as he wrote to her : "Sans toi je ne sçaurois goûter que des plaisirs imparfaits," and with tender courage says, "Ne t'embrasse l'esprit d'aucune affaire bonne ou mauvais, ma plus chère amie et laisse-moi supporter les contretemps que la fortune peut nous prépare." [1] Though in this same letter he says that he will extricate her from her troubles, this was impossible. He died leaving her in absolute destitution. Her torments at the hands of pitiless creditors, until she left Louisbourg were, says St. Ovide, a harrowing spectacle.[2]

On the death of Costebelle he was succeeded by St. Ovide, a dithyrambic petition having been sent to the Government asking for his appointment. " Oui, Monseigneur, l'officier et le soldat, le marchand et l'habitant, les pasteurs, et leurs troupeaux, tous élèvent leur voix, tous forment des vœux en sa faveur." [3] The King's lieutenancy, made vacant by his promotion, was given to de Beaucours.

The work on the fortifications had engaged the attention of the authorities, but up to this time they had been carried on by day's labour under the supervision of the engineer, the force employed being the troops and various artisans sent out from France for this purpose. Verville complained of the extravagance and slow progress made, and the council determined to carry on this construction by contract. The work was put up to tender "à l'extinction de bougie." The successful bidder was a Sieur Isabeau who proceeded to Louisbourg on the first King's ship which went out in the following year, and took over the work.[4]

The Council of the Navy had promised, after the disastrous winter of 1715–16, that such conditions would not be permitted to occur again ; but after a famine in 1717 so bad that the troops at Port Toulouse were, in the spring, reduced to bread and water,[5] in 1718 conditions were again so desperate, there being in the colony only two hundredweight of bread for four thousand people, that after contemplating sending the entire garrison back to France or Acadia,[6]

---

[1] Bib. Nat. N.A. F, 3283.

[2] Madame Costebelle found on presenting her claims to the Regent that Costebelle had taken the gratuity referred to in satisfaction of them. She, however, received a pension which she drew for many years. The Alphabet Laffilard says he died in France, but in this seems inaccurate. His effects at Louisbourg were sold in 1720 for the benefit of his creditors.

[3] I.R. vol. 2, f. 217.   [4] B, 40, f. 538½, June 28, 1718.   [5] I.R. 2, f. 243.

[6] St. Ovide abandoned the idea of sending them to settlements about Chignecto, as it might give umbrage to the

St. Ovide took the step of sending most of it to Quebec for the winter. He thus left in Louisbourg, at a time which the events to be recounted in the next chapter will show was a critical one, only some one hundred and forty-one soldiers. The change, however, in economic conditions was so swift that the next year, October 1719, Barrailh, who was again out in Isle Royale, says that there were seventy vessels in the island, which made bread, wine, and brandy cheaper in Louisbourg than in France. This is generally confirmed by Bradstreet, an officer of the English garrison at Canso, writing to the Board of Trade in 1725 saying, " he was familiar with Louisbourg, and had found there so many vessels from New England and Nova Scotia that two sheep could be bought there for the price of one at Canso.[1]

The development of the town is seen not only in the increase of its population but by the various regulations which were made from time to time ; on the military side forbidding the erection of any buildings or the planting of trees within a distance of three hundred and fifty toises from the fortifications ; on the commercial, by the regulations against the erection of houses higher than seven feet in the post in order that the free circulation of air, essential to the successful drying of fish, might not be hampered ; on the civil side by forbidding, on account of the danger of fire, the covering of the houses with bark. The town was laid out and a plan made,[2] and lands were granted to the people under the condition that within a year and a day the land should be occupied (*d'y tenir feu et lieu*).

The streets of the new town were narrow. Outside of Italian cities of this period but few towns were drained, and had it not been for the salubrity of the air of Cape Breton conditions at Louisbourg would have been unwholesome. The fishing industry is not a cleanly one ; the sheep and goats of the people were kept by a public herd, who received soldier's ration and small pay, but the pigs ran at large. An ordinance was passed empowering any one to kill them if they destroyed property. The regulation states that " they damage the drying fish and the poultry, and are even so ferocious that there is danger sometimes for little children."

The necessity for an hospital was recognized from the first, although the tax proposed by Soubras for its support was disallowed. The treatment given was unsatisfactory to the people. The Bayle et Jurats of St. Jean de Luz and one La Mothe, a merchant representing the people of Louisbourg, appeared before the Board. In the course of their representations they stated that the hospital was useless, as the people went to the ship's surgeons or used Indian

---

English.   That he contemplated doing so would seem to bear the same construction as La Ronde, Denys, and de Pensens not visiting these settlements in 1714, namely, that there was no doubt in the minds of any of them that they were in French territory.

[1] B.T.N.S. vol. 2.   [2] The plan ordered in 1718 did not finally receive ministerial sanction until 1723.

remedies in place of those supplied by the two local surgeons, and they did not hesitate to say that Soubras turned the funds to his own use. The Board endeavoured to improve matters. They ordered that one of the best surgeons be sent from Brest, as the reports of La Grange and Le Roux, who had come from Placentia, were unsatisfactory. It was also decided to place the hospital in the charge of the Frères de la Charité,[1] four of whom had come out in 1716.

A conflict of jurisdiction had arisen in ecclesiastical matters. Spiritual affairs in Placentia had been under Recollets of Brittany, and Father Dom. de la Marche had come with the first settlers; but the Bishop of Quebec, whose diocese included Nova Scotia and Isle Royale, had appointed the Recollets of Paris to this cure. The civil authorities temporized with the matter, and allotted the spiritual care of the Acadians and the services of the King's chapel to the latter, while the general population was served by monks of Brittany, who finally remained in possession of the field.[2] The importance of the Basque element in the population was recognized by sending out a priest of that nationality.

The chief drawback to the prosperity of Louisbourg was unquestionably drink. It impressed Verville so much that he says, in explaining the ineffectiveness of the work going on, that the troops who should be at work escape daily to roam the woods and to get drunk, far in excess of these European nations who were given to drink.

Soubras battled with the evil and proposed and tried many expedients. Fines, rewards to informers, and severe punishments of those who would not tell where they obtained drink, were the obvious measures. He tried also the prohibition of the officers' canteens, in which drink was sold to the soldiers, but found that this simply increased the number of groggeries. He endeavoured to restrict the sale to six of the principal people of the place, but found that these would not act, and he anticipated the Gothenburg system by proposing that the sale should be exclusively in the hands of the Government. In some of these proposals he received the support of the Board, but the result justified Costebelle's view that nothing effective could be done until more settled conditions prevailed.

The echoes of the Regent's experiments were heard in Louisbourg, and Law's Mississippi Company was imitated in these northern islands. M. Poupet de la Boularderie, formerly an officer in the Navy and in the troops of Acadia, but for many years a trader, was given a grant of that beautiful and fertile island which lies between the great and little entrances to the Bras d'Or Lakes. It still perpetuates his name. His grant also included the opposite southern shore to a league in depth, the island at Ingonish, exclusive beach

---

[1] This was a religious fraternity founded in 1540 by the Portuguese, St. Jean de Dieu, at Granada in Spain, thence it spread to Italy and in 1601 to France. It was of sufficient eminence to have charge of the hospitals de la Charité in Paris and at Charenton.   [2] Their letters patent were not sent out until 1731 (B, 55, f. 577).

rights for one hundred fishers, and the use of the King's ship *Le Paon* for two years.[1] He undertook to place one hundred settlers the first year, fifty the next, and employ one hundred fishermen. He was given command for the King in his lands, and a "safe conduct" for three months, that delightful opposite of the *lettre de cachet*, which during its currency made its holder superior to all judicial and police mandates. He proceeded vigorously to the development of his grant, first by his unaided efforts, which were undertaken on so great a scale that he contemplated the building of a ship of twelve hundred tons ; but, hampered by the shipwreck of one of his vessels in the St. Lawrence, and the exhaustion of his funds, he turned his grant over to a company of Malouin merchants, with whom he quarrelled.[2] He formed another company in Havre and Rouen, which accomplished little, so that at his death in 1738 it was a question whether the grant of the property would be confirmed to his son.[3] There had been obtained for his son in early life a position as a page in the household of Her Royal Highness, the Duchesse d'Orléans. When he had outgrown this position at Court, he obtained a lieutenancy in the regiment of Richelieu, and after a service of seven years obtained a company therein. When the aged Berwick, that able general whom the deposed Stuarts had given to France, led her armies to victory over the Austrians, Boularderie went through the campaigns of Kehl, Phillippsbourg, and Clauzen. Then, through a reverse of fortune, he had to sell his company, but retained the assistance of that grand Seigneur, the Duc de Richelieu. The death of his father followed shortly afterwards, and the concessions being confirmed to him, Boularderie came out to Isle Royale, with the remains of his personal fortune, the proceeds of the sale of a house in Paris. He brought with him husbandmen and craftsmen from Normandy, and according to his own account was most successful. " I have in my employment twenty-five persons, a very handsome house, barn, stable, dairy, dovecot, and oven, wind and water-mills, twenty-five cows and other live stock."[4] He grew wheat, in 1740 he had 150 bbls. of fine wheat and vegetables as in Europe, and had a large orchard and a garden, but disasters befell him in this charming establishment.

The earlier grants of the islands in the Gulf, St. Jean and the Magdalens, having been finally revoked in 1710, a Count St. Pierre took advantage of his position at Court, that of first Equerry to the Duchesse d'Orléans, to obtain a grant and found a company for the development of these islands. His enterprise was unsuccessful. The merchants of St. Malo protested so vigorously against the exercise by the company of its exclusive fishing rights, and their protection

---

[1] Feb. 15, 1719, B, vol. 41, f. 565. [2] Cor. (Canada), C, 11, 64, 1724.
[3] One account speaks of the older Boularderie as captain in Acadia in 1702, his grant describes him as Enseigne de Vaisseau. He was given a frigate in 1713 for trading. [4] *Derniers Jours de l'Acadie*, p. 287.

by an armed vessel (1722)[1] that these rights were curtailed, and notwithstanding the loan of artillery and an officer, the enterprise was abandoned in 1724 and these islands reunited to the royal domain in 1730, the fear of a seignorial establishment having, in the interval, retarded the settlement of the island by the Acadians.[2] M. Ruette D'Auteuil, after a stormy career in Canada, where he had been at one time Procureur-General at Quebec, also received a grant of Isle Madame on substantially the same conditions of settlement, but no vigorous efforts were made at colonization. After some years St. Ovide reported that it had also failed, and expressed his disapproval of the system. These companies, like their great prototype, added three to the long list of failures, both French and English, to establish in America the profitable corporate administration of land.

At last the question of the chief establishment of the colony was to be permanently settled. St. Ovide had been much impressed by the advantages of Port Toulouse on his tour through the island, thus confirming the good opinion it had made on him in 1714, and now recommended it warmly to the Council, and asked them to hear Rouville, who was in France, and to appoint a commission to make a report on the matter.[3]

This suggestion was supported by two petitions. One, which described Louisbourg as a bottomless pit for funds, was signed by officials ; the other by the principal inhabitants. The latter stated that so soon after coming from Placentia and other places, they were unable to bear the expense of a second moving, but if the King would pay the actual cost, they would gladly go to Port Toulouse, and leave behind the tavern-keepers, who made up two-thirds of the population of Louisbourg.[4] The reply to these petitions, which reflect, on account of his position, perhaps little more than the personal opinion of the Governor, was in the negative. Louisbourg was made the principal place, the first indication of which had been the mounting of six guns in 1719. But to mark the decision as final, a medal commemorating its founding and fortification was designed and struck, and in the following year it was placed in the foundation of the King's bastion. Six years had passed in uncertainty. Isle Royale had repeated the mistakes previously made in Canada and Louisiana, against which Villien had warned the Minister without success. However, the question was at last settled, the administration was concentrated there, and was coincident with De Mezy's taking the place of Soubras. The troops were brought together from the outports, with the exception of small detachments, and a renewal of discipline was hoped for, and in some measure attained.

---

[1] C, 11, vol. 12, p. 78.   [2] May 1720, I.R. vol. 5, f. 56.   [3] I.R. vol. 4, Jan. 9, 1719.

[4] This indicates again the prevalence of drinking, as does an earlier letter of St. Ovide and Soubras, who speak of "Cabaretiers qui ruinent entierrement la colonnie," Nov. 13, 1717 (I.R. vol. 2).

ARCHIVES DU CANADA—ISLE ROYALE. (I.R. vol. 1 (St.) Ottawa.)

COMPAGNIES

Il y en a sept à l'Isle Royale dans chacune desquelles, il y a un Capitaine, un Lieutenant et un Enseigne, deux Sergents, deux caporaux, quarante-cinq soldats, et un tambour.

Il leur est délivré tous les ans un habillement, une année le grand habillement et l'année suivante le petit.

Le grand habillement consiste en un justaucorps, une culotte, deux chemises, deux cravates, un chapeau, une paire de bas et deux paires de souliers.

Le petit habillement consiste en une veste, une culotte, deux chemises, deux cravates, un chapeau, une paire de bas et deux paires de souliers.

Ces habillements ne doivent estre délivrés qu'aux effectifs et on conserve le surplus dans les magasins pour les recrues.

La ration du sergent et du soldat est par jour d'une livre et demie de pain, quatre onces de lard cru ou demy livre de bœuf, quatre onces de légumes, un quarteron de beurre et cinq livres de mélasse par mois.

Cette ration est plus forte qu'en Canada où il ne se délivre au soldat par jour qu'une livre et demie de pain et un quarteron de lard, cette augmentation a été accordée à Plaisance à cause du mauvais pays et continué à l'Isle Royale par rapport au nouvel Etablissement, quand le pays sera establi on la diminuera.

Il est retenu pour l'habillement et ration par mois au Sergent 9 ff. 10 s., au Caporal 7 ff. 10 s. et au soldat 7 ff. 10 s. de sorte qu'il reste de solde toute déduction faire, excepté celle des 4 s. pour livre, au Sergent 13 ff. par mois, au Caporal 6 ff. et au soldat 30 s.

La distribution de l'habillement, des vivres et de la solde regarde le Commissaire Ordonnateur.

Tout le militaire regarde le Gouverneur de l'Isle et les fonctions de l'un et de l'autre sont les mêmes que celles du Gouverneur Général et de l'Intendant du Canada.

THE CROSS OF ST. LOUIS

The correspondence of all the French officers shows an eagerness for the Cross of St. Louis. This order was founded by Louis XIV. in 1693. There had been up to that time only two orders—that of St. Michel, founded by Louis XI. in 1469, and the Saint Esprit, founded by Henri III., 1578–79, the former of which had fallen into such discredit that Henry gave command that none should be admitted to the splendid order he was founding save Knights of St. Michel ; therefrom springs the expression so common under the splendid portraits of the seventeenth and eighteenth centuries, designating the subject as of "the King's Orders." The restrictions of the Order of Saint Esprit to those of lofty descent left Louis XIV. without means of honouring the many officers who distinguished themselves in his service, so the Order of St. Louis was founded. The King was Grand Master, the Dauphin or heir-presumptive to the throne was a member, there were eight Grand Cross, twenty-four Commanders, who could only be admitted as Knights, and as many Knights as the King might designate. It was reserved to Catholics, officers on sea or land who had served for ten years.

Admission to the order carried pensions of considerable value. As the order was at first constituted the junior Knights, thirty-two had a pension of 800 l.; forty-eight, 1000 l.; twenty-four higher, 1500 l.; and the highest twenty, 2000 l.; but in 1719 the Regent increased the number of Chevaliers from 128 to 413, with pensions decreasing from 2000 l. to 200 l. The recipient at his induction knelt, swore to serve the King faithfully, and no other sovereign without permission, that he was a Catholic, and that he would live as a good, wise, virtuous, and valiant Knight; the Governor drew his sword, touched him on each shoulder and delivered to him the order, which he was to wear on a flame-coloured ribbon on his chest. At the death of a Chevalier his Cross was returned. The large number of Chevaliers of the Order led to abuses, and apparently at Louisbourg it came almost to be a question of length of service. In 1749 it was so common in France that, apparently up to that time there had been no danger in representing oneself as belonging to the Order. In consequence an "ordonnance" was issued forbidding the wearing its Cross without authority.[1] The pensions do not seem to have been paid regularly. An interesting list of the Louisbourg refugees at Rochefort about 1763, which gives particulars of the officers, their families, their debts and resources, in no case mentions the pension of the Chevaliers as a source of income, and in the lively conversation of Le Neveu de Rameau reference is made to the destitution of some of the Chevaliers.

---

[1] Its history in three vols., L'Ordre de St-Louis, has been written by A. Mazas, Paris, 1860. A number of the Isle Royal Chevaliers are not noted in the lists he gives. A list of officers of Louisbourg, 1744–63 (Arch. Col. D 4) shows that the Majors, Aide-Majors, and every Captain of ten years' service had received the Cross, usually at the end of that time.

CHAPTER IV

WHILE fishing was vigorously prosecuted from Louisbourg and its neighbouring outposts, the French fishermen at Isle Madame and the ports to the westward came, during these years, in contact with those of New England in the neighbourhood of Canso. English fishermen had freely used the harbours of Isle Royale, but it soon came to pass that both French and English used the port of Canceau, or, in its modern form, Canso, situated on an island separated only by the narrowest of waterways from the mainland of Nova Scotia. The French had frequented it for a century and a half.[1]

In 1717 there were six French and five English fishing stations there. The next year St. Ovide gave orders to the French to withdraw, but was begged by the New Englanders to leave them, as the latter were threatened by the Indians.[2] In August, George Vaughan, formerly Governor of New Hampshire, was at Canso, and found "all things peaceable and quiet, the French and English fishing with all friendship and love."[3]

Some of the Canso people had, in June, petitioned the Council of Massachusetts to the effect that the French were using Canso, and had threatened the English with removal.[4] The petitioners had thought it their duty to represent this state of affairs to the Council, so that the rights of Englishmen might not be infringed. The authorities thereupon sent to Canso Captain Smart of the frigate *Squirrel*, which had been sent to protect the shipping of North America from pirates. His instructions were to inquire into the truth of the French encroachments. He carried a letter from Shute, Governor of Massachusetts, to St. Ovide, that Shute expected him to "immediately order the French under his command to pull down their Hutts and also not to fish any more upon y't shoar."[5]

Smart arrived at Canso on September 6, left on the 7th for Louisbourg, where he had a conference with St. Ovide. The accounts of this interview

---

[1] A Captain Savalette of St. Jean de Luz was living a little to the west of Canso in 1565.
[2] The French were inclined to believe the territory was English; English authorities that it was French. I.R. vol. 3, and the Commissioners of Trade to Townhend, March 14, 1721.
[3] C.O. 5/867.   [4] C.O. 5/793.   [5] C.O. 5/867. Ad. Sec. In Letters, vol. 2542.

given, on the one hand, by Smart and Southack,[1] and, on the other, by St. Ovide, are irreconcilable. The *Squirrel* returned to Canso on the 14th.[2] On the 18th Smart seized every French vessel and all French property he could find, and sailed away to Boston with plunder valued at 200,000 l.[3]

News of this exploit was promptly brought to Louisbourg, where their understanding with Southack and Smart seemed to have been generally held to be satisfactory, for no preparations had been made to deal with the conditions which confronted the authorities. The news was as much a surprise at Louisbourg as the event had been to the fishers at Canso. St. Ovide at once took spasmodic action. He impressed a Malouin trading vessel of thirty guns, armed her, and put on board forty soldiers, under Ste. Marie,[4] and sailors from other vessels in the harbour to bring her complement up to two hundred and fifty men. Her captain had none of that spirit which made St. Malo *la cité corsaire*. He and his crew made so many difficulties that the condition bordered on revolt, and by nightfall, when it was intended she should sail, she was not ready. The weather the next day was bad, and the expedition was abandoned. Such is the account given in the joint letter of St. Ovide and Soubras,[5] but the latter wrote to the Minister disavowing any share in these preparations, and severely blaming St. Ovide, with supreme authority, for not having overcome the difficulties and delays.[6]

This action of St. Ovide, so deplorably weak that Soubras says he groans while he writes an account of it, was almost inevitable with an ordinary man in charge at Louisbourg.[7] Its wretched condition must have been evident to Smart ; they had no cannon mounted, they had no men-of-war, they had no provisions, and their troops had been reduced to one hundred and forty-one men.

Instead of a warlike expedition, St. Ovide [8] sent Ste. Marie and Laforest, a clerk, to Canso. Laforest was to make on the ground a formal protest, to draw up a careful and accurate account of what had happened, on which, if the facts warranted, the right of reprisals might be based. Ste. Marie was to order the French to withdraw, and to remain on the ground until these instructions were carried out. Ste. Marie was further instructed to tell the Indians to behave, to do justice to the English, and to make the French pay their debts before leaving.[9]

---

[1] Southack was with Smart as a representative of Massachusetts.

[2] B.T.N.S. vol. 2 ; I.R. vol. 3.

[3] The subsequent proceedings outside Cape Breton are too lengthy to be here narrated. The whole incident will be dealt with in a monograph now in preparation.

[4] I.R. vol. 3, Oct. 19, 1718.   [5] I.R. vol. 3, Oct. 1718.

[6] Some suspicion of the accuracy of St. Ovide's version of what the writer calls the "childish conference with Smart" is implied in Soubras emphasizing the fact that he was not present at these interviews.

[7] I.R. vol. 3. f. 186.   [8] Soubras, Oct. 18, 1718, I.R. vol. 3, f. 186.   [9] Letter of Oct. 6.

The part which the Indians of Nova Scotia took in the next incident at Canso makes it desirable to indicate briefly their relations to the European colonists of the Atlantic seaboard.   This was one of extreme friendliness to the French and hostility to the English.   The *Pax Gallica*, which for so long existed throughout so large a part of the wilds of North America, is an enduring monument to the sagacity of French administrators, the self-sacrifice of French missionaries, and the *savoir-faire* of French traders and fishermen. The effects of this have been indicated by reference to the attacks on the English fishing vessels on the coast of Nova Scotia, the safety which the English fishers found at Canso in company with the French, and the fact that at the same time Frenchmen had no fear of living among these savages along this stretch of the coast on which the English only could land in peril.[1]

"MEM'L OF CAPT. CYPRIAN SOUTHACK TO GOV'R JOSEPH DUDLEY AND THE COUNCIL AT BOSTON, SEPTEMBER 15, 1715.

"On 30 Ap. 1715 he sailed with 2 sloops & one two mast vessel for a fishing voyage to Nova Scotia. 14th May arrived at Port Rossway & landed 17th, vessels sailed on their fishing 18th. Welcomed by Mons. Tarranguer & Joseph Muess. 23rd. Welcomed by the chief captain of Cape Sables & 8 Indian Officers. 25th. M. Tarranguer came and threatened to lead 100 Indians to capture all the fishing vessels on the coast. 28th June received news of capture of an English vessel and men. 3rd July. Informed of the capture of another fishing sloop by the Indians, who threatened him with capture and death ; saying Costabelle had given to the Indians a great present. 11th July. 2 vessels came in and told him of a capture of 7 sail at Port Seigneur, that the Indians were on their way to capture him & his, would kill him.   They refused to carry him, his people & effects away, unless he first gave them a bill of 500 current money of Boston & £125 to be p'd in Boston. Agreed to. . . . Loss sustained at Port Rossway—£450 & the fishing season." [2]

This condition of affairs has certain causes which are fairly well defined, chief among which is the different attitude of the French and English to the aborigines.   The former recognized them as independent allies, not as subjects, acknowledging them as sovereign owners of the land, who permitted the usufruct of it to their allies.   Pownall, Governor of Massachusetts, says the English, on the contrary,[3]

"with an unsatiable thirst after landed possessions, have got Deeds and other fraudulent pretences, grounded on the abuse of Treaties, and by these Deeds claim possession, even to the exclusion of the Indians, not only from their Hunting Grounds (which with them is a right of great consequence) but even from their house and home. . . . Upon these pretences they have drove the Indians off their Lands : the Indians unable to bear it any

---

[1] See also Arceneau's account of his voyage to Cape Breton in 1714.   [2] B.T.N.S. vol. 2, f. 7.   [3] C.O. 5/518.

longer told Sir William Johnson that they believed soon they should not be able to hunt a bear into a hole in a tree but some Englishman would claim a right to the property of it as being his tree . . . this is the sole ground of the loss and alienation of the Indians from the English Interest : and this is the ground the French work upon : on the contrary the French possessions interfere not with the Indian's Rights, but aid and assist their interest and become a means of their support."

The splendid heroism of the French missionaries had made these Indians, as well as those of the tribes of Canada, Roman Catholic, and a passion for the orthodoxy of that church made their savage converts more hostile to the heretic than priests and administrators of French origin. St. Ovide objected to the employment of Swiss troops at Louisbourg, as this toleration of heretics would have a bad effect on the Indians.[1] Vaudreuil[2] expresses the French policy in these phrases : " But as Father de la Chasse says, grace among the Indians has often some help from man, and among them worldly gain serves as a channel of doctrine " (" Mais comme me margue le père de la Chasse la grâce parmis les sauvages a souvent de la co-opération de l'homme, et parmis eux l'intérêt temporel sert de la (*sic*) véhicule à la foix.")

The standard form of the " véhicule à la foix " was an annual giving of presents of practical utility to the Indians. These presents were dependent in amount on the number of warriors in the tribe, and consisted of powder, lead, flints, and axes. The occasion of the distribution was an important one for conference, and in the earlier years took place frequently at St. Peter's, but on at least one occasion St. Ovide contemplated going to Antigonish on the mainland of Nova Scotia, but was deterred by the not unreasonable objections which might be made by Phillips.[3]

This system was more potent in keeping the friendliness of their allies than the occasional efforts made by the English to win them over. These efforts were never satisfactory, and the punishments of the Indians for wrong-doings by the English were, as all punishments of that epoch, harsh, and in addition they were humiliating and irritated the Indians. The scalp bounties of the colonies included rewards for the killing of Indian women and children, although a lesser money value was set on the scalp of a woman or child than on that of a man.[4] The strange conditions, in which we find a benign and devout clergyman praying that the young men who have joined the Mohawks in a scalping expedition against the French and Indians may go in the fear of the Lord, and regarding the bringing in of French scalps as a good omen, were such as made it easy for the French to retain the goodwill and affection of their allies. There seemed to have been no resentment among the Indians

---

[1] " Que l'on ne retient que par des motifs de Religion."
[2] To Minister, September 16, 1714.   [3] 1721, I.R. vol. 5.
[4] Reference to this gruesome subject is made in the Appendix. William's Diary, Parkman MSS., May 1747.

when any of their number were punished by the French. The only important case in Isle Royale was the murder of Count d'Agrain by two Indians in his employment ;[1] the criminals were apprehended and executed, without apparently causing any irritation among the other members of the tribe.

The attitude of the French Government was throughout consistent. It is indicated in a reply of the Council to a letter of Costebelle[2] in which he says : "The savages of the French mission on the shores of Acadia are such irreconcilable enemies of the English people, that we cannot, with our most peaceable speeches, impress them not to trouble their trade." The Council's memorandum of reply was to maintain the savages in this state of mind, namely, "to allow no English settlement in Acadia or fishing on its shores, but this should be done prudently and secretly." This was continued for a generation. St. Ovide was reprimanded for having conveyed to the Indians, at a somewhat later time than this, the impression that the small garrison at Isle St. Jean was to help them in their raids against the English ;[3] but in 1727 Father Gaulin was suspected of assisting the Indians in making peace with the English, and although he was an old man, broken with years of service as a missionary, the report seriously irritated Maurepas.[4]

The difficulties inherent in such a situation were increased by braggart and turbulent Frenchmen, who threatened the English at Canso and elsewhere on the coast with Indian attacks and made free in their menaces with the names of Costebelle and St. Ovide. All French accounts of expeditions in which the Indians took a part show that they were intractable, capricious allies, following the French leader when his movements suited them ; at other times, when his persuasions and threats failed, making him yield to their views. Therefore, while the correspondence gives the impression that the earlier French authorities were sincere in not encouraging their allies to deeds of violence, and in protecting the victims when these occurred, with such allies, it was inevitably the more humane side of their policy which failed.[5]

The number of Indians in Nova Scotia was small ; an itemized statement makes in 1721 the total number 289[6] (Isle Royale 36, Antigonish 48, Beaubassin 47, Mines 58, La Have 60, Cap de Sable, 40). The following year,[7] however, in connection with a proposal made by Gaulin the missionary, to remove the Indians to that island in the Bras d'Or Lakes, which is still their rendezvous, the total number of savages bearing arms is spoken of as 265, and the entire Indian population as 838. It seems incredible that so small a number could have caused such widespread dismay among the English, and so seriously

[1] Jan. 22, 1722. [2] Sept. 9, 1715, I.R. vol. 1, f. 336.
[3] B, vol. 54, f. 517. [4] March 11, 1727, I.R. B, 50.
[5] See Journals of Marin and Boishébert. [6] I.R. vol. 5, Sept. 15, 1721.
[7] I.R. vol. 6, Dec. 27, 1722.

hampered their operations. In many cases the crew of a fishing vessel would have been as numerous as any of the bands which attacked them. It is to be expected that fishermen on shore would be at a disadvantage when attacked by savages skilled in the ways of forest warfare ; but it is surprising to find that the Indians of Nova Scotia were bold and skilful at sea. In the outbreak of 1722 the Indians captured trading vessels both in the Bay of Fundy and off the coast of Nova Scotia.[1] They then cruised on the Banks with the captured sloops, forcing the prisoners to serve as mariners. They threatened to attack Canso, and the fishermen were breaking up the fishery, when Colonel Phillips persuaded them to join him in fitting out two sloops, each with a detachment of troops. In the course of three weeks all the sloops and prisoners, with the exception of four, were recaptured. In one of these encounters fifteen Indians fought for two hours with Phillips' schooner manned by sixty men. Ten of the Indians escaped by swimming ashore. The heads of the other five were cut off and stuck on the pickets of the redoubt at Canso.[2]

In the next attack, 1725, which they made on Canso, after the first onslaught, the English armed a vessel to go in pursuit of the Indians who were cruising in two of their captures, in which they had taken eight or nine small fishing craft. In another case[3] they took an English schooner from Newfoundland and brought her back to Isle Royale, while from their establishment on the Bras d'Or Lakes they made annual excursions in open boats to the Magdalen Islands. The advantages to French industry of these raids is shown by the statement that the capture of one English fishing vessel off Isle St. Jean by Indians[4] caused eighty others to leave its waters and return to Canso, and the view of Maurepas, that in this he saw no inconvenience, is easily understood. The success of the Indians against the fishermen of New England was probably the chief reason for the contempt for the military skill of the British colonists, expressed up to 1745 by the Louisbourg people.

Disturbing as had been the exploit of Smart, its effects lasted longer in diplomatic circles than it did at its scene. The French returned, or possibly continued, to fish at Canso. In 1720 Young again visited that port, and says that there were ninety-six English and two hundred French fishermen off Canso. He then went to Louisbourg and saw St. Ovide, who said that he would prevent the French going, as contrary to the Treaty. At the same time it would seem evident that the fishing was held in common, for the English frequented Petit de Grat and other places on Isle Madame,[5] which was unquestionably French territory. But while the conditions were not different from those of 1718, the disturbance of the peace in 1720 came from the Indians.

[1] B.T.N.S. vol. 4, Phillips from Canso, September 19, 1722.   [2] I.R. vol. 6, f. 22.
[3] I.R. vol. 7, f. 179.   [4] B, 54, 517½.   [5] B.T.N.S. vol. 3, f. 20.

"On[1] the 8th of August 1720 the port of Canso was attacked by a body of Indians and some fifty or sixty French. About one or two in the morning the Indians sprang on the English fishermen, scarcely giving some of them time to put on their breeches, and making many prisoners, placed them in the house under guard. The remainder were driven into the boats and then the French stepped in and assisted. Everything was pillaged—fish, goods, clothes, bedding and even pockets, the loss being said to amount to about £18,000. The onset commenced at Capt. Richards' Island, which they made the place of rendezvous. The fishing vessels having assembled, one was manned to save Capt. Richards' ship, which was deemed in danger, but after firing on both sides she was forced to retire.

"During this affair 2 Englishmen were shot dead in escaping to the boats, & one was drowned. At 2 in the afternoon a deputation went to Louisbourg to represent the grievance, but the Gov'r made light of it, saying any Fr. taken in the act sh'd make satisfaction, but was not responsible for the Indians.

"In the mean time Capt. Richards had fitted out two small ships, in which he had pursued the assailants & captured six shallops with plunder on board & 15 Frenchmen. Two captured Indians said M. St. Ovide had encouraged them & ordered them to rob the settlem't.

"One Prudent Robicheau, inhabitant of Annapolis, declared that a rumor had been current in St. Peters that the Indians would fall upon Canso some time in the summer & he had warned 2 Eng. masters bound to Canso. The firing at Canso was heard at St. Peters. He left that place in a shallop, with Father Vincent on board, on the 9th of Aug., & met a shallop with Indians who boasted of having taken Canso & forced the fishermen off their boats, killing 1 and wounding 4. They had much plunder on board, Father Vincent rec'd presents from them & applauded their actions. The Indians stated that 70 Indians in 40 canoes had driven 500 men on to their ships. A master of one of the ships, being set on board his vessel, fired on the Indians & forced them to retire. They seized an Eng. shallop and took some of the plunder in her.

"Not receiving any assistance from the Gov'r of Cape Breton, they sent Mr. Henshaw to Gov'r. Phillips, and five French prisoners with him. Mr. Henshaw returned with Arms and Ammunition & provisions, accompanied by Major Lawrence Armstrong. The latter was directed to go to Canso & take all necessary measures for restoration of peace & security. He was afterwards to proceed to C. Breton & deliver the letter to the Gov'r demanding restitution to the people & the arrest of the principal actors and their ships, until the decision of the two Courts can be received. To return with the Gov'r's answer, calling at Canso on the way.

"Gov'r Phillips' Letter to M. St. Ovide, dated 29th Aug. 1720, acknowledged the receipt of St. Ovide's letter in reply to the deputation from Canso, and informed him that 5 Frenchmen had been captured with some of the Eng. plunder in their possession. From the depositions of these prisoners, copies of wh. are sent to him & also to the King of Gt. Britain, it is evident that the Fr. were not only the framers and promoters of the violation of the peace at Canso, but also the principal actors, the prisoners declaring they were ordered by their Masters, Philibert, Massey, &c., to pillage the Eng. goods, to load the shallops with them, with their Arms in their hands, powder & shot being distributed to the Natives as in a time of war. He stated that one Renaud had previously

[1] B.T.N.S. vol. 3.

arranged the onslaught with the natives, & questions whether this could have been done without support from high authority. The Indians who took part had (all but four) come from Cape Breton, where the affair had been openly discussed for 3 mos. previously. He cannot credit the assertions of 2 Indian prisoners that Mr. St. Ovid was the one who encouraged them. Proofs of his desire to preserve the peace demanded his making full restitution for the losses at Canso, & due satisfaction made on the chief actors, who with their ships, &c., should be arrested & await the decision of the two courts." [1]

Armstrong went to Louisbourg, where, notwithstanding the peremptory tone of his demands, he was received with politeness. St. Ovide, with the action of Smart and the British authorities before him, was determined to show the "road of equity" to the English in this transaction. He sent De Pensens, who was accompanied by Armstrong, to Petit de Grat, where he examined the French who knew about the affair. It was proved by their evidence that the Indians were destroying the cod and other property, or giving it to them. Arquebel thought it only right to make good his losses through Smart, and therefore took cod. Two other men said the Indians forced them. Another man saw Indians destroying a good sail, asked for it and they gave it to him ; and still another had lost by the English in 1718. The property that had been taken was restored to Armstrong to the value of £1600. [2]

As two years had elapsed since the first outrage at Canso, and it was still unatoned for, the English authorities were not in a position to notice this incident, [3] in which, granted the fact that the French had such allies as the Indians, the conduct of their local authorities was honourable, straightforward, and the action that they took towards righting the wrong was all that could be expected of them.

The view which St. Ovide wrote to the authorities at home as to the reason of the outbreak at this particular time was, that the Indians were incensed by British treatment of their brothers, the Acadians. On the face of it this does not seem probable. It receives some confirmation from Phillips, who reports with bitterness that Lieutenant Washington, one of his officers at Annapolis, went about saying that his severity to the Acadians brought on this attack. [4]

Phillips took prompt action. He sent in the autumn a company to remain at Canso all winter. These he reinforced the following year with two companies, built a small fort, which he armed with cannon borrowed

[1] B.T.N.S. vol. 4, Nov. 20, 1720.
[2] The Court approved this action of St. Ovide (B, vol. 44, f. 557, June 20, 1721).
[3] The Commissioners of Trade, nevertheless, wrote to the Lords Justices, speaking of the Indian attack as reprisals by the French, and urged that restitution be demanded before satisfaction be given Mr. Hirriberry, the chief victim of Smart (B.T.N.S. vol. 31, Oct. 18, 1720).   [4] N.S. vol. 4, f. 7.

from the vessels, and thereafter held the place, on the ground that it was necessary to protect the fishermen from Indian hostilities. He thus made Canso, on his own initiative, British territory.

These events at Canso have been set forth in some detail, for they may be regarded as indicating with clearness the course of the future relations of the two peoples in North America, which culminated in the obliteration of French power. On the one hand, there was the commercial aspect ; the people of both nationalities engaged in the peaceful exploiting of the fisheries, which were so rich that both together had ample room, and indifferently used the harbours and waters which belonged to both Crowns. On the other hand, there is the action of the Governments ; that of Massachusetts, energetic and forceful, which took steps on false information, for the French were not on the mainland of Nova Scotia, and in the trouble which followed their action, an unscrupulous naval captain was vigorously supported by the Admiralty. On the French side one marks the leaning on the broken reed of English respect for the law of nations, and a supineness in considering an insult to the French flag in colonial waters as of little consequence. It is not to be wondered at that a writer [1] on French colonial policy, should have a chapter on the contempt for the colonies in the eighteenth century. The history of the French action at Canso would justify the heading of his chapter, as well as the matter he publishes therein.

Again, no comment is necessary on the significance of the action of the officials. St. Ovide waited for instructions from the Court and supplies from France. Phillips, as ill-equipped as the French Governor, threw a garrison into Canso without waiting for instructions, and, without artillery, made those interested contribute guns from their vessels for its defence. These are examples of the working out of the two systems on which colonies were governed, quite as striking as any found elsewhere in the history of New England and New France.

[1] Schon, *La Politique Coloniale.*

CHAPTER V

Louis XV. attained his majority on February 17, 1723. The policy of Du Bois, friendly to England, was succeeded by that of Fleury, more widely pacific. Many years of peace were unmarked by any incidents like that of Canso, which with a more spirited Minister would have led to action, the consequences of which might have been felt far beyond the confines of this little colony.

The immediate effect on it of the King's majority was the substitution for the Navy Board of Maurepas as Minister of the Navy. To his hands, those of a young man of twenty-two, were entrusted the affairs of the vast colonial empire as well as the navies of France.[1] No striking change took place in Isle Royale in consequence of this change at Court. The definite selection of Louisbourg as the chief place of the colony had improved its position. Its population increased, but to a less degree than that of the outports. The growth was:

	Louisbourg.	Other places.
1718	568	815
1720	733	1181
1723	795	1102
1726	951	2180

The number of places at which settlements were made also increased. In 1718 outside of Louisbourg there were apparently only four places, while in 1726 there were settlements of more or less importance in thirteen other localities, the most important of which was Ninganiche (Ingonish), which did not exist in 1720,[2] but in 1726 was much larger than any other place, except Louisbourg, and put out more than twice as many fishing-boats as that port. Four years later the number of settlements was eighteen. While Ingonish was a successful competitor in fishing, in general commerce which employed larger vessels Louisbourg quite surpassed any of the outports or, indeed, all of them together. Of the sixty-one vessels which came from France in 1726,

---

[1] For the character of Maurepas see Chap. XV.   [2] G¹, 467.

thirty-nine came thither ; of fifty-seven from Canada, the West Indies, New England, and Nova Scotia, all came to the port of Louisbourg.[1]

During these years, Isle Royale, like the northern colonies of Britain, suffered from the ravages inflicted by pirates on the commerce of the high seas. The increase in the number of these freebooters, brought about by the disbanding of the men-of-war's men after the Peace of Utrecht, produced its effects in these waters. It will be remembered that, as evidence of the sad condition of Louisbourg in 1715, St. Ovide feared that after the leaving of the King's ships it would lie defenceless to the attacks of pirates.

In the autumn of 1721 the authorities at Louisbourg were dismayed to find that in the town there was no powder or shot, when the pirates were on the coast, and the inhabitants were so badly armed that St. Ovide drew the attention of the authorities to their state. Their condition, in the face of what was real danger, apparently led them to tempt the soldiers to sell their muskets, which the authorities punished with a fine of 200 l. The following year Phillips sent an officer to warn the authorities that a pirate brigantine and schooner were on the eastern coast of Acadia, and had taken ten or twelve vessels.[2] A vessel of St. Malo on the coast of Isle Royale was taken by a pirate schooner, her rigging destroyed, her yards broken, and she was ordered to return to France. She reached Scatari after sixteen days, and reported the outrage to the authorities at Louisbourg. Further havoc was done by a vessel of seventy or eighty tons, eight cannon, sixteen swivels, and one hundred and fifty men. In 1720 the ship of Captain Carey, from London to Boston, near the Grand Banks, was plundered by a pirate of twenty-six guns with a consort of ten. The loss was £8000. Carey brought in the report that they had destroyed the Newfoundland fishery.[3]

So serious was the menace that Bourville, acting Governor after St. Ovide had left for France in 1721, found it necessary to fortify Louisbourg, a town of a thousand people, with a garrison of three hundred against an attack by pirates.[4] He mounted seven large guns of twenty-four pounds on the island, seven near the fortifications, and six at the ancient fort, the site of the first settlement.

Throughout this period, apparently some of the freebooters, whose names have been preserved to history, and throw a lurid glare over modern fiction, left the richer commerce of the West Indies to come northwards to plunder on the coasts of New England, Acadia, and Isle Royale. The force of some of those vessels was so great that it could not have been sent out by the other

---

[1] Its people also owned most of the vessels used for coasting.   [2] I.R. vol. 6, p. 22.
[3] Shute to the Lords of Trade, Boston, August 19, C.O. 5/868.
[4] Bourville had become King Lieutenant in succession to de Beaucours.

pirates who also preyed on this commerce. These were outlaws largely from English fishing vessels frequenting the coasts of Newfoundland, who had been turned adrift for insubordination or drunkenness, or had deserted on account of low wages and poor fare. Their head-quarters were at Cape Ray. While possibly the majority of them were English, their rendezvous received accessions from the French and became the " cave of Adullam " of these coasts. Fishermen stole the boats and gear of their masters, notably from Ingonish. De Mezy's exalted position did not prevent one of his boats being stolen from under his windows. All such malefactors joined the outlaws. They plundered vessels on the Grand Banks and on the coasts of Newfoundland. Although the site of their settlement was known, and the British Government sent out regularly vessels to protect its commerce against the pirates, and a joint French and English expedition was contemplated, no steps were taken to break it up. Throughout the whole period of Louisbourg's history, while the freebooters in its immediate neighbourhood disappeared, both French and English men-of-war visited the fishermen on the Grand Banks, for the purpose of protecting them from pirates.[1]

The incident which marked these years was a shipwreck which de Mezy described as the most frightful which he had known in the five and thirty years of his seafaring life.[2]

The rock-bound coast of Isle Royale is, to the eastward of Louisbourg, free for some distance from outlying dangers. Near Cape Breton, its eastern extremity, currents, which are at times impetuous, rush round the low island of Porto Nova and other rocks and shoals, and so make impossible a safe approach to this shore.[3] At this time, August 1725, the inhabitants of these hamlets, some six or eight score, most of whom were at Baleine, took refuge before nightfall of the 25th, in their rude huts ("cabannes"), from an east-south-east gale which blew furiously on this coast, the steep-pitched beaches of which mark the force of the seas. It was ten the next morning before any of them ventured out, and they found in the sea-wrack on the shore the wreckage of a large vessel. Among it were pulleys marked with *fleur de lys*, which, when this news was brought to Louisbourg on the following day, the 27th, indicated to the authorities that a King's ship had been lost near Baleine. De Mezy himself, de Bourville, Major of the troops, and Sabatier the Comptroller, at once set

---

[1] The lesser value of the commerce of the North made it unnecessary for the pirates to obtain a foothold on this coast, although at more than one place in Nova Scotia and Cape Breton are legends of the buried treasure of Captain Kidd. Rhode Island is the most northern of the colonies whose officials and citizens were accused of complicity in this piracy ; the French certainly had no share in it. See Weeden, *passim*, Channing, vol. ii.

[2] The intimate connection of colonial administration with the Navy is shown in his expression in writing to a minister who knew his record, " depuis trente cinq ans que je vais à la mer," although in many of these years he served in the colonies.

[3] The small harbours of Grand and Petit Lorambec, and Baleine, afford shelter to only smaller craft.

out. They found along the coast, from Grand Lorambec to Baleine, the beach strewn with wreckage, among which was the figure-head which identified the vessel as the *Chameau*, which, under command of M. de St. James, was carrying supplies, money, and dispatches, together with a distinguished passenger list, to Quebec. The first bodies found were those of Chazel, the newly appointed Intendant of Canada; the ship's pilot, Chointeau, and one which they believed was that of young de Lages, son of de Ramezay, Governor of Montreal. Papers came ashore, among them the patent of Chazel. These victims were but the forerunners of many. In two days, forty more were found by men of the three detachments which had been promptly formed to make salvage of what came ashore. The wreck was indeed complete; the ill-fated ship, evidently under sail, had been carried over the outlying reefs. She at once broke up; part of her starboard side came ashore with the main mast and its rigging; another part of the same side with the mizzen mast was found nearly a mile farther along the coast. The suddenness of the disaster was made evident by the fact that most of the bodies were undressed. The fury of the sea was shown by the fact that from the live stock carried on her, not even a pig came ashore alive; "les cochons mesmes qui nagent si bien sont venus morts à la coste." Among the victims who were recognized were two officers of Canada, de Morrion and Pachot, but if L'Hermitte's body was found it was not identified, and De Pensens, who was at one time thought to be on board, had not sailed. The missionary priest at Baleine buried one hundred and eighty; the total loss was three hundred and ten.

The authorities acted with effectiveness in this disaster. They advised those of Quebec, and arranged to lend them ammunition and money from the Louisbourg supplies which were coming on the *Dromedary*. There was no sign of the after part of the ship having come ashore, so it was hoped that some salvage might be made of her guns and treasure, particularly as the rock on which she broke up was covered at low tide by only a few feet of water. Detachments were kept posted along the shore to save what wreckage they could, their men being promised a share of whatever was found. The next season some soldiers who were skilful divers were sent from Quebec and were employed at the wreck. They were in charge of Sabatier and of young Le Normant, then acting as clerk under his father. They lodged in an abandoned house of Carrerrot, a merchant of Louisbourg. It was roofless, except for one room. It had been occupied by his sister, Madame La Salle, a sprightly lady to whose attractions Le Normant lightly refers, and to whom he and Sabatier sent a message of esteem and gratitude in his letter to "Monsieur mon très cher Père." Morpain conducted the actual operations, which were carried on in September, Le Normant whiling away his spare time by shooting when bad weather interrupted the work. He sent to his father the game which he got, and in his last letter from Baleine ends his requisition for supplies with "five or six days of good weather or an order to return." The latter came in due course. No more striking contrast in circumstances is connected with Louisbourg than that between young Le Normant in Baleine and Le Normant at the head of the Navy in attendance on the King, and belonging to the party of Madame de Pompadour.[1] Further search was abandoned, but the wreck left its mark on the colony, although no one connected with it was lost, for almost the latest French maps mark, on the bleak shore of the cove, the cemetery of those of its victims which the sea gave up. It lived in the memory of the French of Isle Royale as the August gale of 1873 is still before the people of Cape Breton, and when two heavy gales in November 1726 swept Louisbourg with great damage, it was vividly recalled to its people.

Isle Royale was at this time, thirteen years after its foundation, described as a colony beginning to be considerable. Its commerce with the West Indies had by 1726 become important, as had its trade with France and Quebec. Its principal export, after fish, was its coal, followed in value by furs gathered at Louisbourg from Nova Scotia.

The trade suffered from a scarcity of ready money not seriously felt within the colony, but for example making trade difficult with Quebec, whither the merchants of Louisbourg had to send cash to pay the duties on goods they exported to Canada.

The regulations which in the earliest stage governed trade between France and her colonies, established by the Edict of 1716, were irksome. Vessels could sail for the colonies from only a few of the ports of France.[2] Bonds had to be given that they would return to the port of departure.[3] The destination had to be named before leaving, and a certificate produced, after the round voyage was finished, that the vessel had been at the port named. This restricted freedom in seeking markets, and in taking advantage of the triangular trade, which for so long was the normal course of shipping between Europe and America. This was modified by an edict in October 1727,[4] which provided that no foreign product, except Irish salt beef loaded at a port of France, should be admitted to Canada or the West Indies, and that none of their products should go directly to a foreign country, with the exception of refined sugars to Spain. Foreign

---

[1] The value, about 6000 l., of the salvage from the *Chameau* was trifling, although she had on board 289,696 l. in cash, for the expenses of Canada (I.R. B, vol. 48, f. 862).

[2] *e.g.* Sables d'Olonne then a fishing port, not, as now, a watering-place, had to apply to the Conseil de Commerce for this privilege. Previously to its being granted its outfitters had to pay local imposts on the goods they sent out, which they brought to their port from Bordeaux (Arch. Nat. F, 12, vol. 75).

[3] Dugard Le Vieux of Rouen was hampered by this regulation, which was modified on his application. The Conseil generally decided in favour of freedom of trade (Arch. Nat. F, 12, vol. 87).

[4] Isambert, Recueil, vol. 26.

vessels were not permitted to enter a port in the colonies nor come within a league of them, under penalty of confiscation, and a fine of 1000 l. Officers were ordered to seek them out, and men-of-war and privateers to capture foreigners or French vessels engaged in illicit commerce. An elaborate scale of division of the proceeds of such confiscation was established, the only relaxation on humanitarian ground of the stringency of these regulations being that a vessel in distress could take refuge only in a port where there was a garrison.

A later chapter [1] deals with the lack of balance of the trade which centred at Louisbourg. The defiance or ignoring of the regulations made by distant authorities, enforced in many cases by officials who had a personal interest in illicit trade, was as important a factor in the economic conditions as official regulations.

If the margin of profit is adequate, any trade will be carried on in defiance of law. Vessels from the British colonies had been permitted to come to Isle Royale from time to time, until, under pressure of necessity in 1726, a proclamation was issued permitting the importation from them of building materials, live cattle, poultry, etc., but prohibiting everything else.[2] This opened one door, for the returns of the permitted vessels would indicate that none of them carried full cargoes, the balance of their lading would be contraband goods. Others apparently depended on corruption, and made no colour of being on a legitimate voyage. We have the record of an agreement made in 1724 at Boston between three merchants,—"Johonnot," P. Evarts, Hough, and one Pierre Grouard,—who undertook to sell the lading of the schooner *Hirondelle* and purchase a cargo of fish and bring back in money or taffetas [3] any balance for a commission of 6 per cent. The *Hirondelle* was seized at Rimouski, suspected of spying. Grouard and others were imprisoned, and were the occasion of charges of official improprieties, and a conflict of jurisdiction.[4] While this cargo went to the Gulf of the St. Lawrence there is no reason to believe that a similar method of doing business was not carried on with Louisbourg, and that the merchants named were the only ones in Boston who conducted trade with the French colonies in this fashion. The ledger of one of the most important of them, Mr. Faneuil, contains may entries of transactions with merchants of Louisbourg. The evidence of Newton, the collector of Customs at Canso, makes this reasonably certain, for in no year during the period under consideration did the number of vessels declared as from British ports come to as many as he says was the normal number. He wrote, as follows, in speaking of eighteen vessels then in that port :

"They will without any Restraint Load and carry from thence to several Ports in his

---

[1] Chap. XII.

[2] 1728, I.R. vol. 10, f. 4.

[3] This is so printed. It unquestionably means taffia (rum).

[4] MSS. Que. vol. 3, p. 106, and B, 48 (Canada).

Majtys Plantations, Brandy, Wine, Iron, Sail Cloth, Rum, Molasses & several other French Commoditys with which there is from 80 to 90 Sail generally Load with in a Year, these Vessels generally carry Lumber, Bricks & live stock there, they commonly clear out for Newfoundland, tho never design to go farther than Lewisburg, often they sell their vessels as well as Cargoes."

The prosperous farmers of Nova Scotia shared in a simple way in trade with Louisbourg. Their shipments were made mostly from Baie Verte on the Gulf coast, although there are instances of vessels of ten tons making the long voyage from the Bay of Fundy to Louisbourg. Ordinarily they were not interfered with, and Verville's theory that the Acadians were of more value to Isle Royale where they were, than if they had migrated, was borne out. At times Armstrong, then in charge of Nova Scotia, attempted to stop this intercourse, and on one occasion his reply to St. Ovide being unsatisfactory, de Pensens was sent to him to declare that they would arm a ship to prevent him making seizures on the high seas. He desisted in face of this threat, which would have been proved, in the contrary case, to have been empty, for Maurepas refused permission to fit out this vessel.[1]

The entrepôt which should flourish by freedom of exchange, foreseen by Raudot, was struggling with the enactments of its rulers to come into existence. The furniture and axes[2] which New England sent there, the winnowing machines with which Louisbourg supplied Quebec, the rum and molasses, the sail cloth and iron she exported to the British colonies, none of them her own production, indicate his sureness of judgment as to the proper foundation for a flourishing colony situated on Isle Royale. The scanty records of the trade which are available make tenable the hypothesis that had the civil population of Louisbourg been left untrammelled to develop its commercial possibilities, it would have been so prosperous and populous an establishment that its later history would have been entirely different.

Raudot's views were as far in advance of his time as was the commercial Treaty of Utrecht, the provisions of which waited until the younger Pitt in 1787 forced them through an unwilling House of Commons. Maurepas' objections to this trade were held in common with all his contemporaries, and the ineffectiveness of his opposition was probably owing to his lack of force rather than a philosophic acquiescence in a state of affairs which was theoretically wrong, but practically extremely profitable. In at least one instance he connived in it. When Ste. Marie was pressing, in 1724, for repayment of his expenses, 1893 l., incurred in 1718-19 in visiting Boston, Maurepas wrote to St. Ovide that Ste. Marie brought back goods presumably to sell, and rejected the claim.[3]

In the earlier days of the colony the merchants of France objected to it, for

---

[1] I.R. vol. 8.   [2] 1100 in 1740.   [3] I.R. vol. 39, B, vol. 48, f. 716.

their chief business was the sale of commodities to the new settlers, later they were silent on the subject. The merchants of Louisbourg objected from time to time, notably in 1728, and again ten years later. On the former occasion St. Ovide was accused with full details of carrying on this trade through De Pensens, under the names of Dacarette and Lartigue. It appeared as if Maurepas intended to take some action, for he wrote to De Mezy sending a list of questions about the trade, with the assurance that his reply would be confidential, so that he might not be restrained by the fear of incriminating St. Ovide.[1] De Mezy replied on the 30th of November and the 2nd of December, in some fashion which was satisfactory to the Minister. His replies unfortunately are not extant. St. Ovide contented himself with a short denial.

In 1738 an anonymous letter was forwarded to the Minister on this commerce and its abuses.[2] It was followed by a new attack against Du Vivier which goes into detail. It says he bought the cargoes of two French vessels which he resold ; that he took a cargo of molasses which he sent to Boston in partnership with Faneuil, who had traded with Louisbourg through one Morel ; that they took money from the country, as they sold for cash ; that they put in quarantine a vessel from Martinique on account of small-pox, because two vessels of Du Vivier arrived shortly afterwards ; that Du Vivier forestalled the market by having early news from Quebec ; and they did not hesitate to say that Le Normant was interested in Du Vivier's transactions ; and that they enriched themselves by taking provisions from the King's stores in the autumn, selling them at a high price, and replacing them the following year when they were cheap.

But however the trade was carried on, it was unquestionably large, profitable, and essential to Isle Royale. The real complaint of its merchants was of the competition of military and civil officials, whose influence and command of information gave them great advantages. The only people to suffer were the Admiralty officials, who found their confiscations overruled by the Governor and the Commissaire-Ordonnateur. Ship-owners benefited by full cargoes. None of them were placed at a disadvantage except vessels with letters of marque, which, relying on the edict of 1727, made these captures.

In trade, like the fishing at Canso before the incursion of Smart, all things were peaceable and quiet, the French and English in defiance of the laws trading " together in all amity and love," a happier state than in the West Indies, where mutual savagery brought on the war between England and Spain. But the protests of Mr. Newton to his Government, the prohibition of Maurepas to his officials, both disregarded, caused less irritation than the *guarda costas* and the pirates of Jamaica. Thus prohibited trade in Northern waters led to a friendly

---

[1] I.R. B, 52, f. 605, 607.   [2] I.R. vol. 20, f. 311. See Appendix.

intercourse between Isle Royale and the sea-ports of the Puritans, not to mutilations which inflamed against the Spaniard both the humanity and the patriotism of England.[1]

The fishermen had in the earliest times placed on the knoll of the eastern side of the harbour a beacon to serve as a guide to its entrance. This proved unsatisfactory as the commerce of the port grew, and it was visited by other ships than those of its ordinary trade. The first foreign ship, other than English, which visited the port, was the Spaniard, *Nostra Signora de la Toledo*, homeward bound from Havana.[2] Three years later the *Mercury*, a ship of the French East India Company, came into Louisbourg with sixty men ill of scurvy, who in the pure air of Isle Royale soon became convalescent. When the project for a lighthouse, to take the place of the beacon, was seriously considered, the difficulty of landing coal for its fire was an objection to the best site. The home authorities proposed on this account placing the light on the clock tower of the citadel, but this project was fortunately abandoned, and the lighthouse was erected on the eastern side of the harbour, where its ruins are still to be seen. It was first lit in 1734, and the statement is that it was visible for six leagues at sea. It was burned on the night of the 11th of September 1736, but was immediately rebuilt of fireproof materials.[3]

St. Ovide and De Mezy acted in harmony in only one matter—their efforts to restrict the excessive consumption of intoxicants. Although De Mezy was effective in the steps taken in connection with the *Chameau*, the laxity of administration in his department shortly thereafter became evident, through the death of Des Goutins the Treasurer. St. Ovide insisted on having particulars of De Mezy's accounts, which he was asked to approve, and of verifying the contents of the Treasurer's chest. It was found empty. Nevertheless, De Mezy took offence at what he considered an interference with his rights. He took high ground in writing to the Minister. He expressed his extreme repugnance, after "thirty-seven years of service, to submitting his documents to a naval officer, who, although meritorious and of easy intercourse, has neither the experience, nor other qualities superior to his in a matter concerning my administration."[4]

Maurepas did not accept his views, but replied that he was wrong in putting the blame on Des Goutins when his own accounts should have been better

---

[1] *Camb. History*, vol. vi. p. 24.   [2] August 10, 1726.

[3] In the new lighthouse the light was supplied from forty-five "pots" (about twenty-two and a half gallons of oil), fed through thirty-one pipes in a copper circle to the wicks which gave the flame. As this oil was held in an open bronze basin, three feet in diameter, and ten inches deep, there was constant danger of fire. This was provided against by sustaining this ring on pieces of cork, which, if fire took place, would burn through and let the ring fall into the oil where it would be extinguished. No wood was used in the construction of the tower.

[4] "À un officier de guerre qui quoique homme de mérite, et de très bonne société, n'a ni l'usage, ni les services, ni autres qualités supérieures à moi dans une affaire de mon ministère" (vol. 9, Nov. 24, 1727).

kept.[1] De Mezy admitted that his books were not in perfect order, his excuse being that the entire financial business for the year was transacted in the fortnight following the arrival of the King's ship with remittances. He further excused himself by saying that the records were in extremely bad order when he came to the colony, and that it had taken them some time to correct them. This is borne out by the documents themselves. By 1724 they are much fuller, and on the surface appear more accurate than in the earlier years of the colony.

But the disregard of instructions was evident in more serious ways than book-keeping. De Mezy admitted having disobeyed orders about rations, not without justification, for he says he had given food from the King's stores to four widows who were destitute, but that hereafter he would execute orders without mercy. Without any charge having been made against him, he assures the Minister that the only funds he can touch are those of the extraordinary expenditures 15,000 or 20,000 livres. He was largely responsible for so important an edict as that of October 1727, in reference to Colonial Trade, not being registered or put in force in Louisbourg until October 1730.[2] Other tangible evidence of neglect of royal instructions was before the eyes of all. An ordinance had been passed establishing the width of the quay, and another forbidding building within 350 toises of the fortifications, yet in a few years one cronier had built a stone house within the prohibited distance, and there were also encroachments on the quay. This took place in so small a town that from any point on the ramparts every house could be seen. That the infraction of regulations, presumably important, could go so far under the eyes of the Governor, the Commissaire-Ordonnateur, and the Engineer, that it required ministerial action to stop it, illustrates the weakness of the system on which the French attempted to administer their colonial empire.

Whether the complaints of the Minister against De Mezy, founded on these irregularities and his quarrels with St. Ovide, led to the change in his department, which was determined on by Maurepas, is uncertain. De Mezy had completed about forty years in the King's service, and when St. Ovide heard that he was to be succeeded he wrote to the Minister, saying that he trusted he would select a new Commissaire-Ordonnateur of a gentle disposition, with whom the merchants and people could carry on business in comfort.[3] The favourable impression the younger De Mezy (usually known as Le Normant) had made, or possibly family influence, led to his succeeding his father.[4] He had been in the colony during the greater part of his father's tenure of office, employed first as a subordinate, and then as principal clerk, and during his

---

[1] B, vols. 52 and 53.   [2] B, 55/570.   [3] I.R. vol. 12, Nov. 25, 1731.

[4] The De Mezys were of the family of that Le Normant who was the husband of Madame de Pompadour, and as a Fermier-General had great influence before she rose to power. Oct. 8, 1733 is the date on which young Le Normant wrote to Maurepas his thanks. The official appointments were made March 23, 1735.

father's leave of absence had in his place administered the office. He was therefore well fitted by experience for the position. But he began his administration with the same quarrels with St. Ovide as had disturbed the relations between the Governor and his father, and in one of his first important acts he displayed a lack of judgment which seriously imperilled the well-being of the colony.

In 1732 the *Ruby* came into port with small-pox on board. Although from time to time there had been regulations establishing a quarantine, once against the plague which raged in Toulon and Marseilles, and at another against a pest in Boston, at this time no precautions were taken, or if taken were ineffective.

The disease spread throughout the colony and many of all ages died, not only sailors and passengers of the ill-fated ship, but residents of the colony and soldiers of its garrison. The ship, however, proceeded to Quebec, leaving those who were sick on shore, replacing them by sailors taken from the merchant's vessels. Further misfortune followed the survivors, who late in the year were shipped to Quebec on a brigantine which was wrecked at Ingonish. This epidemic was followed by a famine, the cause of which Le Normant explained by the method by which the inhabitants supplied themselves. The earliest vessels to arrive were those of the Basque ports. Their captains lent the provisions of their large crews to the inhabitants. These people counted on returning them by purchases from the provisions brought from Canada. If this supply was short, it had for the greater part to be utilized in returning these borrowings, which the Basques required for their homeward voyage, instead of being retained by the inhabitants for consumption during the winter.[1] While the Quebec vessels were there in the summer the inhabitants, living on their borrowings, offered only meagre prices, and therefore, De Mezy said, fewer vessels came from Quebec.[2] This condition was aggravated, as the Quebec authorities explain, by a local regulation that Quebec vessels should not leave port without selling their cargoes. But whatever were the causes the situation was most serious in the autumn of 1733,[3] and with an optimism for which no grounds are shown, Le Normant delayed action. St. Ovide changed from the devotee of Costebelle's description, or justified by the gravity of the situation, says he trusted Providence less than Le Normant ; but it was not until St. Ovide declared that he would send a vessel to the Minister with a statement of their condition, brought about by Le Normant's refusal to supply funds to purchase supplies in New York, that the latter consented to take action.[4]   Two

---

[1] I.R. vol. 14, f. 175.   [2] This is not borne out by the officials' returns which are available.
[3] I.R. vol. 14, f. 126.
[4] " De vous seul monsieur dépend aujourd'huy la conservation ou la perte de cette colonie, que j'alois faire embarquer un officier le lendemain sur un bâtiment qui devait partir pour France à fin d'informer Mgr." (Nov. 14, 1733, vol. 14, f. 77).

small vessels, under charge of De Gannes and Bonnaventure, were sent late in the year for these supplies, New York being chosen in preference to Boston, where the plague had recently existed, but they did not return before spring, and the colony passed a winter in want, mitigated only by the opportune arrival of one vessel from Quebec and one from New England.

In 1734, at the beginning of the outbreak of war between France and the Emperor, the unsettled affairs on the continent gave rise to rumours of war with England, and St. Ovide took up the question of their relations with the New England colonies. He points out in a letter in cipher [1] to the Minister that the English, particularly those of New England, dislike the existence of Isle Royale as a French colony. He dwells on the necessity of being advised early of the outbreak of war, as it is important to take the offensive. In another letter he lays before the Minister the steps which they propose to take to protect themselves, which were to complete the fortifications between the citadel and the Dauphin battery, which, although projected from the first had not yet been carried out, and to protect, by *chevaux de frise*, the quay where a landing from boats could be made. He then gives his opinion of what might occur ; which was, that if England made an attack on Louisbourg it would be by New England militiamen, of whom he had not a high opinion ; that they would be supported by English men-of-war, and that they would come very early in the year in order to prevent the fishermen from France, or vessels of force from entering Louisbourg ; that they would not make their base at Port Dauphin or Baie des Espagnols as apparently some thought, as these points were too distant, but that the landing would be made in Gabarus or Miré bays. His plan of campaign, if the King intends the offensive, with all its advantages, is that two men-of-war and a frigate should be sent early in the year with four or five new companies for the garrison and six hundred regular troops and munitions of war. These, with volunteers from Louisbourg and Indians would make adequate force to take Annapolis Royal, if secrecy and celerity could be attained. He points out, notwithstanding the previous views he had expressed to the Minister, that the Acadians were not to be depended on. He informs him that Annapolis Royal [2] is in a wretched condition, a statement quite within the bounds of truth, and that the English in Canso are in such a poor condition that its commander has instructions to abandon the port at the outbreak of war. He intended further to supplement the force with the forty men of the garrison of Isle St. Jean, and the Indians of that island. He also assured the Minister that not only Placentia, but Boston, would easily fall before such an expedition. He

---

[1] Letters of St. O. to Minister, in particular Oct. 28, 1734 (I.R. vol. 15).

[2] The garrison of Annapolis and Canso was nine companies : 360 officers and men, five at Annapolis, four at Canso (1734, B.T.N.S. vol. 33, f. 361). "Canso lies naked and defenceless" (1734, A. & W.I. vol. 30). Kilby says Canso is so ill-prepared that 100 men could capture it in one hour (1743, A. & W.I. vol. 594).

followed this by a second letter, saying that twenty companies are necessary, part of whom should be commanded by local officers ; repeated earnestly his request for munitions ; and referring to his forty-five years of service, said to the Minister that the experience of the past made him fear for the future.

These representations, made ten years before the war broke out, so accurately forecast the course of events, that St. Ovide in 1745 might, with a sad satisfaction, have recalled to his associates the predictions which he made at this time. St. Ovide hoped, if there was no war, that in the troubled conditions France might again get possession of Acadia by exchange, for it would be of infinite importance to France. He based this hope on the indifference to Nova Scotia of the English Government, as shown by the continuous neglect of that province from 1710, the year of its capture, to 1734, the time of his writing in this strain.

General matters of defence probably engaged the attention of the French authorities at this time. Chaussegros de Lery combated an idea, which he says was prevalent in France, that Louisbourg was the highway " le boulevard " to Quebec and Canada. He said that a naval expedition against Canada would require three squadrons, and that Quebec was more vulnerable by way of the woods. Were it not for the general policy of France in relation to her colonies during this period, it might be thought that the views of Chaussegros had more weight with the Minister than those of St. Ovide and his successors.

In 1737 the colony again suffered from famine, but affairs had so far adjusted themselves that St. Ovide was able to go to France in the autumn of 1738, leaving, as before, the government in the hands of De Bourville, while Sabatier discharged the duties of Le Normant de Mezy, who was promoted to the Intendancy of St. Dominique, as the first step towards the highest position in the administration of the navy. (As Intendant-General he was practically joint Minister for the few months in which Massiac held the portfolio.) [1]

St. Ovide does not seem to have thought that he would not return to Isle Royale. Not long before that he had obtained a large grant at the head of the harbour, and more recently a splendid tract of land on the Miré River.[2] In the ordinary course of business, after his arrival in France, he wrote to the Minister about an increase in that garrison, and Maurepas in January said that he would await his suggestions before dealing with the question of promotions.[3] But between this time and March the Minister had taken a more hostile and determined attitude than he had yet shown. St. Ovide went, or was summoned, to Versailles, and had a painful interview with Maurepas, who charged him with many faults. The Minister told him that he was acquainted with a transaction in which, it was said, that as far back as 1725 St. Ovide had a pecuniary interest in Ganet's

---

[1] La Cour-Gayet, pp. 211-217.   [2] 1737, B, 65, 451.   [3] B, 68, f. 1.

contract for the fortifications.[1]   St. Ovide admitted that the offer of a share had been made to him, but declared that he had declined it.   He said the sworn testimony of two survivors of the transaction, Daligrand, a merchant of the town, and Ganet, the contractor, would bear out his statement.   De Pensens, who was alleged to be his partner, had died, and the incident had become public through a clause in his will.   The Minister does not seem to have been convinced by his explanations.   The charges have this much prima facie evidence in their support, that it was through De Pensens, St. Ovide was said, in the accusations of 1728, to have carried on his illicit trading.[2]   No further steps were taken, and St. Ovide, bearing his wounds[3] and the burden of his forty-seven years of service, was permitted to retire with a pension of 3000 livres.

As a civil administrator he had little success, but the evils of his administration seemed to be as much due to the lack of discipline and inspection as to the personal faults of the man.   His quarrels with both De Mezys, his slackness at the time of Smart's attack at Canso, the reiterated reports, some of them circumstantial, which were made of his complicity in illegal trade, were, beyond occasional reproofs and exhortations to amend his ways, ignored by Maurepas.   During the whole period no report by an independent person seems to have been made on the condition of the colony.   Those familiar with affairs can well picture the slackness and abuses which would exist in a distant establishment, uninspected for nearly a generation, from which no report of irregularity received more than a rebuke from the central administration.   This laxity is the more astonishing as both the colonies and the navy were under the direction of Maurepas, and although the correspondence contains remarks on Louisbourg in the reports of the voyages[4] there is nothing to show that the Minister ever sought information as to conditions in the colonies from the captains of the ships he annually sent out. Whether this slackness was the result of indifference, incompetence, or hopelessness, the results were a demoralized administration and a stunted development.

---

[1] St. Ovide, April 4, vol. 21, p. 290.   [2] B, 52, f. 605.   Cf. Appendix.
[3] These wounds were a shattered shoulder-blade received in an attack on St. John's, Newfoundland, and three others received in action.   [4] Arch. Nat. Marine, B⁴.

CHAPTER VI

THE connection of St. Ovide with Isle Royale began when he landed with the one hundred and forty, founders of Louisbourg in 1713. Four years later he became its Governor. By the time of his retirement he had seen most of the little harbours along the coast become fishing establishments, and the civil population of the island grow to something over thirty-eight hundred, and the commerce, which had begun with the few vessels which the people of Placentia had brought with them, increase to a fleet of great importance. In 1738 seventy-three vessels came from France, forty-two from New England and Acadia, and twenty-nine from Canada and the West Indies. At the latter date some fifty-four vessels of the inhabitants were engaged in coasting and trading, besides sixty odd schooners and one hundred fishing-boats which pursued the staple industry of the coast, cod-fishing. The value of this industry was about 3,000,000 livres, and the overseas commerce of the island, one year with another, was about an equal amount. Shipbuilding was established in the island and was carried on on the Miré as well as at Louisbourg, although many vessels were brought from New England. A little later the British authorities complained that "in the fall, after the British guard-ship has left Canso, the French go to Pictou, build vessels, and cut some of the finest mast timber in the world and take it to Louisbourg in the early spring." [1]

The project of fortifications as originally laid down was finished. Beginning at the water front on the harbour side, the Dauphin bastion and spur protected the principal approach to the town, and swept the water front of the harbour. Between it and the King's bastion ran an ascending curtain wall to the height on which the citadel was placed. Across its opening on the town side stood a stately stone building, the Chateau St. Louis, of four stories with slated roof. The only entrance was across a draw-bridge thus described by a New England observer :

"The entrance is by a large gate over which is a draw-bridge over a small ditch through the whole building, in passing which on the left hand the door opens into a King's

[1] C.O. $\frac{2}{2}$V. Cf. Appendix.

85

Chappell, on the right hand into a dungeon, one of which has a greater resemblance of Hell than the other of Heaven." [1]

The Citadel contained, on the southern side, the apartments of the Governor and the King's Chapel, which served as parish church ; the other half was occupied by the barracks. The whole work was the Bastion du Roy, the centre of the system of fortification. Between this and the sea coast were the Queen's bastion and the Prince's half-bastion. These works by 1735 were in an advanced state, although but a few guns were mounted, for at this time the defence of the town depended on the island battery, protecting the mouth of the harbour with a battery of twenty guns broadside to the narrow entrance, and on the shore of the harbour, facing its entrance, the Royal battery completed with its towers and with its guns mounted. After that date there was taken up by the Engineers the fortifications of the eastern part of the town as shown in the plans.

There is some material to make a picture of the town. Monsieur Verrier, the Engineer, whiled away the hours of the winter of 1731 in making a drawing of the town from the harbour side ; another from the sea, drawn by Bastide, shows it substantially as St. Ovide left it ; but in the way of description little exists, except the few references to the condition of the people, given by Don Antonio d'Ulloa, a Spanish man of science and captain in her navy, who was at Louisbourg in 1745 under circumstances to be recounted later. [2]

Verrier's view is confirmed by the written description, and by those which are found ornamenting some of the maps, notably that of the first siege. The houses were built for the most part in wood on stone foundations, and were from eight to eleven feet in height ; but some of them had the first story in stone, the upper in wood. This description and Verrier's view would seem to indicate that the restrictions as to height had been disregarded, but justify D'Ulloa's description. The hospital would, in the general *coup d'œil*, go far to redeem the appearance of the town, for it dominated it as the Chateau of St. Louis the citadel, and their slender flèches, so characteristic of French architecture of the period, would, from sea, have been a guide as certain and as visible as the lighthouse. It is also characteristic of the methods of the two peoples, that there seems to have been in all the British colonies no buildings so imposing as those which the French Government thought suitable for this little establishment.

Beginning at the water front near the Dauphin gate, the principal entrance to the town, the first buildings were the King's store-houses, and lodged in the space between this and the inner angle of the King's bastion were the dwellings

---

[1] C.O. Ad. Captains' Letters, No. 2655.

[2] B.N. Geo. C, 18,830. Brit. Mus., King's, 119, 95 A. A facsimile is in the Archives at Ottawa, and another in the possession of the writer is given as a frontispiece ; of the former, Bastide's view is opposite.

of four military officers. Next on the water front were the establishments of some merchants, and the official residence of the Commissaire-Ordonnateur, which De Mezy had built for himself in stone at a cost of 20,000 l. Next to this house was one belonging to Madame Rodrigue, widow of one of the principal merchants in the place, which was 22 feet square on a piece of land 44 × 150 feet, which Bigot certified in 1739 to be worth 5500 l.[1] This family, like many others of the merchants, were well off, "fort à leur aise," enriched by their commerce with Europe and America ; their prosperity all founded, to the amazement of D'Ulloa, on their single product the cod of Isle Royale, which he states is the best from American waters.

Next to these came the Chapel and Convent of the Recollets, and then along the water front some properties belonging to the civil staff. About the centre of the town the Sisters of the Congregation had made a somewhat improvident bargain, as it was regarded at the time, in buying from De Beaucours a lot on which they established their convent and school. So large a part of the town was occupied by government buildings and the properties of the military and civil staff, that the working population must have been placed along the shores of the harbour, on which one still sees the foundations of many buildings. Verrier, the Engineer, had a lot on the corner of the Rue d'Estrées and Scatarie running through to the newly opened Rue de l'Hôpital, where his principal neighbour was Cailly, Lieutenant of the Swiss, who had bought from the heirs of Baron de L'Espérance the adjoining property. On this Verrier had built his modest habitation, not much exceeding, he says, the estimated cost of 6000 l.[2] This consisted of a ground floor, which held a kitchen, and annexed thereto a scullery and a room for a servant, a dining-room, a principal bedroom, and two small closets, and in the attic his study, and some small bedrooms for his family. The only other description of a house is that of Delaforest, who came to Louisbourg in 1714 as clerk, and in 1728 had risen to be Procureur in the Admiralty Court. This he had to demolish because it was under the little hill which was to be occupied by the Dauphin bastion. The house was 50 feet long, 15 wide, built with pickets and was covered with boards. The principal room was 15 feet square, with two large glazed windows looking out on the harbour, and a glazed door opening out to the garden. It had two cabinets, each with a window, a kitchen 15 by 14 with two windows, all of them with a loft over. There was a lean-to store-house, 15 by 12, against the gable of the house, a court of 30 by 70 in front surrounded by pickets and with a large gate. At the back was a garden of 60 feet square, also fenced in, which was in an excellent state as it had been well manured.

The normal increase in the population was good. In 1726 it had been

[1] *Ulloa*, vol. ii. p. 140.   [2] Its cost was 28,945 l., for which St. Ovide was reprimanded.

951, in 1734 it was 1116, and in 1737 was 1463. They were a fruitful people. There were 157 families, in which the wife was resident, in 1737, and the number of children 664. The custom of sending women to the colonies did not affect Isle Royale. Many Canadians had come and married immigrants from France, while Acadia supplied all the marriageable maidens the growth of the population required.

These figures include neither the garrison nor the official classes, nor apparently the ecclesiastics, of whom there were five Brothers of Charity at the hospital, three Recollet monks, and five Sisters of the Congregation. The daughters of some of the officers were sent to Canada or to France for their education, but after the establishment of the Nuns at Louisbourg their school seems to have provided adequately for the education of the young people of the place. There does not seem to have been, however, any school for boys, and yet they all seem to have written fairly well, and show no more inaccuracy as regards grammar and spelling than the majority of young New Englanders of the time.

The population also had become, with the growth of the town, somewhat more complex. There was a gardener in the town, a Master of Hydrography, and the ladies of the town had the choice of two dressmakers. One Marie Paris, born in Louisbourg, apparently had the larger establishment, for with her lived three sisters and a maid ; while the widow Radoub, who belonged to St. Malo, lived by herself, and, if her name had any significance, exercised a humbler form of the art. Nor was the gardener the only person who promoted the amenities of life ; one Simon Rondel had come from Namur to carry on his profession as a teacher of dancing.

The earlier disapproval by the authorities of having negroes in Cape Breton had broken down through the intercourse with the West Indies, and several of the families had negro servants brought from the French islands.[1] They were baptized, and in the majority of the cases the godfather and godmother were sons and daughters of the officers of the garrison.

The three bells for the chapel in the citadel were blessed and baptized as St. Louis, St. John, and St. Anthoine-Marie, the last being named for Sabatier, who was acting at the time, 1733, as Ordonnateur, and for Madame Bourville, wife of the King's Lieutenant. The bells for the Recollet church in town were also baptized, with De Lort, a merchant of the town, as godfather, and Marie, the wife of Despiet, an officer of the garrison, as godmother.

The illegitimate children of the town were cared for by people of position taking the responsibility of godfather and godmother to these unfortunates. These were not numerous, considering the fact that it was a large

[1] St. Ovide to the Minister, Nov. 27, 1724, vol. 9.

garrison town, frequented by fishermen for six months of the year, and was the home of families from which the husband was often absent. Practically the full number is known owing to the necessity for baptism among Roman Catholics.

In the environs the twenty-five years of settlement had developed the country, as is shown on a contemporary map. A road "on which two carriages could drive abreast," still passable except for the bridges, had by 1738 been opened through to the Miré, which it reached opposite Salmon River. On the beautiful meadows which form its banks, St. Ovide had his concessions, and in his neighbourhood were settled some few retired soldiers.

The Sieur Jean Milly, a principal merchant of Louisbourg, had an establishment not distant from that of the Governor. It is probable that these were the two estates which were described by Gibson, who led a party to the Miré in 1745.[1]

"We found two fine farms upon a neck of land that extended near seven miles in length. The first we came to was a very handsome house, and had two large barns, well finished, that lay contiguous to it. Here, likewise, were two very large gardens ; as also some fields of corn of a considerable height, and other good lands thereto belonging, besides plenty of beach wood and fresh water . . . . The other house was a fine stone edifice, consisting of six rooms on a floor, all well finished. There was a fine wall before it, and two fine barns contiguous to it, with fine gardens and other appurtenances, besides several fine fields of wheat. In one of the barns there were fifteen loads of hay, and room sufficient for three score horses and other cattle."

Living people have seen the brick floors of a large byre with the bones of many cattle on it on the southern side of the Miré, near Albert Bridge. The properties of M. de Catalogne and the Fathers of Charity ran along the Miré River and shore of the bay, into which it empties, and Lagrange, a sergeant, and Boucher, the Engineer, owned the lands behind the Lorambecs, and caused much dissatisfaction to the fisherfolk by refusing permission to cut the wood necessary for their flakes. The description of these farms would indicate that this outflow of enterprise and population would come from a more thriving town than the official letters described. Scarcity of food is a serious thing, but satisfaction, with her offspring comfort and energy, treads close on the heels of supply. It was only after St. Ovide's time that the accounts indicate stagnation from want.

The officers were approximately of the same social grade, and that noble. They were of different origins : some, as Bourville, were Normans ; the Du

[1] This identification is not certain. Gibson's distances seem all inaccurate, but Milly was the only known proprietor likely to have so important an establishment, unless St. Ovide had built after his absence, which is not likely. The direction by which the scout marched, west-north-west, prevents these being those of the Pères de la Charité and Catalogne. There is some evidence that Du Vivier had in 1745 a farm on the Miré.

Chambon and Dangeac families, as well as St. Ovide, were from the south-west provinces of France ; the Perelles were Parisian, and the Canadian connection was kept up by D'Ailleboust, after the younger Rouville, born in Isle Royale, had returned to Canada ; while the families of De Gannes and De la Tour were Acadian.   Catalogne, a Protestant of Béarn, who had been admitted to the Catholic Church, had come to Isle Royale after a distinguished service as Engineer in Canada, apparently possessed of some means, for he not only bought property in the town, but an extensive tract of land along the slopes of that lake which was then known as the Barachois de Miré and is now called by his name.

Among this little group of people marriages were frequent. It might almost be said that they were all connected. Villejouin, for example, came to Isle Royale in 1714, dying there four years later. After a widowhood of ten years, his wife married D'Ailleboust, connected with the Perelles ; their son married a De Gannes-Falaise, whose mother was a De la Vallière ; while another sister married Couagne, an officer. La Vallière intermarried with the Rousseau Souvigni, and a daughter of the latter family became the wife of Chassin de Thierry, the grandson of an Ecuyer de la Bouche de sa Majesté (Louis XIV.). The daughters of the De la Tour family married, as might be expected ; Jeanne was the wife of Rousseau Souvigni, but the brother, judging from the names of his two wives, married among the bourgeois, and so on through the list. The older Catalogne came to Louisbourg as a married man, and one of his four daughters married before she was of age a De Gannes-Falaise. While these were socially correct marriages, others went outside of their own class. The young Baron de l'Espérance, an officer of the Swiss companies, married a Demoiselle Rodrigue. Young Bois Berthelot married a Des Goutins. Two of the descendants of the Baron de la Poterie married Daccarettes of the superior bourgeoisie. A D'lle la Vallière, apparently after a hasty courtship, for the vessel was not long in port, married Fierrot, a lieutenant of a ship of the East India Company which in 1744 called at Louisbourg. Another sister, Barbe, married Delort, a merchant of the town, an alliance more unusual than the military men marrying the daughters of merchants. The Dangeac family apparently married into the bourgeoisie in the second generation. The first to serve in the colonies was the older Gabriel, who began his career in 1685. He was transferred to Cape Breton, where he died in 1737. His son served in Isle Royale, became Governor of St. Pierre, and died in 1782 after fifty-seven years in the King's service. He made at Louisbourg in 1735 a misalliance which enhanced the vigour of his race, for there are letters extant from his two daughters, one aged ninety-four, and another, Charlotte, aged eighty-nine, written in 1830. As these old ladies, when Queen Victoria was in her teens, could have boasted that their grandfather was alive when Charles the Second reigned in England, it illustrates the extraordinary space of time which can be covered by three generations.

As somewhat unwelcome members of this community came, in 1721–22, two detachments of the Swiss Regiment of Karrer, raised by the King to supplement the naval troops. The officers and men were Protestants, but, notwithstanding the friction at first, they adjusted themselves. Some of the non-commissioned officers married; and the elder De l'Espérance, a Baron of the Holy Roman Empire and son of the Lieut.-Colonel of the regiment of the Duke of Wurtemburg, was admitted to the Catholic Church and married Margueritte Dangeac, a step which he represents as costing him his patrimony.

Complaints were made that the Swiss troops held tenaciously to their privileges as Protestants, but the example of De l'Espérance was followed by not an inconsiderable number of his men, mostly among those who were married and were householders. Other cases occur. A native of " Hampcher," an English Calvinist, a Dutch Lutheran, and one "Gyleis," an Irish Anglican, made their peace with the dominant Church, while here and there occur entries in the register which indicate that the French wandered into New England colonies. Couples remarried after living in Massachusetts, children born in New England were baptized, all this showing the benign influences of mutually profitable trade, and a zeal on the part of the Recollets or their parishioners, which, like the care of the negro and the unfortunate, give fairer impressions of the community than we get from some reports of scandalous conduct.

The high-sounding names of these officers did not imply any great splendour in their way of life. All of these families, by the census of 1734, except that of the Dangeacs, had two servants. In food they had good material to work with. Fish and game were abundant.[1] Voltaire somewhere draws a comparison between the splendid equipages of Lima and their absence in Louisbourg; a more significant indication of the modesty in life in Isle Royale is that although every year one or more men-of-war visited it, remaining usually several weeks in port, none of their officers married into its families, while many daughters of planters in Martinique and St. Domingo became the wives of naval men.[2]

Costebelle was in financial difficulties, but in his time he occupied the first position in the colony. The returns of his goods sold at auction in 1720 for the benefit of his creditors give some details. The first article offered was a yellow satin dressing-gown lined with blue taffeta. It was followed by a scarlet coat embroidered in gold, a suit of coffee-coloured cloth lined with silk and

[1] The latter was cared for, for twice at least the shooting of partridges was prohibited. Forest fires, however, which also made fuel dear, were their greatest enemy.

[2] Among them, two M'Carthys, obviously Irish, and presumably Jacobites, who were in the French Navy, became rich by such alliances.

embroidered in silver, which, bringing ninety livres, made it less valuable than another cloth suit, bordered with gold, which brought one hundred and seventy livres. Twenty-one shirts were sold and nine cravats. In silver there were apparently only ten table spoons and forks, and two silver candlesticks, his table service being made up by three dozen pewter plates and fourteen dishes, while there were only eight table-cloths and three dozen napkins, which would indicate either a meagre supply for the position he occupied, or that not all of his household goods were then disposed of. The proceeds of this sale were distinctly less than those of a ship's captain who died in port and whose personal effects, in which were twenty-four gold buttons, brought 1600 francs.

But there were brighter sides to life in Louisbourg than these details of circumscribed conditions and narrow incomes. It was permanent, for there were very few changes in the garrison or civil officials. There were the pleasures of the chase for those who cared for them.[1] Gaming was common and excessive in the later years of the town, and with its prevalence in France it probably at all times passed away many hours for society.[2] The town appealed to a New England chaplain, who writes of the fine walk along the ramparts.[3]

They had public celebrations which kept them in touch with events in Europe, and made it evident that Isle Royale was a part of a great kingdom. A Te Deum was sung for the restoration to health of the King in 1721, and another for the birth of a Princess in 1728, but the greatest entertainment was at the time of the rejoicing for the birth of the Dauphin.[4] On the 26th of October 1730, at daybreak, there was a salvo of artillery, another during the Te Deum at High Mass, and a third with a discharge of musketry at nightfall. Bourville, the acting Governor, gave a dinner to eighty military officers, followed by a ball. De Mezy, at his house, had a dinner of twenty-eight for the civil officers and the principal merchants, and the following days gave two dinners of sixteen for the captains in port, and of twenty to the staff, his house being too small to entertain, at one time, all whom he wished. The festivities closed by the officers of the garrison giving a feast for eighty, followed, like that of De Bourville, by a ball. No such rejoicings seem to have taken place in Louisbourg since Meschin's dinner in 1716, whereat the tally of salutes was lost in the mists of his exuberant hospitality.

Cape Breton has weather as dreary and disappointing as well can be conceived. There are weeks in autumn when a dull earth meets a leaden sea, in winter when the ground is white, the sea sombre. In spring the sea

---

[1] Le Normant's bag one morning at Baleine was forty birds.

[2] Verrier's picture of the town designates by the local standard a rather imposing house on the Rue du Port as "le billard." We have no indication as to whether this was a club or a public place for the game.

[3] William's Journal.   [4] Vol. 11, f. 21.

is white and glistering with drift ice, the land dreary with dead vegetation. In early summer sea and land are dank with fog, and at any time occur gales of wind which are always blustering and often destructive. Although by the accounting of the meteorologist the difficult or unpleasant conditions predominate, the good weather so far surpasses in degree the bad, that, the latter past, it seems but naught. On fine days the moorland is a sheet of glowing russet and gold, the rocks are so noble a background, for the most pellucid of seas, the clouds which hang in the overarching blue are so monumental in shape, the line of coast which dies down to the eastern horizon is so picturesque in outline, that they, seen through an air sparkling, limpid, exhilarating in the highest degree, make of Louisbourg a delight which must have appealed to its people in the past, as it does to the visitor of to-day. Above all, when the inhabitant reached the turning-point of his promenade at the ramparts, he looked out over an ocean which stretched unbroken to southern polar ice. That ocean was the only highway of important news. On it mysterious sails appeared in the offing and pirates plundered. Each ship which worked in from its horizon might bring tidings of adventure or of consequence to the onlooker or the community. With such a prospect life might be hopeless but it could not be permanently dull.

CHAPTER VII

MAUREPAS had contemplated improving the administration of Isle Royale before matters had come to a head with St. Ovide. On his dismissal, the Minister acted in the best interest of the colony, for from the applications for the position of Governor he selected Isaac Forant,[1] a captain of the ship of the line. He offered the place to him privately, so that in the event of his declining, the choice of a successor would not be more difficult. Forant did not consider the position worthy of his rank, as Isle Royale was only a dependency of New France, and the Governor-Generalships of New France, St. Domingo, Martinique, and Louisiana were held by naval officers of his own standing. After the intimation to him that it was the King's wish that he should go, he made no further difficulties, and set sail on the *Jason* for Louisbourg, where he arrived early in September 1739.[2]

For the first time the colony was placed under a new administration, for on the same ship was the new Commissaire-Ordonnateur, belonging to a family distinguished in the magistracy, but untried in colonial administration.[3] He had been principal clerk at Rochefort, and began, as the associate of Forant, a colonial career which for ever links his name, François Bigot, with the darker passages of the latest years of French rule in Canada.

The ample instructions to Forant and Bigot indicate that the Minister was familiar with the condition of affairs at Isle Royale, but do not disclose whether the self-reliance which these officials displayed was the result of instruction or of personal qualities. The contrast between their administration and that of St. Ovide shows clearly how far a system may be modified by the character of the men it employs. St. Ovide and both the Le Normants constantly quarrelled.

---

[1] Isaac Louis Forant was the son of Job de Forant, Premier Chef d'Escadre des Armées Navales. He passed through the ordinary course of naval instruction and promotion, in the course of which he visited Louisbourg and other ports in American waters beginning in 1724. In this year he made charts of the Grand Banks, A. N. Marine, C⁷, 108, and B⁴, 48. The *Habitant* says that the family was of Danish origin and left their country on account of their religion.

[2] His commission was dated April 1, 1739.

[3] His father was a councillor of the Parliament of Bordeaux, akin to Puysieulx, Minister of Foreign Affairs, so that the son entered the King's service in 1723 under favourable auspices.

They lacked initiative, and found, when they did make decisions, that these were frequently overruled. The merchants, fishers, and officers of the Admiralty complained of their acts. Their official reports to the Minister seem, at times, to have been intentionally inaccurate. The new officials took up their duties in harmony, with vigour and self-confidence, and seem to have had no hesitation in laying before the Minister the exact condition of affairs under their charge.

Immediately after his installation Forant, calling together the troops at Louisbourg, which consisted, including the garrison of the outports and Isle St. Jean, of eight companies of sixty men and one hundred Swiss, told them that any complaints that any of them might make would be carefully considered and justly dealt with. His report on them was far from satisfactory.

"With the utmost sincerity I may say that I have never seen such bad troops. We would not keep one hundred soldiers, if we discharged all those who are below the regulation height. But without regard to stature and physique I believe that it is better to discharge invalids, who are pillars of the hospital and occasion much expense, and are of no use whatsoever, as well as rascals who not only are incorrigible, but are even capable of leading others into vicious ways. . . . It is better to have fewer men than to have them of this character."[1]

He deals severely with the conditions in which the troops live. In the stately barracks their quarters were wretched. They slept two in a bunk, and Forant immediately requested for them a supply of mattresses and bedding, for the hay on which they slept was changed but once a year, and, therefore, was so infested with vermin that many preferred to sleep during summer on the ramparts. Notwithstanding such conditions and the relations of the men with their officers, so low a standard had the soldiers, that, in response to his invitation, no complaints were made.

He then called together the officers of the garrison in his apartment, and laid before them the complaints of their conduct which had reached the Minister. These were, that not all the troops were carried on the rolls ; that verbal leave of absence was given to the soldiers, so that it was said privates had been twelve or fifteen years in the colony and had never mounted guard ; that new recruits had to buy unnecessary clothing, which the officers supplied from the uniforms of the soldiers who had died in the hospital ; that their canteens encouraged the soldiers to drink ; and that the officers obtained provisions in excessive quantities from the King's store. The officers seemed much affected by these charges, and assured him that they were not so bad as they had been represented. They instituted on the spot certain reforms, and he closed the interview by saying that the best way to discredit the bad impressions of the past was to see that in the future no grounds for complaint should occur.

[1] I.R. vol. 26.

Forant on his previous cruises had visited Louisbourg and was familiar with its requirements. Knowing its dependence for defence on artillery, he had provided in France a wooden cannon to serve as a model. He brought it with him on the *Jason*, mounted it in the barracks, and thereafter gun drill took place every Sunday. This he did as preliminary to the establishment of an artillery company, the necessity of which he urged on the Minister as the troops were unskilled in serving artillery.

The unsettled state of affairs in Europe directed the attention of Forant and Bigot to the military condition of Louisbourg. They wrote that in a time of peace it was suffering from the scarcity of provisions,[1] and in time of war a privateer or two in the Gulf and the Strait of Canso could reduce them by famine, unless there were more ample stores. It was necessary to send out more guns with their equipment, and to remount those already on the ramparts, as their carriages had decayed. They pointed out that it would be inadvisable to attempt the preservation of guns by dismounting them for the winter, as, if they were attacked, it would be very early in the year before they could get them remounted. Forant wrote to urge the Minister to begin the war by attacking Acadia. With two frigates, two hundred regular troops, two thousand muskets for the Acadians, whom the English would probably disarm, the expedition under his command, he would answer for the result. Acadia joined to Isle Royale would make a flourishing colony,[2] and desiring secrecy he wrote in his own hand a letter,[3] displaying his eagerness for attack : " I have the honour to say only, that in the situation in which we find ourselves we require fewer forts and less outlay to attack than to defend ourselves." [4] The principle was sound ; when war came it was, however, the enemies of Isle Royale who acted on it.

The garrison needed strengthening. He pointed out, as St. Ovide had often done, that it was inadequate to do more than ordinary duty, but he could get on with the increase of two or three companies and the artillery company. He begged the Minister not to be deterred by the expense of more barrack accommodation, for he could provide for eight more companies by giving up his own house, and utilizing for himself that of Verrier, who was to go to France the following year.

Bigot was not less active, on his side, in carrying out the Minister's instructions. He introduced a system of supervision of the King's stores which was, in his view, called for in a country where officials owned boats, and in consequence had crews to feed, and were interested in other commercial ventures

---

[1] Vaudreuil, who commanded the *Jason*, had supplied several vessels with provisions which they could not obtain in the town.

[2] Nov. 14, vol. 21, f. 72.   [3] Nov. 16, f. 86.

[4] " J'ay l'honneur de vous dire seulement que dans la situation où nous nous trouvons il nous faut moins de fortes (?) et de depances pour ataquer que pour nous defandre."

which they had more at heart than the interest of the King. He established an office at the warehouse to supervise the distribution of stores, and made an attempt to introduce the contract system in the purchase of supplies. His first effort, asking tenders for molasses for three years, was unsuccessful, on account of the high price asked by the merchants, who feared war. During the course of the war with Spain the French merchants had enjoyed the benefit of Spanish markets for fish over those of England, but its ending would throw them open to competition with England. This caused Bigot to look to the West Indies for an extension of the trade in fish, and he suggested to the Minister the imposition of a duty on salt beef to promote in these islands the consumption of cod, if it would not hurt the commerce of France.

He promoted experiments for the manufacturing of fish-glue, which seemed to be successful. He was the first persistent friend of the Cape Breton coal trade, which seems to have languished, for he at once sent a sample to France, and, as it again proved good, he continued in later years his attempts to develop this important industry. He supported his case by pointing out that the coal mines of Cape Breton supplied New England, and that their produce would be two-thirds cheaper in France than the coal which the King was then buying.

While their letters of instructions had carefully defined their respective duties, Forant and Bigot seemed to have worked in entire harmony and acted together on matters which, strictly, were exclusively entrusted to one or the other of them. Bigot gave his opinion on military matters, and we find not only a desire to secure the best interests of the traders of the place on the part of Bigot, but that he associated Forant in his dealings with these matters. Le Normant had left an elaborate memoir dealing with the fisheries, which for some years had been unprofitable. He proposed in it various remedies. Bigot and Forant, before making any report on the matter, called together the principal traders of the place, and discussed the subject with them. They also called a general assembly of the inhabitants and arranged with them the rates to be established for wintering boats in the little harbour, which had been made in the Barachois de Lasson.

The business of the colony went on in a satisfactory way. Twelve vessels had been built in Isle Royale during the year, eight had been bought from New England, and Bigot urged on the Government to give the same shipbuilding bounty, 5 l. a ton, as was given in Quebec. The Minister was informed in relation to foreign trade that only one English vessel had come, which was sent by Armstrong, Governor of Nova Scotia, with a little flour, the proceeds of which had been exchanged for French goods. Permission had been readily granted for this trading, as Forant and Bigot were desirous of placating Armstrong on account of the missionaries of Acadia. The abundant crops of

Isle St. Jean, where there was now a considerable Acadian population, encouraged there the further clearing of land.

They secured, by employing these judicious methods, a willing acceptance of their proposed regulations before they were issued, and in the only case of conflict of jurisdiction, Forant asserted his supremacy over the officials of the Admiralty so tactfully that there was no friction about this matter, nor over the release by him and Bigot of a vessel from the western shore of Newfoundland, which the Admiralty officials had condemned on technical grounds.

There was no disagreement between them when it came to the consideration of a most important proposal made by Beauharnois and Hocquart to establish a warehouse at Louisbourg which, kept permanently supplied, would prevent the famines to which the colony had throughout its existence been exposed.[1] They said, with sound judgment, that if the storehouse were the King's every one would depend on it, while if it belonged to a company it would ruin commerce.

The following year, 1740, was opening with plans for further development when the career of Forant was cut short, in the inclement spring of Louisbourg, by an attack of pneumonia, to which he succumbed on May 10, after an illness of thirteen days. He was buried, at Bigot's instance, and in spite of the criticism of some of the military, in the chapel of the citadel, Bigot considering that his position as Governor entitled him to this unusual honour. His eulogy of his late associate was handsome. Forant knew character, he recalled to better courses his subordinates who had fallen away, was upright, and inspired by a sense of justice which was all-important in an establishment full of cabals. Bigot begged that a successor like him should be sent out. Forant testified in his will to his high opinion of Bigot, for the latter was made his executor; and in the disposition of his property showed his interest in the colony where he had ruled so short a time by bequeathing a fund for the education of eight daughters of officers in the Convent of the Sisters of the Congregation. After a short interval this bequest was made effective.

The few months in which they administered the colony were too short to show many results, but the harmony with which they worked, the intelligence with which they grasped the situation, their interest in trade, their conciliatory attitude to the people, make it reasonable to believe that had Forant been appointed at the time St. Ovide became Governor, and ruled as long, the condition of Louisbourg would have been very different.

Bourville again took charge. At different intervals he had served six years in all as acting Governor. He now unsuccessfully applied for the position. While he discharged its duties he continued to make plans for defence, and representations of the needs of the place in the same strain as his predecessors.

[1] Vol. 21, p. 23.

He arranged to put, in event of attack, the fishermen and sailors at the outlying batteries, and reserve his troops, unfamiliar with artillery, for the defence of the walls. The successor to Forant chosen by Maurepas was Du Quesnel,[1] who hurriedly left France for his new post, where he arrived on November 2, 1740, and at once assumed the duties of the position.

When Du Quesnel was installed the defence of the town at once occupied his attention. He stumped forth to inspect the work, for he was one-legged, a cannon-ball having carried away one leg and shattered the other when he was on the Admiral's ship in the action off Malaga in 1704. He found the works of the town in good condition, agreed with the view expressed in one of Forant's latest letters (February 8), that the royal battery was unsatisfactory on account of the lowness of the embrasures on the landward side, important in a place where a surprise was more to be feared than a regular attack. He repeated the complaints of St. Ovide, Forant, and Bourville, that the garrison was inadequate.[2] He asked for fifty more Swiss, as some of the troops knew not their right hand from their left. Their supply of arms was short, and Bigot joined him in asking for fifteen hundred more muskets, that the inhabitants might be armed.[3]

Du Quesnel and Bigot represented that the supply of powder should be kept up to its present quantity, so that the five tons they had recently received would be available for privateers should war break out. They asked for six twelve-pound guns of the new model, which had commended itself to Du Quesnel.

---

[1] Jean Baptiste Louis Le Prévost, Seigneur du Quesnel, de Changy Pourteville et d'autres lieux. I have found little about his professional advancement. He was made captain, October 1731, and had evidently been in the West Indies, for his wife was Mademoiselle Giraud de Poyet, daughter of the Lieutenant de Roi at Martinique. The *Habitant* says, " Poor man, we owe him little ; he was whimsical, changeable, given to drink, and when in his cups knowing no restraint or decency. He had affronted nearly all the officers of Louisbourg and destroyed their authority with the soldiers. It was because his affairs were in disorder and he was ruined that he had been given the government of Cape Breton." There is no evidence in other sources to confirm this view.

[2] An analysis of the guards made in 1741, after the troops had been increased by 80, shows how they were disposed :

Guards and Reliefs—	
Citadel, King's Bastion	94
Queen's Bastion	94
Port Dauphin Gate	76
Maurepas Gate	76
Store-house, Treasury	...
Hospital Battery	103
Artillerymen	16
In Hospital	20
Royal Battery	70
Island Battery	10
At Port Dauphin	25
At Port Toulouse	26
Isle St. Jean	41

A total of 651, while the whole force was 710. With the Island Battery ungarrisoned, it certainly left no effective combatant force. Bourville wrote in August 1740 that 556 men could not fill the posts (vol. 23, p. 71).

[3] They had in store only five hundred at this time.

These cannon were intended for the defence of the town ; but in addition they asked for a supply of guns and shot, for the same purpose as the extra supply of powder, the use of privateers.[1]

The condition of affairs continued so threatening that he asked the officers who had received permission to go to France (Verrier, Cailly, Commander of the Swiss, De Pensens, and Sabatier) to remain at their posts, to which they all cheerfully consented. He also took up a scheme of attack after consultation with Du Vivier, Du Chambon, the senior officer being at Isle St. Jean.[2] They discussed Forant's plan of attack on Annapolis. They emphasized the necessity of sending the two men-of-war for which he asked at the same time as the Basque fishermen who left France in February. They called the Minister's attention to the fact that, as the English would probably not remain passive, and Louisbourg would be their objective if they took the field, that the defences of that place should not be weakened. Du Vivier presented an alternative scheme to that of Du Quesnel. It was to select two hundred men of the Louisbourg troops, who were to proceed late in the autumn to Acadia, and lie hidden in the forests until snow made travelling possible. Then, reinforced by the Indians and Acadians, the latter being induced to join the expedition by the payment of lavish prices for their provisions and supplies, these forces should rush the feeble defences of Annapolis over its snow-filled ditch, and overpower its small garrison.[3] They would require for the expedition two hundred troops, eight hundred muskets, two hundred haversacks, and 40,000 l. in cash. These, if the plan was approved, the Minister was asked to send.

While these military matters, being of the most vital concern, were engrossing the attention of the authorities, the ordinary commercial business of the colony was being carried on. The energy of the administration in the colony seemed to have been reflected in the bureau of the Minister, for the reports from Isle Royale now received a more careful examination than they had in the past. Bigot's attention was called to the fact that although the catch of fish in 1739 was valued at 3,061,465 l., and in 1740 at 2,629,980 l., seventeen more vessels had come from France in the latter year. These either had returned not fully laden or had bought English cod. Bigot dealt with the matter with his accustomed openness.[4] He admitted that smuggling went on.

---

[1] They asked ior 6 of six pounds with 900 shot, 24 of four pounds with 4500 shot, and copper ladles for hot shot (I.R. vol. 22, p. 215). As the letter of the *Habitant* is the most generally known contemporary account of these years it may be pointed out that in reference to sending out privateers, as well as in other matters, the actions of the local officials, of which the writer complained, were known to and encouraged by the Minister.

[2] Letter, December 1, 1740.   [3] Five companies each of 31 men.

[4] He further points out that the captain's personal ventures are not included in returns, nor those of the exports of Ingonish, the most important place after Louisbourg. I have found no evidence that the practice was different this year than at previous times, and hazard the surmise that it was the ease with which the excuse passed scrutiny that opened to him the possibilities of enriching himself by improper means.

The new England vessels brought mostly tar, pitch, and planks, and in return bought rum and molasses, for which there would be an inadequate outlet if it were not for this trade. He informed the Minister that Sieur Lagarande, the richest and most charitable merchant of Ingonish, was concerned in this contraband trade, but that the principal place where it took place was at Petit de Grat. This could easily have been prevented by efficiency on the part of the officer at Port Toulouse, Du Bois Berthelot. A boat to watch this commerce which was carried on with Canso should be kept, but that unless manned and officered from a man-of-war, it would be useless. Somewhat later he pointed out that French and English vessels were accustomed to meet at Martengo,[1] a port to the westward of Canso, where they exchanged cargoes without molestation from either French or English officials. The new vigour in the home administration, or confidence in Bigot's representations, is shown by the removal, when these reports were received, of Du Bois Berthelot from Port Toulouse, and by the authorization given to Bigot to arrange with D'Aubigny, captain of the man-of-war on the station in 1741, for the proposed coast-guard, for which a barge of thirteen oars was sent out. This searching statement of the actual state of affairs, the proposal of remedies, and the immediate acceptance of the suggestions by Maurepas, are without counterpart in the previous history of Isle Royale.

The first dispatch received in July by the Louisbourg authorities intimated to them that the political situation was unchanged, that only through necessity would the King be drawn into war, but if France should become involved, the two men-of-war which the King proposed to send to American waters would be dispatched to Louisbourg to protect the fisheries, and carry out plans Maurepas had previously sent them. He referred them also to his instructions to Forant, and with a confidence for which his own acts had given little ground, expressed the view that while the English might make an attempt on Louisbourg, the reports he had received led him to the opinion that it would be without success. Instead of establishing two more companies he increased the eight already at Louisbourg by ten men each, sent fifty more Swiss, and enough recruits to bring all the companies up to their full strength of seventy men. Fifteen thousand pounds of powder, eight hundred muskets, and some cannon-ball were shipped out with them. Du Quesnel accepted these supplies, only as an instalment of what was necessary. They had, he reported, in their armoury, not a pike, pistol, or sword, and needed mortars as much as small arms. They were, however, doing all they could. Satisfactory progress was being made on the fortifications.[2] They had increased the number of workers by bringing in

---

[1] I.R. vol. 23, p. 17.
[2] The transfer of this work from Ganet to Muiron, the new contractor, was made without loss of time.

the soldiers from the outposts, while abolition of Monday as a holiday, and their efforts to prevent the soldiers getting drunk on rainy days, made the work more effective.   The population was divided into militia companies of fifty men each, and Verrier projected a small bastion on the landward side of the Royal Battery [1] to overcome the weakness of that fortification.   The only disquieting reports received, except those from headquarters, were rumours which reached them from the West Indies of depredations on French commerce by English privateers, and the appearance off the port of a suspicious vessel.   They sent out Morpain, the port captain, in search of her.   He cruised along the coast and entered the smaller harbours without any result.

The Swiss had always given some trouble in their dealings with the Governor, as they were tenacious of the privileges granted to their regiment the Karrer, possibly because the Louisbourg detachment included its leading company, "la compagnie Colonelle"; but this year Cailly, their captain, made the most serious disturbance by refusing, on a question of precedence, to assemble his men when ordered by Du Quesnel.   His refusal was formal and in writing, so that Cailly was dismissed; but his wife having made intercession for him with Du Quesnel, the latter brought his influence to bear on the Minister, which led to Cailly's reinstatement.[2]

The necessity of pushing on the works, and of safe-guarding the morals, not only of the troops, but of the people of the town, led the authorities to make, after a long interval, efforts to limit the sale of drink.   St. Ovide had never found the settled season which Costebelle thought was necessary before it could be effectively dealt with.   Du Quesnel and the captains agreed that the canteens which they had kept, and were a considerable source of profit to the company commanders,[3] should be suppressed.   He noted that Du Vivier had never kept one, having taken the course of giving his men a little money when they wished to divert themselves, an indication of his being well off; the result possibly of those commercial ventures of which the merchants of Louisbourg had complained.   They dealt with the public sale of drink by regulations which prohibited traffic in it to any who were capable of earning a livelihood in some productive employment.   Those who engaged in it must have a licence and display a sign; they were forbidden to sell to soldiers on duty or working, to sailors and hired fishermen who were supplied by their masters, or to any one during the hours of divine service, and after the retreat had been beaten; the penalty for an infraction of any of these rules being the confiscation of their supply and a fine of 100 l.   Further efforts to improve the morals of the place

---

[1] This was not built.   [2] Vol. 23, 60, 72.

[3] Du Quesnel says that they must shut their eyes to the profit which the officers make from supplying their men, as the pay of a captain, 1420 l. is too little.   He also speaks well of Du Chambon, who succeeded him, as he never engaged in trade, he was poor.

were made by the Minister sending from the West Indies a negro to apply the rack to criminals.[1]

The influence for good exerted by Forant was losing its effect. Du Quesnel said that things were slipping back into bad ways, that his efforts to right them had made him unpopular, but that he carried with him the best of the officers and citizens. He praised Bigot, who, he added, had no other object than the good of his service. The Minister showed his confidence in them in the most satisfactory way. Du Quesnel received an indemnity of 5000 l. for the expenses of his removal to Isle Royale, and Bigot, making his request with a statement that he had never expected to ask for anything but advancement, says he was compelled, by the expenses of living at Louisbourg, to solicit an increase in his salary. The Minister sent to him an additional 1200 l. with a commendation of his zeal. Somewhere in the man were the potentialities of the Bigot of Quebec. They do not appear in the frank, intelligent letters of one who was a favourite with his associates, who asked for a second Forant as Governor, from whom a Minister demanded no more than to continue as he had begun, who placed in him, as years went on, increasing confidence, and, unsolicited, gave him promotion.

In 1742 Bigot had to deal with those economic conditions which so often had injured the colony. In May they sent an express to warn Maurepas that Louisbourg was again on the verge of starvation. They had attempted to obtain flour at Canso, but without success, and they were further disquieted by the report that the exportation of provisions from New York and New England was forbidden. Nevertheless, in the emergency, they sent a vessel there with some hopes of obtaining a cargo for it, as an officer [2] of Canso was interested in the venture.

Du Quesnel and Bigot suggested that to avoid the recurrence of these periods of scarcity a store-house for flour from New England should be established at Louisbourg. This would have given no immediate relief even if permission were given to undertake its founding. The situation demanded prompter remedies. In June the soldiers were persuaded to submit to the limitation of their bread to a pound a day, which set free about three hundred-weight of flour to be distributed among the needy. The fishermen also cut down their consumption, which helped matters ; but the curtailment of food was uncomfortable, and the dearth of vegetables produced ill-health among the

---

[1] Vol. B, 72, f. 10.

[2] It seems a fair surmise that this was Bradstreet, then an officer of this garrison, who was related to several of the officers at Louisbourg. Bradstreet says that he was thoroughly familiar with Nova Scotia, so that this connection would have arisen probably through the De la Tour family. He was certainly interested in trade, for in 1741 he visited Louisbourg, carrying to Du Quesnel the congratulations of Cosby. He there sold his schooner, bought rum with its proceeds, and laid out two thousand crowns in the port (I.R. vol. 23, f. 57).

people. This distressing condition continued until August, when some relief was obtained by the arrival of small vessels from New England and Quebec, and in September the arrival of the store-ship from France brought abundance. But to fully justify Du Quesnel's description of Isle Royale as an unhappy colony, as the fishing had been a failure, the people were too poor to buy food at the high prices asked. Bigot, who had previously seen the agricultural resources of the Miré, and regretted that so fair an estate on its banks had been given to St. Ovide, saw this year, on a tour of inspection to the northern parts, the agricultural lands along the Bras d'Or lakes, which made him certain that the island might become self-sustaining. The Minister sent a prompt reply which denied approval to the recommendation of a store-house for New England flour, although he had previously been told that the merchants of Quebec did not fear the competition of New England. In this he followed the same policy as the Navy Board of the Regency which had disapproved in 1716 of Costebelle's suggestion of a permitted trade with New England. Costebelle had accepted the decision without protest. Bigot did not hesitate to warn Maurepas that, if his views were carried out, the colony would be injured. Crops in Canada would in the future fail, as they had in two successive years. If Isle Royale must depend on France alone, without drawing any part of its supplies from New England, the cost of living would be so permanently enhanced that it would carry on its business at a great disadvantage. He returned to the matter the following year, and showed that flour from New England delivered at Louisbourg cost less[1] than French flour delivered at Rochefort. In addition to this disadvantage, the shipment of flour with which he made comparison was so poor in quality that it could only be used by mixing it with that from the British colony.

Such periods of scarcity as this had been passed through not infrequently. Nothing, however, had arisen in the past to affect the fundamental advantages of Isle Royale in its great industry, but in these years complaints of the quality of the fish it sent to European markets were heard. As we learn from English sources[2] that the curing of fish at Canso was bad, these complaints of the poor quality of French shipments give basis for a confirmation of the reports that the merchants of Louisbourg bought Canso fish, as they were cheaper than their own catch.[3] In the midst of these discouragements, the promise of a new trade gave encouragement to its people. It had been thought that Louisbourg would prove an admirable port of call for French merchantmen on long voyages. This year the Baleine of Nantes, from Vera Cruz to Cadiz, called at Louisbourg for provisions and a convoy for the remainder of her voyage. Her cargo consisted of treasure and such

[1] 16 or 17 l., as against 17 l., 18 l., 18 l. 10 s. (vol. 25).   [2] C.O. 5/5; B.T.N.S. 5.   [3] Weeden, p. 595/6.

valuable commodities as cochineal and indigo. She was followed by other vessels of the same kind, but this course proved disadvantageous to the port and disastrous to most of the vessels.[1]

The possibilities of war seemed in Europe no nearer, although, in July, Du Quesnel was warned that they might change at any moment. Du Vivier's plan had been considered, and Du Quesnel was told to get all the information he could. In reply he informed the Court that an engineer had come to fortify Annapolis Royal in brick, and to erect fortifications at Canso, which should not be permitted. He asked for orders, either to openly stop the work, or to stir up the Indians against the English. A further cause of uneasiness was the action of an English man-of-war which had prevented the French from fishing off Canso, but Du Quesnel was not in a position to act firmly. The Minister had not responded to their demands for further troops and supplies. He would not consider their proposals for additions to the fortifications. Those already projected, he wrote, must be completely finished before any new work should be undertaken. The King was surprised that after so many years there was so much work in an incomplete state. Moreover, the state of the Royal treasury was such, that they could not send out the supplies and munitions for which the Governor had asked. Du Quesnel's answer was reasonable : they would do the best they could, although the supplies were essential. He accepted a suggestion of the Minister to minimize their demands for artillery, by moving the guns from one battery to another, which they would do if the field carriages were sent. His view was that the outlay already made on Louisbourg, as well as its importance, demanded that he should be put in a state to respond to the confidence placed in him.[2]

With the long break in its activities caused by the winter season it was easy for the hopeful to trust that when the season reopened things would be better, for they had closed in gloom. The colony was in the most miserable condition it had ever been. The purchases of supplies at exorbitant prices to avoid starvation made it impossible for the people to carry out the engagements into which they had entered. Bigot looked forward to a certain loss on the shipments of provisions which had been sent out to sell to the people in the two preceding years. The French merchants complained to the Minister that they could not continue shipments to Isle Royale unless they were paid for previous ventures. Moreover, they were also deterred by the fear of finding their market forestalled by arrivals from New England, and although official information had been given to all the shipping ports of

---

[1] The treasure ships which called in 1744 hampered the military operations and reduced the number of men in the town by shipping many in their crews. In 1745 the ships were captured.   [2] Vol. 24, Oct. 7, 9, 22, 24.

France in the previous autumn of the need of supplies at Louisbourg, this official intimation produced little effect. Bigot rose to the situation and was able to report that he had collected from the people 32,000 l.,[1] more than he had expended for supplies, and in the autumn the French ships which had come out had sold their cargoes well.[2]

The torpor of malnutrition affected the commerce of the country. The people would not take up the manufacture of glue, nor the shipment of "noûes de morues," for which a market had been found in France. Bigot's efforts to push forward the coal trade had not met with much success. The coal was too light for the heavy forging on which it had been again tested at Rochefort. Its export was further hampered by the prohibition to take it on men-of-war or the store-ships of the navy, on account of the danger of spontaneous combustion, although merchant vessels made no objections to carry it to the West Indies. Above all, the fishery was a failure. A fortuitous circumstance relieved the military aspect of the food supply. Alarmed by the appearance of caterpillars in Canada, its authorities wrote in July 1743 to those of Isle Royale that they must obtain for them from New England at least 4000 barrels of flour. They acted promptly, for Hocquart said that on them depended the salvation of Canada. Du Vivier was sent to Canso with a credit of 80,000 l. to buy this supply. He had completed the purchase before a second letter came from Quebec informing them that the pest had disappeared and the harvest promised well, so there was no longer a necessity for the supply. Sixteen or seventeen hundred barrels were delivered that autumn, and more would have been sent had the authorities of Boston and New York not been advised by the English court to be on their guard. They had in consequence prohibited further shipments to Louisbourg. The anonymous Canso agent of the French was at Louisbourg when this news was received. He said the authorities would not have interfered with further shipments had he been on the spot, as he would have cleared the vessels for Placentia, and further promised, should it be at all possible, to continue shipments the following year even if war broke out ; an incidental verification of the view that commerce was a more dominant factor in the eighteenth century than national animosity. Bigot proposed, and the Minister consented, to use this extra supply as a reserve which would give rations for the troops until October 1745. There were other foreshadowings of the strained relations with England than the forbidding of exportation to Louisbourg. The English man-of-war at Canso captured a vessel of Du Chambon on her voyage from

---

[1] On previous occasions of the same kind his predecessors had never succeeded in making more than trifling collections.
[2] The returns of commerce do not indicate as serious a falling-off in vessels as might be expected from the phrasing of these letters.

Isle St. Jean to Louisbourg, and Du Vivier returned to Canso, this time in his military capacity, and made such representations that the vessel was released. The slackness with which the colonial affairs of England and France were administered, is shown by the fact that Cosby and Du Vivier had copies of the Treaty of Utrecht which differed in the points of the compass determining the fishing boundaries, as had the documents to which Smart and St. Ovide referred in 1718. In a score or more of years this needless cause of mis-understanding had not been cleared up.

The year was unsatisfactory in a military way. Men were scarce in France ; the King's treasury was low and this affected the strengthening of Louisbourg, but the Minister promised to do the best he could the next year, when they might expect enough cannon for one flank of each battery. Signals were arranged for the men-of-war, which were to be dispatched as soon as the rupture took place. The companies were full, so only thirty recruits were sent out, which left unanswered Du Quesnel's insistent demand for reinforcement. Their efforts to push on the work had produced results, the walls were complete, the parapet and one gate on the quay were finished, as well as the supplementary batteries at the Prince's Bastion and the Batterie de la Grave. He pointed out again that the work at the Dauphin Gate was necessary as well as the razing of Cap Noir, which commanded all the southern fortifications. This, Du Quesnel said, had never been proposed by the engineers, as the recommendation of this course would have exposed their mistake in not in-cluding this eminence within the walls of the town.

As in all emergencies, the ordinary business of life went on much in its accustomed way, funds were allotted, ecclesiastical and civil matters dealt with, promotions were made, gratuities distributed. Six young ladies were enjoying the advantages of Forant's bequest ; and two *chats-cerviers* were sent from Louisbourg for the King's menagerie, to succeed in La Muette the one whose fondness for music had been the delight of the Royal children.[1]

The condition of Louisbourg was in the highest degree unsatisfactory. It was the key to Canada, it gave a base for fishery, but it was inadequately supplied with provisions and munitions of war ; its garrison was not only inadequate, but of poor quality ; its artillery required an increase of seventy-seven guns to make all its fortifications effective. For ten years the plan of attack, if an attack was to be made, had been laid by its Governors before the Minister, and these documents had not all been pigeon-holed. They were known to Maurepas himself, and there exists a memorandum which is marked "presented to the King" (*porté au roi*), dated June 20, 1743, which gives a *résumé* of the history of Louisbourg.[2] This places the responsibility of its

---

[1] De Goncourt, *Portraits intimes*, p. 8.   [2] I.R. vol. 26, p. 219.

condition on Louis XV. himself. So much of evil in his career has been attributed to the malign influence of Madame de Pompadour, that it may be noted that at this time when, more than in later years, he neglected his colony, she was Madame d'Étioles, and had never seen His Most Christian Majesty, except in the hunting field.

CHAPTER VIII

THE declaration of war with England was made on March 18, 1744, and expedited to Louisbourg by a merchant vessel of St. Malo, which arrived on May 3. It was accompanied and followed by letter after letter to encourage privateering. Blank commissions were sent out to Du Quesnel, as Maurepas was alive to the advantage of being first in the predatory field. His encouragement, however, stopped short of making a gift of the powder and shot which was sent out for the use of these vessels, for he sent instructions that they must pay for these supplies. A prompt shipment of food was promised, and permission was given to Bigot to send to New England for an additional supply. Orders were given for the two men-of-war to go to Louisbourg, and referring to the fortification of Canso, Maurepas said that the best way of settling the question was by the capture of that outpost of the English. The King, he added, wished that Du Quesnel should use the Indians to continually harry the English in all their settlements. These instructions, involving carrying the war into the colonies, and, if they were to be successful, demanding vigorous execution, found Louisbourg ill-prepared to do its part.

On May 9 there was food in Louisbourg for no longer than three weeks or a month, although the people were living largely on shellfish.[1] This condition, unusual in the spring, had arisen through the Basque fishermen not coming out. The authorities foresaw that if help did not speedily come they would have to send the inhabitants back to France, unless they should migrate in a body to some foreign country. The fisher folk of Baleine and the Lorambecs, under the pressure of famine and the fear of war, had come in, and were plotting with those at Louisbourg to force the government to supply them from the military stores. Du Quesnel took steps to prevent an uprising, and lessened its possibility by giving some provisions to prevent the people dying of hunger. Some vessels arrived, and reduced the distress, although again in September it was only the receipt of the stores from Quebec which prevented their abandoning the colony, and even then Du Chambon wrote that "to-day

---

[1] Du Quesnel to Maurepas, vol. 26.

it was more than ever to be feared that this accident would arrive." They were in no condition, said Du Quesnel in his letter of May 1,[1] to undertake an enterprise against Acadia. He was anxious to send out privateers, but he had only Morpain, who was already at sea, and Doloboratz, then engaged in the expedition to Canso, and therefore applied to the Governor-General of Canada for men. It seemed superfluous to say that as they had no pistols or cutlasses the men of Louisbourg were loath to go unarmed on such expeditions. He again pointed out to the Minister that their request for troops, artillery, arms, and provisions had not been granted, and the condition of the place, no less for defence than offence, was pitiable. Their difficulties were material. It required no more than the receipt of some further provisions and munitions of war to cause the Governor and officers to undertake the aggressive operations suggested to them by the Minister.

Canso was the first object of attack ; its condition was to the last degree indefensible. Its garrison consisted of about one hundred and twenty men, commanded by Captain Patrick Heron of Phillips' regiment. In the harbour was a sloop of war of unspecified strength, in command of which was Lieutenant George Ryall,[2] detached by Captain Young of the *Kinsale* for the protection of the fisheries and the prevention of trade with Isle Royale. Its defences were a blockhouse built of timber by the contributions of the fishermen and inhabitants, in so poor a condition that to its repair, and that of the huts in which the soldiers lived, their officers had frequently contributed from their private purses.[3] The military authorities of England were as slow as those of France. It was not until July 19, 1744,[4] that the Master of the Ordnance was directed to order that the Fort of Annapolis be put into a good posture of defence without loss of time, and that a fort of sod-work be erected at Canso with the assistance of some of H.M. ships of war, and that General Phillips' regiment be forthwith augmented to the highest establishment.

On the 23rd of October 1744, a warrant was passed to add 10 sergeants, 10 corporals, 10 drummers, and 392 privates to Lieut.-General Richard Phillips' regiment serving in Nova Scotia and Newfoundland ; establishment to take place from 25th August 1744.

Statement annexed of the cost of maintenance of "A Regiment of Foot commanded by Lieut.-Genl. Phillips."[5]

---

[1] To Vaudreuil. Du Quesnel's spirit is shown in a letter to Maurepas : "trois points de mon discour Monseigneur troupes vivres et munitions de guerre avec quoy vous devez estre persuadé que cette Place ne craindra rien et que je la deffenderay au delà de ce qu'on peut espérer" (May 11, vol. 26, pp. 55-56).

[2] Captain's letters.

[3] Such was its condition as reported by Mascarene, Governor of Nova Scotia, and confirmed by the letters of Captain Young of H.M.S. *Kinsale*.

[4] B.T. Jls. vol. 52, p. 137.

[5] Consisting of companies of 70 private men in each.

Field and Staff Officers	£2 7 10 per day, *i.e.*	
Colonel, 12s. 2d. in lieu of servants . . .	0 14 0	
Lt.-Col.	0 7 0	
Major, 5s.; Chaplain, 6s. 8d.; Adjnt., 4s. . . .	0 15 8	£2 7 10
Quarter-Master, 4s. 8d. in lieu of servant . . .	0 4 8	
Surgeon, 4s.; Mate, 2s. 6d.	0 6 6	

One Company, £3 : 18 : 6 per day, including—

Captain, 8s. 2d. in lieu of servants	£0 10 0	
Lieut., 4s. 8d. „ „	0 4 8	
Ensign, 3s. 8d. „ „	0 3 8	
3 Sergeants at	0 1 6 each	
3 Corporals at	0 1 0 „	
2 Drummers at	0 1 0 „	£3 18 6
10 Privates at	0 0 8 „	
Other expenses	0 4 0 „	

Eight other Companies do.   31   8   0

One Company of Grenadiers.

Pay and numbers the same as last, except they had two Lieuts. and no Ensign.

Expense P. diem   .   .   .   £3   19   6

Total for Regiment [1] .   .   .   £41   13   10

For the first time, in May of this year, the officers of Louisbourg set out on a warlike expedition.[2] The command was given to Du Vivier, one of the sons of the first officer who died in Louisbourg, where he and his brother were brought up by their mother in a modest house on the Place du Port with dependencies extending to the Rue Royale. In the peace of that place he had spent his entire life. The force was made up of 22 officers, 80 French and 37 Swiss soldiers, and 218 sailors, mostly the crew assembled for manning the man-of-war *Caribou*, built at Quebec. They embarked on the schooner *Succès*, Doloboratz' privateer, a vessel of Du Chambon, and fourteen fishing boats. They met no resistance when they appeared before Canso.[3] On May 24 a capitulation was signed by which the garrison and inhabitants surrendered. They were to remain prisoners of war for a year, their property was to be spared and carried to Louisbourg on the schooner of Bradstreet, and Du Vivier undertook to use his best efforts to have the ladies and children sent at once to Boston or Annapolis. The same terms were given to the crew of the guard sloop. News of this exploit was sent to Boston. Shirley asked to have Heron sent back, but the latter would not abandon his troops. Du Quesnel returned all those

[1] In all 815 men, officers included (War Office, 24/232).

[2] Boularderie says that, as none of the officers had any experience in war, he was asked by Du Quesnel to go on the expedition (*Derniers Jours*, p. 188).

[3] A. M. St. M. vol. 50. The *Habitant*, never trustworthy, says Du Vivier had 600 soldiers and sailors. The total force was 351.

captured at Canso, on condition that they would not bear arms against France for a year from September 1, the time of their release, and forwarded to Shirley an agreement duly signed.   Shirley at once repudiated this action, on the ground that Heron and his men acted under duress ; but Heron and the other officers intimated that they felt themselves bound by the agreement into which they had entered, and when there was need of their services the next year it apparently required official action to free their consciences.[1]   The vital part of the transaction was the cost of maintaining these troops, which Shirley did not care to assume, and of which, in the conditions of Louisbourg, Du Quesnel was anxious to be rid.   Shirley did not accept the views of Du Quesnel, but their correspondence was courteous, and was accompanied by an exchange of presents.   Du Quesnel sent with one of his letters a barrel of white wine.   Shirley's reply was supplemented by a cask of English beer and three turkeys.   The Governor of Massachusetts, notwithstanding these marks of good feeling, was firm in maintaining the position he took in regard to the prisoners.   He also refused Du Quesnel's proposition that in any warlike operations the fisheries of both nations should, as in the beginning of the century, be neutral and undisturbed, his ground for this being that the French had been the aggressors.[2]

It was not expected that Canso would make any resistance, but the conditions at Annapolis were not favourable to a brilliant defence.   Its fort was built of earth of a sandy nature, "apt to tumble down in heavy rains or in thaws after frosty weather."   It had been repaired from time to time with timber, and there was then assembled on the ground material for its permanent reconstruction. It was, however, laid out on such a scale that it would require five hundred men to defend it, and the garrison consisted of five companies, each, at its full complement, of thirty-one men.   The conditions of defence were therefore not different, except to the disadvantage of the English, from those of Louisbourg. Its small garrison, commanded by Mascarene, was, for example, so ill-supplied with arms that there were not enough muskets to arm the reinforcements it received.   Its troops were so ill-clothed that they were permitted to wear a blanket when on sentinel duty, and the provision of six or seven "watch coats" made of duffle, worn in turn, added much to the comfort of the garrison during the next winter.   Its people had been thrown into a panic on May 18 by the report that Morpain, port captain of Louisbourg—so renowned a privateer in the wars of thirty odd years before, that his name still struck terror into an English population—was to appear before the place at the head of a band of five hundred French and Indians.   The inhabitants of the lower town, among whom were the families of several officers and soldiers, began to remove their

[1] An order in Council was passed, 11th of April 1745, directing both officers and men to disregard the capitulation forced on them by Du Quesnel (B.T. Jls. vol. 53).   [2] C.O. 5/909.

goods into the fort. The report proved unfounded, but the arrival of the Massachusetts galley shortly after, bringing news of the declaration of war, gave an opportunity for some of the officers to send their families to New England. These were followed by as many as two other vessels could carry, but even after they had left, seventy women and children were quartered within the fort. Bastide, the engineer, had come on the Massachusetts galley, and under his direction temporary repairs were made to the fortifications, which work was carried on by the aid of the French inhabitants, until a band of Indians, on July 1, caused the withdrawal of the French. Mascarene had only a hundred men in the garrison fit for duty. The workmen from " Old and New England " on the whole behaved well, but the grumbling of some of the New England men, who took the ground that they had come to work, not to fight, " Caus'd a backwardness and dispiritedness amongst their fellows." The loss was small in the first attack by the Indians, who reached the foot of the glacis, but were dislodged by the cannon of the fort, which kept them from doing further harm than marauding, until the arrival of the first reinforcement of seventy men from Massachusetts caused them to retire. This reinforcement was followed by a second detachment of forty. Both of them, however, were sent without arms, and the supply on hand was not enough to furnish them with efficient weapons.

The capture of Canso being effected, the next point of French attack was naturally Annapolis. Du Vivier set forth early in August.[1] He had with him thirty soldiers and various munitions of war on the schooner *Succès* and another vessel. At Isle St. Jean he took on twenty more soldiers. His first duty was to quiet the Indians at Baie Verte, who were pillaging the Acadian inhabitants. His instructions from Du Quesnel for his later operations, were to confine the troops of England within Annapolis Royal, so that the assistance the French expected to receive from the Acadians should appear to the English as forced from them, and, still further to protect and encourage the inhabitants, to pay those who gave them any assistance. The hope of any Acadians joining Du Vivier was meagre, for only two hundred and fifty muskets were sent to arm them. Du Vivier was to approach Annapolis Royal, and if he found it possible to make a sudden attack, " À faire quelque coup sur Eux," he should do so, taking care, nevertheless, not to compromise the troops or the inhabitants of the country. If his report was favourable, and no contrary orders were received from France, Du Quesnel promised to send him some vessels to attempt the taking of the fort. If it could not be done without endangering themselves too much, and with a moral certainty of success, he was to withdraw, leaving one or two officers with the soldiers, and a hundred picked Indians, so as to prevent the English

---

[1] His expenses at Mines began on the 29th, which may be taken as the date of his arrival in the settlements of Nova Scotia.

disquieting the Acadians. He was to retire by September 15, unless he had then received word from Du Quesnel; and he was again cautioned to display the utmost prudence, to expose no one needlessly, and to protect the Acadians as far as possible. These instructions, which, it will be seen, were in effect simply to confine the English within the fort, that the Acadians might be unmolested, to make a reconnaissance and to report, were not such as to lead to a dashing or determined attack.

Du Vivier arrived before the fort with colours flying, and then retired to his encampment about a mile distant. His Indians made disquieting attacks, night after night, on the little garrison, the commander of which had no intention of troubling the Acadians, who were left to gather in their harvests, which Du Quesnel feared they would not be permitted to do. Du Vivier sent word to Du Quesnel that the attack should be made, and was informed in reply that the *Ardent* and *Caribou*, two ships of force, would be dispatched to his aid. Du Vivier thus completely carried out his orders. He prepared scaling-ladders and combustible materials in preparation for the event, and on his own initiative entered into negotiations with Mascarene.[1] He sent his brother, who was serving with him, on September 14, to Mascarene with a letter saying that he expected reinforcements by sea, and proposed that Annapolis should surrender, offering very favourable terms, which were not to be effective until his good faith had been proved by the arrival of the French ships. He thus evidently expected no more resistance than he had found at Canso. His views were so far justified that when Mascarene consulted his officers he found that the majority of them were in favour of accepting the French proposal.[2] Mascarene, feeling that his hand was being forced, made the heads of the various departments sign a statement of the condition of the works and of the garrison, and then permitted, through chosen officers, various negotiations to go on, and consented (purely as a preliminary) to an acceptance by these officers of Du Vivier's terms; but although "desired and pretty much press'd" to sign himself, he absolutely refused. The truce, which had been arranged for carrying on these negotiations, was then broken off. Mascarene found that the men of the garrison, whom their officers had represented as dispirited, were really uneasy over these negotiations with the enemy, and, to cut them short, had threatened to seize their officers "for parleying too long with the enemy." He "immediately sent the Fort Major to acquaint them with what was past, and that, all parley being broken off, hostilities were going to begin again, to which they expressed their assent by three cheerful Huzzas to my great satisfaction." Fifty more men of Gorham's Rangers arrived from Boston, and Mascarene threatened to

---

[1] Mascarene to Shirley, Dec. 1744, N.S. Archives, vol. 1, p. 140.
[2] "All the officers, except three or four, very ready to accept the proposal."

visit Du Vivier at his camp.   Before he did so, word was brought to him that the French had gone.   His first idea was that it was a feint, but he found to his astonishment that they had left the country, which, not unnaturally, he attributed to their fear of his making an attack.   Thereafter the British were only disquieted by the Indians, who were dispersed by the rangers of Massachusetts, incited thereto by scalp bounties which Shirley went beyond his powers as Governor of Massachusetts in guaranteeing them.[1]

Du Vivier had withdrawn, not fearing conflict, but on account of orders he had received from Louisbourg.   Capt. De Gannes, who felt that he had claims to lead the expedition superior to those of Du Vivier, had been appointed to take charge of the detachment which was to winter in Acadia.   He set out, after making some difficulties, and, as his conduct shows, with no intention to allow any credit to Du Vivier, but with the purpose of asserting to the utmost limit his authority over him.   He insisted on an immediate withdrawal, would not wait to destroy the storming materials which Du Vivier had prepared, nor to hear Mass, although the time of their leaving was a Sunday morning.

Both expeditions returned to Louisbourg, where De Gannes found himself "sent to Coventry" by his brother officers and the people of the town.   He demanded a meeting with the officers in the presence of the Governor.   De Gannes' excuse at this assembly was that he had no orders to carry on the siege ; that he had retired from Port Royale because they had no provisions, and from Mines because the inhabitants begged them to do so.   He presented certificates from his officers, that even when they went armed, to obtain bread from the inhabitants, they had scarcely any success ; as well as one from the inhabitants of Mines begging them to withdraw.   The officers remained silent with the exception of Du Vivier, who absolutely denied everything De Gannes had said.   They then examined Abbé Maillard and Du Vivier.   Maillard sustained Du Vivier's story and denied that of De Gannes.   He explained that the refusal of the inhabitants to give them bread began only when De Gannes announced that they were to retire ; that previously there was abundance in the French camp.   The Abbé added that when De Gannes arrived at Mines,

[1] "For which Reason I think it of such Consequence to his Majesty's Service that the Indians and other New England Auxiliaries enlisted in it at Annapolis Royal should have premiums for scalping and taking Captive the Indian Enemy as the People within this Province have, and, as I am inform'd, as promised to the French Indians by Mr. Du Vivier, that I am determin'd the present Demands of Captain Gorham and his Indians for three Scalps and one Captive already brought in shall be satisfy'd in some Method or other upon the hopes of a Reimbursement from his Majesty, and shall endeavour to procure for 'em the same premiums for the future from the Assembly upon the prospect of their being reimburs'd in the same Way, since I find I can't prevail upon 'em to extend their own Bounty to those enlisted in his Majesty's Service within his Government of Nova Scotia, which they seem to have an unalterable persuasion ought to be given at his Majesty's Expence" (Shirley to Newcastle, Nov. 9, 1744, C.O. 5/900).

I have found no reference in the French documents to any bounty offered by Du Vivier.   It does not seem probable that if a bounty had been offered this proof of zeal on the part of the authorities would have passed unnoticed in letters to the Minister.

the latter held a council with himself and the other priests, Miniac, Lagoudalie, Leloutre ; that he represented to them the pitiful situation of the Acadians, whom it would better serve to join with the English than to enter again into allegiance with France, as Louisbourg was incapable of helping them. De Gannes had gone on to make the same statement to the principal inhabitants, with whom in the presence of the priests he arranged for presenting to him the request to withdraw his force, on which De Gannes relied as a justification,[1] and notwithstanding a letter from Du Chambon blaming him for being so precipitate, he persisted in his withdrawal. So when, in default of the ships of the line, which for a variety of causes had not been sent, on the night of October 25 the frigate *Le Castor* and two vessels with French troops arrived before Annapolis, they found all quiet. Bonnaventure went ashore. He, to find out the situation, aroused an inhabitant and brought him and a companion on board the frigate, and from him heard the astonishing story that De Gannes had remained only two days at the camp. The Acadians said that the fort, which contained only provisions for eight days, was ready to surrender, and that the women and children were prepared to fly to the head of the river, at the time the situation was relieved by the departure of the French. After a stay of three days the expedition returned to Louisbourg, taking with them their captures, two small vessels with supplies from Boston. The deputies of the Acadians promptly made their peace with Mascarene.

It is difficult to account for the conduct of De Gannes. His views were justified by events, but unsuitable to be proclaimed by a French officer. Under any administration less lax than that of the French Navy at that time, his conduct would have met with the severest punishment. Du Chambon, who had succeeded Du Quesnel after the latter's sudden death on October 9, instead of deposing De Gannes, simply reported to the Minister. Bigot, ready enough generally to express his opinion, brought no influence to bear on Maurepas, and De Gannes continued to serve, and eventually passed to higher positions.

The only ones to suffer were the priests. Year after year the priests of Acadia had been cautioned to confine themselves to their sacerdotal functions and respect the British power. But the three priests who fell in with De Gannes' views were deprived of their allowance from the French Government. Desenclaves was not present, but a captured letter forwarded by Warren expresses his views on the expedition :

"Surtout après trop de Légèreté que avoit fair paroître du Tems de Monsr. Du Vivier. Il est étonnant que l'on se soit mis dans L'Idée, qu'avec une petite Poignée du Monde qui n'avoit aucune Idée de la Guerre on Voulut essayer de réduire un Province aux Portes

[1] Oct. 10, 1744, N.S. Archives, vol. 1, p. 135, printed on p. 125.

de Boston " . . . and, thus, on the way they were treated as priests, "Le Point le plus Important est celui de la Religion mais nous sommes entièrement libre là-dessus, n'ayant eut d'autre Empêchement dans nos Exercises, que celui qui est devenu de la Part de François ; Je pense Monsr. que ces Egards que l'on a là-dessus ne laissent pas d'atterer les Bénédictions de Ciel sur les Puissances qui nous commandent." [1]

Returning now to the events which had taken place at Louisbourg, we find that the proceedings of the French men-of-war were as ineffective as those of the land forces. Meschin was in command of the *Ardent*, a vessel of sixty-four guns, which, although her departure had been planned for April, did not leave Rochelle until June 18, and then convoyed twenty-six vessels for the West Indies and Canada. After leaving them, he lost his bowsprit in a gale, shortly before arriving at Louisbourg on August 16. He found that the *Caribou*, a vessel built at Quebec, had been rigged and manned and was privateering under the command of Morpain. He promised to be ready to sail for Annapolis by the 5th or 6th of September after his repairs were made and his crew refreshed ; but when the time came, his version is that Du Quesnel said that it was undesirable to go, as the English had been reinforced, and that it was important to guard their own coast from privateers. On the 9th they went cruising, captured a privateer of twelve cannons, twenty-one swivels, and ninety men, attempted to find three other Boston privateers at Newfoundland, and returned unsuccessful on October 11.

Bigot and Du Chambon proposed to him to attempt Annapolis, to which he willingly agreed. The news of this venture having spread abroad, the captains of eight vessels of the Compagnie des Indies made formal representations to him, and, as well, to Du Chambon and Bigot, in which they said that they had orders to come to Louisbourg to be convoyed thence to France by the King's ships. Meschin proposed that they should accompany him to Acadia, as he might not be able to regain Louisbourg on his way to France. As these vessels from China and India were without moorings, their captains justly said that it would be an enormous risk to their valuable cargoes to accompany him into the Bay of Fundy. It was decided that he should take them to France, but, as the voyage turned out, he might as well have gone to Acadia, for the fleet of fifty-two sail which had left Louisbourg under his convoy became dispersed, and he arrived towards the end of December without any of them.

A knowledge of this fleet of East Indiamen comes to us through a deposition made by two men "of full age" who appeared in Boston in September.[2] They had been in the East Indies, and being minded to return

---

[1] Desenclaves to the Superior of St. Sulpice, Sept. 25, 1765, Ad. Sec. In Letters, No. 2655. Desenclaves was a severe critic of his compatriots. Maillard also was not hopeful about French prospects ; see Canadian Archives, 1906, p. 45.
[2] C.O. 5/900, f. 122.

home, had taken passage in the spring on a French East Indiaman the *Mars*, and sailed for France in company with the *Baleine*. Five other ships left the undesignated port in the East about the same time : three of which were from China, loaded with tea and porcelain ; two others from Bengal and Pondicherry, loaded with piece goods and coffee ; and the fifth from the Isle De Bourbon. Off the Cape of Good Hope they fell in with a French vessel, which advised them that war was about to be declared. At Ascension, where they arrived about the latter end of May, a packet boat from France was waiting for them with orders to proceed direct to Louisbourg. They arrived there, with one exception, in July and August, and in the latter month also came in two armed vessels of the company, with three or four merchantmen with provisions and reinforcements for the armament and crews of the ships from the East. The *Mars* and *Baleine*, after this strengthening, mounted upwards of fifty guns, each with a crew of three hundred and fifty men. The *Fullavie* (?), *Philibert*, *Argonaute*, and the *Duc d'Anjou* mounted thirty guns with a crew of one hundred and fifty. The deponents seem to have returned from Louisbourg with the Canso prisoners, and at once gave this information to Shirley.

Meschin was an officer of good reputation, and his letters shows willingness to act. The moral effect of Shirley's unarmed and untrained reinforcements, in deterring Du Quesnel from sending vessels against Annapolis, was of vastly greater importance than the services of these levies in the actual defence against the skirmishing of Du Vivier.[1]

The New England colonies had remained on the defensive during the year. All that they did was to lay an embargo with very severe penalties on trade with Louisbourg and Martinique. Dissatisfied as were the officials of Louisbourg with the number of privateers they were able to send out, those that they did, as well as the privateers from France, making Louisbourg or ports in the West Indies their head-quarters, seriously interfered with the extended commerce of New England. Even with the towns of Isle Royale there were eighty or ninety vessels regularly employed. The fishing fleet of New England was very large, and their coasters plied along the littoral of the North Atlantic from Newfoundland and the Gulf of St. Lawrence to the West Indies. In addition to Morpain, Doloboratz was in command of a privateer of twelve cannon and as many swivels, in which he assisted at the reduction of Canso, and then proceeded to cruise on the New England coast. There he was captured, after a spirited encounter in which no one on either side was injured, by Captain Tyng in the *Prince of Orange*, the first "man-of-war" of Massachusetts.[2] Nine vessels

---

[1] In addition to documents referred to, see also others in I.R. vol. 26 ; Acadie, vol. 8 ; Marine, B⁴, vol. 56, and C.O. 5/900.
[2] Printed in full on p. 124.

were taken on the banks by two Louisbourg privateers early in June, and a merchantman coming from Ireland,[1] with a number of women on board, who were sent on to Boston with the Canso prisoners. These unhappy women were thrown into terror by the statement of the master of the vessel on which they were to make the voyage, that he had the right to sell them as slaves. Du Quesnel informed Shirley of this, and begged his offices on their behalf, which the latter effectively used. In another detachment Shirley received one hundred and seventy prisoners, and Du Quesnel sent in addition seventy-seven to Placentia, which would represent a not inconsiderable loss inflicted on the commerce of New England.[2] Some measure of it is shown by the fact that the sale of eleven vessels taken at sea, and at Canso and Annapolis Royal, produced at Louisbourg a total of 114,409 l., according to the account rendered by the treasurer of Louisbourg.[3] These were the vessels taken on the King's account, others were captured by private parties, and Bigot in his defence says that he sold, to the great advantage of himself and partners, the prizes which he sent to France instead of to Louisbourg.

The damage inflicted by the English during this year was vastly greater than the losses suffered by her maritime commerce, although it was greater than that of France. The *Kinsale* (44), Captain Robert Young, was again sent out to this station. She left Plymouth on the 7th of May. On her way to St. John's, Newfoundland, where she arrived on the 23rd of June, she captured five vessels. By the 2nd of August, on a cruise to the westward, she had destroyed St. Peter's and everything between Cape Ray and Placentia, and had sent an expedition northwards, about Trinity, to take, sink, burn, and destroy what French they met ; a kindly office which was also performed by Louisbourg privateers for the abandoned English fishing stations on Newfoundland. At Fishott, Young's expedition met with resistance, which lasted for five hours, but they were rewarded with 18,000 quintals of cod and " 80 ton " of oil, and another expedition captured five French privateers.[4] The nature of these exploits justifies their inclusion in the record of privateering rather than that of military operations.

On the coast of Isle Royale and in the Gulf of St. Lawrence English privateers were most active, and interrupted the commerce between Quebec, Louisbourg, and Martinique, so that Beauharnois and Hocquart wrote that it was necessary to have a convoy to protect their trade. Their representations were supplemented by petitions of the syndics of the merchants of Quebec and Montreal,

---

[1] Possibly the *Hope*. Cork to New England, reported in London, Nov. 8.

[2] " A List of 769 Ships taken by the Enemy which the merchants of London have received an account of, from the Commencement of the War, March 31, 1744, to the 11th of March 1745-6 inclusive," gives the name of six taken to Cape Breton, all on deep-sea voyages.

[3] I.R. vol. 27, f. 116.

[4] Captains' Letters, No. 2732.

who stated that, on account of Boston privateers, the previous year there had been only half the ordinary trade, and that in the next year there would be none. In September four of these privateers had taken five St. Malo fishermen, and had other prizes even in sight of Louisbourg. The situation was so serious that these officials did not hesitate to refer to the complaints of the merchants against ships of the navy. These vessels arrived late in the season, their officers were indifferent and remained in port. They went so far as to say that four vessels manned by sailors of St. Malo, commanded by a townsman to be selected by the King, would be a more efficient protection to commerce.

Boston had sent out since June, when the news of the declaration of war was received, fifteen privateers, and four more were being built. Rhode Island, a nursery ground (Pépinière) of privateers, sent out twenty - three, and Philadelphia seven or eight, which were fitted out with money borrowed from Quakers, whose scruples did not permit them to engage directly in the lucrative sport. Captain Jeffo, in the *Swallow*, brought to Boston not only the declaration of war, but the news that he had captured a French merchantman bound for Isle Royale, and set free an English ship homeward bound from Jamaica.[1] New York gave a great reception to Commodore Warren, who in the *Launceston* brought in the *St. François Xavier* with a rich cargo of sugar and specie. Captain Spry of H.M. ketch *Comet*, received at Boston a handsome piece of plate in recognition of his capture, off Nantucket, of a noted French privateer fitted out at Louisbourg. She was more heavily armed and carried a crew of ninety, compared with sixty-four men of the *Comet*. The fight lasted over five hours, and was in doubt until Le Gras, the privateer captain, described by Shirley as a brave commander, was shot through the temple by a musket-ball.[2]

A Massachusetts privateer did almost as much damage as H.M.S. *Kinsale* and the expeditions Captain Young sent out. He broke up eight fishing settlements within the space of five leagues, burned the houses and works, sunk nearly one thousand boats, took seventeen ships, five of which were armed with from eighteen to twelve carriage guns, and took nearly seven hundred prisoners.[3] French accounts do not permit the identification of the scene of these exploits. They would appear to have taken place in the Gulf, and the sufferers to have been the vessels of St. Malo and the shore fisheries at Gaspé. Even allowing for exaggeration, for there do not seem to have been outside of Louisbourg any settlements which would have yielded so rich a spoil, it seems probable that this one vessel did more damage to the French than was inflicted by all the Louisbourg privateers on British commerce.

[1] Shirley to Newcastle, Nov. 9, 44, C.O. 5/900, f. 135.

[2] Among her crew were twelve Irishmen, one of them lately a soldier at Canso. They were detained in jail, and the others exchanged at Louisbourg for the men of New England privateers captured by the French.

[3] Shirley to Newcastle, C.O. 5/900.

The practice of privateering lacked official encouragement as little on one side as on the other. Newcastle's letter to the Governor of Rhode Island enclosing the declaration of war, ends with a command to do everything in his power to encourage privateering, and to distress and annoy the French in their settlements, trade, and commerce.[1] The authorities of Massachusetts broke up the comfortable custom of the old war by which privateers avoided each other, and made those to whom commissions were given give bonds that they would fight privateers as well as capture merchantmen.[2] Governor Shirley sent for the owners of a vessel commanded by one Captain "W.," who had allowed a small French privateer to escape, with the result that the latter had since captured several American vessels. This the Governor pronounced to be "scandalous behaviour." The minutes of Council,[3] August 16, less discreet than the newspaper, says Capt. Samuel Waterhouse, of the brigantine *Hawk* privateer, was severely reprimanded for "not vigorously attacking a French privateer of much lesser force." Having promised "to manage his affairs for the future more agreeably to the honour of his Commission," his commission was continued on trial (*News-Letter*, August). This rebuke, or the chances of war, led, the next week, to his sending three prizes to Boston.

The occupation was so attractive that one hundred and thirteen privateers were sent out by the British colonies the next year.[4] It was difficult to obtain crews, as they were fitted out faster than they could be manned, so that special inducements had to be offered to obtain a crew for the *Prince of Orange*, the ship of the Commonwealth.

The effect of war naturally told on the commerce of Isle Royale, although the chances of the sea gave some opportunity, even amidst privateers and men-of-war, to carry on trade. In 1743 one hundred and seventy-two vessels from other places than Nova Scotia and New England had come to Isle Royale. In 1744 there were fifty less, while the intercourse with these British colonies almost completely stopped, for in place of seventy-eight in the last year of peace only twelve came, and it is possible that these were prizes brought in and not traders.

War, however, was the predominant interest of the time. Doloboratz was captured in the vicinity of Boston, and while there as a prisoner a great deal of liberty was given him. After his return to Louisbourg he presented to the authorities a memoir stating the condition, not only of Boston, but of other towns as far south as Philadelphia. He said that he knew Boston perfectly, had previously been at Rhode Island, and had spent five days there at this time, where

---

[1] R.I. Records, vol. 5, p. 80.   [2] *News-Letters.*   [3] C.O. 5/808.
[4] The Boston *News-Letter* proudly says that this is a greater fleet than the Royal Navy in the time of Elizabeth. The *Gentleman's Magazine* says one hundred were fitted out.

he consulted with a native of France, residing in that place (Newport), from whom he had bought a thousand barrels of flour to be delivered in April. His view was that the defences of these places were weak. He would risk his life on laying them under contribution if he had five or six vessels of war, a fireship, and some small merchant vessels. He excepts from these New York, which, being under a Royal Government, would be more difficult to attack, as order is well maintained there, better than in those other towns where every one is master.

Although Du Chambon's experience had been entirely at Isle Royale he seems to have done what he could with vigour. As to warning the Minister, he did so as forcibly as his predecessors, and had more specific information to give him.[1] He sent on Doloboratz' memoir,[2] which contained the report that an enterprise against Louisbourg was being prepared in England, and that the four northern colonies had offered the English Government the services of six hundred men and a money contribution amounting to £800,000 of provincial money, if they would send fifteen men-of-war for an expedition against Louisbourg. The merchants of Boston believed so firmly that this offer would be accepted that they had laid in extra stores to sell to this fleet. Du Vivier also brought back word from Acadia, that an enterprise against Louisbourg was to be attempted in the spring, and the matter had been so fully discussed with his English acquaintances that he was able to add that the English hoped to arrange devices by which the Island Battery could be shrouded in smoke long enough for their ships to enter the harbour. The authorities impressed on the Minister that if he did not forestall the English, who would follow the ice to blockade the port and prevent their receiving any help, the position of Louisbourg would be a sorrowful one, as the English intention was to starve out the inhabitants, and thus compel the reduction of the place. Du Chambon was doing all he could for its defence, and attempted to provide a large quantity of faggots on the quay for the use of the fire-ships. He proposed a battery on the top of Cap Noir, and asked the Minister to send out more cannon and bar iron for use in the guns of the Island Battery. Their efforts were not confined to preparations for defence. They sent a new memorandum of the requirements for an expedition against Annapolis more powerful than the preceding ones, as Annapolis was to be strengthened, and recommended for its command Du Vivier, who, on account of his health, had been allowed to go to France for the winter.[3] They also pointed out that an expedition could be sent against Placentia with fair prospects of success, for its defences consisted of pickets, a battery in bad order, and a garrison of forty-five soldiers and three officers. These

[1] See p. 124.   [2] MSS. Que. vol. 3, f. 211.
[3] The Minister was urged to send him out with the first vessel in the spring

were the final events of the active season of Louisbourg and this warfare of unwilling amateurs.

The somnolent condition of a Louisbourg winter was broken into by an extraordinary event. Serious efforts, which have been recounted, were made by Forant and Bigot to remedy the conditions of the troops, and there is no evidence in the official correspondence to show that after this time, and the subsequent steps taken by Du Quesnel to suppress the canteens, there was any unusual degree of dissatisfaction among the troops. But as told by Du Chambon and Bigot,[1] on the 27th of December, in the dreary dawn, the Swiss troops armed themselves, and took their ranks in the parade ground of the citadel. Their one officer who was on duty made them return to their quarters, after having promised them all they wanted. Instead of remaining quietly there, they went into the quarters of the French troops and so effectively reproached them for not having joined them as they had promised, that the whole garrison formed up in the court. They then sent the drummers of the garrison, threatened by the bayonets of twenty men, to beat to arms throughout the town. All the officers rushed immediately to the citadel, which some of them entered only by craft or supplication. The others were unable, even sword in hand, to move the sentinels, whom the mutineers had placed. De la Perelle, the major, placed himself before the drummers in the town in an effort to stop them, but was unable to do so, as he was covered by the muskets and bayonets of the soldiers. They even surrounded him and carried him off his feet to some distance, but he at last prevailed on them to cease the drumming, and by agreement followed them into the fort, where the officers by this time had got the soldiers to form themselves in their companies.

Order being restored, they promised to recognize De la Perelle as their major, and Du Chambon, who had been on the scene, asked them the reasons why they had so signally failed in their duty to the King. They said that each company required half a cord more wood, the return of five cords which had been kept back from them on account of their having stolen the same quantity ; that there should be given their proper rations to those soldiers who had been in the expeditions to Canso and Acadia ; that the recruits of 1741 should receive their clothing, which had not been given them, as it had not been sent out for the extra ten men then added to each company. All this was accepted, and Bigot at once began to carry out the agreement. The Swiss again came out under arms after the dispersal of the French troops, although their officer had promised them all they demanded, and they refused to recognize M. Cherrer (Cailly) for their commander. They had been uneasy for some time, and he had been in bed for a month, which prevented him appearing in person.

The officials thought the object of the troops was to take possession of the

---

[1] Letter of Dec. 31, vol. 26, pp. 231-234.

magazines and of the treasure and to yield the place to the enemy in the spring. They had not given up this idea of rebellion, although their demands had been complied with. The situation was intolerable. All the officials were their slaves ; the mutineers caused all the disorder which they wished ; made the merchants give them, at their own prices, all they asked for ; for as there were only forty or fifty of these merchants and these not armed, they were unable to join together to resist. They were in consequence more dead than alive, and intended to go to France the following autumn, if they were permitted to live so long. The revolt was complete, for there was not a single soldier who had not joined the mutineers. All the Swiss corporals and sergeants had sustained their soldiers, and the only men who stood firm were the sergeants of the French companies and the small company of French artillerymen. At the time, the 31st of December, when Du Quesnel and Bigot wrote this letter there happened to be in the Port two small vessels bound for the West Indies. They wrote it secretly, as they were under observation night and day, and they did not send the vessels direct to France for fear that some vessel coming out would warn the mutineers that they had asked for help. If this were known the soldiers would first ransack the town, and then deliver it to the enemy, for they were aware of their strength, and knew that the six hundred civilians in the colony would be easily overpowered. The situation became less alarming, and the soldiers behaved not badly during the winter, owing to some extent to the tact of Bigot, and the fact that nothing was required of them by their officers.

The condition of the King's finances was so low that in February Maurepas felt that he could do little for Isle Royale ; he accepted all the suggestions that had been made, even to sending a captain of St. Malo to cruise with Morpain in the Gulf, which the syndics of Quebec and Montreal had thought desirable. The *Vigilant, La Renommée,* and *Le Castor* were intended for Isle Royale, and as M. Chateaugué, who had been appointed Governor, was too ill to leave France the command of the colony was given to Perrier de Salvert, who was commander of the *Mars,* in which ship he was to proceed to Louisbourg.

APPENDICES

A. Boston Weekly News-Letter, *June* 29, 1744

On Monday last Capt. Tyng in the Province Snow, returned from a Cruize, and brought in with him a French Privateer Sloop with 94 Men, mounted with 8 Carriage and 8 Swivel Guns, burthen between 70 and 80 Tuns, commanded by Capt. Delebroitz, which was fitted out from Cape Breton, and sail'd about 3 Weeks before : Capt. Tyng discover'd her last Saturday Morning about 9 o'Clock, as he was laying too off of Crab

Ledge, 15 Leagues from Cape Cod, it being very Calm : Perceiving she had a Topsail and was bearing down towards him, Capt. Tyng took her to be the Province Sloop commanded by Capt. Fletcher ; but soon after, as she drew nearer, he suspected her to be a French Cruizer under English Colours, whereupon, in order to prevent a Discovery he ordered his Colours to be struck, his Guns to be drawn in and his Ports to be shut close, and at the same Time the Bulk Head to be taken down.   When the Privateer had got within about Gunshot of Capt. Tyng, taking the Snow to be a Merchantman, they fired upon him : upon which Capt. Tyng threw open his Ports, run out his Guns, hoisted his Colours and fired upon them : Perceiving their Mistake, they tack'd about, put out their Oars and tug'd hard to get off after firing two or three Guns more.   It continuing very calm, Capt. Tyng was obliged to order out his Oars and to row after her, firing several Times his Bow Chase at her, in which the Gunner was so skilful, that 9 Times the Shot did some Damage either to her Hull or Rigging : About Two o'Clock the next Morning he came up pretty close with them being very much guided by 4 Lanthorns which they had inadvertently hung out upon their Rigging in the Night ; finding they were bro't to the last Tryal, attempted to board Capt. Tyng, which he perceiving, brought up his Vessel and gave them a Broadside, they having before thro' Fear all quitted the Deck : The Mast being disabled by a Shot, it soon after broke off in the middle : Upon firing the Broad-side they cry'd for Quarter ; and then Capt. Tyng order'd them to hoist out their Boat and bring the Captain on board, but they answered that their Tackling was so much shatter'd that they could not get their Boat with it ; they were then told they must do it by Hand : Accordingly they soon comply'd and the Captain being brought on board deliver'd his Sword, Commission, &c. to Capt. Tyng, desiring that he and his Men might be kindly us'd, he was promis'd they should, and then the other Officers, being a 2nd Captain, 3 Lieutenants, and others Inferiour, were brought on board, and the next Day the rest of the Men who were secur'd in the Hold.

The Night after Capt. Tyng brought them into this Harbour, they were convey'd ashore and committed to Prison here ; and the next Morning 50 of them were guarded to the Prisons at Cambridge and Charlestown : The Officers and Men are treated with Humanity and Kindness.

'Tis remarkable that notwithstanding the great number of Men on either Side, in the attack and surrender, there was not one kill'd or wounded.

Capt. Morepang in a Schooner of 110 Tuns, mounting 10 Carriage Guns, 4 Pounders, and 10 Swivels, with 120 Men, came out with Delebroitz from Cape Breton, and we hear is appointed to Guard the Coast there till a Vessel of greater Force arrived for that Purpose.

B. Acadian Petition to De Gannes

To M. De Ganne, Knight, Captain of infantry commanding the troops and the savages united, at present in the country.

We the undersigned humbly representing the inhabitants of Mines, river Canard, Piziquid, and the surrounding rivers, beg that you will be pleased to consider that while there would be no difficulty by virtue of the strong force which you command, in supplying yourself with the quantity of grain and meat that you and M. Du Vivier have ordered, it would be quite impossible for us to furnish the quantity you demand, or even a smaller, since the harvest has not been so good as we hoped it would be, without placing ourselves in great peril.

We hope, gentlemen, that you will not plunge both ourselves and our families into a state of total loss ; and that this consideration will cause you to withdraw your savages and troops from our districts.

We live under a mild and tranquil government, and we have all good reason to be faithful to it. We hope, therefore, that you will have the goodness not to separate us from it ; and that you will grant us the favour not to plunge us into utter misery. This we hope from your goodness, assuring you that we are with much respect, gentlemen,

Your very humble and obedient servants—acting for the communities above mentioned.

Oct. 10, 1744.

Then follow the names of ten signers.

Mr. Alex Bourg, Notary at Mines,

I am willing, gentlemen, out of regard for you, to comply with your demand.

DE GANNE.

Oct. 13, 1744.[1]

Estat des pieces d'artillerie qui sont en Batterie pour la deffense du port et place de Louisbourg, et des poudres de Guerre qu'il Faut pour tirer cinquante coups par canon, et autant par mortiers et le moindre nombre d'hommes que L'on peut mettre à chaque Batterie pour Les Servir.[2]

	Canons et Mortiers.		Poudres.	Hommes.	Boulets.	Bombes.
Batterie Royalle	de 36	28	19,600	196	1400	...
Mortier	de 12p.[3]	1	750	7	...	50
Mortier	de 9p.	1	650	4	...	50
Batterie de L'Isle . . .	de 24	32	15,200	192	1600	...
Mortier	de 9p.	2	1,300	8	...	100
Batterie de La pce. . . .	de 36	12	8,400	84	550	...
de la grave	de 24	6	2,850	36	300	...
Batterie dauphine . . .	de 24	10	4,750	60	500	...
Barbette	de 12	6	1,650	30	300	...
Eperon	de 6	6	1,500	24	300	...
Bastion de Roy . . .	de 18	6	2,250	30	300	...
sur le cavalier du cap noir } . . .	de 8	4	900	20	200	...
Bastion Maurepas Mortier } . . .	de 12p	2	1,200 }	14	...	100
Bombe poudre quil Faut . . .			1,300 }			
		116	62,300	705	5450	300

---

[1] Translated in N.S. Archives, vol. 1, p. 135.   [2] I.R. vol. 26, f. 60.

[3] p. = inches in calibre. From this statement it is clear that the representations of the Governors from St. Ovide to Du Chambon, that Louisbourg was undermanned and inadequately supplied with munitions of war, were well founded.

| Total des munitions de guerre en provision dans cette place | 66,921 l. de poudre
1,772 Bombes de 12 pouces
833 Bombes de 9 pouces
284 Bombes de 6 pouces
1,867 Boulets de 36
2,147 Boulets de 24
2,520 Boulets de 18 | 1670 Boulets de 12
1214 Boulets de 8
280 Boulets de 6
1929 Boulets de 4 |

Du Chambon.

A Louisbourg, Ce 10ᵉ 9ᵇʳᵉ 1744.

CHAPTER IX

THE events of 1744, and the condition of New England at the close of that season, did not indicate that so remarkable an event as the expedition against Louisbourg would take place in the following year. Massachusetts, the most enterprising and the most important of the northern colonies, had placed herself in a "posture of defense," and levies from her people had succoured Annapolis. There does not seem to have been any disposition to do more. The *Memoire du Canada* for this year states that an Indian Chief sent by Vaudreuil to Boston brought back a report that Shirley took an oath in the presence of eighty Councillors that he would not begin operations against the French, but that if even a child were killed, he would exert all his powers against them and their savage allies.[1]

Massachusetts was in no condition to undertake any serious expenditures. Her treasury was empty. A lottery was authorized by the legislature (Dec. 14, 1744; Jan. 7, 1745), to raise £7500 for the pressing necessities of the province in "its present difficult circumstances." Her debt was excessive. Through her issues of paper money, the rate of exchange was much more unfavourable than that in the other colonies, and was sinking to a rate of ten to one, which was reached in 1747. Her fisheries were declining; and but one favourable material condition existed—the harvests of the year had been abundant.

There had been, however, talk of military movements. A Boston newspaper published, on August 2, a London letter stating that a body of troops was to be sent to the northern colonies, "to undertake an expedition of great importance against France on that side." This is probably the basis for the report of Doloboratz, for it might well have risen to his definite figures in passing to the social stratum in which the privateer moved during his detention in Boston. Du Vivier brought back to Louisbourg from the Annapolis expedition the same report; and the Malouin fishermen taken by New England privateers

---

[1] June 30, 1744, " Divers Delegates from the Six Nations of Indians living to the Westward of Albany . . . had a conference this day with his Excellency in the Council Chamber in the presence of both Houses " (Minutes of Assembly, Mass., C.O. 5/808 ; MSS. Que. 3, p. 215).

were told by their captors that an expedition against the French was in con-
templation for the following year. As indicating the temper of the people
of Massachusetts, it may be noted that Doloboratz said that it was only those
engaged in the fisheries who were interested, that while the country folk would
like to see such an expedition succeed, they did not seem to him inclined at
all to support it in person, and but little as taxpayers. After speaking of
the difficulty of getting men for Annapolis he goes on :

"I have talked to many of these people. I believe on the whole that the townspeople,
except the bourgeois and the superior artisans, are privateering, and that the country people
will not engage without large promises and rewards. It is true that there was very easily
found plenty of men to engage in the expedition to Carthagena and elsewhere in the
Spanish Indies, but beyond the fact that they were disgusted with the ill success of this
enterprise, they were attracted to it by the hope of the gold and silver of that country,
and they are persuaded that there are more blows to suffer than gold pieces to capture
in an expedition against Isle Royale, and they are free men (maistres de leur volonté)."
Of two hundred and fifty sent away from Rhode Island in the West India expedition not
twenty had returned.[1]

The impressions of Doloboratz seem reasonable. He underestimated the
resources of these plain people, " masters of their will," acting under the influence
of two men, the one the Governor of the province, the other its principal
citizen, President of the Governor's Council.

William Shirley, the Governor of Massachusetts at this time, was an
Englishman who emigrated to Boston in 1732, where he practised as a barrister
and occupied subordinate official positions, until in 1741 he was appointed
Governor. His preliminary experience was of great value to him, for he
gained from it a knowledge of the people, among whom he was to represent
the Crown. He was tactful, and thus found it easy to deal with the representatives of the people. He was as keen to persuade them to courses which
he believed to be in the interests of the province, as to strain the authority
of his commission in carrying them out. His policies were progressive, and
in these troublous times expensive, and were based on the fundamental view
that there was not room enough on the continent for colonies of both France
and England.[2] He was industrious, a voluminous, persuasive, and clear writer,
undismayed by responsibility, and to these solid qualities added a taste for
military strategy, the results of which in the Seven Years' War tarnished the
reputation gained by his antecedent career.

William Pepperrell was a merchant of Kittery, born in 1697, the son
of a Welsh or Devonshire man who had founded the business, which his son

---

[1] R.I. Rec. vol. v. p. 146. Massachusetts also suffered severely.

[2] Douglass is his bitter critic. He says that the financial condition of the colony was due to his policy, and that
the Louisbourg expedition was a source of gain to Shirley.

prosecuted with such success that he was one of the richest men in the country. He was not born in the purple of New England life, among those who, in the ordinary course of family events, go to Harvard College ; his education was that of the country school, with some special instruction. His biographers note that his grammar was imperfect in early life, a thing not uncommon in more exalted circles in the eighteenth century, and certainly not unique in New England. He had received that splendid practical training of an old-time merchant, whose dealings brought him into contact with men of all conditions in his own country, and with many foreigners. No occupation is more broadening in its effect on a mind weighted by responsibility and capable of learning from a life widely diversified in its daily occurrences. His sense of responsibility to public duties is shown in his acceptance of office. At the age of thirty he was elected to the House from his own district, and after one term was appointed to the Council, to which he was annually called until his death, thirty-two years later. For eighteen years he was President of the Board. He was also colonel of one of the militia regiments of Maine. Any man whose dealings extended from the lumber camp and the fisheries to the transportation and exchange of their products in the markets of the world, a man of wealth and of position, must possess great influence in any community, the people of which are largely dependent on his activities. The fact that Pepperrell's command of the Louisbourg expedition made enlistment popular, indicates that his character inspired confidence and his disposition liking, not only in his neighbourhood, but wherever his reputation extended.

The prominence given to these two names is not meant to reopen a discussion as to the person to whom is due the credit for proposing the expedition. The project had for years been considered as possible by French and English. When in November 1744 Shirley wrote to Newcastle proposing that an expedition against Louisbourg should be sent out from England, he was following up what Clark, Governor of New York, had written home in 1741. The latter, in his turn, held the same views as his predecessor Crosby.[1] At the same time as Clark's second reference to the matter, Shirley had sent through Kilby a description of Louisbourg and the means of attacking it, which the latter vouched for, as it was made by a kinsman of his own. Kilby, who was agent of Massachusetts in London, wrote the 30th of August 1743, recommending projects against the French, and closed his letter by urging an early attack upon Cape Breton, " the situation, Strength, & every other Circumstance relating whereto, I am possess'd of a perfect & Minute account of . . ."[2] Warren was in possession of this document or similar information, for he discussed this project not only in his letters to Corbett, Secretary to the

---

[1] N.Y. Col. Doc. v. 961, 970 ; vi. 183, 229.   [2] C.O. 217/31, p. 157.

Admiralty,[1] but also in private letters. Therefore, the proposals of Vaughan,[2] of Bradstreet, of Judge Auchmuty, the writer of a valuable pamphlet on the *Importance of Cape Breton*, of a Merchant of London, who wrote in 1744 to the Ministry urging the reduction of Louisbourg, dealt with a matter that had been much discussed.

The project was in the air. The British colonist of the eighteenth century turned his back on the potential opulence of the vast continent on the shores of which he lived, exploiting it only for a sustenance and for material with which to engage in maritime trade, of which the fisheries were the foundation. French and English from before the time that Louisbourg was settled pictured to themselves the superb monopoly which would fall to the nation which succeeded in dispossessing its rival.

Such play of the imagination is the poetry of practical affairs, and the spring of political events. The people of New England were of an intellectual temper to feel this speculative impulse. It is as certain that the capture of Isle Royale was the theme of discussion long before conditions made the project at all practical, as that many then held the opinion that the colonies, if prosperous, would not remain faithful to the Crown; although a score of years elapsed before events brought these slowly germinating impulses to a head. In the same way the startling accuracy of French forecasts of the method of attack on Louisbourg came from the discussions with which St. Ovide and the others relieved the dreariness of their idle hours.

Shirley's proposition to Newcastle in December had been that six or seven ships could force the harbour and land troops, of which 1500 to 2000 would be enough. At this time he contemplated a regular expedition sent out by England, but the knowledge he gained in the next few weeks led him to propose, and finally to carry through, the expedition which was the crowning achievement of his career.[3]

The General Court of Massachusetts was in session on January 9. Shirley, apparently without taking any one into his confidence, asked its members to take an oath of secrecy as to the subject of a communication he desired to make.[4]

---

[1] Ad. Sec., In Letters, 2654, Sept. 1744.

[2] Vaughan's work in promoting the expedition, and in self-effacing services therein, were unquestionably great. His own account of them is given in pp. 360–9. Read in connection with other accounts, they give the impression that he was a man of great energy, public spirit, and self-sacrifice, but lacking in judgment and the power of working with others. The type of man in our times most likely to be found among inventors. These documents make interesting reading, and throw some light on the events narrated, and are on this ground commended to the attention of the reader.

[3] This was based on the reports of the Canso prisoners, and of other persons who had visited Louisbourg. In New England there must have been many scores of sea-faring people who knew Louisbourg as well as any but their native towns, all of which confirmed the news that the garrison was small, all of it discontented, the Swiss on the verge of mutiny, and the inhabitants suffering from a scarcity of provisions, the result of Shirley's own policy.

[4] Parkman, *Half-Century*, vol. ii. p. 85.

This they did, and he presented an address on the subject of an expedition against Louisbourg. This document begins by recounting that in the course of the present war Massachusetts must expect from Louisbourg "annoyance in trade, captures of provision vessels, and destruction of fisheries"; that the interest of the province would be greatly served by the reduction of the place; that the time was opportune, for from information which Shirley had he believed that if two thousand men were landed on the island, they could damage the out-settlements and fisheries, and lay the town itself in ruins, and might even make themselves masters of the town and harbour. He asked for suitable provision for the expenses of the expedition, which if partially successful would pay for itself, "and if it should wholly succeed, must be an irreparable loss to the enemy and an invaluable acquisition for this country."

The next day the House appointed a Committee of eight, of whom four were Colonels and one a Captain, and the Council added seven to their number, with instructions "to sit forthwith and report as soon as may be." The result of their deliberations appears in a short address to his Excellency from both branches of the legislature, on January 12, in which, while they express approval of the scheme, they are convinced that they are unable to raise a sufficient sea and land force, and "dare not by ourselves attempt it." They pray the Governor to lay before the King the danger of the colonies from Louisbourg, and to express the disposition of the province to aid in its reduction in conjunction with other Governments.[1]

During this time Pepperrell was presumably absent from Boston. He at all events was not present at these sittings of the Council. Shirley had, unaided, made his proposal, and had failed in carrying the legislature with him. He was much cast down by their refusal. James Gibson, once an officer in the British army, then a merchant in Boston, tells that the Governor came to him and asked him if he felt like giving up the Louisbourg expedition. This led to Gibson undertaking to obtain signatures for a petition from the merchants of Boston and Marblehead, asking for a reconsideration.[2]

Pepperrell came back to town, if he had been absent, and presumably was won over by Shirley. Gibson's influential petitions were presented to the Legislature, which was addressed on the 19th and 22nd by Shirley. A new Joint Committee, with Pepperrell at its head, was appointed. It examined witnesses, and reported on the 25th, to the effect that they were convinced that it was incumbent on the Government to embrace this opportunity, and proposed that the Captain-General, Shirley, issue a proclamation to encourage the enlist-

---

[1] Shirley at once took the matter up with Newcastle in a long letter about the advantages of Cape Breton, the danger of an attack from Louisbourg on British ships and colonies. He lays more emphasis on the advantages which would follow its capture than on these dangers (Shirley to Newcastle, Jan. 14, 1744/5, C.O. 5/900).

[2] Vaughan was active in this work. See Biographical Appendix.

ment of three thousand volunteers under officers to be appointed by him. It recommends the rate of pay of the men, that they shall have all the plunder, that warlike stores be provided, and provisions for four months, that a transport service be organized so that the force could leave by the beginning of March, and that application be made to the other colonies to furnish respectively their quotas of men. This report was concurred in by both branches the day of its presentation, and consented to by Shirley. The House voted that half a pound of ginger and a pound and a half of sugar be given to each soldier, and unanimously voted against impressing any part of the three thousand men. The majority was small. It is said that it would have been a tie had a member not broken his leg as he was hastening to vote in opposition. Other accounts say that the majority was narrow, some members known to be opposed having remained away from the House, a result which might well have been produced by the influence of important merchants who favoured the project.[1]

It seems certain that the influence of Pepperrell, exerted personally and through his associates, was paramount in bringing about this result. His later statement,[2] "it must be confessed that there would have been no Expedition against this place had I not undertook it," must refer to his course at this time rather than to his acceptance of the chief command which immediately followed. Shirley could unquestionably have found another leader. Without Pepperrell's influence he failed with the General Court. When it was exerted in support of his scheme, Shirley obtained for it the necessary legislative sanction.

Both French and English historians for the most part agree that the attacks on Canso and Annapolis Royal, the interruption of fisheries, and the devastation of privateers led the colonies to take a desperate step to avert an impending calamity.[3] There is much in a superficial reading of the official documents, e.g. Shirley's address already quoted, to sustain this view. This aspect, moreover, would be the most serviceable one to present to the legislators of provinces in acute financial distress. An expenditure to protect the state from an impending danger is always legitimate, but with a vigorous people the hope of gain is a stronger incentive than the fear of loss. It may be maintained that the real motives which led to the acceptance of Shirley's proposal, when all the facts were before the Assembly, were aggressive, not defensive.[4]

[1] The House Journals do not mention the oath of secrecy or the majority. Governor Wanton says it was one (R.I. Rec. vol. v. p. 145).

[2] Pepperrell to Stafford, Nov. 4, 1745, Preface to *An Accurate Journal and Account*, etc.

[3] "Lettre d'un Habitant," Parsons's *Life of Pepperrell*.

[4] "The Motives, which have induc'd the Assembly to set this Expedition on foot before Spring, are the weak Condition of the Garrison and Harbour of Louisbourg in comparison of what it will be when they shall have rec'd their supplies of Provisions, Stores and Recruits from Old France by that time, besides that the Season of the Year

It is said also that fishermen thrown out of employment by the war formed a considerable part of the troops raised ; but the fact that New England privateers could not find crews, that the press-gang was organized, if not used, to secure sailors for the vessels of the province,[1] is not compatible with this statement. When the British colonies sent out about ten times as many privateers as the French, the latter being vastly less effective, it is not reasonable to believe that New England was seriously dismayed by French privateering or failed, in irritation at her small losses, to calculate her surpassing gains.

These considerations lead to the conclusion that, describing Louisbourg as the Dunkirk of America as an oratorical flourish, New England had no real fear of invasion, but that the monopoly of the fisheries meant such prospective wealth,[2] that sound business insight in the leaders of her people led to their grasping an opportunity to benumb French competition in the markets of the world. This opportunity presented itself when war existed: Louisbourg was short of provisions,[3] its fortifications weak, its garrison small and mutinous.

Shirley carried with him the most influential merchants, for their care for public advantage was stimulated by the prospect of private gain. They found a following, for at no time in its history were the people of Massachusetts more recklessly enterprising. Every motive was appealed to, as is always the case when the success of a policy depends on the support of an independent people. The expedition against Louisbourg, to the fanatic was directed against Romanism ; to the timorous was a preventive of invasion ; to the greedy a chance for plunder ; and to all, an object for the self-sacrifice of every patriotic Briton.

Shirley's activity in the week which followed the decision to undertake the expedition was prodigious. On February 1 he wrote a long dispatch to Newcastle. He laid before him plans for the expedition, informed him about the artillery he could provide.[4] He had also communicated with the other governments, and had received a favourable reply from New Hampshire and Rhode Island. The plan for the expedition was based on that handed into the Committee,[5] but modified by Shirley with the help of Bastide, the engineer of Annapolis Royal, who was in Boston at the time.

Shirley had already discovered the impossibility of arranging matters for

---

will be most Advantageous in March for Attacking the Town, the present Spirit of the People in this Province to attempt it at this time, and the Advantage which the Surprize of such an Expedition as well as from New England and Great Britain (in case his Majesty shall support it from thence) will give his Majesty against the Enemy " (Shirley to Newcastle, Feb. 1, 1745, C.O. 5/900, f. 157).   [1] Parsons.

[2] " Besides we had not the same dependence upon, and expectation of advantages from the fishery as Massachusetts and New Hampshire had, which undoubtedly was a main inducement to their people to list so cheerfully as they did " (Governor Wanton, R.I. Records, vol. 5).

[3] The burden of Shirley's reproaches to Captain W. was that the privateer he let slip captured several vessels laden with provisions, to the benefit of the French at Louisbourg, " who so much wanted 'em."

[4] Eight 22's, one 24, two 9 and 11 inch mortars.   [5] Apparently by Vaughan (Parkman, Half-Century).

the expedition to sail by March 1, as recommended by the Committee, and at this time was in hope to get it away by the middle of the month. All saw the great importance of blockading the port before the arrival of the ships from France, which, from what was known of Louisbourg and its condition, the New Englanders felt would be sent out at the earliest moment. Some merriment has been created by the proposal of Vaughan to take Louisbourg by surprise. It may be said the plan with undisciplined men under untrained officers required too many accurate conjunctions to be successful. In defence of its projector, it may be recalled that Du Vivier, certainly familiar with the conditions of Nova Scotia, proposed to enter Annapolis when its ditches were filled with snow ; that the drifts at Louisbourg, at least once, were deep enough to make it necessary to dig sentries out of their boxes, and that its Governors had united in holding that a surprise of the place was more to be feared than a regular attack. It is to be noted that this element in the preliminary plan on which the legislators voted to undertake the expedition was abandoned by Shirley. "As to that Part of the Scheme, which is propos'd for taking the Town by Surprise, so many Circumstances must conspire to favour it, and so many Accidents may defeat it, that I have no great dependence upon it, and shall guard as well as I can by Orders against the Hazard that must attend it." His project was at this time, February 1, to make a base at Canso, land near the town and make an attack on the Royal Battery, the weakness of which on the landward side was known to him and his advisers. The bombardment of the town was to follow, without, it would appear, any prospect of carrying it, but with fair hope of holding the position until the arrival of an English naval force.[1] In event of being unable to do this, he felt sure that the buildings and fishing gear, not only of the environs of Louisbourg, but of other places on the island, could be destroyed, and that the colonial forces could retire to Canso and there encamp until advices were received from Great Britain as to whether or not the King would support the expedition with ships and troops.[2]

Shirley carried with him Benning Wentworth, Governor of New Hampshire, so far that he was induced to strain the credit of his province in a case of such urgency, by issuing more paper money, Vaughan being his representative in these delicate negotiations. Having succeeded in this, Shirley complicated the situation by a flourish of diplomatic courtesy, in intimating to Wentworth that had it not been for his gout, Shirley would have appointed him to the chief command. Wentworth assured Shirley that this would not prevent him serving. Shirley was thus forced to throw the onus of not accepting this offer on various people of consideration whom he consulted in the matter.

[1] To Newcastle, Feb. 1, 1745.

[2] Although Shirley did not think well of a surprise, it is included in his instructions to Pepperrell, as he was about sailing (M.H.S. first series, vol. 1).

They were clearly of the opinion that a change in the command would be prejudicial.[1]

The pay offered was 25s. per month and a blanket, besides the ginger so promptly voted by the House. Other inducements were offered, such as that those who enlisted were not liable to be pressed for service on the vessels of the province, and for them processes of law for the collection of debt were suspended until their return from the campaign.

While the determination of causes which led to the taking up of an expedition like this is hypothetical, there is no question that the decision having been made, the people threw themselves heartily into the project. The complete militia system of New England made this easy, and it was along the lines of an existing organization that recruiting proceeded. There was some hesitation in certain districts at the outset, on account of doubt as to whom the command of the expedition would be given, as well as about the company officers. Various officers took active steps to secure their men ; one Captain Sewall began his work by giving the men of his militia company a dinner ; he also increased their pay from his own pocket, and offered to provide for any wives and families that might be left destitute. Others were as eager, if less free-handed, and very shortly complaints arose of the officers poaching on each other's companies. The allotment of commissions gave trouble to Shirley as well as to Wentworth, who said he would rather be a porter than a Governor. But these are the drawbacks of earnestness and activity. Shirley was active and foresighted, his legislature prompt in passing acts, and the officers of the forces and members of committees were efficient. The course of events as detailed in the records of these busy weeks displays the actions of a capable people, trained to the dispatch of business. Chief among the active was Vaughan, who was too unbalanced to be trusted with an executive office, but whose zeal had done much to ensure the undertaking of the expedition, for he had gathered witnesses, secured signatures to the petitions, and harangued. When it was determined upon he rode post here and there, and his impetuous haste must have appeared to Shirley and Pepperrell, who considered means as well as ends, that of a meddler.

" I have desired ye gentl at York to march one compa next Mondy to Boston, to give life & Spring to ye affair. I hope yoou'l encourage ye same. I have written to Doctor Hale to desire ye Govr. to ordr. to be at Boston next week, for dispatch is ye life of businesse. I have proposed ye 2000 men, if no more, be ready to sail by ye twentyeth day of ye month. Portsmo, Feb. 8, 1744." [2]

The general eagerness to serve and the importance of Pepperrell's opinion are shown in the letters received by him from willing participants in the

---

[1] *Half-Century*, vol. ii. p. 91.

[2] M.H.S. sixth series, vol. 10. Vaughan accompanied the expedition as a member of the Council of War.

expedition. One gentleman, rejected as a surgeon, wrote begging that he might go in any capacity, and reported to the General that he had already made some progress in enlisting. A clergyman informed Pepperrell with inexpressible pleasure, that he had been appointed a captain ; another friend expressed his regret that the legislature of New Hampshire, of which he was a member, would not allow him to serve. A gentleman, whose iconoclastic zeal has been quoted by Parkman in *Half-Century* (vol. ii. p. 98), wrote in terms of such perfervid piety that it is difficult, with our changed standards, to find in them the note of sincerity ; particularly, as his excuse for not going on the expedition is the only one of those given which seems inadequate.[1]

Mr. John Gibson followed up his work in stirring up the merchants of Boston and Marblehead to approach the legislature, by raising a company at his own charges and commanding it on the expedition. He had the unusual distinction, when the Parliament of Britain defrayed the expenses, to be named in the Act with the colonies. The response of the other Northern Colonies was considerable and prompt. In view of the emergency Wentworth ignored the royal prohibition to issue any more paper-money, and the little Province of New Hampshire sent a regiment of 500 men, 150 of them being at the charges of Massachusetts.[2] Connecticut raised 516 men, and to their commander, Roger Wolcott, was accorded the rank of Major-General, which made him second to Pepperrell.

Rhode Island on the 5th of February authorized her sloop *Tartar*[3] to assist in the expedition ; a month later, the raising of 150 men. Its legislature reconsidered this action on learning that Shirley was acting on his own initiative,[4] but later, at an unspecified date, passed an act encouraging soldiers to enlist for service in the expedition. The full regiment of 500 men authorized by this act did not serve, but apparently three companies went, which were incorporated in Pepperrell's regiment, under commission from the Governor of Rhode Island, which was dated early in June. They thus arrived at Cape Breton too late to take part in the siege. The response from the Southern Colonies was much less satisfactory. New York loaned some guns to Shirley ; but its legislature debated ten days as to what they could do, and voted £3000 ; but a new legislature being elected, this sum was by it increased to £5000.[5] New Jersey

---

[1] M.H.S. sixth series, vol. 10, contains letters which display the attitude of Massachusetts and New Hampshire.

[2] 304 men were in the New Hampshire regiment.

[3] The *Tartar* was the colony vessel. She carried fourteen guns and twelve swivels.

[4] Their defence, a sound one, is in R.I. Rec. vol. 5, p. 145. Extracts therefrom at the end of this chapter.

[5] ADMIRAL WARREN TO GOVERNOR WANTON

LOUISBOURG, *September* 13, 1745.

. . . " You see, sir, I speak here as an American and a well wisher to the colonies : and am therefore really sorry the particular one I mean, New York, to which I am nearest related, has not had a greater share in this great acquisition ; for it's a mistaken notion in any of the colonies, if they think they are not greatly interested, even the remotest of them, in

gave £2000 in July, which was laid out in provisions, and Pennsylvania, prevented by the peaceable principles of some of its people from providing arms, gave £4000 for provisions and clothing.

The brigadiers to the expedition were Samuel Waldo, like Pepperrell a large land-owner and merchant, and Joseph Dwight, who was Colonel of the artillery. Its active head was Richard Gridley, to whom we owe that map of Louisbourg which has been so frequently copied. The success of the enlistment was so great that 3250 men were raised. The Committee of War, whose chairman was Mr. John Osborne, was active in providing for these troops. A naval force and transport was of the utmost importance. Massachusetts bought a new brig of about four hundred tons, armed her as a frigate, and placed her under the command of Capt. Edward Tyng, who had previously served the Commonwealth, and distinguished himself as the captor of Doloboratz. He was in command of the flotilla.

Pepperrell discharged the military duties he had assumed as he would carry on any business operation. He asked advice from Mr. J. Odiorne,[1] a merchant of Portsmouth, who was familiar with the coasts of Acadia and Cape Breton. Odiorne urged a prompt attack, at which he thought their men would be better than at a regular siege, and, as a second resort, to hold their ground until reinforcements arrived, "if itt should cost us halfe our substances." Advice was volunteered to him by the Rev. John Barnard, probably on the ground that that gentleman had in 1707 been at the siege of Annapolis. In the universal enthusiasm and the certainty that the expedition was favoured by Heaven,[2] it may be noted that he is one of the few who modified his statement on this point by saying, "I doubt not but the cause is God's, so far as we can well say any cause of this nature can be." Shirley made efforts in every direction to obtain armed vessels, as the colonial armed vessels were inadequate to protect the transports or themselves from the forces they might expect to meet. The men-of-war on the American station which were within easy reach were under orders from the Admiralty to act as convoys,[3] and he found himself without any promise of assistance from them with the exception of the *Bien Aimé*, a prize commanded by Captain Gayton.

---

the reduction and support of this conquest, which will quiet them all in their religious and civil rights and liberties, to latest times, against a designing, encroaching, and powerful enemy, and increase our trade in the fish, fur, and many other valuable branches, to such an advantageous degree to the colonies, and our mother country, as must ever induce them to be extremely grateful to those who have opened so fair a channel for the increase of wealth and power " (Rhode Island Colonial Records, vol. 5, p. 144).

[1] Mr. Odiorne spells the name of the place " Lewisbrug," possibly a phonetic effort, for the same pronunciation is still extant locally. The New England form of " Chapeau Rouge," which appears in the documents for the Bay, always spelled by the French Gabori or Gabarus, seems to have come from the " little knowledge " of the " linguisters " of the expedition, who would be more familiar with the spoken than the written name. The local pronunciation of Mainadieu preserves its more ancient form of spelling Menadou.

[2] M.H.S. vol. 10, pp. 108 and 114.   [3] *Eltham, Rippon's Prize.*

Shirley applied to the Commodore of the station for assistance,[1] sending a dispatch to him to the West Indies, where the fleet was then cruising. This officer was Peter Warren, a native of County Meath, who had entered the navy at fifteen as an ordinary seaman. His professional advancement was rapid and at forty-two he found himself a Commodore, somewhat broken in health, and anxious to obtain an appointment as Governor of the Jerseys or to reach the "pinickle" of his ambition by succeeding Clinton as Governor of New York. Mrs. Warren, a native of New York, did not care for the "Beau Mund," so that at this time he looked forward to retiring from the sea and spending the remainder of his days, if a Governor's chair were denied him, on a property he owned at Greenwich, Long Island.[2] Notwithstanding these views, he had applied in September for command of all ships in North America, which was given to him.[3] Before he received Shirley's letter the project of an expedition against Louisbourg was familiar to him. As already stated, he also wrote about it to Corbett, Secretary of the Navy,[4] and to his friend the Hon. Geo. Anson, then Lord of the Admiralty, with whom, notwithstanding the differences in social and professional rank, he was on terms of frank intimacy. Warren was fully alive to the importance of reducing the French power, and set forth clearly in a letter to Anson its many advantages. He goes on :

"Yet I think it wou'd be in vain to attempt Lewisbourg, without a moral Certainty of Success. As it is a very regular fortification, and has always a Strong Garrison of regular troops in it, I submit whether it is not likely, that it will hold out a Siege longer than the season will allow the Besiegers (if not numerous enough to take it by storm) to keep the Field, and what can they do in that case in the winter ?—It is certain if Ships go into the Harbour to attack it the people must determine to Succeed or dye. Where that is the case, there shou'd be (I believe the world will allow) a Strong possibility of Success.

"What I have here sett forth, being granted, how is it to be effected ? What number of ships from England of Regular troops or artillery and other Ordnance Stores will be necessary ? And what quantity of Provisions, and other Stores, of all kinds, will be proper for such an undertaking ? And what part will the Colonies themselves take in such an attempt ? Whether they will assist in it heart and hand ? What assistance, and in what Shape, will each different Government that is willing to assist give its assistance. Whether in Money, Shipping, Men or Provisions ?

"By forming all this into a proper plan, it will not be very hard to judge of the probability of succeeding, or not, in such an attempt. And the formation of it previous to the Execution, cannot be any Expense to Great Britain, or the Colonies. And when it is form'd, and approv'd, then let it be Executed with all the Intrepidity, that becomes good Officers, and Men, both of Sea and Land.

[1] Jan. 29, Ad. Sec., In Letters, No. 3817. He also asked assistance from Sir Challoner Ogle and Admiral Darvers, who replied in the negative (Ad. Sec., In Letters, vol. 233).

[2] In an article on Greenwich Village by T. A. Janvier, *Harper's Magazine*, Aug. 1893, is a pleasant account of Warren's life there.

[3] In Letters, 2654 ; Out Letters, 486.   [4] Sept. 8, 1744, from New York (Ad. Sec., In Letters, vol. 2654.

" But to undertake an affair of such consequence and Expence, too rashly, that must, if they fail in it, Involve both England and the Colonies, in a large debt to no purpose, I think wou'd be madness, both in the Advisers, and the Executors, of such an attempt.

"What you mention with regard to an Expedition in Embrio against Cape Britton, is what I have long consider'd as of the greatest consequence to our Country, this my good friend Mr. Corbet and myself have exchang'd some private letters upon, and I have, tho' in a very Inaccurate manner, formerly run over some of the benefits that wou'd accrue from it, and some steps necessary to be taken previous to the attempt, which I beg leave to address to you, for your Private and Candid opinion, as the Inaccuracy of it will not bear the light, tho' the matter, if well digested, is worthy of the Ministrys most serious deliberation.

" What the event will be of Mr. Shirleys scheme, who is a very worthy man, I won't take upon me to prejudge, but when time lets me more into it, you shall know.

" I beg leave to assure you, nothing shall be wanting on my part, so farr as I have power or Capacity to serve my King and Country, and I am persuaded, I can do it in no shape better, than in that scheme, if attended with success, and I have none more at heart, tho' I cou'd have pitch'd upon none attended with a prospect of greater uneasyness, and less personal advantage, I mean where Booty is esteem'd so, which I hope will never be so with me." [1]

Shirley's letter to Warren, dated January 29, went over much the same ground as his dispatch to Newcastle of February 1, but dwelt, as was natural, on the military aspect of the expedition, and clearly set forth the importance of the naval assistance, which he assumed Warren would send. " I must acknowledge that the hopes I have Entertained of it have been of no small Encouragement to me in forming this Expedition." He goes on then with the arts of the politician, displayed as in the case of Wentworth, to say, "and if the service in which you are engaged would permit you to come yourself and take upon you the command of the Expedition, it would, I doubt not, be a most happy event for His Majesty's service and your own honour." [2] Two fifty or forty gun ships in March were what Shirley asked for, or even one, and with Warren to follow with his force, Shirley was persuaded the place might be taken in May, or invested until help from England could be received in June.[3] This letter found Warren in trouble, his effective force diminished by the loss of the

---

[1] B.M. Add. MSS., 15,957, f. 152.

[2] Shirley's care to placate all who could help him makes inexplicable to the writer his springing the project on the Assembly.

Shirley, had he to deal with a touchier man than Pepperrell, might again have gratuitously created embarrassment as in the case of Wentworth. He placed himself in a position to make trouble with Pepperrell and with Warren. He wrote to the former, April 22: "I doubt not, Sir, from the extraordinary conduct and vigilance with which you have hitherto acted for His Majesty's service, that you will instantly give orders to Tyng and the other cruisers to follow the Commodore's directions and orders to them, and omitting of which may create a most unhappy disagreement and variance between you and Mr. Warren, which may prove fatal to the service. Had I not received these precise orders from his Majesty, which so evidently give Mr. Warren a general command at sea, in all expeditions from hence, I should have insisted upon my command given you over the sea forces (which, as it is, is only suspended during Capt. Warren's presence, and would revive upon his going off) against every person whatsoever, and you must be sensible that this is not a preference given to him by me, but only acting in obedience to his Majesty's orders" (M.H.S. 1, p. 19, Shirley to Pepperrell).

[3] Ad. Sec., In Letters, No. 3817.

Weymouth. Warren consulted his captains,[1] who unanimously reported that the proper course for Warren was to send the North American ships to their stations, the *Mermaid* to New York, and the *Launceston* to New England, and to forward Shirley's letter to the Admiralty by an express; and that, until receipt of a reply, Warren should not alter the ordinary course of proceeding, but remain cruising in the West Indies. The grounds for this decision were that the expedition had not received his Majesty's approbation, nor had they received orders thereon from the Admiralty; that taking the ships off their stations would greatly weaken the British West Indies, at a time when a report was current that a French squadron was expected shortly at Martinique, "*and can be of no great service in such an undertaking.*"

This italicized expression of opinion is so extraordinary over the signatures of the captains of a naval squadron, that it must be interpreted in the light of Warren's opinions that Louisbourg was a strong place, defended by a garrison of regular troops, with no convenient anchorage in the vicinity for ships of war and transports, that the expedition had been hastily planned, and might be abandoned before they arrived,[2] so that the opinion was held by them that it was foredoomed to failure. It has never been the opinion of seamen that in conjoint expeditions their branch was of lesser importance. Warren gave orders to the *Launceston* and *Mermaid* to go north, and was on the point of setting out on a cruise when Capt. Innis arrived in the sloop *Hind*.[3] He had been dispatched from England, early in January, with orders for Warren, which, if he were in danger of capture, he was instructed to sink.[4]

The instructions in the usual sources[5] contain only Warren's commission as Commander-in-Chief, for which he had asked power to hold court-martials and warrants to impress seamen; but Warren's letter speaks of definite orders to proceed with *Launceston, Mermaid, Weymouth,* and *Hastings* to Boston. Corbett, Secretary to the Admiralty, in sending these documents[6] heartily wishes him success in all his operations against the enemy. The colonial Governors were advised by Newcastle that Warren had been ordered to go northwards to protect the colonies and fisheries, and, "as occasion shall offer, attack and distress the enemy in their settlements, and annoy their fisheries and commerce."[7] This we may take as the substance of the orders which Warren received, for his intention, when he left Antigua on March 13, was to act in concert with Clinton and Shirley. He took for his flagship the *Superbe,* which gave great offence to Knowles, her former captain, his irascible and influential second, from which Warren feared disagreeable consequences. He sailed for Boston with

---

[1] Feb. 23, 1744/45, Harbour Antigua.   [2] Warren, March 10/45, In Letters.
[3] March 8.   [4] Out Letters, 486 and 63, f. 55.
[5] Ad. Sec., Out Letters, vol. 486 and 63, also the Newcastle correspondence in the British Museum.
[6] Jan. 4., Ad. Sec., Out Letters, 486.   [7] R.I. Doc. vol. 5, p. 132, Shirley, April 3; C.O. 5/809.

her, the *Launceston*, and *Mermaid*, on March 13, in company with two small armed vessels and ten sail of merchantmen.[1]

If Warren's preliminary views were cautious his actions were eager. Unless his instructions were more definite than those of which records are extant, he interpreted them in the widest sense, and put into adequate action the opinions he had a few days before expressed to his friend. " These are considerations worthy of a discreet Officer, who should not, but upon the best grounds, attempt to put his Country to Expence, and probably himself to shame. When these difficulty's that occur to such an Officer are obviated, by the Sound reasoning of others, or by Self conviction, he will then go on with becoming Vigour and Gallantry, that cannot fail to have a good effect upon all that serve under his command." His fleet fell in, on April 10, with a schooner from Marblehead, " who Informed us that a Fleet of 63 Sail had sailed 14 days on Sunday last with 5000 Men for Canso under the Command of ' Generall Pepperall.' "[2] Warren took the master on board to act as pilot, as he was unfamiliar with the waters,[3] and proceeded direct to Canso. He sent word to Shirley of his course, greatly to his relief,[4] for Warren's refusal to join the expedition had been communicated by the former only to Pepperrell and one or two important people. Shirley had, however, pushed on with his preparations, amid difficulties and delays. At last he saw the troops gathered together and embarked on the transports, which with the armed vessels lay in Nantasket Road, whence, much to the relief of the wearied Governor, the Massachusetts contingent sailed on March 24 for Canso, which had been selected as their base.

Warren also gave instructions to Captain Durell of the *Eltham*, which had wintered in Boston, to act as convoy to mast ships from Piscataqua. On the 16th of April the ships he was to protect had dropped down the river, and the next day they all were actually under way when Warren's orders arrived,[5] so " that 5 minutes delay would have put him out of our reach." Durell's account is, " Just as I was ready to sail with the Mast Ships from New England to return Home I received orders from Commodore Warren to join him off this Harbour (Canso), which commands were so agreeable that I made all despatch possible."[6]

Newcastle's response to the representations of Shirley, and others which have been noted, did not stop with sending Warren for the defence of the Northern Colonies. When he was informed of the Louisbourg expedition, he sent out

---

[1] His letter of March 10.   [2] R.O. Logs, vol. 820.   [3] He had been once there in the *Squirrel*.

[4] Shirley in a speech, April 17, thus acknowledged Warren's action : " The cheerfulness and zeal with which Mr. Warren undertakes this Service, & the great Concern he had for the success of it, & the Prosperity of these Provinces . . . greatly recommends him to our respect & affections." £50 worth of live stock were presented to Warren by the Assembly of Massachusetts as a token of respect (C.O. 5/809).

[5] M.H.S. vol. 10, p. 129.   [6] A Particular Account.

with the utmost dispatch no less than eight men-of-war to augment Warren's force before Louisbourg and as guardships.[1]

The vigour of Pitt had been so often contrasted with the sloth of Newcastle, that it is interesting to note that in this matter Newcastle's Government acted with the greatest promptness. Captain Joshua Loring arrived in London with four letters of Shirley's [2] on March 16. The Admiralty met at once, ordered the *Hector* and *Princess Mary* to sea to assist Warren, and sent Loring, who had only been in London a few hours, with the express " at half-past midnight " to return to Cape Breton on the *Princess Mary*.[3]

After a passage,[4] which the General describes as "rough and somewhat tedious," the Massachusetts contingent arrived at Canso on the 4th of April, where the New Hampshire troops had landed on the 1st. The day after landing Pepperrell called together his Council of War, which, even without any representatives of Connecticut, had seventeen members present. He submitted to them the instructions he had received, and the army was divided into four sections, to land at a selected point on Gabarus Bay, three miles from the town and four from the Grand Battery. Canso was seen to be a suitable place. A blockhouse, brought with them ready framed, was erected, armed with eight-pounders, and called " Cumberland " in honour of that Royal Duke. It was resolved to push on to Gabarus Bay with the first favourable wind and weather, although the train of artillery and part of the troops had not arrived.

A projected attack on St. Peter's, about eighteen miles across the Bay, was deferred, but the expedition to cut off the vessels with provisions believed to be at Baie Verte was sent out. The ice on the coast fortunately prevented them from pushing on to Louisbourg without artillery, and with their provision vessels, so uncertain in their arrival, owing to the prevailing winds, that Pepperrell writes on the 10th " that they soon would be put in greater danger of famine than sword." Their two principal cruisers, the *Massachusetts* and the *Shirley*, had provisions for only ten days, and, by computation, the army only for a month. This was a situation serious enough to justify Pepperrell's appeal for help to the Chairman of the War Committee. But the activity of their cruisers brought some aid : two vessels with rum and molasses, both valuable commodities to their army, were captured and brought to Canso. Captain Tyng and the other armed vessels had been sent to cruise off Louisbourg. There they had a running fight with a French frigate, the *Renommée*, Captain Kersaint, which left France for Cadiz on the 7th of February, where she waited

---

[1] These vessels were the *Lark, Hector, Princess Mary, Princess Louisa, Canterbury, Chester, Sunderland,* and *Wager* (Ad. Sec., Out Letters, vol. 63).

[2] 5-9-14th Jan., 1st Feb.   [3] C.O. 5/900 ; Ad. Sec., Out Letters, 50, 63.

[4] " Our men was exeding sick and did vomet very much as they would Dy the seas running mountaining," is the account of another diarist.

until the 10th of March, and after crossing the Atlantic had this encounter in the fog and ice off Louisbourg. She then cruised to the westward. On the Cape Sable shore she fell in with the seven transports carrying the Connecticut troops under the convoy of the Connecticut sloop and the *Tartar* belonging to Rhode Island. The ever-active Shirley had suggested that the *Tartar* should make the voyage with the Connecticut forces as a safeguard. It was fortunate that his proposal was accepted, for Fones, her captain, was a bold and skilful sailor. He led Kersaint to chase him away from the little fleet, which reached Canso in safety, and having accomplished this, the *Tartar* escaped from the frigate after nightfall.[1] Kersaint then proceeded to the Baie des Castors in Acadia, and after remaining there attempted to make Louisbourg, but was driven off by contrary winds, and then returned to Brest on June 19.[2]

The situation was changed on the 22nd by the arrival of the *Eltham*, followed the next day by Warren and his other ships. No time was lost in visits or exchange of courtesies between the Commanders. Letters passed between them, and Warren sailed at once to blockade Louisbourg. The Connecticut contingent reached Canso on the 25th. With the forces thus complete, the first part of the movement had been carried through with remarkable celerity. They were in possession of their base ; their armed vessels were off Louisbourg ; the provincials were on the eve of putting to the test the value of their preparations and the steadfastness and skill of the officers and men.

APPENDIX

GOVERNOR WANTON TO THE AGENT OF RHODE ISLAND IN LONDON

NEWPORT, ON RHODE ISLAND, *Xber* 20, 1745.

Sir : The conduct of this colony relating to the Cape Breton expedition having been, as your letters advise, very unjustly misrepresented at home, with a view to prejudice the ministry against us, the General Assembly have directed that a true account thereof should be transmitted to you, which, we doubt not, will enable you fully to vindicate our colony, which hath always distinguished itself by joining with readiness and zeal in all expeditions ordered by the crown.

---

[1] R.I. Rec. vol. 5, p. 138 and 155.

[2] A.M.B.[4] vol. 56, p. 228, and vol. 57, p. 291, contain the précis of this voyage, and that of De Salvert's squadron, which returned to Brest on the 12th of October. The latter took some prizes, among them the *Prince of Orange*, from whom they learned of the fall of Louisbourg, and the large fleet on the coast of Isle Royale. De Salvert attempted to meet the vessels of the India Company, but in bad weather and fog missed them all. He made for Newfoundland on his return to France, in which two of his ships were dismasted. The documents themselves are wanting, so that this is the little information which can be given of the French expedition to relieve Louisbourg. From a captured letter we learn that Du Vivier had come on De Salvert's squadron, and had been placed by him in command (although he had never been at sea) of the frigate *Le Parfait*. He took *The Two Friends*, which was again recaptured off Louisbourg (Ad. Sec., In Letters, No. 2655).

The reduction of Louisbourg, we always thought, would be of very great importance, as well to the trade and commerce of Great Britain, as of the northern plantations, and therefore expected and hoped it would be undertaken at home in the course of the war ; but we judged the attempt to reduce that prodigiously strong town, regularly fortified, and furnished with a garrison of regular forces, to be much too hazardous, as well as too expensive for New England, as not having one officer of experience or even an engineer, and the people being entirely ignorant in the art of encamping and besieging towns, and were therefore greatly surprised at hearing that the Province of the Massachusetts had voted to make said attempt.

At first, while it was supposed that Governor Shirley had secret instructions to raise men, and an assurance of a sufficient addition of sea and land forces from Great Britain, our people were zealous in the affair ; but when it was known that he had no orders at all, not so much as a discretionary power to stop some of His Majesty's ships then at Boston, a thing of the last importance to the blocking up the harbour of Louisbourg, no assurance that the ministry would approve of the undertaking, or make any provision to support it, or that the state of affairs in Europe would permit the sending such a force from Great Britain, as seemed necessary, to render the expedition successful, surely, 'tis no wonder that our zeal abated, and that we were not very forward to precipitate an attempt, in which a failure must needs have been a fatal consequence, as it would have exposed the weakness of the northern plantations, and disabled them from assisting, if the crown should think fit to order such an expedition ; that the Massachusetts themselves were very doubtful of success, cannot be denied, for the undertaking of the expedition was carried but by one single voice, in their house of representatives.

. . . But notwithstanding all this, the General Assembly voted to send our colony sloop well manned, permitted the Governor of Boston to endeavour to raise men in the pay of the Province, and voted an additional bounty of forty shillings a man to induce them to list, but to no effect.

On further application to us in March last, the General Assembly voted to raise three companies of fifty men each, exclusive of officers ; and offered a large pay, and a higher bounty than the Province of Massachusetts had given ; but it being found impracticable to fill the companies in season, the then Governor, after we have been at a considerable expense, ordered the men that were raised to be disbanded. However, our colony's sloop, mounting fourteen carriage and twelve swivel guns, well fitted and manned, convoyed the Connecticut forces, and proved of singular service, by preventing their entire ruin from a French two-and-thirty gun ship ; and afterwards in the Gut of Canso, by repelling, in conjunction with two other cruisers, a large body of French and Indians, who were going to the relief of Louisbourg.

. . . In May, we had advice that the ministry approved of the expedition, and that Commodore Warren was arrived off Louisbourg with a squadron of His Majesty's ships. The General Assembly did then renew their vote to raise three companies ; and that it might be effectual, increased the bounty, and raised the pay to £10 per month a man, double of what the Massachusetts allowed theirs. But to complete said companies (we) were notwithstanding obliged to order that men should be impressed into the service, as several actually were ; a thing not done by order of Assembly in any other part of New England, and scarce ever practised here before ; and on notice that seamen were wanted to man the ship *Vigilant*, voted to raise two hundred, allowing a bounty of £17 to a man. But such was the scarcity of men, that though the bounty was so large, and the most effectual means used (for we had again recourse to impressing, and allowed said bounty even to the impressed men), that we could raise only about seventy. The good news of the surrender of Louisbourg had reached Boston before our transports sailed from thence, having lain there some days for convoy ; yet they proceeded (on) the voyage, and are now in garrison ; and we have lately sent a vessel to Louisbourg, with clothing and provisions sufficient for their support till late in the spring.

This is the assistance we have given, which was really the utmost we were able to give, the colony having never exerted itself with more zeal and vigour on any occasion ; and it ought to be observed, that no other of the neighbouring governments, besides Connecticut and New Hampshire, could be induced, at the first, to give any assistance at all ; nor afterwards, of all of them together, to give so much and such effectual assistance, as this little colony cheerfully afforded, at the hazard of leaving our sea coast unguarded, and our navigation exposed to the enemy's privateers, from the beginning of April to the latter end of October, during which time our colony's sloop was in the service.[1]

[1] Rhode Island Colonial Records, vol. 5, pp. 145-147.

CHAPTER X

PEPPERRELL had many causes for anxiety. His stores were inadequate, and many of the small arms were in bad order. Rioting had taken place at Canso, so he had to find, and did fïnd, that middle way between a severity to which his levies would not submit, and a laxity perilous to the success of the expedition. The detachment which was sent against St. Peter's had acted without dash, "which party returned without success, not having carefully conformed to their orders, for landing in whale boats by night, and finding there several vessels, which though of no force, yet well manned for trade, and a number of Indians being alarmed ; their whole force appeared so considerable, that our party did not think it safe to land."[1]

These were indications that neither his materials nor his men would stand much strain ; and yet his officers had urged him to push on to Louisbourg without waiting for the transports laden with his artillery. The ice on the Cape Breton coast made impossible this advance. The vessels with this part of his armament had arrived before the sea cleared. As soon as navigation to the eastward became practicable, the movement on Louisbourg began. The expedition started from Canso early on the morning of the 29th of April. That day, the most warm and pleasant since their arrival at Canso, opened with light winds, which, after a calm, rose again to a gentle breeze from the north-west. It, being a fair wind, enabled the fleet of about one hundred vessels to reach along the coast to their appointed position in Gabarus Bay. Here, after passing Warren's cruising ships, they arrived in the morning of Tuesday the thirtieth.[2]

Du Chambon had been in doubt as to what was going on, or perhaps was in that frame of mind which tries not to see indications of a crisis to which he felt himself unequal. The vessels in the offing, and reports that there was unusual activity at Canso, were disquieting. But the former, it was hoped,

---

[1] Pepperrell to Shirley, Massachusetts Historical Society vol. 1, p. 24.

[2] The large map of this siege can be used with great advantage in following its course. Its comparison with written accounts shows its substantial accuracy.

It is necessary to collate the letters which passed between the officers and the minutes of the Council of War. The latter and some of the letters are in Massachusetts Historical Society, sixth series, vol. 10. Other letters are in vol. 1 of its first series. These are referred to as vol. 1 and vol. 10.

might be the succour from home for which they had asked ; the latter the carrying out of English plans for the fortification of Canso, of which they had knowledge.   He ordered Benoit in command at Port Toulouse (St. Peter's) to ascertain what was going on.   The latter sent out a civilian, an Indian, and a soldier, who captured four of the enemy.   These in turn overpowered their captors, and brought the Frenchmen in as prisoners, the Indian having escaped.[1]

The miscarriage of this scout left Du Chambon still uncertain.   Nor could the people of Louisbourg tell the nationalities of the combatants, in seeing from the land the running fight between the *Renommée* and the provincial cruisers. There was little room left for doubt when a vessel from St. Jean de Luz arrived safely, and reported that on the 25th she had exchanged three broadsides with the enemy.   Whatever uncertainty still existed in their minds was dispelled by the capture of three coasting boats.[2]

Du Chambon, thus driven from the position that there was no cause for alarm, in conjunction with Bigot, sent word to France of their condition.[3]   The *Société* slipped successfully through the blockade, and bore to the court their evil tidings, which falsified the optimistic previsions of Maurepas.   The preparations for defence which Du Chambon had made in the autumn seem to have been held in abeyance by the mutiny of the garrison.   Officials, officers, and townspeople feared the purpose of the troops was to deliver the place without striking a blow, so its condition was one of suspended animation.   The conduct of the soldiery during the winter had been orderly.   When the crisis came it was spirited.   Du Chambon and Bigot appealed to their patriotism, and promised, in the name of the King, a pardon for their past offences.   The troops responded to their appeal, returned to their duty, and behaved well during the siege.[4]

Although arrangements had been made for calling in the people of the outlying settlement of Baleine and Lorambec, who joined the townspeople in a militia for its defence, there seems to have been no settled plan of action in event of these threatening appearances proving to be the prelude of an attack.

Du Chambon was Governor by accident.   Neither Chateaugué, appointed to succeed Du Quesnel, nor De Salvert, his substitute, had been able to reach Louisbourg.   Du Chambon was inexperienced.   Neither he nor any of the officers of the troops had even been in action, so that this siege is the culminating event of that warfare of amateurs which began at Canso a year earlier.   The New Englanders at least made plans ; Du Chambon seems to have been incapable of

[1] Mass. Hist. Soc. vol. 1, p. 23 ; Que. Hist. Mass. vol. 3, p. 238.   [2] One was a large sloop loaded with game.

[3] Bigot does not seem to have been in doubt.

[4] Bigot says none deserted.   This is almost literally true, there were only two desertions.   The promise of pardon was repudiated after the return of the garrison to France.   Certain of the soldiers were executed.   The alleged ringleader had died in prison.   Bigot made a statement in favour of the soldiers, which the court-martial did not admit (Colonies, B, vol. 82).   Bigot, however, wrote to the Minister, Oct. 9, 1745, taking a different view.   He said, it is of the utmost importance to the colonies that an example be made (" Qu'on fasse un exemple d'une pareille sédition ").

foresight. His disastrous lack of judgment was shown in his dealing with the force of Marin. This officer had been sent with a strong detachment from Quebec for a winter journey to Acadia, there to act against Annapolis or to help Louisbourg. It left on January 15. Du Chambon informed Marin in April that it was unnecessary for him to come to Louisbourg. He consequently attacked Annapolis. It was not until the provincial artillery had begun to fire on the town, May 5, that Du Chambon attempted to avail himself of this reinforcement. At this late day, Du Chambon sent a messenger on the long journey to Annapolis. Marin set out, penetrated to Isle Royale, after an encounter with provincial cruisers in the Gut of Canso, and arrived too late to be of any help.[1]

It was not until the French saw from the ramparts on the morning of the 30th a disembarkation begun, its boats moving towards two points, one near, the other much more to the westward of Flat Point, that the question of resistance was raised. Two civilians were the spokesmen of those who desired action. One was the retired officer of the Regiment de Richelieu, de la Boularderie, who, on hearing of the cruisers off the port, had come in an open boat from his estate at Petit Bras d'Or. Morpain, now port captain, but at the beginning of the century a privateer of Port Royale, was the other.

De la Boularderie said that, under cover of the woods, a force could advance within half a pistol-shot of the beach ; that half of the garrison should be sent out to fall on the enemy, who would be in that confusion which always attends landings ; that they would be chilled from exposure, and that they were, moreover, but poor creatures (" misérables "). Morpain recounted his exploits in 1707 and appealed to Du Chambon to give him leave to go out with those of the towns-people who were willing. Du Chambon, who had taken the view that he had no men to spare, at last gave way. Fifty civilian volunteers and twenty-four soldiers, the latter under Mesillac Du Chambon, the Governor's son, the youngest officer of the garrison, set forth from the town with vague instructions and under uncertain command.

When they were about half-way across the marsh, Boularderie thought the attempt was hopeless, as fifteen hundred men had landed and were taking regular formation. Morpain was for keeping on. Marching in solid formation, they came under the fire of the ships,[2] and alarmed the landed troops. The French had reached a depression when the enemy closed in on them. Morpain, heedless of De la Boularderie's expostulations, withdrew all the men except twelve soldiers. These momentarily withstood the provincial attack made in

---

[1] The first news they received in Quebec of the fall of Louisbourg was from the younger Marin, who was dispatched by his father with this disappointing intelligence (MSS. Que. vol. 3, p. 217).

[2] " We were covered in our landing by Fletcher, Bush, and Saunders, who fired their cannon smartly on the enemy " (Pepperrell's Journal).

overwhelming force. De la Boularderie was twice wounded and surrendered, five of the soldiers were wounded, but escaped, and seven were killed. Morpain was wounded, but watched over by a faithful negro slave, was later brought into the town.[1] The losses were trifling : only two or three provincials wounded, and on the French side sixteen or seventeen killed and wounded. From the English accounts there does not appear to have been the delay of which the French speak, nor the number of men landed at the time the attempt at a repulse was made.

The provincial troops, after dispersing this tardy and ill-led expedition, were emboldened to advance freely. In a few hours irregular groups of them emerged from the woods overlooking the town, in which their exultant cheering could be heard. Order was maintained among some others, for regular squads advanced through the woods, and came into the open in the neighbourhood of the Grand Battery.

Two thousand were landed before nightfall, and the work of encamping was begun. The site of the camp was on either side of a small brook which runs into Gabarus Bay, between Flat Point and the boggy plain which stretches to the outworks of the fortress. The land is dry, and the wisdom of Pepperrell's officers is shown by the fact that Amherst's engineers in 1758 found no better place for the encampment of a much larger force.[2]

While morning of this day brought to Du Chambon these perplexities, the evening brought another, of no less moment. This was the report of Chassin de Thierry, Captain in command of the Grand Battery, that, in his opinion, the post was not tenable. He proposed to blow it up, as it would be of great value to the enemy, and spike the cannon. A council of war was held, and the opinion of the engineer, Verrier, confirmed Thierry's statement. At its best, the fort was commanded by higher ground ; in its present state, difficult to defend, for on the landward side its defences had been levelled preparatory to their repair. The council without a dissenting voice voted for its abandonment, and, with the exception of Verrier, thought that it should be blown up. His protests against the destruction of the work were so vigorous that the point was given up, and Thierry was ordered to spike the guns and withdraw his men and as many provisions and warlike stores as he could bring away. This he did with such haste that the guns were not properly spiked, and the garrison was back in the town about midnight. A detachment had to be sent to complete the evacuation. Other detachments, on the 1st and 2nd

---

[1] Morpain set free the man as a reward. Boularderie was taken to Boston, made a good impression on its authorities and people, took charge of the other prisoners, and left for France with a certificate that he had behaved like a gentleman, and was of great service to the prisoners. This was signed and sealed on September 2 by various distinguished gentlemen, among whom were members of Council and B. Pemberton, its Secretary (C[11], Canada, vol. 87).

[2] The earthworks which enclosed the latter camp are still quite visible.

of May, sunk at their moorings the vessels near the town, those at the head of the harbour, and brought away from the lighthouse its supply of oil. A third force, a mixed detachment of French and Swiss, protected those who demolished the houses between the Dauphin Gate and the Barachois, and while at this work beat off an attack.

The disembarkation was completed on the 1st, but for a fortnight the troops, landing stores and artillery on an exposed shore in cold and foggy weather, and in bringing the artillery over rocks, through woods and bogs, suffered the severest hardships. They worked so effectively that, on the fifth day after the descent, a battery was in position opposite the citadel at a distance of 1550 yards, and then opened fire on the town.

On the night of the 1st a strong detachment marched through the woods and destroyed the houses at the head of the harbour. The next morning, William Vaughan, returning from this expedition, reconnoitred the silent Grand Battery, and, preceded by an Indian, entered its court and found it deserted, a condition which scarcely justifies the opening of his letter to Pepperrell:

"May it pleasure your Honour, to be informed yt with ye grace of God and ye courage of about thirteen men I entred this place about nine a clock and am waiting here for a reinforcemen^t and flag." [1]

Another account speaks of this event from a different standpoint, and incidentally illustrates the conditions of the troops in these early days.

"This Morning we had an alarm in the Camp suposing there was a Salley from the town against us We Ran to meet them but found ourselves Mistaken: I had a Great Mind to se the Grand Battery So with five other of our Company I went towards it and as I was a Going about Thirty more fell in with us; we Came in ye Back of a hil within Long Muskitt Shot and fired att ye s^d fort & finding no Resistance I was Minded to Go & Did with about a Duzen men setting a Gard to ye Norward Should We Be asolted who Espied two french men whom we Imeadately Took Prisners with two women & a Child then we went in after some others to ye s^d Grand fort & found itt Desarted." [2]

Before Vaughan was reinforced, he beat off four boat-loads of men, covered by the fire of the town and island batteries. Colonel Bradstreet was sent with a reinforcement, and began at once getting the guns into order, in which he was so successful that the next day, the 3rd of May, at noon, one gun had fired on the town, and a second was in service at seven the same evening. This, Colonel Waldo, who had taken over the command, reports with satisfac-

---

[1] Vol. 10, p. 138.
[2] Gidding's Journal, Essex Inst. vol. 48. The "some others" I take to be the men under Vaughan.

tion, and enlivens his letter to the General by a jest in the manner of the times over the poor quality of the bombs fired at them by the French.

His regiment continued to garrison this fort, and the artillery officers soon had enough cannon drilled and in service against the town to amply justify, by the effects of their fire, the view of the importance of this position held by the planners of the expedition. Waldo made daily reports to Pepperrell while he was at the Grand Battery, in which the most striking feature was the constant clamour for rum. Day after day it was asked for, and it was not quantity alone, for in one letter they beg for French rather than the home-made drink. The quantity required apparently seemed excessive to the Commissariat, for Waldo writes :

" The short supply of rum, the severall Captains tell me, is of prejudice to the people. Should one from the dead tell the soldiery anything, in the prejudice of it, 'twould have no weight." [1]

In warlike stores the supply was short. Waldo was constantly on the point of being left without powder, and feared at one time that their battery would have to be silent, which he felt sure would lead to a revival of the drooping spirits of the besieged, and possibly to an attempt to retake it.[2] He reported that its cannon were twenty-eight of 42 pounds and two of 18 pounds, " as good pieces as we could desire. I fear the only badd quality in them will be in the opinion of our principalls that they devour too much powder." He wrote to Pepperrell that his men were poor, and " we are in great want of good gunners that have a disposition to be sober in the daytime " ; and again, that he would answer for the flag provided he had men and good officers. " Three fourths of the men which you apprehend . . . are here are partly employed in speculation on the neighbouring hills and partly employed in ravaging the country."

While the excessively arduous work of establishing batteries and serving them was going on, it is evident from the journals of individuals, that the troops were not all engaged in this legitimate work, but parties of them went out on expeditions, the purpose of which was plunder and destruction of property, as well as taking prisoners. It is quite evident from the numbers taken, either that, owing to the short notice given by signals, all the inhabitants of the outports did not come in, or that people of the town passed to and from their properties on the shores of the harbour. The scanty records show that both the dwellers in the environs, and those who left the town, fell into the hands of these roving bands, who apparently had at best no other commission than the permission of

---

[1] Vol. 10, p. 158.

[2] One diarist notes that a sermon was preached on the morning of the 5th in the chapel of the Grand Battery from the text : " Enter into his gates with thanksgiving, and into his courts with praise."

their regimental officers. The records of one diarist[1] begin on the day of landing with the capture of five cows, from which, as only three of them were killed, follows in natural sequence, that he breakfasted the next morning on milk. Horses and cattle were both taken and killed; houses were plundered. Forty-eight hours later he says again, that "our men keep continually plundering," and on the first Sunday they were on shore, May 5, he records that one of the General's men killed himself with drink in a house he was looting. The same day two unhappy Frenchmen, clearly non-combatants, for they were carrying their goods from the city to a hiding-place in the woods, were killed by a party numbering a score. Their boat-loads of property and two bags of gold became a richer booty to a more unscrupulous squad than was usual. Another writer, in recounting the events of May 2, says, "and after that (we) took the grand Batry and several cows and horses and sum plunder viz. sum pots sum kitles sum grid irons sum one thing and sum another."[2] The value of the spoils impressed the enemy. Gibson later describes handsome farms on the Miré. It is said that in one house, burned at St. Peter's, there were 1000 bushels of wheat,[3] and more than once the good looks of the women captured are mentioned, "4 of which is hansom ladeys,"[4] but it was not always so easy as in these instances.

Friday 10, Gibson's Journal:

"A small scout of twenty-five men got to the north-east harbour. I and four more being in a house upon plunder, 140 French and Indians came down upon us first, and fired a volley, with a great noise. Two jumped out of the window and were shot dead. With great difficulty the other two and myself got safe to the grand battery. They afterwards killed nineteen of the remaining twenty."[5]

The authorities were seriously concerned about this plundering. Waldo wrote to Pepperrell soon after he went to the Grand Battery:

"I fear yr Honr will be under necessity of appointing a moroding officer with ye powers, & without it, should an obstinate siege be our portion, a train of ill consequence must ensue which I doubt not you'll be pleased to consider of."

Pepperrell was evidently determined to arrange some means of dealing with the matter, for he wrote to Warren the same day:

"The unaccountable irregular behaviour of these fellows (the masters of transports) ot some moroders is the greatest fatigue I meet with; hope to reduce them to a better discipline soon."

War is a cruel thing even with a disciplined army; with irregular troops it

---

[1] Bradstreet.   [2] Giddings, p. 6.   [3] From French sources there is no evidence of such abundance.
[4] Vol. 10, p. 155.
[5] The next day forty prisoners were taken by the force which set out to bury the dead. It made a clean sweep of the place, chapel, fish stages, and a hundred fishing-boats.

is a scourge to the people of the invaded territory. Neither Pepperrell's correspondence, nor the journal of the Council of War, shows what measures were
taken, but the later entries of the diarists narrate no such barbarities on the part
of the provincials as the records of the earliest days.[1]

Having abandoned a surprise on the town, in the securing of the Grand
Battery, and the encampment of the army, Pepperrell had carried out in the
main the instructions of Shirley. He was left, supported by his Council, to
devise further action ; except in one respect, the destruction of all French
property. This work was steadily prosecuted, until in three or four weeks,
either by land expeditions or the forces of Warren, no hamlet or settlement on
the island was left unravaged.

The question of sending a summons to Du Chambon was the first considered
by the Council on the 3rd. The matter was under consideration intermittently
until the 7th, when it was decided on. Some of the seniors, among them
Waldo, held that Du Chambon would be justified in hanging the bearer of their
message, "unless we had made a more formidable genl. appearance than we
have yet been able to make."[2]

The Council took up the erection of batteries. Beginning at the Green
Hill, these were pushed forward with a celerity which was possible only among a
force made up of men, some with the dexterity of seafarers, others with that of
woodsmen accustomed to handle mast timber from the stump in the forests of
New Hampshire to its berth in the vessel. By the 20th, a fifth battery,
sweeping across the little Barachois, completed the attack against the fortifications towards their northern end, where the ground was most suitable for these
operations and an assault. (The boggy grounds south of the citadel protected
the place from attack on that side.) Other projects against the town were considered and attempted. Warren proposed an operation against the Island
Battery, which guarded the mouth of the harbour. It was tried unsuccessfully,
as the boats withdrew on account of the surf. It was determined in the Council
on the 9th to storm the town that night. When news of the decision spread
through the camp, so much dissatisfaction was expressed that a hastily
summoned meeting of Council was held in the afternoon, and abandoned the
project. There were seventeen members present in the morning and six in
the afternoon. The latter passed the following :

"Advised, that in as much as there appears a great dissatisfaction in many of the
officers & soldiers at the design'd attack of the town by storm this night, and as it may

---

[1] The only officer whose diary shows any sympathy with plundering was Gibson, who was not a New Englander,
but had held his Majesty's commission in the Foot Guards at Barbadoes (Gibson's Journal, p. 21). Pepperrell and his
second, Waldo, were strongly opposed to it.

[2] Vol. 10, p. 141. This, written by Waldo on the 3rd, confirms the impression given by other records that the
disorder was great.

be attended with very ill consequence if it should not be executed with the utmost vigour whenever attempted, the said attack of the town be deferr'd for the present.[1]

Warren was present at both meetings.

The outlook was not as brilliant as the leaders had hoped. Du Chambon had returned a spirited answer to the summons to surrender. The guns of their siege batteries were burst by overloading,[2] and, firing at long range, did little damage to the French defences ; and it was found impossible to arrange an attack on the Island Battery. Discouragement dictated the decision of the Council of War which met on the 11th ; for this was virtually to abandon the offensive, and to attempt no more than to hold the harbour until reinforcements were sent to them. The Council decided at its meeting as follows :

"Advized, that the battery begun at the west part of the Town be compleated with all possible expedition, and the eight 22lb cannon be mounted there.

"Advized, that two regiments be posted on the west part of the town to guard the batteries there, and to intercept succours that may attempt to get into the town that way.

"That one regimt be posted at the Grand Battery.

"That a battery be thrown up, and the New York train of artillery and some cannon from the Grand Battery be mounted between the light-house and careening place, and that the remaindr of the army with the stores encamp in some proper place abt the North East Harbour, & intrench there and place the field pieces round the camp, that so they may be able to keep possession of the harbour till measures can be taken for the effectual reduction of the town.

"That some guard-boats be prepared & kept in readiness in the North East Harbour to intercept small vessells from getting to the town with succors."[3]

It was also decided that Shirley send down a reinforcement of one thousand men. The battery was begun, no steps were taken to remove the troops, and by the 18th the action was reconsidered in Council and the project abandoned. Vaughan wrote, on the 11th, that he could take the Island Battery if given control of an expedition against it. He busied himself with preparations, but was obliged to write Pepperrell that the indiscipline of the men made the expedition impossible. A bungling attempt to burn a vessel from France, which had passed through the cruisers unhurt by their fire and that of the Grand Battery, and had been anchored or was beached close under the walls of the town, was also made and failed.

Warren was getting uneasy. He pointed out to Pepperrell that the St. Lawrence was open, and that reinforcements might be sent down from Quebec as well as from France. Pepperrell's letters to Shirley became apologetic in their tone, for he and his officers were receiving letters which showed that at home hopes were held that they were in Louisbourg when they had not landed.[4]

---

[1] Vol. 10, p. 17.
[2] Many accidents of this kind took place to their own guns and men.
[3] Vol. 10, p. 18.
[4] Parkman, also vol. 10.

Warren proposed an attack on the town, by the combined land and sea forces, for which he secured the approval, not only of his own captains, but of Rous and Fones, of the colonial cruisers. The Council determined that the circumstances of the army did not justify its immediate undertaking. Warren was unquestionably disappointed, and some irritation appears in his letters to Pepperrell. Before this had risen to any plain expression one event occurred which materially affected the course of the siege. This was the capture of the one ship sent out from France which could have helped Du Chambon in his defence. The *Vigilant* was a new ship mounting sixty-four guns. It was said that she was so heavily laden that her lowest tier of guns was not available in battle. Her command was given to Maisonfort, who was given instructions to succour Louisbourg without uselessly exposing his vessel.[1]

The *Vigilant*, on her voyage from Brest, captured two British vessels, on which she put prize crews to bring them in to Louisbourg. On the 20th of May she was off the coast of Isle Royale, proceeding with a fair north-east wind for her destination. She fell in with and chased the *Mermaid*, of forty guns, Captain Douglass. The latter, replying with his stern guns to the fire of the Frenchman, was pursued towards the northwards where Warren's ships lay. Douglass signalled to them the presence of the enemy. When Maisonfort[2] (at 2 P.M.) discovered the British ships, conditions were reversed. He turned south-westwards to sea, and was chased by the *Mermaid*. He crowded on all sail. The British ship was joined at six by Rous, in command of the *Shirley*, who "Ply'd his Bow Chase very well." At eight the *Eltham* and *Superbe* came up, and after an hour's action Maisonfort struck. In the darkness of night-time and fog they all but lost the prize. Maisonfort had made a gallant fight, and did not surrender until his ship was unworkable, and was so much shattered that she had to be towed into Gabarus Bay the next day, so that he had no chance of escaping. Sixty of her crew of 500 were killed or wounded. Douglass was put in command of her, and with difficulty a crew was obtained from the transports and army.[3] The *Superbe's* master's log, No. 722, has a slightly different account, agreeing that the *Vigilant* fought until completely disabled. "She could make no sort of sail." The logs all show that she inflicted considerable damage on the three ships which overpowered her.

Had the *Vigilant* successfully entered the harbour the effect on the siege must have been great.[4] Its crew would have about doubled the number of the defenders of the town. The stores she carried would have most opportunely

---

[1] I.R. B, vol. 82, f. 59 and 70.   [2] See Biographical Appendix.

[3] This in brief is the account of the *Mermaid's* log (R.O. Captains' Logs, 820).

[4] If she had got in, I believe she would have put them in such a condition as to prevent any Fleet in the World's coming in the Town " (Capt. Ph. Durell of the *Superbe*). "If the Ship had got into the Harbour we should never have taken the place " ("an officer of Marines " in Durell, Captain M'Donald (?).

supplemented those of the defence, which were so low that the powder was sparingly used. The rashness of De la Maisonfort would have animated the defence with the spirit it needed. The courage and tenacity with which he and his crew fought on the *Vigilant* until she was completely disabled, we must believe, would have proved too much for the few and unskilled gunners of the Grand Battery. Had they silenced these guns, then, from some such position as the *Arethuse* occupied in 1758, the siege batteries would have been laid open to the devastating broadsides of the *Vigilant*.[1] The fortunes of France suffered grievously from the rashness of her commander.

Powder from her stores was found very useful by the provincials in adding to their stores, which, like those of the French, had run low. But the fire of their batteries was not very effective. With regard to other operations, the officers had not enough control over their men to order them to the attack on the Island Battery, and to have that order obeyed. The organization of this expedition was being attempted continuously from the time that it was first spoken of, but night after night it was put off. The first of the attempts which were serious was made on the 21st. Warren had two hundred men ready to assist, but the disorderly mob which appeared at the Grand Battery was in no condition to make an attack.

"The night, owing to the moon and the northern lights, was not so agreeable as may happen the ensuing one, and the appearance of small detachments of men without officers was much less pleasing, many of which only under the conduct (not influence) of a sarjeant & many others only centinells without any officer of any kind, & not a few of them noisy & in liquor."[2]

Waldo wrote that only fourteen of his men would go; although he claimed that the spirit of his regiment was better than others. The men believed the French had wind of their design. D'Aillebout, in command of the island, was erecting a fascine battery to protect its landing-place. The council had an examination of witnesses the next day. Their decision was that Colonels Noble and Gorham, who were in command, were not chargeable with misbehaviour in the affair. The council also " advised, that if a number of men to the amount of three or four hundred appear as volunteers for the attack of the Island Battery, they be allowed to choose their own officer and be entitled to the plunder found there." [3] This offer produced some effect.

---

[1] See map.   [2] Vol. 10, Waldo to Pepperrell, p. 213.

[3] Vol. 10, p. 21. Had plunder been much of an inducement, the adventurers would have been sorely disappointed had the island been taken. Young d'Estimauville was burned out when in command of the detachment at Fort Guillaume, at Table Head, in September 1752. His claim for reimbursement of his losses represents that he had the following property : 10 shirts, 10 handkerchiefs, 11 stockings, 2 vests, 2 shoes, 8 towels and bedding ; also an overcoat, a silver couvert, and a goblet, a hunting knife, etc., a canteen of 5 bottles, demijohn of wine, 8 glasses, 2 flasks, etc. He was probably better supplied than any officer in 1745, and the four or five on the Island Battery and their eighty men would have given little to divide.

The officers chosen found over four hundred adventurers assembled at the Grand Battery on the night of the 26th. As they embarked they gave the impression to Waldo that the greater part of them never intended to land in the attack. The surf was as heavy as any Warren had known on the coast.

"I am very sorry for the miscarriage and loss of men in the attempt on the Island Battery. There was as great a surff the night it was undertaken as I have known here, and I desired Captain Durell to acquaint you, if you wou'd lend us your whale boats we wou'd attempt it from the ships the first favourable opportunity, tho' I must own I think wee ought not to unmann them upon any account, as the sea force of the enemy may be daily expected, whom we ought to be in a condition to receive." [1]

The foremost boats reached the island and landed their men. The garrison was ready for them and a conflict began. The garrison was small. One account says 60 to 80 soldiers. There were also about 140 militiamen. After three hours of fighting, which ended at four in the morning, the victory was with the French. The loss was 189 men,[2] and it paralyzed for the moment the besieging forces. The next day the batteries were silent for some time; that of the Grand because it had no powder, nor men to work it; the others presumably on account of the confusion. Waldo sent one of his vigorous letters to Pepperrell:

"The silence of all our batterys after the misfortune of last night is very prejudicial to our interests. I humbly apprehend we ought rather to have doubled our zeal ye way." "From all accounts from shore we learn the men are prodigiously discouraged." [3]

Warren's impatience increased. On the 24th he again sent a plan approved by his captains. It proposed that 1000 men from the army should embark on the vessels, that 600 men more should be found from the land forces to man the *Vigilant*, that the harbour should be forced, the transports to be under cover of the men-of-war, and that a vigorous attack in boats should be made from the ships, and that Captain M'Donald should land the marines and lead the land attack.[4]

The council on the 25th "maturely weighed" this plan, pointed out that the reduction of the Island Battery, and of that circular battery with which Du Chambon [5] had replaced and reinforced the guns at the Dauphin Gate, would be of great service to the attack on the town, and that they would endeavour it,

---

[1] Vol. 10, p. 233.   [2] Pepperrell to Warren, May 28, vol. 1, p. 33.

[3] Diary of Rev. Joseph Emerson, Chaplain of the *Molineux* frigate; published by Sam. A. Green.

[4] The marines on the men-of-war were about 300 in number. Capt. James M'Donald came to Shirley highly recommended, and received from him a Colonel's commission to command the marines under Pepperrell, if they served on shore (Shirley to Pepperrell, May 10). Pepperrell thought he was boastful and a martinet. "I am well assurd. he never was, put it all together, one hour in any of ye trenches, & he might be on shore before we came in ye citty three days at a time in ye camp, & then to be sure we were glad to get rid of him, for ye most he did was to find fault that our encampment was not regulr., or yt the soldrs. did not march as hansome as old regulr. troops, their toes were not turned enough out, &c." (Pepperrell to Shirley, vol. 10, p. 330).   [5] Lartigue, a civilian, was very active in this work.

while the *Vigilant* was refitting.   They then summarized the difficulties of the situation :

"That as the difficulties of communication between the army and shipping are often so great that boats cannot put off nor reland for several days together ; there being a considerable degree of sickness in the army ; there being reason to apprehend that a number of French Indians may be dayly expected on the back of our camp ; also that our men being unused to the sea would be soon unfitted for service by being on shipboard ; it is by no means advizeable to send off any number of the land forces to go into the harbour in the ships, lest if by any accident the ships should not go in at the time proposed, the land men might not be able immediately to repair on shoar, which might be attended with the worst consequences to the army.

"That a general attack be made on the town by the army and naval force as soon, and in such manner, as shall be determined upon by their united Councils [and submitted an alternative plan] :

"Vizt.   That five hundred men be taken out of the cruizers and transports, and distributed in the ships of war, in order to facilitate the manning the *Vigilant*.

"That the ships and other vessels proceed into the harbour at the time agreed upon in such manner as Com^re Warren shall direct.

"That five hundred land men and what men can be spared from the cruizers be in readiness at the Grand Battery to put off in boats upon a signal, and to land and scalade the wall on the front of the town, under the fire of the ships' cannon.   The marines and what seamen Com^re Warren thinks proper to attack at the same time and place.

"That five hundred men, or more if to be had, scalade the wall at the southeast part of the town at the same time.

"That five hundred men make an attack at the breach at the West Gate, and endeavour to possess themselves of the Circular Battery.

"That five hundred men be posted at a suitable place to sustain the party attacking at the West Gate." [1]

Warren's impatience showed in his letters.   He transmitted his plan of the 24th in a letter beginning with these words :

"I am sorry to give you the trouble of so many plans of operation against the garrison of Louisbourg, and beg leave to assure you, most candidly, that they all have been such as appeared best to my weak judgment, under the several circumstances that you were in, at the different times of my proposing them." [2]

Pepperrell replied in a calm tone on the same day in transmitting the report of the council, which drew from Warren a brusque answer, the basis of which is in two of its passages.   "For God's sake, let us do something, and not waste our time in indolence," showed Warren's frame of mine.   The reasons for this impetuous appeal Warren stated as follows :

"I sincerely wish you all the honour and success imaginable, and only beg to know, in what manner I can be more serviceable, than in cruizing, to prevent the introduction of succours to the garrison. I fear that if that be all that is expected from the ships, or that they can do, Louisbourg will be safe for some time ; for my part I have proposed all that I think can be done already, and only wait your answer thereto."[1]

Pepperrell replied on the 28th with a statement of what the army had done and its condition.

"In answer to yours of 26th inst. I beg leave to represent to you that this is now the 29th day since the army first invested the town of Louisbourg, and drove the inhabitants within their walls. That in this time we have erected five fascine batteries, and with hard service to the men, drawn our cannon, mortars, ball, etc. ; that with 16 pieces of cannon, and our mortars mounted at said batteries, and with our cannon from the royal battery, we have been playing on the town, by which we have greatly distrest the inhabitants, made some breaches in the wall, especially at the west gate, which we have beat down, and made a considerable breach there, and doubt not but shall soon reduce the circular battery. That in this time we have made five unsuccessful attempts upon the island battery, in the last of which we lost about 189 men, and many of our boats were shot to pieces, and many of our men drowned before they could land ; that we have also kept out scouts to destroy any settlements of the enemy near us, and prevent a surprise in our camp . . . that by the services aforesaid and the constant guards kept night and day round the camp, at our batteries, the army is very much fatigued, and sickness prevails among us, to that degree that we now have but about 2100 effective men, six hundred of which are gone in the quest of two bodies of French and Indians we are informed are gathering, one to the eastward, and the other to the westward."[2]

He promised that he and some of his council will wait on Warren as soon as possible, but told him that an attempt on the Island Battery by boats was impracticable ; a tribute to the vigour of D'Aillebout's defence on the 26th.

Warren writes again on the 29th after being

"three days in a fog that I could not see the length of my ship, nor one of my squadron ; when that is the case I look on myself to be as far from you as if I were in Boston." He quotes Shirley's letter in which the Governor refers to Warren's command. This Warren says he mentions "but to show that my opinion, which I shall ever give candidly to the best of my judgment, might have, in conjunction with the captains under my command, some weight and force with you."

A most important step was now taken, one which might have been earlier begun, had the technical skill at Pepperrell's disposal been more adequate.[3] The nearest point to the Island Battery was the land across the mouth of the harbour on which the lighthouse was placed. A distance of about one thousand yards separated these points. It was not, however, until towards the end of May that it occurred to the besiegers to attack the Island Battery from

---

[1] Vol. 1, pp. 34-35, May 26.   [2] Pepperrell to Warren, vol. 1, p. 35.
[3] "We being poorly provided with persons experienced in engineering" (Pepperrell to Bastide, June 2, vol. 10, p. 239). Bastide arrived at Louisbourg about June 5. The lighthouse battery was then under construction.

Map of the Province of Nova Scotia, parts adjacent and showing the situation of Cape Breton, 1760

(author : James Turner — photo courtesy William L. Clements Library, University of Michigan.)

A map of Royal or Cape Breton Island by Thomas Kitchin

(author: Thomas Kitchin — photo courtesy The Beaton Institute, College of Cape Bret

Plan of the Town of Louisbourg, Isle Royalle, 1730
(author: Etienne Verrier — photo courtesy Archives Nationales, Paris.)

Plan of the First Siege of Louisbourg, 1745
(author: Richard Gridley — photo courtesy Public Record Office, Surrey, England.)

A PLAN of the
CITY and HARBOUR of LOUISBURG,
with the French Batteries that defended it
and those of the English, shewing that part
of GABARUS BAY, in which they Landed,
and the Ground on which they Encamped
during the Siege in 1745.

A New Battery
erected since 1748

GROUND

Settlements which were destroyed May 2 on which the
Garrison and Royal Battery immediately Deserted it.

North East
Harbor

North Cape

The Royal
Battery

Mariesema

HARBOR OF LOUISBURG

Careening
Place

Light House

Gorham

English Battery

North Cape

Island Battery

Goat or
Green Island

City
of
Louisburg

Black Cape

Willard's Regiment

Moulton's Regiment

Moores Regiment

White Point

A Map of
GABARUS BAY
adjoining to
Louisburg

BAY OF
GABARUS

S BAY

White Point

Scale of Miles

Gabarus Point

La Guion

Sold at Charing Cross April 20. 1757.

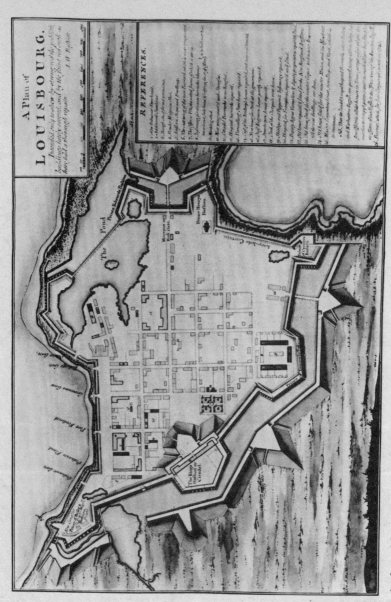

A plan of Louisbourg, English occupation, 1746

(author: John Henry Bastide — photo courtesy Yale University Library.)

Second Siege, view from the Centre Redout, 1758

(author: Thomas Davies — photo courtesy Public Archives of Canada.)

Old print of the Second Siege, showing Lighthouse, 1758

this point. The first mention of the project in letters to Pepperrell is in that of Waldo, who wrote on the 26th :

"I have been over to the Lighthouse side, where have found a very convenient place for electing a fine battery to the seaward . . . and a flank or bastion to ye said battery that will mount four or five guns that will range the Island Battery . . . I have determined as Col. Gorham's have leisure enough that they this evening and the ensuing night thrô up another . . . which will greatly annoy the Island Battery, being the best-situated in my poor apprehension for the purpose." [1]

Guns and materials were conveyed by sea to the position, and the work carried on. No movement made by the besiegers was more effective. Warren's ships were held outside the harbour by the Island Battery. The injuries to the walls of the town were being repaired as the damage was done, or when the permanent works were destroyed, they were, as at the Dauphin Gate, replaced by newly erected defences of earthwork and fascines. The French thus deferred the possibilities of a successful land attack. They guarded, in the event of the harbour being forced, against boats landing from the ships or from the Grand Battery on the beaches and quays, by stretching a chain between the Dauphin Works and the Batterie de la Grave. Du Chambon and his men, with dogged tenacity rather than Gallic dash, were doing all they could to hold the place. Eager as Warren was, his captains had on June 7 declared that it was inadvisable to attempt to force the harbour without silencing the Island Battery, nor would the pilots then with them bring the ships close enough to bring their guns to bear effectively on it.[2] Warren's captains added that if they could get pilots who would anchor the ships half a cable length from the battery, and they had five hundred men from the army with officers, who would land where Warren directed, they would attempt its reduction. Such pilots did not exist, and Pepperrell replied :

"I cannot think it advisable to attempt it again in whale boats which a few musket balls will sink." [3]

The progress of the siege was almost blocked when the Lighthouse Battery began its work.

Shirley's account of the later days of the siege clearly and briefly sets forth the conditions and course of events.

"And by the 14th, four more Guns were placed on the 11th, sustained by 320 Men. Powder growing short, the Fire had for some days been very much slacken'd, and the French began to creep a little out of the Casmates and Covers, where they had hid

---

[1] Vol. 10, p. 224. As Waldo gave orders to proceed with the work, it is likely that the project had been discussed before. There is no entry in the minutes of the Council of War about this battery until June 9, then only about transferring to it one of their largest mortars.

[2] June 7, vol. 1, p. 41.　　　　[3] Pepperrell to Warren, June 8.

themfelves, during the greateft Fiercenefs of it; but this being the Anniverfary of his Majefty's happy Acceffion to the Throne, it was determined to celebrate it as became loyal Subjects and good Soldiers; and Orders were given for a general Difcharge of all the Cannon from every Battery, at Twelve O'Clock, which was accordingly done, and follow'd by an inceffant Fire all the reft of the Day: which much difheartened the Enemy, efpecially as they muft be fenfible what muft be the Confequence of this new Battery. It was now determined, as foon as poffible, after the Arrival of the *Canterbury* and *Sunderland,* to make a general Attack by the Sea and Land: Accordingly they arriving the next Day, all the Tranfports were order'd off to take out the fpare Mafts and Yards, and other Lumber of the Men of War. The Soldiers were employ'd in gathering Mofs to barricade their Nettings, and 600 men were fent on board the King's Ships at the Commodore's Requeft. The large Mortar was order'd to the Light-houfe Battery; and a new Supply of Powder arriving, the Fire was more fierce from this Time to

"The 15th, than ever. When the Mortar began to play from the Light-houfe Battery upon Ifland Battery; out of 19 Shells, 17 fell within the Fort, and one of them upon the Magazine, which, together with the Fire from the Cannon, to which the Enemy was very much expofed, they having but little to fhelter them from the Shot that ranged quite through their Barracks, fo terrified them, that many of them left the Fort, and run into the Water for Refuge.

"The Grand Battery being in our Poffeffion; the Ifland Battery being fo much annoy'd by the Light-houfe Battery; the North-Eaft Battery fo open to our Advance Battery, that it was not poffible for the Enemy to ftand to their Guns; all the Guns in the Circular Battery except three being difmounted, and the Wall almoft wholly broke down; the Weft Gate demolifhed, and a large Breach in the Wall adjoining; The Weft Flank in the King's Baftion almoft ruined; all the Houfes and other Buildings almoft torn to Pieces, but one Houfe in the town being left unhurt, and the Enemy's Stock of Ammunition growing fhort, they fent out a Flag of Truce to the Camp, defiring Time to confider upon the Articles of Capitulation. This was granted till the next Morning when they brought out Articles, which were refufed, and others fent in by the General and Commodore, and agreed to by the Enemy: Hoftages were exchanged and

"On the 17th of June, the City and Fortreffes were furrendered, and the Garrifon and all the Inhabitants, to the Number of 2000, capable of bearing Arms, made Prifoners, to be tranfported to France with all their perfonal Effects. During the whole Siege, we had not more than 101 Men killed by the Enemy and all other Accidents, and about 30 died of Sicknefs. And according to the beft Accounts, there were killed of the Enemy within the Walls about 300, befides Numbers that died by being confined within the Cafemates."[1]

This was brought about by the hopelessness of the situation, well described by Shirley. The principal inhabitants of the city begged Du Chambon to capitulate. Verville, the engineer, at his request, made a report on the battered state of the fortifications; Ste. Marie, another on their exhausted munitions of war. A council of war met, and unanimously decided the proper course was to offer to capitulate.[2]

[1] Shirley, p. 30.   [2] The originals of these documents or at least contemporary facsimiles are in M. St. Mery, vol. 50.

Du Chambon sent an officer, young Eurry de la Perelle, who had recovered from his wound received in the defence of the Island Battery, with a letter asking for a suspension of hostilities to arrange terms for a capitulation. It was high time. We know the condition of the town. There were but forty-seven barrels of powder in its stores. The men-of-war cleared for action, their crews supplemented by 600 provincials lay ready in Gabarus Bay, over against the camp, to force the harbour. The land forces were prepared with scaling ladders and fascines to storm the breaches in the walls. Warren had landed, and the regiment drawn up on parade listened to his inspiring words. The suspension was granted until nine the next morning. Negotiations were carried on during the 16th, Sunday, and resulted in the following letter from Warren and Pepperrell, which was modified by later arrangements : [1]

"We have before us yours of this date, together with the several articles of capitulation on which you have proposed to surrender the town and fortifications of Louisbourg with the territories adjacent, under your government, to his Britannic Majesty's forces, now besieging said place, under our command, which articles we can by no means conceed to. But, as we are desirous to treat you in a generous manner we do again make you an offer of terms of surrender proposed by us in our summons sent you the 7th may last ; and to further consent to allow and promise you the following articles," viz. :

First.—"That if your own vessels shall be found insufficient for the transportation of your persons and proposed effects to France, we will provide such a further number of vessels as may be sufficient for that purpose. also any provisions necessary for the voyage which you cannot furnish yourselves with."

Secondly.—"That all the commission officers belonging to the garrison, and the inhabitants of the town may remain in their houses with their families and enjoy the free exercise of their religion, and no person shall be suffered to misuse and molest any of them till such time as they can be conveniently transported to France."

Thirdly.—"That the non-commission officers and soldiers shall immediately upon the surrender of the town and fortresses, be put on board of his Britannic Majesty's ship till they also be transported to France."

Fourthly.—"That all your sick and wounded shall be taken tender care of in the same manner as our own."

Fifthly.—"That the commander in chief now in Garrison shall have liberty to send off covered waggons to be inspected only by one officer of ours, that no warlike stores may be contained therein."

Sixthly.—"That if there are any persons in the town or garrison which shall desire may not be seen by us, they shall be permitted to go off masked."

"The above we do consent to, and promise upon your complyance with the following conditions : "

First.—"That the said surrender and due performance of every part of the aforesaid premises, be made and completed as soon as possible."

Secondly.—"That as a security for the punctual performance of the same, the Island

[1] See end of chapter.

Battery or one of the batteries of the town shall be delivered together with the warlike stores, thereunto belonging unto the possession of his Brit. Majesty's troops, before six of the clock this afternoon."

Thirdly.—"That his said Brit. Majesty's ship of war now lying before the port, shall be permitted to enter the Harbour of Louisbourg without any molestation as soon after six of the clock this afternoon as the commander in chief of said ships shall think fit."

Fourthly.—"That none of the officers, soldiers, non-inhabitants in Louisbourg who are subjects of the French King shall take up arms against his Brit. Majesty, nor any of his allies until after the expiration of the full term of twelve months from this time."

Fifthly.—"That all subjects of his Brit. Majesty who are now prisoners with you shall be immediately delivered up to us."

"In case of your non-compliance with these conditions we decline any further treaty with you on this affair, and shall decide the matter by our arms, and are, Sir, Your humble servants,   P. WARREN,
                                                                          W. PEPPERRELL."

The point on which Du Chambon held out to the last was the granting the honours of war, that is marching out with their arms and colours flying. An interchange of letters between Pepperrell and Warren showed that their sentiments agreed on this point, "the uncertainty of our affairs that depends so much on wind and weather make it necessary not to stick at trifles."[1] Hostages from the town were sent to them. It was arranged that Warren should take possession of the Island Battery and Pepperrell of the town. The inexperience of the civilian General led to precipitancy, of which Du Chambon complained to Warren. Pepperrell did not, apparently, know that taking possession was irregular until after the ratification of the articles of capitulation. These were hastened to completion, and on the 17th the town was yielded up.

"Monday, 17. This day, the French flag was struck, and the English one hoisted up in its place at the island battery. We took possession early in the morning. We hoisted likewise the English flag at the grand battery, and our other new batteries; then fired our cannons and gave three huzzas. At two o'clock in the afternoon, Commodore Warren, with all the men-of-war, as also the prize man-of-war of sixty guns; (the *Vigilant*), our twenty guns ships; likewise our snows, brigantines, privateers and transports, came all into Louisbourg harbor, which made a beautiful appearance. When all were safely moored, they proceeded to fire on such a victorious and joyful occasion. About four o'clock in the afternoon, our land army marched to the south gate of the city, and entered the same, and so proceeded to the parade near the citadel; the French troops, at the same time, being all drawn up in a very regular order. Our army received the usual salutes from them, every part being performed with all the decency and decorum imaginable. And as the French were allowed to carry off their effects, so our guards took all the care they possibly could to prevent the common soldiers from pilfering and stealing, or otherwise giving them the least molestation. The guard and watch of the city, the garrisons &c., were delivered to our troops" (Gibson, p. 52).

[1] Vol. 1, p. 45.

The terms gave little satisfaction to the rank and file. The prospect of booty was as potent an influence in favour of enlistment as it was in all other armies to a much later time than 1745, and the troops, after a campaign which was full of hardship, if not of fighting, saw French property secured to its owners. Warren had foreseen the possibility of disorder. He wrote to Pepperrell on the 16th :

" I rejoice at our success : be assured, sir, that I shall always be glad of your approbation of my conduct. I beg we may all behave to the prisoners that fall under our protection by the chance of war, with the humanity and honour becoming English officers, and be persuaded it will add greatly to the reputation which we acquire by the reduction of this formidable garrison." [1]

His words of caution were justified by the result. The French had been irritated by irregularities in the official conduct of affairs. They commented on Bradstreet being sent in at the head of the detachment which took possession of the town. He had broken, from their point of view, his parole, given at Canso, by serving in this campaign. They later laid stress on the infraction of the terms of capitulation in some of the prisoners being sent to France by the way of Boston instead of directly from Louisbourg. They had now more substantial grievances. The arrangements to protect the inhabitants were inadequate. Pillage, rioting, and insult were the lot of these people who had already been subjected to the hardship of so long a siege. Du Chambon complained to the authorities. Pepperrell entered in his diary on the 19th, " Many complaints of abuses done by the English soldiers to the French inhabitants." Rejoicing took place and dinners. Haste was made in removing the troops to the town and destroying the entrenchments, for there were rumours that a large force of French and Indians were close at hand. The inhabitants were shipped to France as rapidly as possible. Eleven transports sailed on the 4th of July. It was found that as there was scarcely accommodation in the vessels for the people, they had to leave behind much of their property, so that to a great extent they lost the benefits of the capitulation. They were deprived of their own vessels, which fell as spoils to the victors. Bigot, however, secured the King's cash, 200,000 l., by representing it as the property of private parties.[2]

---

[1] Vol. 1, p. 45.

[2] Bigot Memoire. The losses of this siege were not great in men. About one hundred on the English side. A French return gives their force and losses as follows :

Statement of the soldiers, inhabitants, sailors, and fishermen who were in the town of Louisbourg at the beginning of the siege :

Soldiers	500		
Inhabitants, sailors, and fishermen	762	1262	

AT ILE DE L'ENTREE

Soldiers	90		
Inhabitants, etc.	138	228	

1490

The garrison of St. John's Island resisted an attack made by provincial cruisers, and the younger Du Vivier, its commander, carried off his soldiers in safety to Quebec.[1] The inhabitants, unlike those of Isle Royale, were allowed to remain undisturbed.

A joint letter to the Prime Minister was dispatched. Shirley and the other Colonial Governors were advised of this victory.[2] The mother country and the colonies rejoiced over the capture of a fortress the reputation of which for strength had been supposed to be much more nearly commensurate with its strategic importance.

Britain was not ungrateful. Warren was promoted and made Admiral of the Blue, and hoisted his flag amid the salutes of his ships when the news was received at Louisbourg on the 25th of September. It had been proposed to make him a Baronet, but apparently his own representations caused this offer to be withheld. The prospect of an hereditary title brought too closely to him, as the full tide of his success was in flood, the disappointment of his most personal hopes. " Lord Sandwich in his letter mentions the intention to create me a Baronet. I have no son, therefore if that cou'd without offence be let alone, I shall take it as a favour." [3]

Pepperrell was made a Baronet. To him and Shirley was given the right to raise regiments. This in itself was a large pecuniary reward, as the perquisites of a colonel were very considerable. Pepperrell, although Warren, a little later, thought that he on no account would accept the Governorship of the new dependency, had on July 30 applied to the Duke of Newcastle for the position.

"My Lord Duke, I beg leave to trouble yr. Grace to request yr. favour in my behalf to His Majesty, that if my Services in ye Expedition against this place have merit'd His Majesty's Gracious Notice, I may obtain His Royal Commission for ye Government hereof." [4]

Now that the expedition had been found a success, the outlay incurred by the provinces in raising and supplying it became of the first importance to them in their impoverished condition. Massachusetts could not have undertaken it had ready money not been supplied by contributions of its citizens.[5]

To be deducted :					
Killed during the siege .	.	.	.	50	
Wounded	.	.	.	80	130
					———
Remaining after the siege	.	.	.	1360	

Besides the Srs. de Souvigny, la Fresilliere, and Loppinot, officers, killed (M. St. M. vol. 50, p. 495). This seems to include only the combatants, the actual number of inhabitants, including those of the outports, was nearly 8000.

[1] He arrived there on August 7.

[2] The news reached Boston early on the morning of July 3.

[3] Warren to Anson, Oct. 2.

[4] Pepperrell to Newcastle, Louisbourg, July 30, 1745. C.O. 5/.

[5] Mr. Dudley Pickman was the largest subscriber to this fund, with the exception of Pepperrell. A handsome piece of silver presented by Massachusetts in recognition of his services is still extant.

The custom in the old wars had been to reimburse the colonies for such expenditures. All their expeditions had been undertaken by authority from home, but in this case, Massachusetts having been its prime mover, the question was raised as to whether the reimbursements should be a matter of grace or justice. There was considerable delay in the verification of accounts, and when the amounts were settled there were again difficulties on account of exchange. While the negotiations were in progress, the value of the bills of the Province of Massachusetts had fallen so materially that it was a question as to whether one hundred and eighty-three thousand pounds or one hundred and four thousand pounds sterling should be remitted. Bollan, who was acting for Massachusetts, displayed ability in dealing with all these matters. Finally the larger amount was paid over and divided among Massachusetts, New Hampshire, and Rhode Island. The share of the larger province was wisely used in reducing its paper money.[1] Pepperrell's contribution to the expedition was ten thousand pounds. It was presumably repaid, but it is probable that Pepperrell's perquisites of two and one-half per cent commission on the disbursements made the expedition not unprofitable to him. Douglass does not hesitate to say that it was remunerative to Shirley.[2]

When the French garrison and inhabitants had left, some attempt to clean the town was made, and to put it in a state to resist an attack which might be made by the squadron of de Salvert.[3] Colonel Bastide now became important. The return which he and Gridley made of the warlike stores in the town bore out the contentions of Du Chambon. There were but 27 bbls. of powder found in it. Bastide made an estimate of the cost of repairs which were immediately required. This amounted to £9000 sterling. While the army, defrauded of their hopes of plunder by the capitulation, were engaged in unexciting tasks, they saw the navy, which from their point of view had done little, now reaping a rich harvest. The day after the capitulation a well-laden French vessel found itself becalmed off the mouth of the harbour. It was towed in, a capture, to

---

[1] The sums paid over were :

Massachusetts	.	.	.	£183,649 2 7½
New Hampshire	.	.	.	16,355 13 4
Connecticut	.	.	.	28,863 19 1
Rhode Island	.	.	.	6,332 12 10
James Gibson	.	.	.	547 15 0

[2] Waldo had to write to the home authorities in Feb. 49/50 for £1339 pay due him. He says Pepperrell was also unpaid. C.O. 5/.

"As writers and preachers forbear publifhing . . . which are fingular, rare or new, left they fhould prove of bad example, I fhall only fum up thefe perquifites in this manner : In the fpace of four years, viz. 1741, the introductory gratuities from the province, and from . . . of many thoufand of pounds and the unprecedented perquifites in the three expedition years of 1745, 1746, and 1747, from a negative fortune, was amaffed a large profitive eftate and the loofe corns built a country-houfe at the charge of about fix thoufand pount fterling" (Douglass' *Summary*).

[3] De Salvert heard at sea of the fall of Louisbourg and returned to France.

the port, which its master had thought French. The ships of the French East India Company had been ordered to rendezvous at Louisbourg. Three of them came to that port, where they expected to find refitment and a convoy across the Western Ocean. Warren's dispatches tell their fate :

" On the 22d June a large Ship appear'd in the Offing which I took to be a Sixty Gun Ship, and the next morning at daylight I sent out the *Princess Mary* & *Canterbury*, & had the pleasure to see them from the Remparts take her, without opposition, they brought her in the day following, & she proves to be the *Charmante*, a French East India Ship of about five or Six Hundred Tuns, Twenty Eight Guns & Ninety Nine Men Commanded by Mr. Nouoal of Contrie, who assures us that she is except Mr. Ansons, as good a Prize as has been taken this war."

Thus Warren wrote to the Secretary of the Admiralty on the 25th of July. By the fortunes of war he was able in his next letter, that of August 1, to go on as follows :

" And have now only to acquaint you that the *Chester* & *Mermaid* have brought in here the *Heron*, a French East India Ship from Bengal, pretty rich, by her we learn that the *Triton* is on her passage, and that this is the appointed Rendezvous for their Indian Trade."

Again :

" On the 2nd inst. the *Sunderland* and *Chester* brought in the French ship, *Notre Dame De la Deliverance*, Capt. Pierre Litant, Twenty two Guns, and about Sixty men, from Lima in the South Seas, for which place she sail'd from Cadiz in the year Forty one, she has on board in Gold and Silver upwards of Three hundred thousand pounds Sterling, & a Cargo of Cocoa, Peruvian Wool, and Jesuits Bark ; She came from Lima with two others, each of them much richer than this."

These were Warren's official accounts of these events so interesting to him and to the crews of the ships concerned.[1]

The personal aspect he touches on in the letter to Anson :

" The Captains that I now send home under Captain Edward's Command carry home the South seamens money, and they will pay one hundred thousand pieces of Eight, to my Attorneys, and the Eighth of her cargo, and that of the two India Ships when sold, and settled, and also of the *Vigilant*, all of which you will please to vest in the best Funds you can for my advantage." [2]

[1] Ad. Sec., In Letters No. 2655.

[2] Warren to Anson, October 2, Brit. Mus. Add. MSS. 15,957, f. 160.

From the 6th to the 18th of August the *Canterbury* took on board, according to her Captain's Log, R.O. No. 161, the following treasure :

" Came on board from the *Deliverance* South Seaman 39 bags said to contain 1000 Dollars & 9 bags, each bag said to contain 300 ' Double Loons in Gould.'

Received from *Deliverance*   3 boxes sd. to contain 2000 dollars each.

    „   „   1   „   „   1000   „
    „   „   7 pigs of virgin silver.

Such captures as these show the enormous growth of Law's one success, the French East India Company, founded less than thirty years before, as well as the effect of the system of prize money, which made a naval command during these wars one of the most remunerative enterprises in which one could be engaged.[1]

Warren was appointed Governor, but his commission not arriving, he and Pepperrell remained at Louisbourg until the spring of 1746 and jointly administered the affairs of a new establishment. The problems with which they had to deal were as trying, if not as critical, as those which arose during the siege. The rank and file, as well as many of the officers of the provincial forces, began as soon as they had entered the town to turn their thoughts to getting back to their homes. Shirley's proclamation for raising the troops was loosely worded, but the preservation of this important capture, open, it was felt by the authorities, to attack from France or from Canada, made the retention of these forces at Louisbourg until the arrival of regular troops absolutely indispensable. Pepperrell dealt as well with the matter as was possible. The sick were sent home ; as many as could be spared of those whose affairs urgently required them were also returned, and, showing the importance of one of the principal industries of New England, those who had contracts for the supply of mast timber were also allowed to go.

The temper of the troops was, however, unsatisfactory. Shirley was sent for, and he arrived, together with Mrs. Warren and his own family, on the 17th of August. The troops by this time were mutinous. However, they received the Governor with due form and ceremony.

" The whole army was mustered and placed in the most Genteel manner to Receive the Govr. the Genl. walk't foremost the Governors Lady at his Right. Then his Excellency &c. The men Stood on Each Side with their arms Rested from ye Gate By ye Comondores To ye Barracks att ye Govrs : Landing ye Cannon fir'd from ye Batterys & from ye men of war ; when the Battallian was Dismissed there was fireing with Small arms for two Hours. His Excellency's arrival was verry Rejoycing To us all." [2]

The dissatisfaction of the troops was at its height in September. On the 17th they had plotted to lay down their arms on the next day. Acting after consultation with the Council, Shirley addressed the troops and promised an

---

Received from *Deliverance* 32 boxes sd. to contain 2000 dollars each.
     ,,   ,,   1   ,,   ,,   1140 doubleoones.
     ,,   ,,   18 bars of gold sd. to weigh 65½ lbs.
     ,,   ,,   1000 dollars in silver & 39 bales of wool.
     ,,   ,,   22 chests sd. to contain 2000 dollars each.
     ,,   ,,   11   ,,   ,,   3000   ,,
     ,,   ,,   40   ,,   ,,   3000 dollars each."

[1] Warren also retained of his specie 100,000 Spanish dollars to meet the immediate expenses of the ships
[2] Bradstreet's Diary, p. 33.

increase of pay to forty shillings a month.[1]   His efforts to placate the soldiers were successful.   On October 2 the members of Council, answering his inquiry,

"Unanimously declared that it was their opinion that His Excellency's said declarations and measures had quite appeased and delayed the spirit of discontent, and that the soldiers appeared well satisfied with his declaration to them, claiming that many of them were uneasy in their prospects of being detained here from their families till Spring, some of them for want of cloths."[2]

When these exciting events had ceased to occur, the garrison settled down to what to them would have seemed a dreary winter, with their only occupation, the repair of the fortifications and buildings.   It proved more than a dreary autumn and winter.   Louisbourg at its best was a town of narrow streets and lanes.   The interruption to ordinary life of the siege had resulted in an accumulation of filth that turned the town into a midden.   The change from sleeping in the open, to infected barracks and houses was unwholesome, and the entries in the diaries of these months is a dreary repetition of sickness and burials.   Warren, in addition to the "scorbutick disorder" which afflicted him, had a touch of the prevailing disease from which he recovered.   The Rev. Stephen Williams was at death's door for weeks with sufferings which he bore with fortitude, ceasing his ministrations to the men only when his strength was completely spent.

In October the garrison, reduced by mortality and the return of the troops to New England, was nominally two thousand men.   About one-third of them were on the sick list.   Warren, who was recovering, more than once, in a long letter, touches on the danger of an attack on a garrison of this size where from eight to fourteen of its members die daily.[3]

There were causes for alarm.   Some of de Salvert's smaller ships touched at a port in Newfoundland, which Warren thought might be a base from which an attack would be directed.   Word was brought that a force of six thousand men would be sent down from Canada to retake Louisbourg.[4]   It followed the same lines as the first scheme for the British attack in 1758, namely, a landing in Miré Bay and an advance overland.   The town itself was strengthened as much as possible.   A boom was made ready to protect the mouth of the harbour.   Guns which could be spared from the ships were mounted on the walls and the Grand Battery was dismantled.   The adequacy of these preparations was not tested.[5]

[1] Vol. 10, p. 45.   [2] Vol. 10, p. 47.

[3] Douglass' estimate that New England lost two thousand of its able-bodied people as the price of this victory was not exaggerated.   Warren said in the spring that two thousand had died since the occupation.

[4] This project, that of Beauharnois and Hocquart, was set forth in a letter to the Minister, Sept. 12, 1745, A.N. C¹¹, vol. 83.

[5] Warren was dismayed at the expense, and assured the Lords of the Admiralty that the utmost economy was practised by Pepperrell and himself.

One loose thread may be fastened in. The friction between Pepperrell and Warren was only during the period when the troops were inactive, and Warren saw that unless more progress was made the expedition would fail. Then, irritated by the lack of attention paid to his proposals, the inefficacy of the Council's actions, his letters lose their courteous phrasing. It is fair also to infer that his bearing in personal intercourse during these days may have been very different from that which made him so great a favourite with the colonists among whom he had been stationed.[1]

Pepperrell's tone in his letters never varied. It commands admiration. He retained his calmness in his dealings not only with Warren, but in those with his Council. He was undismayed by the failure of plan after plan, shaken neither by the jealousies of his officers, the recklessness of some, the sluggishness of others, nor by the unreasoning rashness nor the equally unreasoning despondency of his men. For some weeks, under less momentous circumstances, for diplomacy made their victory ephemeral, the colonial merchant-general displayed many of the qualities which have made immortal the name of William the Silent. Pepperrell and Warren busied themselves in providing for the future of the colony. They urged that it should be made a free port in so far as the Acts of Trade would allow, confirming in this the soundness of the view of Raudot and Costebelle. They thought Louisbourg would be an admirable port of call. They insisted that it must have a civil government, for settlers would not come under a military governor and toleration for all Protestants, and they parted with mutual esteem, Pepperrell to dignified colonial activities, Warren to professional advancement and an early death. There was opportunity later for misunderstandings, had these men been of different calibre.

New England had taken fire when the news came that the town had surrendered to Warren. The Legislature of Massachusetts was precipitate in stating its dissatisfaction. The keys were delivered up by Du Chambon to Warren. He apparently handed them to Pepperrell, who in turn, at the parade on Shirley's arrival, delivered them over to the Governor.

Pepperrell sums up the matter in a letter to Shirley on July 17:

"I am very sorry you should meet with anything to damp yor. joy relating to any dispute between the Comodore Warren & myselfe, & considering that we are both quick in our tempers, I do think ye land & sea have agreed in this expedition as well as ever they did on ye like occasion, & if it had not been for some who have had yor. favours I dont think there would have been any, and I was well assurd. that before we got possession of this place and since that it was of absolute necessity to keep from disputes & differences (or otherwise ye grand design might have sufferd.) & I have strove to my uttermost to keep things easey. It is true Mr. Warren did tell me he was the chief officer here. I

---

[1] He certainly placed Pepperrell's character, position, and conduct in the most favourable light in all his letters to the home authorities.

told him, Not on shoar. I look upon it that these disputes are all over, as we both aim at ye good & security of this place."

Warren wrote to Anson about the attitude of Massachusetts :

"As it is very probable you will see in some of the New England papers, or hear of an address from the Council & General Assembly of the Massachusetts Bay to Governor Shirley, upon his departure for this place, I think it proper as it carrys a reflection in it, both upon the General, and me, upon him for submitting to, and upon me for assuming (if it had been true), an undue authority to tell you of it as my Friend, to prevent any Ill impression with regard to my Conduct, this was done without any manner of foundation by Ill dispos'd people, to make a breach between the General and me, to serve some dirty end. The General, and I have resented it both to Governor Shirley, and his Council and Assemble, who all declare their concern at it, and say they are now convinc'd it was done too rashly, upon a misrepresentation, and that they will give us publick satisfaction for it when the two houses meet ; I resented this treatment so warmly, that I have had many letters of excuse from numbers of the people concern'd in the address." [1]

A curious afterglow is thrown on Warren's dealings with the provincial officers and men by a posthumous quotation of his opinion of them, given by Lord Sandwich in the House of Lords during the troubles with the colonists in 1775.

"As to their prowess, I remember very well, when I had the honour to be at the Board at which I now preside, I had the curiosity to inquire about the surprising feats said to be performed by those people (the Americans) at the siege of Louisbourg, of the great naval officer who commanded on the expedition, as able and honest a seaman as ever lived (Sir Peter Warren), who told me very frankly they were the greatest set of cowards and poltroons he ever knew ; they were all bluster, noise, and were good for nothing. I remember a particular instance he told me, which, from the ludicrous circumstances attending it, made a very deep impression on my mind. Soon after their landing, there was a battery, called the Island Battery, which commanded the entrance of the harbour. Sir Peter having ordered them to attack it, they engaged to perform it ; but what was the consequences ? They ran away on the first fire. And how did you manage ? Did you employ them afterwards, or upbraid them with their cowardice, says I ?—No, answers Sir Peter, neither would it have been prudent ; I formed the marines and part of the ship's crews into a body, to act on shore ; and instead of upbraiding them, I told them they had behaved like heroes ; for, if I had acted otherwise, I should have never taken the town, as their presence and numbers were necessary to intimidate the besieged." [2]

This is at best a free report of an off-hand statement by Warren, obviously inaccurate as a statement of facts. Its tone differs completely from all we know of Warren's expressions. Still, this may well have been his opinion of these troops. We have instances of individual recklessness like that of the man, who enraged by the injury to a borrowed coat, killed many Frenchmen

[1] Warren to Anson, Nov. 23, 1745 ; Add. MSS. 15,957, f. 164.   [2] Vol. 1, p. 109.

on the walls from a position he took in the open ; and like that privateer, who in his eagerness in the chase of the *Marguerite* was driven under and disappeared in the Gulf. The indifference they displayed to ineffective fire from the walls is common among raw soldiers. But if with the qualities of cheerfulness, ingenuity, and self-will they did not display military virtues, it makes more significant the course of events. The aggressive upholding of colonial claims which we associate with the name of Pitt gave in the next war seven years of training to these men and their fellows. This training, and the inspiration of a nobler cause than the capture of Louisbourg, turned a population, in their first essay as soldiers such as Sandwich describes, into troops before whom, at Saratoga and Yorktown, the armies of England laid down their arms.

The winter wore away. In the spring the provincial troops were relieved and returned to New England in May. Their places were taken by two regiments from Gibraltar, and Pepperrell's and Shirley's newly raised regiments.

Until the return of the island to France, the garrison was maintained at an effective strength of twenty-five to eighteen hundred men. The force of June 2, 1746, was :

Fuller .	613
Warburton	613
Shirley .	517
Pepperrell	417
Artillery	64
Framlon	300
	2524 [1]

On September 1, 1747, the effective strength was 1919, of whom 1709 were fit for duty.[2]

Pepperrell and Shirley found great difficulty in getting recruits. Shirley said it was easier to get 10,000 men for an expedition against Canada, than 1000 for garrison duty.[3] The state of these regiments in May 1746 shows that recruiting had given them

	Pepperrell's.	Shirley's.
Massachusetts	...	400
Pennsylvania	...	150
New York	20	70
Connecticut	50	...
New Hampshire	50	...
Louisbourg	300	150

When one notes that 890 had died in Louisbourg between December and April, and that for weeks, in the weather described by Knowles, living and dead

---

[1] C.O. 5/13.   [2] C.O. 5/901.   [3] Shirley to Warren, Sept. 22, 1745 (C.O. 5/900).

had remained under the same roof, it is not surprising that the adventurous preferred a campaign in the open to such service.[1]

Vice-Admiral Townsend took Warren's place in the sea command. Commodore Charles Knowles, Warren's former junior, became Governor. Warren returned to Boston with Shirley on the *Chester*, sailing June 7, 1746, and all misunderstanding having been cleared away, the warmth of his reception was scarcely less than that of Sir William's.

One-tenth of the forces destined by a mortified minister to rescue Louisbourg and deliver a counterstroke, which might restore in America the prestige of French arms, would have saved the place from capture. Slowness in gathering together this great armament prevented its dispatch until June 1746.

The command of the expedition was given to De Roye de la Rochefoucauld, Duc d'Anville, then in his thirty-seventh year, described by one subordinate as worthy to be loved and born to command. In the latter capacity he succeeded his father as Lieutenant-General of the Gallies at eleven years of age. Without any sea service he was made Lieutenant-General of the Naval Armaments of the King, than which but one grade higher was held by those not of royal blood.[2] Whatever may have been his qualities, every disaster known to the seafarer was the lot of his armada. Tempest, the thunderbolt, collision, an appalling epidemic, and starvation ruined the expedition. D'Anville died in Halifax of apoplexy, or, some said, poison. D'Estournel, who succeeded him, overwhelmed by responsibility committed suicide, and it fell to La Jonquière to bring back to France the ships and men which had survived. Those who would read its fate will find in Parkman[3] pages in which lucidity no less than picturesqueness adorn the tale of its ill fortune.[4]

Not only Louisbourg and Annapolis, but New England was alarmed by the news of this expedition. The hardy provincials marched from their inland homes to defend Boston with an eagerness that they had not displayed before the Island Battery. Townsend and Knowles prepared to hold Cape Breton and Nova Scotia. The best disposition possible was made of their resources. Knowles, looking back over the events of the summer, thought that if the French fleet had arrived before August, Louisbourg might have fallen, as there were but five or six guns mounted to the land and the breaches made were not repaired.[5] But so sturdy was his spirit that with a garrison of only 2015 effective men, he wrote on September 19, when the arrival of D'Anville was expected, " M. le Duc with all his force shan't have Louisbourg this Trip "[6]

Knowles knew of the movements of the French fleet. He sent a flag of

---

[1] C.O. 5/901 and C.O. 5/13.   [2] A.N. Marine, C¹, vol. 161.   [3] *A Half Century of Conflict*, ch. xxv.
[4] The official documents on the French side are in A.N. Marine, B⁴, vol. 59. Bigot was a commissary in the fleet (*Mémoire pour Messire Francois Bigot*, Paris, MDCCLXIII).
[5] Ad. Sec., In Letters, No. 234.   [6] C.O. 5/44.

truce to D'Anville with prisoners, and learned something of their condition.[1] Spies whom he sent later gave him the information, that La Jonquière, who had succeeded to the command, sailed to attack Annapolis.[2] Warren at Boston got the same news, and while he felt that Louisbourg was secure, grieved for poor Spry[3] at Annapolis. Spry awaited the attack which never came, with more solicitude for chances of British victory than about what might befall him. He wrote to Knowles, "Good God, Sir, if you had but Ten Sail of Ships now how easy it would be to compleat the Destruction of this Grand Armament."[4]

No further warlike alarm disturbed Knowles. The administration of Louisbourg occupied his attention. He did not share the optimistic views of Shirley, Warren, and Pepperrell. He held the worst possible opinion of the place. It would cost five or six hundred thousand pounds to put it in proper condition. He thought the soil barren, the climate either frost or fog for nine months of the year, and within a few weeks of his taking command had stopped the carrying out of the designs of Pepperrell and Warren, except completing the necessary barracks. He had sound views of the command of the sea, and therefore thought little of the importance of Louisbourg as a fortress.

"Neither the Coast of Accadia nor any of the Harbours in Newfd. (except St. John's and Placentia) are fortifyed and these but triflingly and yett we continue masters of them, and whatever nation sends the Strongest fleet into these seas will always be masters of the Cod fisheries for that year whether there be a Louisbourg or not."[5]

Of the people who came he also had a poor opinion. He sent back the parish beggars of New England who hung about. He said that rum was the chief trade in which were engaged every one in the New England army from the General down to the Corporal,[6] and he describes vividly the ravages of alcohol.

"As the Commerce of this Place was changed from Fish to Rum and the loss of so many of the New England troops last year was principally occasioned by that Destructive Liquor, I found myself obliged for the preservation of His Majesty's Forces to endeavor to put a stop to the vending of it in such unlimited quantities and as Admiral Warren just before his Departure had published an order for every suttler to lodge what spiritous Liquors they were possessed of in the Cittadel casements,"[7]

he got possession of 64,000 gallons; but from secreted stuff, often as many as one thousand men daily were drunk, until the supply ran short. A rate

---

[1] Capt. Scott, C.O. 5/44.   [2] Co. 5/44.
[3] Spry was an officer of whom Warren thought highly, and had been sent to Annapolis in the *Chester* to guard that position. He was followed by Rous, now a captain in the navy in command of H.M.S. *Shirley*, bought from Massachusetts. On Nov. 4, 1744, Spry had gained reputation among the people of New England by his capture of a Louisbourg privateer. Shirley to Newcastle, Nov. 9 (C.O. 5/900).
[4] Chester at Annapolis, Oct. 4 (C.O. 5/44).   [5] C.O. 5/44.   [6] Letter of July 9.   [7] C.O. 5/44.

of consumption which had such results must have rapidly depleted the stores of the traders.

His judgment in certain respects was sound. He foresaw that a change in the stoppages of the regiments would lead to disturbances and mutiny. He was right in this, for when about June 26 Knowles communicated to the mustered troops instructions he had received with regard to stoppages, and gave an order that they should be deducted from their pay,

". . . in a few hours after the whole garrison was in a general mutiny & the troops ran & returned their provisions into store in a tumultous manner & swore that they were no longer soldiers. It was impossible to discover any leader, for in an instant there were more than a thousand assembled together; as I thought no time was to be lost to prevent the threatening danger I immediately order'd them under arms & met them upon the parade & informed them it was His Majesty's Order & that nothing but the exigencies of the state for money to carry on the War could occasion this stoppage being made. They remonstrated regiment by regiment that they were ready to obey His Majesty's commands with their lives, but they must perish in this climate if those stoppages were made, that it was scarce possible for them honestly now to supply themselves with necessarys and the Common Refreshments of Life in this Scarce and dear place but it would be absolutely so with those deductions & that therefore, if they had not their full Pay they could be no longer soldiers, all reasoning proving ineffectuall, and perceiving many to be heated with drink, I found myself obliged to order their pay & provisions to be continued to them till His Majesty's further Pleasure should be known, when they huzza'd & said they would serve faithfully. I told your Grace in several of my former letters that I dreaded the consequences of such an order being issued & I may now rejoice that nothing worse had happened, for I will venture to affirm that had four hours been neglected to have given them satisfaction no reasoning would have been able to have stopped their rage & force we had not to quell it with." [1]

Much to his delight he was relieved to take command of the West Indies squadron. On the 18th of September 1747 he resigned the government to Col. Peregrine Hopson, the senior officer of the garrison, and sailed the next day for Jamaica. Hopson's occupancy of the position was not marked by any events more serious than an attack on a block-house at Table Head, erected by the English to protect the coal mines. The occasional capture by bands of Indians of an imprudent officer, and the incursion of Marin into Cape Breton in 1748, which Hopson claimed was a breach of the peace which had then been established, broke the monotony of the place. While the officers of its garrison were still uncertain as to their fate,[2] diplomacy had dealt with the situation.[3]

[1] Knowles to Newcastle, June 28, 1747, C.O. 5/901, p. 128. Choleric and unpleasant as Knowles was, he acted in this instance with excellent judgment.

[2] "Some say we shall battle the elements in this damned place for six or eight months longer" (Lawrence to Knowles, Oct. 12, 1748, B.M. MSS. 15,956, f. 177).

[3] The forecasts of Knowles proved nearer correct than those of Shirley or Warren. The holding of Cape Breton had not proved the advantage to New England which they and many others had hoped. The settlers were few, but

APPENDICES

A. The Capture of the "Vigilant"

The principal accounts of the engagement are in the Logs. That of the *Mermaid* is as follows :

MERMAID, 20*th May*.

Hazey Wear., Gave Chace to the S.W. at 1 wore Ship to the No. Wd. the Chace hoistd. a French Ensign & Pendt. We fired our Stern Chace on her wch. she returned from her Bow we made ye Sigl. of Discovering a Strange Ship to ye Fleet who were all in shore at 2 the chace perceivg. our Fleet wore to ye So. Wd. & gave us his Broadside we wore after him and returned it he made all the Sail Possible we kept Close under his Starboard Quarter he kept Plying his stern Chase as we did our Bow we Portd. our Helm twice and gave him two Broadsides at 6 Came up Capn. Rouse in a Privateer *Snow* who Ply'd his Bow Chace very well at 8 the Commodr. in the *Superbe* and *Eltham* Joyn'd us the Chace Engaged us Large the *Superbe* on the Starbd. & we on the Larboard quarter at 9 the Chace, struck sent on bd. our boats and brot. from thence the 1st and 2d. Caps. & part of the Officers it being a Thick Fogg could see no other Ship but the Prize wch. was a French Man of War of 64 Guns & 500 Men Called the *Vigilant* Capn. Maisonfort Am Imployed shifting Prisoners & Securing our Riggin Recd. on board 130 Prisoners at 8 A.M. the Commodr. Joynd us. . . .

21st May.—Modt. & Foggy sent on board the 1st Mate 1 Midshipman 20 Men Laying too in Compy. the *Eltham* and Commodr. at 4 A.M. the Commodr. stood in for the Land sent on bd. the Prize 1 Midshipman and 15 Men to Assist she being much shattered (R.O. Captain's Logs. No. 820).

The Captain of the *Eltham* on the 20th enters :

At 7 P.M. came up with chace she tackt. & Came Close to our Larboard side & Discharged a broad Side & A Volley of Small arms which killed one man & wounded two : we immediately Returned a broad side a low & a loft with a Volley of Small Arms which Shott his fore top saile Yard & mizon Yard away in ye Slings and he called out for good quarters. we had Several Shott holes in all our Sailes ye fore Spring Stay was Shott away Main braces Driver yard : ye Cacsce (*sic*) proved to be a french Ship of Warr called ye *Vigilant* of breast of 64 guns bound to Lewisbourg : Recd. much damage in ye rigging (R.O. Master's Logs No. 393).

Pepperrell, than whom none could be better authority, as he would get an authentic account from Warren, thus relates the incident :

About noon a large French ship (which proved to be the *Vigilant* a ship of war

this was accounted for by the disturbed conditions of these few years. At least two thousand men died as the result of the siege, a large proportion of the young and adventurous of the people of sparsely settled Colonies. The projected expeditions against Canada in 1746 and 1747 so upset the normal course of events that New England was unable to adequately exploit industries her people had already developed. War and commercial depression rather than any local conditions accounted fully for the stagnation of Louisbourg during the years it was under the British flag.

mounting 64 guns) came up with the *Mermaid* (in sight of the camp) & fired upon her, & soon after with Capt. Rouse in ye Shirly Gally.   Both of those ships fired frequently at the *Vigt.* but did not care to come too near therefore bore away towards the Commodore & other of our ships which were nearer ye shore.   The Com. & other ships soon discovered yr. fire and motions & being to windward of her bore down & in the evening came up with her.   We heard a pretty constant firing all the Afternoon & in ye evening at a considerable distance & hopd they will be able to give a good acçt. of her to-morrow. . . . After some dispute the Frenchmen having about 20 men killed & abt. as many wounded, strook, but it being foggy & a large sea, the Com. not hearing ye cry for qr. gave him a broadside & then lost the prize, it being dark, but the *Mermaid* being near and knowing she had strook sent her boat with 4 men on board the prize where yy. stayed all nt.   The next morn. the Com. discovd. her at a little distance in much confusion her rigging, yards & masts much hurt & soon went to work to make ye proper distribution of the prisoners & rectifie the ship in order to bring her in.   [The discrepancies are illuminating.]

B. The Summons and Reply

Letter from Messrs. Pepperrell and Warren to Mons. Du Chambon

The Camp before Louisbourg, *May* 7, 1745.

Whereas there is now encamped upon the Island of Cape Breton near the city of Louisbourg, a number of his Brittanic Majesty's Troops under the Command of the Honble. Lieut. General William Pepperrell, Esq., and also a Squadron of His Majesty's Ship of War, under the Command of the Honble. Peter Warren, Esq., is now lying before the Harbour of said city ; for the reduction thereof to the obedience of the Crown of Great Britain.   We, the said William Pepperrell and Peter Warren, to prevent the effusion of Christian Blood, do in the name of our Sovereign Lord George the Second, of Great Britain, France and Ireland King, etc., Sommons you to Surrender to his said Majesty's obedience, the said city, fortresses and territories ; together with the Artillery, arms and stores of War, thereunto belonging.

In consequence of which surrender, We, the Sd. William Pepperrell and Peter Warren, in the name of our said Sovereign do assure you that all the subjects of the French King, now in said city and territories, shall be treated with the utmost humanity ; have their personal Estates secured to them and have leave to transport themselves and sd. effect to any part of the French King's Dominions in Europe.   Your answer hereto is demanded at or before five of the clock this afternoon.

Wm. Pepperrell.
P. Warren.

To the Commander in Chief of the French
    King's troops, in Louisbourg, on the Island
    of Cape Breton.

Lettre de Monsieur Du Chambon a MM. Warren et Pepperrell

A Louisbourg, le 18 mai 1745.

Nous, Louis Du Chambon, Chevalier de l'ordre militaire de St. Louis, Lieutenant du

Roy, Commandant pour Sa Majestié Très Chrétienne des Isles Royale, Canso, St.-Jean et terres adjacentes.

Sur la sommation qui nous a été faite ce jour septième may vieux stylle, de la part du Sieur honorable Pepperrell, Lieutenant Général, commandant les troupes qui forment le siège de Louisbourg, et du Sieur honorable Pietre Warren, commandant l'escadre des vaisseaux du Roy de la Grande Bretagne, mouillés près du port de la dite ville, que nous ayons à lui remettre la dite ville, avec des dépendances, artillerie, armes et munitions de guerre sous l'obéissance du Roi leur maître.

Le Roi de France, le nôtre, nous ayant confié la défense de la dite ville, nous ne pouvons qu'après la plus vigoureuse attaque écouter une semblable proposition ; et nous n'avons de réponse à faire à cette demande que par la bouche de nos cannons.

C. Letters relating to Capitulation

Letter from Messrs. Warren and Pepperrell to Gov. Du Chambon

Camp, *June* 15, 1745, at 1/2 past 8 o'clock, P.M.

We have yours of the date proposing a suspension of hostilities for such a time as shall be necessary for you to determine upon the conditions of delivering up the garrison of Louisbourg, which arrived at a happy juncture to prevent the Effusion of Christian Blood as we were together and had just determined upon a general attack. We shall comply with your desire until eight of the clock to-morrow, and in the meantime you surrender yourselves prisoners of war, You may depend upon honour and generous treatment.—We are, your humble servants,

P. Warren.
W. Pepperrell.

Letter from M. Pepperrell to Gov. Du Chambon

Camp before Louisbourg, *June* 16.

Sir,—I have yours by an hostage signifying your consent to surrender of the town and fortresses of Louisbourg and the territories adjacent, etc., etc., on the terms this day proposed to you by Com. Warren and myself; excepting only that you desire your troops may march out of the garrison with their arms and colours flying, to be there delivered into our custody till the said troop's arrival in France, at which time to have them returned to them which I consent to, and send you a hostage for the performance of what we have promised, and have sent to Com. Warren that if he consents to it he would send a detachment on Shore to take possession of the Island Battery.—I am, Sir, your humble servt.,

W. Pepperrell.

Letter from Com. Warren to Gov. Du Chambon

"Superbe," off Louisbourg, *June* 16.

Sir,—I have received your letter of this date, desiring that His most Christian Majesty's Troops, under your command, may have the honours of war given them so far as to march to my Boats at the Beach, with their musquets, and Bayonets, and colours flying, there to deliver them to the officers of his Brittanic Majesty whom I shall appoint for that purpose, to be kept in my custody till they shall be landed in the French King's Dominions, then and there to be returned to him, which I agree to in consideration of your gallant defense, upon the following conditions.

First.—That you deliver up immediately to the officers and troops, whom I shall appoint, the Island Battery with all the ammunition, cannon warlike and other King's stores belonging in the condition they now are.

Secondly.—That all the ships of war and other vessels do enter the Harbour without molestation at any time after daylight to-morrow morning, and that the keys of the town be delivered to such officers and troops as I shall appoint to receive them, and that all the cannon, warlike and other King's stores in the town be also delivered up to the said officer.

I expect your immediate complyance with these terms and beg to assure you, that I am with regard, Sir, your most obt. and humble servant,   P. WARREN.[1]

[1] Quebec MSS. vol. 3 ; Moreau St. M. vol. 50.

CHAPTER XI

THE Treaty of Aix-la-Chapelle was finally signed October 18, 1748. Its main provisions were arranged in the preliminaries of peace definitely agreed to by the contracting parties on the previous 30th of April, and forthwith communicated to their colonial governors. The places taken during the war were mutually restored, which gave Cape Breton back to France. This disappointed bitterly its New England captors, and blasted the hopes of making it the seat of a prosperous English colony, of which Shirley and Warren had been the most prominent exponents. Pamphleteers of the metropolis expressed the public dissatisfaction.[1] Public opinion was dissatisfied with the terms of the Treaty, the language, French, in which it was expressed, and the indignity to England of giving hostages for the fulfilment of her agreements.[2]

The terms of the Treaty were not better thought of by the French, and with more reason. Louis XV. returned the Austrian Netherlands, Maestricht, and Bergen-op-Zoom, the two frontier fortresses of Holland, Madras, and with it command of the whole Coromandel Coast in India. The former concessions, giving up the command of the narrow seas, which it was England's secular policy to hold inviolate at any cost,[3] made the action of Louis XV. a kingly largess, rather than a business transaction. More humiliating to French self-respect were the renewal of the agreement to dismantle the fortifications of Dunkirk, and the public withdrawal of the long support given to the House of Stuart by the expulsion from France of Charles Edward.[4]

---

[1] The London *Evening Post*, from October 25 to November 12, 1748, deals frequently with this matter, and severely criticizes the terms of peace. On November 10-12 it publishes verses, of which the following is a specimen :

"A NEW BALLAD, ON THE GLORIOUS TIMES

(*To the tune of ' Derry Down.*')

Cape Breton's expensive, as well hath been prov'd,
And therefore, the *Burthen* is wisely remov'd ;
Which *Burthen French Shoulders* we settle again on,
And *add*—our own *Stores*, our *Provisions* and *Cannon*."

A history of the negotiations and the text of the Treaty are in *La Paix d'Aix-la-Chapelle*, par le Duc de Broglie, Calman, Levy, Paris, 1892.

[2] *E.g.* "A Letter from a Gent in London . . . " 1748, B.M. 101, K, 58 ; "The Advantages of the Definite Treaty," 1749, 8135, aaa 20 ; "The Preliminaries Productive of a Premunire," 101, K, 57. The references are to the British Museum Library.   [3] Corbett, *England in the Seven Years War*, vol. i. p. 10.   [4] La C. G. p. 205.

Louisbourg was duly returned. The advantages of a port in Acadia had been made evident to British administrators by the three years of possession. Louisbourg being no longer available, made necessary the development of Nova Scotia, which had lain fallow since 1710. Chebuctou Bay was decided on as the site for its capital, to which, in honour of Lord Halifax, President of the Lords of Trade and Plantations, his name was given. Colonel the Honourable Edward Cornwallis was named the first Governor. He and the first settlers arrived in June 1749. The project was carried on with such vigour that in three years, Halifax had over 4000 subsidized and more or less satisfied inhabitants, about as many as had been gathered in forty years at Louisbourg.

That town, until the actual breaking out of hostilities, was in an eddy of the stream of pregnant events which took place elsewhere. These events demand a brief statement even in a history of Louisbourg of the narrowest scope, for they, more than any local cause, determined its fate as part of the great colonial empire which France was holding with so loose a grasp.

Commissioners were appointed for the delimitation of the American boundaries of the possessions of the two Powers.[1] Their sittings were dragged out. Disputes as to procedure, and the language in which documents were to be presented, occupied undue time. Claims, widely different, were presented. Much irrelevant matter was produced. Little disposition was shown to arrive at a common ground of fact, or to abate pretensions which made impossible any fair chance of development for the rival. Failure was the inevitable result of such procedure. Their deliberations proved fruitless to form a basis for a lasting peace, as their records fail to give the later student any clear view of the merits of the controversy.[2] It was also agreed that, pending the findings of the Commissioners, the *status quo ante* should not be disturbed by such acts on either side as the erection of fortifications, or the placing of troops on the disputed territory. The two courts agreed expressly to this stipulation, " that no fortification, new settlement, or innovation, should be attempted in those countries the fate of which was to be finally determined by their sentence." [3]

The boundaries of Acadia and of the territories to the westward of the Alleghanies were the two principal subjects of difference in America. The action which England took assumed that her greatest claims to both these territories were sound. This action was not that of the active colonial administrator eager to distinguish himself by straining his instructions. It was carried out by him under specific warrant of the highest authority.

[1] La Galissonière and Silhouette for France, Mildmay and Shirley for England. Their proceedings opened in September 1750, and the English Commissioners left Paris in the latter part of 1754. Shirley returned to America to tarnish a brilliant reputation by his military exploits ; La Galissonière to active service and the defeat of Byng off Minorca, and Silhouette to carry on private efforts to adjust the differences between his country and England.

[2] For the diplomatic correspondence see R.O. State Papers, Foreign, France, vols. 232 and 233. The suggestion seems first to have been made by France, June-July 1749.   [3] *History of the late War*, p. 7, Glasgow, 1765.

The first question which arose was that of a grant to the Ohio Company. This was an association of Virginians of the highest standing, with English partners, of whom John Hanbury, a London merchant of great repute and influence, was the chief.[1] It petitioned in 1748 for a grant of 200,000 acres on the western side of the Great Mountains, upon some of the chief branches of the Mississippi. Gooch, Governor of Virginia, "was apprehensive such Grants might possibly give Umbrage to the French, especially when we were in hopes of entering into a Treaty for establishing a General Peace, which was the only Objection he had, and made him and the Council (of Virginia) think it advisable to wait His Majesty's pleasure and Directions." This, in part, is the memorandum of the Lords of Trade to the Committee of the Privy Council (September 2, 1748) on which is based the recommendation of the former that the grant be made.[2]

Instructions were given to Gooch to issue the grant,[3] and it was recommended, on the 23rd of February 1749, by the Lords of Trade to be extended to 500,000 acres on the Ohio, one of the conditions being that on the first 200,000 acres a fort must be erected and the Company place therein a sufficient garrison for the security and protection of the settlers.[4] This was agreed to in Council on the 16th of March.

It was, it may be noted, the colonial Governor who, before the Treaty was signed, recognized the territory as disputed. It was the highest administrative body in the realm which, after peace was concluded, ignored the implications, if not the words, of the agreement so recently executed by one of their number.[5] With this spirit informing the Privy Council it is not surprising to find the pamphleteer discussing the development of the northern colonies from the standpoint of one who expects a new war; nor that the proximate cause of that war was the operations of the Company so brought into being;[6] nor, that succeeding historians have described the conditions between 1748 and 1756 as an imperfectly kept truce rather than a peace.

The *Evening Post* praised the French management of colonies as superior to the English, and urged war, as Great Britain is as yet superior to France in naval power :

"Let us therefore strike when we are able, without regarding the conveniency of the

---

[1] "The Ohio Company established and composed of merchants belonging to Virginia and Maryland and several rich commoners and lords in the Mother Country" (Burk's *Virginia*, 1822, vol. 3, p. 170).

[2] C.O. 5/1366, pp. 411-417.   [3] Pp. 422-425, December 13, 1748.   [4] Pp. 427-433 and 434-439.

[5] Lord Sandwich, Minister Plenipotentiary at Aix-la-Chapelle, was admitted to the Privy Council, 1st February 1749, and was present at the meeting of 16th March.

[6] "Meanwhile, the English traders were crossing the mountains from Pennsylvania and Virginia, poaching on the domain which France claimed as hers, ruining the French fur trade, seducing the Indian allies of Canada, and stirring them up against her. Worse still, English land speculators were beginning to follow. Something must be done, and that promptly, to drive back the intruders, and vindicate French rights in the valley of the Ohio. To this end the Governor sent Celoron de Bienville thither in the summer of 1749" (Parkman, *Montcalm and Wolfe*, vol. i. p. 37).

Dutch, the Views of the Austrians or the safety of H—— (Hanover), lest the time come when we are not able to help them nor ourselves." [1]

The claims of England in Acadia were as extensive as in the Ohio, but not as promptly made. There was no pressure from " rich commoners and lords " to expedite matters. But within a few weeks after Cornwallis arrived in Halifax he had instructions from the Lords of Trade in reference to the northern part of the province : [2]

" And as there is great reason to apprehend that the French may dispute the right of the Crown of Great Britain to these territories, we further earnestly recommend to you to have a watchful eye to the security thereof and upon the proceedings of the French." [3]

England stated her rights even more strongly in the instructions to the Commissioners, Shirley and Mildmay :

" And therefore you are to insist that his most Christian Majesty has no right to any Lands whatsoever lying between the River Saint Lawrence and the Atlantick Ocean, except such Islands as ly in the mouth of the said River and in the Gulph of the same name." [4]

La Galissonière, then Governor of Canada, was equally clear that these lands, now the province of New Brunswick, and that part of Quebec lying between the northern boundary of New Brunswick and the St. Lawrence River, were part of Canada and not of Acadia.

Leaving untouched the pretensions of the Powers, we can deal with the facts. The population consisted of a very small settlement on the St. John River, and some hamlets to the north of the isthmus peopled by the overflow of the Acadians on the peninsula of Nova Scotia, as well as somewhat important fishing stations on the Miramichi, the Baie des Chaleurs, and the south shore of the St. Lawrence. In 1732 the people of St. John River had taken the oath of allegiance to England. [5] In the same year the people of Chippody, one of the settlements of Acadians, had applied to Armstrong for grants of land. [6]

La Galissonière admitted that this was the case :

" Most of the poor people are of Acadian stock, they have been almost entirely abandoned by Canada and France since the Peace of Utrecht, and the English have made them believe that, having been subject formerly to the French Governor of Port Royal, they owed the same obedience to the English Governor." [7]

As regards sovereignty, it would appear that there was not much difference between the Powers. France abandoned, as regards administration, the people

---

[1] Sept. 17, 1745.

[2] The Duke of Bedford wrote Cornwallis on September 26 and November 6, 1749. One of these letters dealt probably with this matter. These letters are not now in the Record Office.

[3] N.S. Arch. vol. I, p. 362.   [4] C.O. Nova Scotia, vol. 39.

[5] N.S. Arch. vol. I, p. 98.   [6] Ibid. p. 92.   [7] Can. Ar. Report, 1905, vol. ii. p. 304.

along the northern shore of the Bay of Fundy. The officials of England never penetrated to the more northern settlements of the territory which she vigorously claimed. It was, however, used by France down to what the French claimed was its extreme southern limit, the isthmus of Chignecto, as the route between Canada and Isle Royale ; while, owing to economic and ecclesiastical conditions, the intercourse of the people living thereon was closer with Louisbourg than with Annapolis. At an earlier time in the winter of 1718, St. Ovide considered placing part of the troops of Louisbourg at the isthmus. His choice of Quebec was not apparently influenced by any notion that the territory was not French.[1]

The territory, it is clear, was disputed. Mutual distrust, the curse of international relations, began to work its evil effects. Gorham, that active and seasoned leader of New England levies, visited in force the St. John River in the autumn of 1748, alarmed the inhabitants and carried off to Boston two Indians. Their return was demanded by La Galissonière, and became the subject of a pungent correspondence between himself, Mascarene, and Shirley, and led to the instructions to Cornwallis already cited.

La Galissonière sent in the spring of 1749 Boishébert and a detachment from Quebec to hold the St. John River as French territory. His successor as Governor of Canada, La Jonquière, sent the Chevalier La Corne in the autumn to hold inviolate the territory on the north of the isthmus. In the spring of 1750 Cornwallis dispatched an expedition under Major Lawrence to dislodge La Corne, who was encamped on the isthmus with a military force, supported by Indians and Acadians. The numbers of the last were augmented by the burning of Beaubassin by the Indians as the forces of Lawrence appeared. Its inhabitants were driven to the French side, where, alone, they felt safe from the threats of the savage allies of their country.

La Corne met Lawrence in a parley, April 22, and maintained that he was to hold and defend his position till the boundaries between the two Crowns should be settled " by Commissioners appointed for that purpose."[2] In short, " his replies were so perimptory and of such a nature as Convinced me he was determined in his purposes." La Corne's force was superior, " his situation in respect to ground was properly chosen, and an argument of his good judgement " . . . " til I (Lawrence) to much feared we had no pretensions to dispute that part of the country with him."

Lawrence withdrew to his vessels in the pouring rain, and gave himself up to unpleasant reflections. He saw that to dislodge the enemy was impossible, and was of opinion that " to have Sat down on one side of the River and Leave

---

[1] I do not find any reason why Mascarene and Bennett, and the French envoys Denys and De Pensens, did not visit in 1714 Beaubassin and more northern settlements. It leaves open, to the bold, the view that both French and English, before any question of boundaries had arisen, held that this territory was French.

[2] *Canadian Archives Report*, 1905, vol. ii. p. 321.

the Enemy possession of the other was a tacit acknowledgment of the Justice of his claim." After considering "whether we could Annoy or Molest them further elsewhere at Chipodie or Memim Cook" (Memramcook), against which his officers were unanimous, the force returned to Minas Basin on the 25th. It would seem that in Lawrence's mind, if not in that of his superiors, the scope of the expedition under his charge embraced the harassing of non-belligerent inhabitants, as much as dispossessing an armed French force from territory claimed as British. Lawrence's superiors evidently did not agree with him, that occupation of the isthmus was a tacit acknowledgment of the justice of the French claim, for he was sent back in September, and he erected a fort on what the French admitted was English territory.

La Corne was recalled to Canada, and was replaced by St. Ours des Chaillons (October 8), who, in the following spring, began the erection of a fort on the French position, which was given the name of Beauséjour.[1]

Skirmishes took place between the English garrison and the Indians and Acadians. Captain How was treacherously murdered, but eventually the garrisons settled down to a peaceful and friendly existence, broken at times by friction, cemented at others by friendly offices on either side, and with illicit trade as a constant bond.[2]

When Vergor[3] took charge, he at once notified Du Quesne that the position was not capable of successful defence (November 1754).

Boishébert, on the St. John, took the same position as La Corne when he was visited by Rous, and as successfully held it. Rous, in command of the *Albany*, captured French vessels on the high seas.[4] This led to friction and reprisals as well as to diplomatic correspondence.[5]

The activities of French and English on the Ohio and the adjacent territories did not reach a condition of stagnation as in Nova Scotia, but passed on to conflict so serious, that in the end of 1754 Great Britain took the momentous step of sending out regular troops to support its Virginian levies, repulsed in their advances into the debatable land. Parkman gives a vivid and picturesque account of De Bienville's expedition to strengthen the effective occupation of this

---

[1] Lawrence's account and that of La Corne are printed in the *Canadian Archives Reports*, 1905, vol. ii. pp. 320 *et seq.* There is also in it a Journal of the events, from September 1750 to July 1751, written by De la Vallière, who was detached from Louisbourg with fifty picked men in response to La Corne's appeal for reinforcements. De la Vallière was the descendant of an Acadian seigneur, and from the heights of Beauséjour looked down on Isle la Vallière, midway between Beauséjour and Fort Lawrence, once the home of his family.

[2] The building of Beauséjour proceeded very slowly. After La Corne (1749-50), its commandants were : St. Ours des Chaillons (1750-51), De Vassin (1751-53), De la Martinière (1753-54), and De Vergor du Chambon (1754-55).

[3] He was the son of the Governor of Louisbourg in 1745, and it was through his lack of vigilance that Wolfe's army gained its foothold on the plains of Abraham.

[4] They were returned.

[5] The first four vessels which arrived in Louisbourg in 1751 were seized and eventually sold (C.O. 217/39 ; Captains' Letters, vol. 2382).

territory by France, as well as some description of the forts and settlements which previously existed.[1]

It is not necessary to carry further the narrative of events elsewhere than in Isle Royale. Louisbourg had felt only the indirect effects of these occurrences, for it was so unquestionably a French possession, that any action against it was not considered within the scope of British operations.

The transfer of Isle Royale and its dependencies to France had been made without difficulty. Charles des Herbiers, Sieur de la Ralière, a naval captain of distinction, was chosen as French Commissioner and Governor, and furnished with voluminous instructions, which included drafts of the letters he was to write. He left France with the men-of-war *Tigre* and *Intrépide*, which convoyed transports, carrying about five hundred troops from Isle de Rhé and civilian inhabitants of Isle Royale. The frigate *Anémone* was dispatched after him to make more imposing his important mission.

On the 29th of June 1749 the *Tigre* was a league off Louisbourg. Des Herbiers transcribed his model letter to Hopson, its Governor, and sent it into the town by two officers. He chose as his envoys Des Gannes and Loppinot, both of whom had been officers in its former garrison.[2] At noon the next day the flotilla entered the harbour and exchanged salutes with the shore batteries. That afternoon Des Herbiers and his staff were received with all the honours, by Hopson and his officers. There were difficulties about the transport of the British troops and people and other minor matters. In the end they were satisfactorily settled. The opportune arrival of Cornwallis at Halifax set free British transports which came to Louisbourg. They were supplemented by French ships, and so effectively were the arrangements made and carried out, that on the 23rd of July Des Herbiers marched into the town, and received its keys from Hopson. The French flag replaced that of England over the citadel and batteries. Hopson received a certificate that the transfer was complete and satisfactory, and the English forces and people withdrew to Halifax.

The English ships did not begin to sail, however, till the 30th, and the Te Deum for the return of peace was deferred, out of consideration for them, until August 3.[3]

---

[1] See *Montcalm and Wolfe*, chap. ii. On colonial wars and reprisals, see Corbett, vol. i. p. 24.

[2] Des Gannes was to be major and Loppinot adjutant of the troops in the new establishment (B, 90, p. 42).

[3] Des Herbiers' account of the transfer is printed in Quebec MSS. vol. 3, pp. 439 *et seq.* He acknowledges handsomely in it the courtesy of Hopson, and the zeal and efficiency of his own officers. The French version of the certificate is given in *Canadian Archives*, vol. ii., 1905, p. 282. See also R.O. France, vol. 233. The difference in the calendars used by the French and English, accounts for the apparent discrepancy of eleven days in all dates up to 1752.

An incident shows the disorders to which such upheavals of population tend. On the 27th of July was baptized, and no doubt cared for, an English child aged about three months, abandoned by parents of whom the new-comers could find no trace :

The same care to make prosperous and safe the returned colony as to provide for its proper transfer was shown by the Minister. Bigot, who had gained with Rouillé, now Minister of the Navy, the same standing as he had held with Maurepas, was sent to Louisbourg to reorganize the civil service. On his recommendation, Prévost, who had been his chief clerk, succeeded him as Commissaire-Ordonnateur. Bigot went there on the *Diane*, and for some weeks gave Des Herbiers and Prévost the benefit of his great abilities.[1]

The former inhabitants returned from Canada and France. They found the houses in poor condition, as but few of them had been repaired by the English during their occupation. Bigot ordered two hundred cows for distribution among the people, and for two years they were supplied with rations from the King's stores. The fishing was good, but they were hampered by a lack of boats. They did their best to make up for the deficiency, by buying the boats of the departing English and by activities in the building yard. Ninety to one hundred boats were built by October, and many were still on the ways. The French who had remained during the English occupation[2] sold boats to the new-comers, and row-boats and canoes were used as substitutes for fishing-boats.

The partly cured cod of the English merchants was bought by the French, but, even with the abundant fisheries, there was too small a catch to load the unusual number of ships which had come out from France. The merchants of Louisbourg, as well as the shipowners, pressed Prévost for permission to buy from the English. Notwithstanding the justice of the request, and the hardships involved, he refused, but, with a frankness in which he imitated Bigot, he adds that in the confusion of the new settlement it is probable some infractions of the laws against trade with the English took place.[3]

An augmented garrison, twenty-four companies of fifty men each and a company of artillery, were placed at Louisbourg and its dependencies. This force was made up from new companies formed for the purpose, and the old companies, which had been in Canada since their return from the English prisons, after the defeat of La Jonquière by Anson. Instructions to Des Herbiers

---

[1] Bigot was in Louisbourg from about the time of Des Herbiers' arrival until August 21. He then went to Quebec. Bigot succeeded Hocquart as Intendant of Canada in March 1748.
[2] In all, 94 people.
[3] C[11], vol. 28, f. 160.

recounted the abuses which had created such disorder among the troops before the capture of the town, and asked for such reorganization as would remedy these evils.   The most important step he took in this direction was the suppression of the canteens kept, as a perquisite, by the captains, recognizing as legal only that of the Major.   In the meantime Des Herbiers received Franquet, an engineer of distinction, who was sent out to Louisbourg as director-general of the fortifications. The Marquis de Chabert, detached from sea duty, was instructed to correct the maps of Acadia, Isle Royale, and Newfoundland, and to fix by astronomical observations the principal points therein.   He made Louisbourg his headquarters in 1751–52, and the results of his labours, endorsed by the Royal Academy of Sciences and by the Académie de Marine, were printed in a handsome volume in 1753.[1]

The ordinary courtesies were exchanged with Cornwallis at Halifax.   Good feeling on the part of Cornwallis was further marked by his co-operation in sending to Louisbourg the body of the Duc d'Anville.   *Le Grand St. Esprit* bore it from Chibuctou to French territory, and, with fitting ceremony, it was reinterred at the foot of the high altar in the chapel of the citadel.[2]

The general instructions of the Minister were to co-operate with La Jonquière in maintaining the rights of France to the disputed territory, to repel force by force,[3] and to harass, by the Indians, the new settlement in Halifax, but to do so secretly.   He was also directed to encourage the settlement of Acadians on Isle St. Jean, many of whom had been driven from their homes by the disturbed state of the border-land, and the menaces of the Indians against those who remained on British territory.   They readily passed over to the island in such numbers that its population rapidly increased.   The instructions to the Governors of Isle Royale and of Canada as to their dealings with the English might be quoted many times.   One memorandum dated August 29, 1749, shall suffice, as it sets forth the policy of France.   It was read to the King, its apostille states, and presumably received his sanction, for the policy it lays down was not departed from.   After stating briefly the advantages to England and the disadvantages to Isle Royale, in particular, of the settlement of Nova Scotia, it goes on :

" Such are, in general, the unfortunate consequences which will necessarily spring from these projects if the English can succeed in accomplishing them.   As it is impossible to openly oppose them, for they are within their rights in making in Acadia such settlements as they see fit, as long as they do not pass its boundaries, there remains for us only to bring against them as many indirect obstacles as can be done without comprising ourselves, and to take steps to protect ourselves against plans which the English can consider through the success of these settlements.

[1] Franquet and Chabert were fellow-passengers on the *Mutine*, which sailed from Brest, June 29, 1750.

[2] Sept. 3, 1746, Quebec MSS., 3, p. 455.   [3] To Des Herbiers, Sept. 11, 1750, B, vol. 91, p. 49.

" The only method we can employ to bring into existence these obstacles is to make the savages of Acadia and its borders feel how much it is to their advantage to prevent the English fortifying themselves, to bind them to oppose it openly, and to excite the Acadians to support the Indians in their opposition (to the English) in so far as they can do without discovery. The missionaries of both have instructions and are agreeable to act in accordance with these views." [1]

A fortnight before this memorandum was prepared for the King, Des Herbiers and Prévost wrote from Louisbourg (August 15, 1749) that the Abbé Le Loutre was carrying out this policy. Bigot had given him, as supplementary to the ordinary presents to the Indians, cloth, blankets, powder and ball, in case they might wish to disturb the English in their settlement in Halifax. " It was this missionary's task to induce them to do so." [2]

The history of these wretched years on the border-land shows with what ardour, self-sacrifice, and cruelty he encouraged the Indians under his charge to carry out instructions which had the Royal sanction.[3] In this course the priest was not alone. Young Des Bourbes gave Surlaville, April 15, 1756, a budget of news from Louisbourg containing this passage :

" Four savages, two Abenaquis and two Miquemacs, arrived here from Quebec, on the 31st of March. They informed us that a band of outaouvis and chaouenons had raided Virginia, they took about 600 scalps, burnt many villages, and took five hundred prisoners, all women and children. . . . On the 2nd of April our Governor feasted these savages ; they danced before him and presented him with a dozen scalps, taken in the neighbourhood of Chibouctou ; they were handsomely paid for their journey and given several presents besides." [4]

This continued during the season, for Du Fresne du Motel wrote on the 1st December :

" Our savages have taken a number of English scalps, their terror of these natives is unequalled, they are so frightened that they dare not leave the towns or forts without detachments, with the protection of these they go out for what is absolutely needed." [5]

Des Herbiers had accepted with reluctance the post of Commissioner and

---

[1] French text in Can. Arch. vol. ii. p. 292.   [2] " Ce missionaire doit les y engager."

[3] Vol. 28, f. 160. It was later felt at Court that Le Loutre must be restrained. The Minister wrote him on Aug. 27, 1751, that he must not give the English any just cause of complaint, although he praises Le Loutre's wisdom in this respect.

[4] " Quatre sauvages, dont deux Abenaquis et deux Miquemacs, arrivèrent icy, de Québec, le 31 mars. Ils nous ont appris qu'une partie de sauvages outaouvis et chaouenons, avoient fait coup sur la Virginie, qu'ils avoient levé environ six cents chevelures, bruslé plusieurs villages et emmené cinq cents prisonniers, tous femmes et enfants. . . . Le 2 avril, notre Gouverneur régala ces sauvages, ils dansèrent et luy présentèrent une douzaine de chevelures qu'ils ont faites aux environs de Chibouctou ; on leur a payé leur voiage fort grassement et fait, en outre, plusieurs présents " (Derniers Jours, etc. p. 187).

[5] " Nos sauvages ont beaucoup levé de chevelures anglaises, qui (sic) ont une terreur sans égal de ces naturels du pais, dont ils sont si effréiés qu'ils n'osent sortir de leurs villes ou forts, sans avoir des détachments à la faveur desquels ils vont chercher leurs besoins les plus urgents " (Derniers Jours, etc. p. 205). (For the English use of Indian methods see Appendix.)

Governor, and as soon as his functions as the first were finished, he began to press for leave to return to sea duty.[1]   The Minister was not ready to make a change until 1751.   The Minister then named as Des Herbiers' successor the Comte de Raymond, Seigneur d'Oye, Lieut.-Colonel of the Vexin Regiment ; so for the first time a military officer governed Isle Royale.   To add weight to the position Raymond was promoted to the grade of Maréchal de Camp (Major-General), and, to give effectiveness to his administration on its military side, he was accompanied by Surlaville, Colonel of the Grenadiers of France, to whom was given the position of Major of the troops and the commission of disciplining them, as well as to report on the coasts of the island and Acadia.[2]

Raymond set forth from Angoulême, of which town and its castle he had been the King's Lieutenant, towards the end of May, embarked on *L'Heureux*, and, after a voyage of fifty days, landed in Louisbourg on the 3rd of August 1751.   He took over the reins of government, and at once Des Herbiers returned to France by the same ship.[3]

There was thus a girding of the loins in the bureaux of the French Admiralty, when Louisbourg was again under its care.   Stores were abundantly supplied.   The arts of peace were fostered by the expedition of the Marquis Chabert.   The presence of an engineer of such eminence as Franquet, of a soldier of such experience as Surlaville, the raising of the garrison until it approached in number that of Canada,[4] showed that a high value was set on Louisbourg and its security.

Raymond was an active man, who made many efforts to improve the colony.   He visited its various ports and those of Isle St. Jean.   He established settlements on the Miré River, he was interested in the crops, and looked with optimistic eye on the yields of cereals in the rude clearings of the settlers.   He also proposed the building of redoubts and the opening of roads which were strongly opposed by Franquet, Surlaville, and the home authorities.[5]   He was apparently vain, for he bought the property of St. Ovide, and desired it should be erected into a seigneury and countship.   While his administration was apparently honest, his request for a gratuity of 20,000 livres so astonished the Minister that in Raymond's own interest he did not put it before the King.[6]

He was fully alive to the ceremonial side of his functions, and found an

---

[1] In this he brought to bear the influence of his distinguished kinsman, De l'Etanduère.

[2] An outbreak took place in the small garrison of Pt. Toulouse in 1750.   See vol. 29, p. 369.

[3] Raymond brought with him, as secretary, one Thomas Pichon, a native of Vire in Normandy, to whom we owe the *Lettres et mémoires pour servir à l'histoire naturelle, civile et politique de Cap Breton*, published La Haye, 1760, and London, an engaging and valuable book.   He was able and brilliant, but his papers in the library at Vire, and those from his hand known as the Tyrell papers, preserved in Halifax, show him as a libertine, and a spy, completely selfish and sordid.

[4] Louisbourg, 1200 ; Canada, 1500.   [5] *Derniers Jours, etc.* p. 14.

[6] According to Prévost, Raymond overdrew his account 26,417 l. (C[11], vol. 33).

opportunity for ingratiating himself with the Court in the instructions he received to have a Te Deum sung for the birth of the Duc de Bourgogne :

"On Sunday 28th of May this important news was announced at day-break by a salute from all the artillery of the place and the King's ships, the frigates, *Fidele* and the *Chariot Royal*, which had dressed ship.

"M. le Comte de Raymond gave a dinner to the staff, the engineers, the officers of artillery, and to the other principal officers, to the Conseil Superieur, the Baillage, the Admiralty, and to the ladies of the place.

"He had two tables with 50 covers, served in four courses, with as much lavishness as elegance. They drank in turn freely every kind of wine of the best brands, to the health of the King, Queen, the Dauphin, Mme. la Dauphine, M. le duc de Bourgogne, and to the Royal Princesses.

"Many guns were fired, and the band increased the pleasure of the fête.

"About 6 o'clock, after leaving the table, they repaired to the King's chapel to hear vespers. At the close of the service, the Te Deum was sung to the accompaniment of all the artillery of the town and of the ships.

"They then went in a procession, as is the custom in the colonies, to the Esplanade of the Maurepas gate.

"The governor there lit a bonfire which he had had prepared ; the troops of the garrison, drawn up on the ramparts and the covered way, fired with the greatest exactness, three volleys of musketry, and the artillery did the same. After this ceremony, the Governor distributed several barrels of his own wine to the troops and to the public.

"The 'Vive le Roi' was so frequently repeated, that no one could doubt that the hearts of the townspeople, the troops, and the country folk, which this festival had attracted, were truly French.

"He had given such good orders in establishing continual patrols in command of officers, that no disorder was committed.

"About 9 in the evening, the governor and all his guests went to see set off the fire-works and a great number of rockets, which he had prepared, and were very well done.

"On his return home, the ball was opened, and lasted till dawn ; all kinds of refreshments, and in abundance, were handed round. His house was illuminated with lanterns placed all round the windows, looking on the rue Royale and the rue Toulouse.

"Three porticoes, with four pyramids, adorned by triple lanterns and wreaths of flowers, rare for such a cold climate, were erected opposite the rue Royale.

"At the opposite angle, where the two roads cross, two other pyramids were also illuminated ; and on the frontal of the three porticoes were painted the arms of the King, the Dauphin, and the Duc de Bourgogne.

"At the end of the same street, opposite the three porticoes, were also represented, by means of lanterns, three large fleurs de lys and a 'Vive le Roi,' very visibly placed on a border above.

"Between these two principal illuminations is situated the large gate of the Government House, which was also adorned at the columns and cornices, by triple lanterns ; above was the King's portrait.

"All round the courtyard there were also fire pots and triple lanterns, as high as the retaining wall of the garden. These illuminations were charming in their effect and lasted till the end of the ball ; all the houses in the town were also lit up as well as the frigate la *Fidele*.

" The government house being too small to accommodate all the distinguished members of the colony, M. le Comte Raymond gave a big dinner the next day to the clergy and the Sunday following to several ladies, officers, and others who had not attended the first fête.

" It can be said that the Governor spared nothing for these festivities and that he gave on that happy occasion very evident proof of a rare generosity." [1]

This account is anonymous but it so closely resembles, both in style and self-praising, the other writings of Raymond, that there seems no doubt it is his. It accounts in part for the overdrawing of his salary, of which Prévost complained.

In spite of his good will, his activities were ineffective. He found the difficulties of his position excessive, for he alienated all with whom he had to work. Prévost had many griefs against him. Page after page of Raymond's memoirs and letters are annotated by the bitter and often unjust pen of Surlaville, whose pocket he had touched in the disposition of the canteens.

He dismissed Pichon on account of an affair of gallantry, which the latter resented, as quite outside the Governor's province, for in his view a tender heart was perfectly compatible with official capacity. Pichon became his bitter enemy, and later wrote in substance that his former patron was " perhaps the most foolish of all animals on two feet." [2] Raymond gave him a certificate, however, on the 10th of October 1753, that he had discharged his duties with " all the intelligence, fidelity, exactitude, and disinterestedness possible."

Surlaville's administration was apparently effective. He lost no time in beginning his duties, but the material he had to work on was not promising. He visited the fortifications the day following their landing and the official reception of Raymond which took place at Prévost's house. The works were in a worse state than he imagined. When he held a review, the troops performed their evolutions badly, some of them did not know how to handle or carry a gun, they were noisy in the ranks, their uniforms were worn and dirty, and were badly put on. Surlaville increased the number of drills and made the cadets take part in them. He enforced the rules about coming into barracks at night, and in a few days was able to note some improvements. [3]

The improvements instituted continued, for, although Johnstone found the works " with more the look of Antient Ruins than of a modern fortification,"

---

[1] This anonymous account is dated May 28, 1752, but we cannot vouch for it being an official date. See Moreau St. Mery, vol. 50, pp. 420-423.   [2] Tyrell Papers, N.S. Archives, vol. 341.

[3] Surlaville went as the official representative of Raymond to announce to Cornwallis his arrival in Isle Royale, and brought back a full statement of the military and civil conditions at Halifax. The impression he made there found an echo on the frontier, for the English officers at Fort Lawrence sought to obtain from the French at Beauséjour confirmation that the functions of Surlaville at Louisbourg portended war (*Derniers Jours, etc.* p. 31).

he also bears testimony that "the service was performed at Louisbourg with as much regularity as in any fortified place in Europe. . . . This made the town to be looked upon as the Athens of the French colonies."[1]

Surlaville endeavoured to enforce the regulations made by Des Herbiers and Prévost (October 10, 1749) establishing the price which soldiers should be charged for articles supplied by their officers, and made a strong statement of the defects of the uniforms worn by the troops. The cloth and linen were poor in quality and badly made, the shoes were thin, and it cost a private six months' wages to buy a new pair. He rightly thought white was a bad colour for uniforms, as it soon got dirty, and the soldier himself followed it. The strictures on the clothing supplied for the barracks, in which the men slept two and two in unclean box beds, and on the exactions of their officers, make quite credible his statement that their recruits were drawn from the dregs of the people, for such service could not attract the self-respecting or the ambitious.[2]

Surlaville also busied himself in trying to improve the condition of the officers, by economies in the lighting and heating, and to benefit both officers and men by a better canteen system. He also dealt ably with the purchase of the King's stores. His memoranda on these subjects show that he was an active and intelligent officer, who remained in Isle Royale too short a time to carry into effect any serious part of the reforms he saw there necessary.[3]

The improvement in the troops, which unquestionably existed, even if less marked than that described by Johnstone, had been helped, not only by the attention given to it by the home authorities, but by the new elements introduced into the garrison. The new companies were officered in the main by subalterns of the regiments disbanded at the Peace. These gentlemen had served in good regiments in the campaigns of Germany and the Netherlands, and brought to Isle Royale standards and a point of view different from those of the "family" officers who had alone held these positions before this time. There was also more interchange with Canada, arising from the alternating garrisons of Louisbourg and Canada at Beauséjour and Fort Gaspareaux, its dependent establishment on the Gulf side of the isthmus of Chignecto.

These years were for the inhabitants of Louisbourg probably the best they had ever seen. It was obvious that the settlement was valued by the Government,

---

[1] Johnstone ascribes this to Des Herbiers. Quebec MSS. 3, p. 482. Des Herbiers says he set for Louisbourg the standard of a French fortress.

[2] The following sums up his criticisms : (1) cloth too thin ; (2) badly cut and costly to make over ; (3) white bad colour ; (4) stockings bad ; (5) shoes thin ; (6) paying only once a year bad ; (7) only three sizes of gaiters sent out, making many misfits ; (8) hats bad ; (9) no distinguishing marks for corporals ; (10) bad linen for shirts ; (11) should have caps, and (12) black instead of white collars (Pap. Surlaville in Laval Univ., Quebec).

[3] Papiers Surlaville. His comments on letters of Raymond and others show him as a severe and meticulous critic. His collection of sixty-six "sottises" of Raymond, if alone preserved, would indicate that he was a malevolent trifler.

and this gave confidence to the people. The expenditure was large ; the fisheries in some of these years gave an abundant yield. Commerce flourished ; many vessels were built and bought from New England.[1] And while smuggling vessels were condemned and sold, it is not probable that these seizures seriously interfered with the trade. The official statements show that it was large, and Surlaville says, in one of his notes, that these were untrustworthy in minimizing the imports from New England. The trade with Canada largely consisted in French and foreign goods, and that with New England, of products of the West Indies.

The Governors promoted the settlement of Acadians in Isle St. Jean, and Baie des Espagnols (Sydney) and other points in Cape Breton, returned and received deserters from Nova Scotia, and on the whole kept on terms of courtesy with its Governor. Raymond retired from the Governorship in 1753, and was succeeded by the Chevalier Augustin Drucour, who came in 1754, and was but little more than installed in his office when occurrences in the west produced a condition in which war seemed inevitable.

The British Cabinet followed the news of the defeat of Washington at Fort Necessity (July 1754) by a decision to reinforce the American colonists, driven again, as a consequence of this French victory, to the eastward of the Alleghanies. General Braddock was ordered to America with two regiments of the line. Newcastle hoped that this might be done secretly, but it was made public by the War Office, and was soon known in France. The action of England in pressing her rights to the debatable land has been noted.[2] The French were now to be driven from all positions which they held on it, by expeditions against Beauséjour, Crown Point, Oswego, and the Ohio. Never- theless Newcastle urged Lord Albemarle, the British Ambassador at Paris, to assure the French Ministry that the sending out of Braddock was purely a defensive measure. The French determined on their side to dispatch forces to Canada and Louisbourg. For the latter point two battalions, the second of the regiments of Artois and Bourgogne, were embarked at Brest on April 15, 1755.[3] These forces and the four battalions for Canada were in excess of the forces previously sent out under Braddock, but as it was a move of the same kind, and but little greater in number, it does not seem that the British Ministers were justified in finding it as offensive as they did. Parliament had acquiesced in the King's "securing his just rights and possessions in America," and voted him a million to that end. The Cabinet, fortified by the public feeling, which Mirepoix, the French Ambassador at London, recognized as bellicose, determined to send a squadron to cruise off Louisbourg, with instructions to "fall upon any

---

[1] In 1749 there were twenty-four, of which three were for the West Indies.
[2] *Ante*, p. 183.   [3] Arch. Guerre, vol. 3404, 89.

French ships of war that shall be attempting to land troops in Nova Scotia or to go to Cape Breton or through the St. Lawrence to Quebec." [1]

The strength of this squadron was first fixed at seven ships, but as the gravity of the step impressed itself upon the Cabinet, its number was afterwards increased to fifteen. Its command was given to the Hon. Edward Boscawen. He had seen service under Anson and Vernon, and had been the commander-in-chief of the fleet in Indian waters in 1749, when the results were in favour of Dupleix.

Mirepoix was assured at his own dining-table by Lord Granville and by Robinson,[2] who had just come from Council, that "the information I had of the offensive orders given to Admiral Boscawen was absolutely false." [3] When one remembers that Granville was the Minister who, "in one of his occasional bursts of strong rugged speech which came from him, and a good deal of wine taken into him," [4] objected to "vexing your neighbours for a little muck," [5] who also was revered as a master by Pitt, it became obvious that the charges made by France against the Punic faith of England were not the mere effervescence of Gallic sensitiveness. The Ministry took apparently the view of Monk at the outbreak of the Dutch War in 1665. "What matters this or that reason? What we want is more of the trade the Dutch now have." [6]

The basis of the orders given to Boscawen has been quoted. Those given to the French commodore who was to escort the fleet for Canada, off the coasts of Europe, were in the ordinary terms :

"You should, if possible, avoid meeting English squadrons. If you do fall in with them, be on guard against their manœuvres, and if they give ground for supposing that they mean to attack, I shall be content that you avoid an engagement in so far as it is possible without compromising the honour of my flag." [7]

The troops for Louisbourg were on the *Defenseur*, *Chariot Royal*, and *l'Espérance*, which did not fall, like the *Alcide* and *Lys*, as captures to Boscawen off the banks,[8] but arrived safely at Louisbourg on June 14. Their debarkation was mostly effected by the 19th, although the barracks were not ready for them.[9]

Admiral Du Bois de La Motte went to Quebec and returned by the Straits of Belle Isle, a daring feat, while De Salvert conducted the Louisbourg ships.[10] Boscawen, letting the French fleet slip through his fingers (with the exception of the *Alcide* and *Lys*) in the bad weather off the banks, hurt the standing of

[1] In the Secret Committee, March 24 ; in Cabinet, April 10, 1755.
[2] One of the two Secretaries of State for Foreign Affairs.   [3] Corbett, p. 46.   [4] Carlyle.
[5] Corbett, vol i. p. 61.   [6] Jane, *Heresies of Sea-Power*, p. 151.   [7] Waddn. i. p. 106.
[8] Boscawen, post, p. 206.   Guerre, 3404, 159.   [9] Guerre, 3404, 161.
[10] A.N. Marine, C^1, 170, sub nom. Pellegrin.

England, and produced the minimum of damage to France.[1]   After sending his captures to Halifax, he cruised with his fleet off Louisbourg.[2]   Many captures were made, mostly of French ships with provisions, which seriously curtailed the food supply of the town.

On June 18, the *Somerset*, for the second time, ran in close, and the log of Captain Geary reports that she was fired on.[3]   The *Somerset* bore away, not knowing the effect of the shot.   It was from a gun on the battery upon the island.   "On its discharge the carriage and the platform flew into a thousand pieces, and if the English had known our position their fleet might have come into the Harbour without any risk from our batteries not having a single cannon fit to be fired."

"They might have burned all the vessels in it and battered the town from the harbour, which must have immediately surrendered.   But luckily for us they had no knowledge of our infirmities." [4]

Thus Johnstone describes the incident, and says that it showed to all "the dismal situation of Louisbourg."

The events elsewhere in 1755 were more important than at Louisbourg. To the west of the Alleghanies the sanguinary defeat of Braddock threw the command of the region and the alliances of its Indians to the French.   The capture of Dieskau at Lake George was a barren victory for the English, and Shirley tarnished the laurels he had won as an administrator by his conduct of the absolutely unsuccessful expedition against Niagara.   In the east Beauséjour and Gaspereaux had fallen.   "Seven bombs which fell in Beauséjour have obliged Vergore to yield," [5] and the Acadian population, suffering like Issachar from the difficulties inherent in choosing either burden, was deported.

The blockade of Louisbourg roused Franquet from his lethargy.   Five years had passed since he had come to the country.   A diarist thus speaks of

---

[1] He was dissatisfied himself with the operation ; see Appendix at end of this chapter.

[2] It consisted of fifteen ships : *Torbay, Gibraltar, Terrible, Grafton, Augusta, Monarque, Yarmouth, Edinburgh, Chichester, Dunkirk, Arundel, Somerset, Northumberland, Nottingham,* and *Anson.*

[3] On July 3 Boscawen left for Halifax.

BOSCAWEN, MOSTYN, AND HOLBURNE

July 3, 1755.—Boscawen sailed from Louisbourg, leaving Mostyn with the *Monarch, Yarmouth, Chichester, Edinburgh, Dunkirk,* and *Arundel.*   To be relieved by Holburne.

The *Torbay* was accompanied by the *Somerset, Northumberland, Nottingham,* and *Anson,* to Halifax.

July 9, 1755.—Mostyn sailed from Louisbourg, arriving at Halifax on the 11th.

Holburne was left off Louisbourg with the *Terrible, Grafton, Defiance, Augusta,* and *Litchfield.*   The *Edinburgh, Dunkirk,* and *Arundel* were to join him in a few days.   They did so on August 10, and the *Success* in September.

Sept. 15, 1755.—Holburne and his fleet entered Halifax harbour.

Oct. 19, 1755.—Boscawen sailed from Halifax with Mostyn, Holburne, and fleet.

(Taken from the logs of *Torbay* and *Terrible,* and Boscawen's letters to Cleveland of July 4 and 12 and Nov. 15, 1755).

[4] De Salvert's ships escaped Boscawen and Holburne, who succeeded him in the station (Quebec MSS. 3, p. 470).

[5] *Derniers Jours,* p. 146.

him, and what he says perhaps explains the little Franquet accomplished during that time : "He was a man of military experience, loving good, all his actions tended towards it, an honest man, a good citizen, but unhappily a malady so ravaged him, and had so enfeebled his bodily energies, that we find only now and again the man he was." [1]

Every observer is agreed that the fortifications were in wretched condition. Des Herbiers, Surlaville, Pichon [2] are all unanimous. [3] Franquet had sent home alternative plans of new works on the scale of the great frontier fortresses of Europe, but little had been done to make effective the existing defences until Boscawen's blockade indicated the seriousness of affairs.

In Europe the action of England was even more energetic and unscrupulous than in America. Three hundred French mechantmen were seized on the high seas and in English ports. France contented itself with protests, and with an accumulation of evidence of England's improper action, which her Ministers hoped would stir Spain to take part with her against the violator of international laws. In this she did not succeed, although Spain had griefs of her own against England. The sole benefit of the representations of France was that Holland did not take the side of England, as by treaty bound, for by the treaty between them neither party was to assist the other in a war in which either was the aggressor. [4] This the Dutch declared was the position of England.

It is hard to credit that a nation which in America was arming savage allies secretly against the settlers of the rival power, could be so meek and magnanimous in Europe. Hawke ravaged French shipping. France sent back to England the frigate *Blankford*, captured off Brest, and instructed the Intendant of Toulon to provision an English fleet cruising in the Mediterranean should it call at that port. [5] This was only some two score years before Burke, lamenting in rolling cadences the sorrows of Marie Antoinette, exclaimed that the age of chivalry was dead. Under Louis XV. it survived in this fatuous and futile treatment of an enemy which had proved itself insensible to the influences *d'un beau geste*.

The comparative insignificance of colonial events as compared with those in Europe, to which reference has already been made, is demonstrated by the fact that, while in 1755 there was armed conflict at every point where the French

---

[1] Le Chef du Génie est homme de Guerre, aimant le bien, toutes ses actions sont portées à Cela, honnête homme, bon citoyen, mais malheureusement une maladie qui le minoit avoit tellement affoibli la machine qu'on ne Retrouvoit plus l'homme en lui il n'avoit que des momens " (Journal du Siège de Louisbourg, 1758, Arch. de la F. 236 F.).

[2] See the latter's reports to Captain Scott when he was in the pay of England (Tyrell Papers).

[3] See the letters to Surlaville from his friends at Louisbourg.

[4] Corbett, vol. i. p. 20.   [5] La C.-G. p. 242.

and English came in contact in America, it was not thought necessary by the Powers to declare war until operations began in Europe. The action between Byng and Galissonière took place only two days later than the declaration of war by England, signed by the King on the 18th of May 1756, and followed by that of France on the 9th of June.

Minorca fell on June 29, and the brilliant operation of the French terminated in the triumphal re-entry of La Galissonière and Richelieu into Toulon on the 16th of July, three months after setting out. The outcome of this disappointing opening of a war, for which the English people had clamoured, was the execution of Byng "for failure to do his utmost." He was shot on the quarter-deck of the *Monarque*, which had been one of the fleet with which Boscawen had begun hostilities.

France occupied herself with land operations and projects for the invasion of England. She contented herself with regard to America in reinforcing the garrison of Canada. Beaussier de L'Isle was given command of a squadron which took out the regiments of La Sarre and the Royal Rousillon ; with them went, to gain immortality, le Marquis de Montcalm, as successor to the captured Dieskau.

The English ships, *Fougeux*, *Litchfield*, *Centurion*, *Norwich*, and the smaller *Success* and *Vulture*, had wintered in Halifax, and were joined in the spring of 1756 by the *Grafton* and *Nottingham*. The squadron was placed under the command of Commodore[1] Holmes, who detached the *Grafton* and *Nottingham* with their tenders to blockade Louisbourg.

The appearance of Beaussier's ships, returning from Quebec to Louisbourg, put to flight the tenders of the English, which were on the point of capturing a French merchantman, driven into Mainadieu. The ships of the line came in sight of each other on July 26, off Louisbourg.[2]

Beaussier's impulse was to engage, at the risk of repeating the mistake of Maisonfort. Wiser counsels prevailed. He went into Louisbourg, landed the treasure he had for the place, and cleared his ships of hamper. The next morning he engaged the English ships, having supplemented his crews by only 200 men, although the whole garrison volunteered. Beaussier's ship *Le Héros*, a seventy-four, had only forty-six guns mounted, and was not supported by Montalais in the *Illustre*. The action was indecisive.[3]

After this action Holmes returned to Halifax for a few days, but on the 7th of August was back again. However, he did not get in touch with

---

[1] Admiralty List, Book 30.

[2] French ships : *Le Héros*, 74/46 ; *L'Illustre*, 64 ; and the frigates *La Licorne* and *La Sirène*. English ships : *Grafton*, 70 ; *Nottingham*, 60 ; and tenders *Hornet* and *Jamaica*.

[3] It is, however, so interesting that accounts of it are printed verbatim in Appendix at end of chapter.

Beaussier when he sailed for France on the 13th.   Holmes carried his operations
further than along the coasts of Cape Breton.   He dispatched on August 7
the *Fougueux* and *Centurion* to the St. Lawrence, the *Success* to Newfoundland,
and the *Litchfield* to Ingonish,[1] to distress the enemy.   The larger ships
destroyed the village of Little Gaspé, flakes, stages, and shallops ; Spry adding
in his report, superfluously it would seem, as the inhabitants were defenceless,
" without the least accident." [2]

   Things were dull and unpleasant in Louisbourg.   The English ships cruising
off the port made various captures, the most important of which was the
frigate *L'Arc - en - Ciel*, bringing out money and recruits for the garrison.
Louisbourg itself was unmolested, but at least three descents were attempted
on its outports.   "They hoped to burn all the dwellings, but, unfortunately
for them, troops and Indians, placed in ambush in these harbours, hacked a
number of them to pieces and took the remainder prisoners ; not one escaped,
and many scalps were taken."

   [The only landing mentioned in the log-books is that from the *Norwich*,
September 1, at the Gut of Canso :

   "6 A.M. sent our Barge & Yaul in Compy. with the *Success's* Barge and Cutter in
shore after a shallop about 1/4 past when the Barges got along side of the shallop we
observ'd they rec'd a very brisk Fire of small Arms from the Shore, which oblig'd them
to put off, on which the Shallop was shoo'd afloat & pursued the Boats, the Fire continuing
incessantly from the shore as well as the Launch, One of the Barges by this Time row'd
only 2 Oars, which the Shallop came up with & took in a little Time, the other Boats
came along side in about 3/4 of an Hour after viz. our Barge in which 2 Men Killed & 3
dangerously wounded, 2 of the *Success's* Bargemen who had jump'd into the Shallop &
when the attack was made into the Sea & Swam to our Barge One of whom was
dangerously wounded, our yaul was safe & the *Success* Cutter had one Man wounded,
several Shot went through the Barge & not a Mast or Oar in her but had one or more
Shot in or thro' them."

   The other landings must have been from English privateers.]
   In consequence of the stringent prohibition of commerce with the French,
enforced as far as was possible by the English Governors, and the presence of
these men-of-war off the port, the French believed that the policy of England
was trying to reduce the place by famine.

   "Some of our fishermen, taken prisoner and then liberated at the beginning of this
campaign, relate that the English intend to intercept all aid and provisions which may come
to us from Europe, they wish to subdue us by famine and oblige us to give up the keys
without striking a blow.   In spite of the fact that this squadron has seized our ship *L'Arc-
en-Ciel*, a 54, with 150 recruits on board . . . they will not succeed in their enterprise.

---

[1] Ad. Des. 1/481.   [2] The *Grafton* and her consorts remained cruising off Louisbourg until October.

We have at the present moment food enough to last the entire colony nearly two years."[1]

The optimism of Des Bourbes was repeated by M. Portal, an engineer, who about the same time wrote, " Du monde, des vivres de l'argent, de la bonne volonté, voilà notre position."[2]

Facts, however, seem not to have justified this cheerful statement; the fortifications were wretched, the garrison was inadequate, and within a twelve-month the lack of provisions in the town was causing the greatest anxiety.

The perspective of time enables us to accurately gauge the relative importance of the events of this year.

It was not the loss of Minorca, which Newcastle felt equal to that of any possession in the world except Ireland, nor the alarm of the country over this loss, nor the fear of invasion, which has always been so potent in its effect over the mind of the English people, nor the fall of Calcutta, though it heightened the alarm, nor the capture of Oswego by Montcalm, thus closing one of the avenues to Canada ; the event of the year was the coming to power of Pitt.

Newcastle had resigned after his long tenure of office as Prime Minister. His place was taken nominally by the Duke of Devonshire, but the real head of the administration was Pitt, for whom the people of England had persistently clamoured.

At once a new spirit animated the Ministry, new confidence was felt in the nation. The importance of warfare in America was recognized, and preparations were made for carrying it on with vigour. Pitt's policy was sound in that he had no intention of "trying to win America in Europe." A French observer saw the justice of his views : " The victory over M. Braddock, which has been made so much of in Europe, has done nothing to decide our fate. The naval strength of the English was a hydra against which we had to try and oppose a like hydra. France should have built and equipped a number of ships equal to those of the English, with her gold and her men, instead of seeking for them a tomb in Germany, an abyss which has always been our ruin."[3]

---

[1] " L'intention des Anglais, suivant le rapport de quelques-uns de nos pêcheurs, qui ont été pris et relâchés dans le commencement de cette croisière, est d'intercepter tous les secours et les vivres qui peuvent nous arriver d'Europe, de réduire notre place par la famine, et de nous forcer de leur en porter nos clefs sans coup férir. Quoyque cette escadre nous ait pris le vaisseau L'Arc-en-Ciel, de 54 pièces de canon, dans lequel il y avoit cent cinquante hommes de recrue . . . ils ne réussiront pas dans leur entreprise. Nous avons actuellement pour près de deux ans de vivres pour toute la colonie" (M. des Bourbes à M. de Surlaville, 10 Aoust 1756, Derniers jours de l'Acadie, p. 190).

[2] Derniers Jours, etc. p. 195.

[3] " La victoire contre M. Bradock qu'on fait tant valoir en Europe, n'a rien moins que décidé de notre sort. Les forces maritimes des Anglois sont une hydre à laquelle il fallait tâcher d'opposer une hydre semblable. C'étoit à la construction et à l'armement d'un nombre égal de vaisseaux qu'il fallait employer les hommes et l'or de la France, et non leur chercher un tombeau en Allemagne, gouffre qui a toujours été notre ruine" (Pichon, Histoire du Cap Breton, pp. 268-269).

Pitt began that prodigious activity which marked his tenure of office. It was devoted not only to affairs of state, but to the military and naval operations which embraced the protection and extension of the Empire, at all points in both hemispheres, where it had a foothold.

Lord Loudon was the Commander-in-Chief in America. His plan of operations, communicated to Pitt, coincided with that which Pitt had himself formed. The most important feature in Pitt's policy was a *coup de main* against the French strongholds in America, the reduction of Louisbourg in the early part of the season, to be followed by an attack on Quebec. Pitt urged on this work, and attempted to animate and unite the colonial Governors in raising forces to assist the regular troops, not only in this expedition, but in land attacks on the outlying French positions.

Before his retirement Newcastle had determined to send one regiment to America. This was quite inadequate for Pitt's schemes. Early in February he wrote to Lawrence that the second battalion of the Royals and six regiments, each of 815 men, are ordered for embarkation, and he hoped would be able to sail by the end of the month.[1] The base of operations against Louisbourg was Halifax, and, with the expectation that the fleet would sail before the end of February, Lord Loudon's plan that he could capture Louisbourg and then proceed to Quebec in June was not unreasonable. However, the vigour of Pitt was not equal to expediting matters as he had hoped. There was great lack of organization in the military services.[2]

Conditions improved, but all the movements were behind the time set in Pitt's plans. Loudon had concentrated his forces in New York, and was ready at the end of April with a body of about 6300 men and abundant siege material. No news came of Holburne, who was to bring out the fleet ; and the naval forces in New York, a fifty-gunship and four small cruisers under Hardy, were inadequate to cope with the French squadron.

In June they embarked the troops, but just as they were on the point of sailing, they got news that De Beauffremont had been in the West Indies and was probably coming north. Further delay took place, for it would have been grossly imprudent to move this force without adequate protection. The impatience of Loudon and Hardy increased. Finally Hardy sent out two cruisers, who reported that the sea was clear of the French between New York and Halifax, and in the last third of June they successfully made the voyage.

There was no sign as yet of Holburne, but the troops were disembarked at

[1] Kimball, vol. i. p. 2.

[2] This last is indicated by the conditions in the previous year. The troops for Loudon lay at Portsmouth until June, without transports being hired for them. Cannon were shipped on one vessel, their carriages on another, ammunition on a third, and powder on a fourth. The loss of one vessel would make useless the safe arrival of the other three. The powder was bought without a test, and proved to be no better than sawdust (Entinck, vol. i. p. 488).

Halifax, and exercised in attacks on such positions as they would be likely to meet ; they were taught to grow vegetables, and later, when an indignant and disappointed nation reviewed the failure of Loudon's expedition, this was part of the source of ridicule. Holburne's late arrival in American waters (July 9) was the chief cause of failure which so completely characterized the movements of the British forces in this campaign, but French seamanship and French strategy accounted for the decided advantage her fleets had over the enemy.[1]

While Pitt, in February, was vainly pressing on the elaborate preparations for attack, France was preparing her forces for defence. A squadron of four ships under Du Revest sailed from Toulon to Louisbourg in April. Saunders' attempt to stop them with an equal force in the Straits of Gibraltar was unsuccessful, and Du Revest arrived at his destination on June 19.

On January 27 De Beauffremont sailed unmolested from Brest to the West Indies, the English Admiralty not having perfected its arrangements to blockade that port by the time the French squadron was ready to sail. He had a force similar to Du Revest's, and arrived in St. Domingo on March 19 after very heavy weather, and left on May 4, reaching Louisbourg on the 31st of the same month.

Du Bois de la Motte left Brest with nine of the line and two frigates. Temple West, who was then blockading the port, had been driven off in a gale of wind ; so that the English efforts to destroy any part of the French reinforcements failed through the unpreparedness of the Admiralty or the fortunes of the sea.

Du Bois de la Motte, Lieutenant-General, arrived in Louisbourg on the night of the 20th of June. He was in command of the united squadrons, which gave him a force superior to that of Holburne's.[2]

The junction of the three French squadrons at Louisbourg was ascertained by scouts sent out from Halifax. The men from the English ships were

---

[1] Holburne received a sharp letter from the Admiralty for indulgences granted to his captains (Ad. Out Letters, vol. 518).

"I believe you have never heard of this A. Holburne, and are anxious to know from whence he came, he is a Scot, you know I don't think well of that nation for upper leather, nor was he ever thought much of in our service, he is rich and has contrived to insinuate himself into the good graces of Lord Anson, made an Admiral and sent here in my assistance, you see by this I don't like him or ever did, having known him from my first entering into service. . . ." (Boscawen to his wife, June 26, 1755, Falmouth MSS.).

[2]

Le Formidable, 80.	L'Hector, 74.	Le Vaillant, 64.	La Brune, 30.
Le Tonnant, 80.	Le Glorieux, 74.	Le Superbe, 70.	La Fleur de Lys, 30.
Le Deffenseur, 74.	Le Dauphin Royal, 70.	L'Inflexible, 64.	L'Abenaskise, 38.
Le Duc de Bourgogne, 80.	Le Bizarre, 64.	Le Belliqueux, 64.	La Comette, 30.
Le Héros, 74.	L'Achille, 64.	Le Sage, 64.	La Fortune, flute, 30.
Le Diadème, 74.	L'Eveillé, 64.	Le Célèbre, 64.	L'Hermione, 26.

(B⁴, Marine, 76.)

sickly, 500 had to be left on shore in hospitals at Halifax, and 200 had died. On the 4th of August, Loudon wrote Holburne a short note, the point of which was : " In view of intelligence recvd. from Louisbourg is there any chance of success in its attempted reduction?" To which Holburne replied on the same day, "that the season is too far advanced, and enemy too strong, for attempt to be successful."[1] Thereupon they determined to abandon the siege. A strong garrison was left in Halifax, as in the forts in the Bay of Fundy ; but most of the troops retired with Loudon to New York. The fleet of Holburne began to cruise off Louisbourg on August 19 ; it kept this position, making more than one attempt to draw La Motte out from the port.

The latter refrained from action ; the point in his instructions which most impressed itself on him was that he must secure Louisbourg from attack. The men from his ships, together with the garrison, occupied themselves in throwing up earthworks and in fortifying every cove, both to the east and west of Louisbourg, where a landing might be effected, and in keeping in them a sufficient garrison to resist a first attack.

The forces which Du Bois de la Motte had at his disposal were :

Artois	.	.	.	.	437
Bourgogne	.	.	.	.	536
Louisbourg Companies	.	.	805		
Militia	.	.	.	.	200
Quebec Soldiers	.	.	.	30	
Acadians and Indians	.	.	260		
Artillery	.	.	.	.	50
Officers	.	.	.	.	150

Volunteers from the Fleet.

Officers	.	.	31
Men	.	.	600

2468

The cannon, 68 in number, and two mortars, mounted in entrenchments, were all served by these forces, with the exception of the Acadians and Indians, who were with Boishébert at Gabarus.

The frigates of his fleet made occasional cruises about the coasts, and the diaries speak of several prizes brought in, mostly by privateers.[2] Holburne kept his position off Louisbourg till after the middle of September. On Sunday the 25th the most violent storm known for years proved disastrous to the greater part of the English fleet, and upset Holburne's plans for any attack on the vessels of Du Bois de la Motte, who after repairing the comparatively slight damage done to the *Tonnant*, returned safely to France.[3]

Holburne got his ships refitted in Halifax, and left there for the winter,

---

[1] Ad. Des. 481.   [2] Marine B⁴, vol. 76. Also journal of *Fleur de Lys*, Ottawa, F, 173.
[3] See Appendix, p. 207, for the account of the storm.

according to instructions, eight men-of-war and brought the others successfully back to England, a highly creditable piece of seamanship, which helped to lessen the resentment of Pitt.[1]

APPENDICES

A. List of Prizes taken off Louisbourg

1755.

June 8. *Torbay* and *Dunkirk* took *Alcide*, 64.

     8. *Fougueux* took French dogger.

     9. *Fougueux* and *Defiance* took the *Lys*, 64.

    19. *Litchfield* took a brigantine from Martinico for Louisbourg.

    20. *Mars* captured a snow, *L'Aigle*, Rochelle to Louisbourg.

    26. *Arundel* took a snow, St. Maloes to Cape Breton.

July 2. *Arundel* took a fishing schooner, G. of Cancer to Louisbourg.

    20. *Defiance* took a French snow, *Prudent*, to Dunkirk, from Bordeaux to Louisbourg.

    20. *Arundel* took a sloop from Louisbourg.

    21. *Terrible* took a schooner from Louisbourg to Nants.

    25. *Arundel* took a schooner from Martinico to Louisbourg.

Aug. 13. *Terrible* took a snow, Bourdeaux to Louisbourg.

    13. *Litchfield* took a snow, also schooner and shallop.

    19. *Dunkirk* took a snow, *Michault*, Martinico to Louisbourg.

    21. *Edinburgh* and *Dunkirk* took two French ships, the *St. Antonia* and *Duke de las Court*, Bourdeaux to Louisbourg.

    22. *Dunkirk* took the *St. Clear*, Bourdeaux to Louisbourg.

    22. *Litchfield* took a French ship.

    23. *Litchfield* took the *Emmanuel*, Bourdeaux to Louisbourg.

 21 to 23. *Arundel* employed sacking and destroying fishing-station at Port a Basque.

    24. *Dunkirk* took a French snow.

Aug. 25. *Dunkirk* and *Litchfield* took the snow, *Three Friends*, St. Malones to Louisbourg.

    26. *Augusta* took a French schooner.

Sept. 1. *Success* took a French snow, Bourdeaux to Quebec.

     1. *Success* took a French dogger, Bourdeaux to Louisbourg.

1756.

May 22. *Success* captured French schooner.

    24. *Success* fired on an Indian boat. Also on Indians on shore.

    29. *Norwich* took French dogger, Rochfort to Louisbourg.

---

[1] Ad. Orders and Instructions, vol. 79, p. 376, see also Ad. Out Letters, No. 521.

    The eight ships were: *Northumberland, Terrible, Kingston, Orford, Arc en Ciel, Sutherland, Defiance, Somerset*, also the frigates, *Portmahon* and *Hawke*. The *Hawke*, which arrived in Halifax on Nov. 5, brought to Holburne the erroneous report that the French fleet was still in Louisbourg. See Holburne to Pitt, Nov. 4, 1757, P.S. Nov. 5, Ad. Des. 1, 481, and Kimball, vol. i. p. 125. In Chapter XV. is a statement of the dismay felt when the news of the storm reached London.

    The *Stirling Castle* and three other ships were ordered on Nov. 11 to cruise for twenty-one days between Ushant and Cape Clear, for the protection of trade and the security of the disabled ships of Holburne's fleet expected from America.

May 29. *Fougueux* took French dogger, *Old France* to Louisbourg.

29. *Litchfield* took *Douchess of Pontchatrain*, Rochfort to Louisbourg.

June 2. *Success* took French schooner.

13. *Litchfield* and *Norwich* took *L'Arc-en-Ciel*, 52 guns, 550 men. *L'Oruebt* to Louisbourg.

16. *Centurion* took storeship *Equity*, Rochfort to Louisbourg.

20. *Hornet* took schooner.

July 8. *Jamaica* captured brig, Rochfort to Louisbourg.

10. *Grafton* took two fishing-boats.

21. *Jamaica* took a French ship which she chased ashore. Seized also a fishing-shallop.

Aug. 13, 14. Schooner and sloop chased on shore—captured by the boats of the *Litchfield* and *Grafton*.

13. *Centurion* drove a vessel into the harbour of Neganish.

14. *Centurion* and *Hornet* captured do., a schooner from Quebec to Louisbourg.

24. *Jamaica* took a schooner, an illicit trader, from Piscadue to Newfoundland.

Sept. 4, 5. *Litchfield* landed at Leganish Bay—took fish, burnt stages, shallops, etc.

7. *Centurion* took sloop loaded with fish.

7. *Fougueux* took three French shallops and a small sloop in Gaspée Bay.

9. *Fougueux* and *Centurion* took a snow, Quebec to Gaspée.

10. *Fougueux* and *Centurion* took a schooner, St John's to Quebec.

11, 12. *Fougueux* and *Centurion* employed in destroying the fishing village of Little Gaspée.

PRIZES TAKEN 1757 BY HOLBURNE'S SHIPS

May 13. Dunviddie recapture.

19. Snow.

June 4. La Hercule, St. Domingo to Bordeaux.

6. Dauphin, Cap. François to Bordeaux.

9. Ship, St. Domingo to Bordeaux.

24. Schooner, St. Eastatius to Salem.

Aug. 24. Ketch, Rochefort, an illicit trader to Louisbourg.

28. Providence, Rochefort to Louisbourg.

Nov. 6. English Snow, recapture.

This statement has been compiled from Log-Books in the Record Office. The spelling has not been changed.

B. LETTER FROM BOSCAWEN TO HIS WIFE

"*June* 26, at 8 A.M., 1755.

"My dearest Fanny cannot think how easy I find myself since I despatched the *Gibraltar* for England, the account I have given of myself good or bad being gone from me, has taken a great burden from my spirits, thus to begin a war between two great and powerful nations, without an absolute order, or declaration for it, now and then gives me some serious thoughts, some will abuse me, but as it is on the fighting side, more will commend me, had I been lucky enough to have fallen in with more of them I should have been more commended, not but that I have the secret satisfaction to know that I have done all that man could do in this part of the world, which no man that has not seen can be any judge of, the sudden and continual fogs the cols [sic] in this Southern latitude at midsummer and our first coming on the coast the dismal prospect of floating islands of ice sufficient to terrifie the most daring seaman, I know what I have done, is acting up to the spirit of my orders, I know it is agreable to the King the ministry and the Majority of the people, but I am afraid they will expect I should have done more, the whole scheme is the demolishing the naval power of France, and indeed the falling in with those that have escaped me and demolishing them, would have been a decisive stroke and prevented a war, but what I have done will add fewel to the fire only, and make them complain at all the Courts in Europe if our great men dare begin first in Europe they will yet take some of them on their return, they have no provisions to stay here all the winter, if they attempt to stay all their men will perish. . . ."

The Storm in 1757

"When the month of September Came, the Equinox brought the most furious tempest ever known in the memory of man. The sea at the same time rose to such a prodigious height, Ferdinand de Chambon, the officer on guard at the "Grave" was obliged to quit his post with his detachment, to avoid being drowned, after standing their ground until the water was up to their knees. It began about twelve at night, and continued with the same force until twelve next day at noon. The evening before being fair, clear and calm, the English fleet was in its usual station near the entry of the harbour, and everybody imagined it impossible for them to get clear of the land and avoid being dashed against the rocks. The next morning we expected to see the coast all covered with wrecks.

"The inhabitants of the Country brought us each moment news of the dismal state of the English fleet.

"All their ships were shattered and dispersed ; five of them were seen together driving before the wind towards Newfoundland without masts.

"Several others were in the same Condition. A fifty-gun ship was lost at the distance of four leagues from Louisbourg; but the crew being saved, a detachment was immediately sent to them to prevent their being butchered by the Indians. In short it was evident that five French men of war, if they had gone out of the harbour in quest of the English, would have been sufficient to pick up and take all that was left of the English fleet. . . ." [1]

An officer on the French vessel *Fleur de Lys* tells the same tale of woe :

"We have gone through the most violent gale of wind seen here for a long time, though they are frequent. Last Thursday (the 22nd) it was fine and quite calm ; out at sea we noticed a mist which spread towards the harbour in the night. On Friday there was a slight S.E. wind with a little fog. Saturday it veered from S.E. to E.S.E. nice and fresh. An English vessel was at that time very near the shore, she set sail as fast as she

---

[1] Chevalier Johnstone, Quebec Hist. Soc., Campaign of Louisbourg.

could for the open sea ; after mid-day the wind veered to the E. so that was in her favour. The wind got stronger from this direction so I let go the big anchor before night fall, very carefully so that it should hold fast. At 11 o'clock at night the wind got very violent, but two hours after midnight it was even stronger, till 11 o'clock this morning, when it veered to the south and soon to the S.W. I have never seen anything like it. At 3 A.M. the *Dauphin Royal* dragged her anchor, fouled the *Tonnant* and broke her bowsprit ; the *Dauphin Royal's* rudder was broken. At 11 the *Tonnant* was ashore, but the wind having changed by then to the South, she floated with the tide, her rudder was carried away, her mizzen mast cut off, and she is now much like the others, but without bowsprit, mizzen mast or rudder, worst of all she is taking much water.

"The hawser of *l'Abénaquise* parted, this frigate has been thrown ashore, and I do not doubt but many of our ships would have had the same fate if the wind had lasted another hour. . . ."—Sunday, 25*th Sept.* 1757. Log-Book of the *Fleur de Lys*.

We read also in the Anonymous Journal written by one of the officers of De La Motte's squadron, on board *L'Inflexible* :

"Since the 23rd the winds in the E. and S.E. parts of the island, were constantly from the S.E. and were fresh enough, with much fog and rain to make us fear a storm, and so it began on the 24th in the afternoon, without much violence at the outset, but at 1 o'clock in the night it turned into a most terrible hurricane, there was not a single ship of our squadron that did not drift, although each had four anchors under her bows ; by daybreak our situation was lamentable. During the night *Le Dauphin Royal* fired a canon as signal of distress. In spite of our wish to assist them, we were unable to do so. The sea was so dreadful that it made us shudder. The cable of the *Dauphin Royal* broke, she was instantly thrown on *Le Tonnant* where she broke her rudder, the whole of the gallery of the poop was destroyed, but these damages were inconsiderable compared with those sustained by *Le Tonnant*, whose bowsprit was broken, also the figurehead and cut-water ; and she was thrown, while thus entangled, on the Royal battery, where she struck with violence. We were even surprised that she could resist the shock, the mizzen-mast was promptly cut away to lighten the stern which was the portion that was suffering most . . . If at noon the wind had continued for another hour and not changed to the south and south-west, nine or ten of our vessels, including that of our Admiral, would have been driven ashore. It is impossible to imagine such a dreadful spectacle as that which met our eyes. The frigate, *l'Abénaquise*, the cable of which was parted, was instantly thrown up on the beach, along with 25 merchantmen, several of them high and dry. More than 80 boats and skiffs of the squadron were tossed by the waves and smashed, most of them on the shore, a number of the men on board them perishing. More than 50 schooners and boats met the same fate. By 3 P.M. the hurricane having greatly abated, I went in our boat to help ours. Sailors, who have been more than 50 years afloat, say that they never saw the sea so awful. The ramparts of the town were thrown down, and the water inundated half of the town, a thing which has never been seen. The sea dashed with such tremendous force on the coast that it reached lakes two leagues inland. . . ."

The incidents connected with her salvage are briefly told as follows by one of the French officers at Louisbourg :

"During the afternoon of the 27th a boat arrived with a report that whilst passing St. Esprit they saw a number of people on the shore, and also many others on the prow. Upon this information we sent, next morning, four schooners with sixty grenadiers and one hundred soldiers, who were forced back by contrary winds, and went by land. The same day a person of the locality brought in his boat Captain Thems (Thane), second captain of the said ship who is on board with us, also two sailors. We learn that it was the *Tilbury* 60 guns, formerly part of the Holburne squadron. The Captain, and the commander of the grenadiers were drowned, as well as half the crew. Our troops had great difficulty in reaching the scene of the wreck, owing to the floods in many localities which the gale had caused the sea to submerge. We were anxious to give the shipwrecked prompt assistance, for fear of the fury of the Indians, who might possibly get there first. This they did, but they behaved very well under the circumstance, their conduct surprising us. When a company of savages, 150 strong, made their appearance, not one of the English, although half dead with hardship, expected to escape, but a chief came forward and reassured them, saying : 'Fear not, since the hurricane has brought you to shore we are coming to your relief, but if you had come to make war upon us, not one of you would be safe, and we would take all your scalps.' The Indians themselves went on board the ship to help the others get off. The living were not plundered at all, but as the dead arrived on the shore they searched them. . . " [1]

The following facts are taken from the log-books of the English squadron :

Captain, *Sept.* 25, 1757.—"Fore stay sail, Main and Mizen stay sail all blown away and Main sail split to pieces . . . . $9\frac{1}{2}$ foot water in the Well, and 9 in the Magazine which washed away all the Powder . . . but the Wind shifting and with the assistance of an Iron Tiller got clear of the Rocks."

Devonshire, *Sept.* 25, 1757.—"At $\frac{1}{2}$ past 3 A.M. the mainsail split all to Pieces. At 6, the Mizen split to Rags, it then blowing a meer hurricane of wind and a very high sea which made a free passage over us."

Lightning, *Sept.* 25, 1757.—"At 4 A.M. it blowing an excessive hard Gale of Wind we split our Mainsail which blew quite away. At 7, we Shiped a Sea Abaft which stove in the Dead Lights, very much damaged our stores and a great quantity of our Bread. . . . The Breakers scarce a cable's length from us."

Newark, *Sept.* 25, 1757.—"Excessive hard gales. Cut away best bower anchor lest it shoud bulge the ship. Threw overboard 6 upper deck guns and carriages to ease the ship, 8 vessels seen with masts gone, etc. . . ."

Terrible, *Sept.* 25, 1757.—"Sunday. The first part strong gales and squally, the middle and latter very strong gales and squally thick weather, with Rain. . . . Saw 15 Sail of Ships, 10 with their masts gone, in Distress. At 10 freed the Ship of Water, $\frac{1}{2}$ past Saw the Land betwixt St. Esprit and Fouché, W.N.W. about 2 miles, and not one mile from the Breakers. . . . Saw one Ship in the Breakers, some near the Shore, Some to an Anchor with their masts gone, and some standing off as we did."

Orford, *Sept.* 25, 1757.—". . . At noon wore ship to the S'ward saw several of our Ships some of them having lost their Masts. Saw the Land from the N.W. to N. distance 4 or 5 Miles the Wind shifted to the Westward."

[1] Moreau St. Mery, vol. 24, f. 3.

State of the Squadron under the Command of Vice-Admiral Holburne, September 28, 1757.[1]

"1757, Sept. 28. — *Windsor, Kingston, Northumberland, Newark, Orford, Terrible, Somerset.* In company with all their Masts standing.

"*Bedford, Defiance.* All their Masts sent to the Eastward to take two ships in tow.

"*Invincible, Captain, Sunderland.* Fore masts and Bowsprits standing, and have raised jury masts to carry them into Port : are in tow.

"*Nottingham.* Spoke to by the *Orford*, yesterday, wants no assistance ; has a Fore Mast Bowsprit and jury mast.

"*Grafton, Nassau.* Have been seen with no Masts nor Bowsprits standing.

"*Devonshire, Eagle.* Have been seen their Fore Masts and Bowsprits only standing.

"*Prince Frederick, Centurion, Tilbury.* We have no certain Accounts, but some of these must be the Ships the *Bedford* and *Defiance* went after.

"*Nightingale.* Has lost her Mizen Mast and Maintopmast.

"It is generally thought that the *Tilbury* is lost, and every soul perished, and we are in some pain about the *Ferret*, as she must have been in the Storm ; We had lost Company for two days, and she is a very indifferent Sloop, sails badly and very crank. The cruizer who I had sent to Halifax to hasten the water out to us was very near foundering having been under water several times, with the loss of his boats, guns, and mizen mast and every one thing above water ; some of the Ships have lost a few Men and guns and Anchors ; Bread and Powder greatly damaged, having had so much Water in them. Booms and Boats many gone.

'(Signed) "FRA. HOLBURNE."[2]

Holburne's fears proved groundless with the exception of the *Tilbury*. She was wrecked on those rocks near St. Esprit, which still bear her name, and it may be that the gold which has been in recent years found on this shore, was cast up by the ocean from the ship's hold. Her Captain, Henry Barnsley, was drowned, but her First Lieutenant, Thane, was among those saved. Her complement was 400 men, of whom 280 were saved.[3]

C. The Fight between Holmes and Beaussier

SIR,—I desire you would please to acquaint their Lordships that on the 26th July I was Cruizing in His Majesty's Ship *Grafton* with the *Nottingham*, *Hornet*, and *Jamaica* Sloop off Louisburg about Three Leagues S.b.E. at Eight A.M., the Man at the Mast head discovered four sail to the N.E. which was directly to Windward, we gave Chace and made our first Board to the Southward, they steering directly for us till within two Leagues we tacked in hopes to have cut them from their Port, and they hauld in for it. Half past one P.M. they came to an anchor in their Harbour and a little after we brought too about a League from it and hoisted our Colours, the lighthouse bearing North where we lay, at four made Sail to the Eastward, soon as it was dark dispatched the *Hornet* with the in-closed Letter to Captain Spry and then stood on as before till three o'clock, when we tacked and stood in for the Land at seven in the Morning (the 27th); the Man from Mast-head call'd he saw six sail under the Land about Eight o'Clock. I could see four ships in chace of us, and I could with my Glass make them to be Men of War, and see the French Commodore's white Pendant very Plain, on which I stood from them to the S.E., about a point from the Wind which drew them from their Harbour and thought it the best of our sailing, for I judged them above our match, or they would not have come out of Port again in so few hours, I believe they only put their Sick and Lumber on Shore and took Troops off for they were very full of Men ; half past One P.M. the headmost of the French Squadron a Frigate of about Thirty-Six Guns, fired on the Jamaica sloop which she Return'd and rowed at the same time, on the *Nottingham* and our firing at the Frigate she hauld her wind and the *Jamaica* bore away to the S.W., which the French Commandant observ-ing made a Signall for the two Frigates to chace the Sloop which they immediately obey'd, about two the *Nottingham* fired her Stern Chace at the French Commandant which he returned with his Bow, and soon after I fired mine, finding our Shott reach'd each other, Hauld up my Courses, bunted my Mainsail and Bore down on the French Commodore, being about a quarter of a mile from him it fell calm and we began to Engage, he being on our Starboard side, the other large French Ship a Stern of him, and the *Nottingham* on our Larboard Bow, the two Frigates a Mile from us and the *Jamaica* something more. Tho' the French Commandant held us so cheap at first by sending his Frigates away, he was so Sensible of his mistake that soon as there was wind he made the Frigates signal to rejoin Him and fearing they did not come fast enough to his Assistance bore down to them, and we followed, at Seven they were all close together, at dusk the Action ceased, they standing to the Southward and we to the S.S.E., light airs, our Men lay at their Quarters all night expecting to renew the Action, in the Morning at day light the French ships bore N.W.b.W. distance four or five Miles, going away with little wind at E.S.E. right before it for Louisburg, we wore and stood to the Westward, but they never Offer'd to look at us, the wind fresh'ning, they sailing much better than our ships and the Weather growing hazey, lost sight of them about noon, their chief fire was at our Masts, which they wounded and cut our Stays and Riging pretty much, I had one Lower deck Gun dis-mounted and one upper, Six Men kill'd, and Twenty odd wounded, which is all the damage the *Grafton* received. I here inclose you Captain Marshall's Letter with his Boatswain and Carpenter's reports of the Damages received in the Action. The *Jamaica's* Mainmast was shott and is Condemned by Survey, I sent her to Halifax with the inclosed letter and the worst of my wound'd men, Employ'd fishing my Main Mast, the 29th being thick Weather could not venture in with the Land as was the 30th till noon, when stood in and at 4 brought too, little wind at South, at 6 Cabroose point N.b.W. ½ W. Three Leagues and Louisburg lighthouse N.b.E. ½ E. Four Leagues no ships off the Harbour nor could I see plain what was in, it being hazey over the Land, soon as it was dark stood away to the Westward for Halifax with the *Grafton* and *Nottingham* the 1st August join'd our ships there and as I wanted much to know the force of the french Ships and from whence they came on my arrival at Halifax I advised with Govr. Lawrence and Detach'd Major Hale of the Garrison to Louisburg with a Flag of Truce in a Schooner on pretence of treating for the Exchange of Captain Lieut. Martin of the Train who was taken by the Indians in the Harbour of Passmaquady, and carried to that place, one of my Petty Officers I have sent as Master of the Schooner, but as she is not return'd I can only give their

Lordships my Opinion of the ships. The Commandant I judge, to be a 74, the other a 64, and two Frigates of 40 and 36 guns. On the 7th I saild from Halifax with his Majestys ships, *Grafton, Fougueux, Litchfield, Norwich, Nottingham, Centurion, Hornet,* and *Jamaica* sloop, the *Success* has since Join'd us and [I] am now with the Squadron off Louisburg,—I am, &c.,   CHAS. HOLMES.

"*Grafton* at Sea,
   "Louisburg N.W.b.N. Six Leagues,
      "the 25th August 1756."

EXT. OF LOG OF THE *Grafton* (70)

July 26, 1756.—". . . At ½ past 10 saw 4 Sail in the N.E. made sail and gave Chace Do. Clear'd ship for Action they bore down to us we kept our Wind which they Observing hauld in for Louisburg. Continued our Chace but they having the Advantage of the Wind of us got into Louisburg Harbour we found as follows a 74 gun ship a 64 with 2 frigates of 32 Guns each Come from Quebeck."

July 27, 1756.—". . . Still Continuing our Chace at ½ past 1 P.M. they Anchord in Louisburg Harbour Brought too and Hoisted our coulers at 5 the *Hornett* parted Company for Halifax . . . in Company the *Nottingham* and *Jamaica* . . . at 7 A.M. saw 4 sail under Scatary which we judged to be the french Squadron Come out wore and bore away they gave us Chace out all reefs and made all the Sail we Could set Clear'd Ship for Action. In Company the *Nottingham* & *Jamaica* the French squadron bearing N.W. about 2 Leagues we being becalm'd & they Having a fresh breeze Coming up to us."

July 28, 1756.—". . . At ½ past 1 a french frigate gave Chace to the *Jamaica* & began to fire at her but upon the *Nottingham* and our fire at him he hauld his wind the french Comodant at the same time began to Engage the *Nottingham* Do. we haild the *Nottingham* desiring he would drop a stern that we might Come to a Closer Engagement with the french Commandant. Continued engageing him with the *Nottingham* on our Larbd. bow & the french Commadant on our Starboard side with the 64 gun ship on our Starbd. quar. till 6 o'clock in the Afternoon at which time the Commadant set his foresl. & bore away Do. set Our foresail & followed him he made Sigl. as we suppose for Assistance by hoisting a white Flag at His Main Topmt. Backstay from His mast head downward, and two white Pendants at his Larbd. main yard Arm on which the 2 Frigates drew Close to him and Engaged till 40 minutes after 7 when they hauld to the So. wd. & we to the S.S.E. being both Sides pretty much Shattered in our rigging we had 5 Men kild & 13 Wounded several Guns Dismounted at 6 A.M. saw them N.W. 5 miles wore Ship & Stood to the Wt.wd. in Company the *Jamaica* and *Nottingham*. . . ."

Aug. 1, 1756.—"In Halifax Harbour."

26, 1756.—"Heard the report of several guns in the harbour of Louisburg."

(Cruizing about Louisburg until 7 Oct. No mention of entering the harbour.)

EXT. OF LOG OF THE *Nottingham* (60)

July 28, 1756.—". . . Begun to fire our Stern Chaces on a Frigate that was Going to Bd. the *Jamaica* & keeping a Continual fire on her Obliged her to Sheer off a short time after we begun to Engage the French Comdr. with our Starbd. Guns Do. hauld up the main Sail at ½ pt. 1 Our Comdr. begun to Engage the 64 Gun Ship at ½ pt. 3. The French Comdr. made the Frigates Sigl. to Chace the *Jamaica* we keept on a Continual fire we Received from them Shott through our Sails two Shott through the Head of the Main Mast, one through the Main Topmast an other that splinterd him abaft, beside several Shott in our Hull. The French squadron Consisted of one of 74 Guns one of 64 one of 40 the other of 36 Guns. At ½ pt. 7 left off Engaging the French hauld the Wind and Stood to the westwd. with a Light Brieze Employed securing the Main Topmt. at 12 getting Pouder filld and getting Shott up and making Wadds ready to Engage at 4 A.M. Tackd to the Wt.wd. the Ship ready to Engage as before. At 7 Empld. overhaulg. the Rigging and Repairing what was Shott away, & Securing the Lower Deck Guns & Gunners Stores at 9 Saw the French squadn. Bearing N.N.W. 4 Leags. Steering for Louisbourg. The Comdr. & *Jamaica* In Company."

Aug. 1, 1756.—" In Halifax Harbour."

7 to 27, 1756.—"Another cruize off Louisbourg. (No mention of her entering the Harbour.)"

" *Grafton* AT HALIFAX *ye* 8th *October* 1756.

"SIR,

" As I had certain Intelligence that the French Men o' War that were in America were sail'd for Europe and there being no Danger to be Apprehended from anything they could attempt on this Coast, I thought it most Conducive to the good of His Majesty's Service and to distress the Enemy to seperate the Squadron. . . . While they were on these different Services I continued with His Majesty's Ships *Grafton* and *Nottingham* on the Station of Louisburg, where I received the enclosed letter from Major Hale of Colo. Lascelle's Regt. who Govr. Lawrence and I prevaild on to go in a Flag of Truce to Louisburg (he being Master of the French Language) in order to discover what we could of their Men of War and to learn if there were more Expected. He went under pretence . . . to treat for the exchange of Capn. Lieut. Martin. As their Lordships will by these letters receive an Account of what Damage the French sustain'd in the Engagement, I inclose you my Officers reports of ours.

"I am, &c.,

"JOHN CLEOLAND, Esq."   "CHAS. HOLMES.

GUNNER'S REPORT OF THE DAMAGES

"An Account of Carriages Disabled, and Powder fired in the Engagement with four French Men of War on board His Majesty's Ship *Grafton* Commodore Chas. Holmes Esqr. Commandt. off of Louisburg on the 27 July 1756."

"32 Pound Axeltrees.

| Broke by a Shot from the Enemy . . . . Fore ... One. |
| Bad Sprung by long firing . . . . . Do. ... Five. |
| Do. Do. Do. . . . . Hind ... One. |

"18 pound Axeltree Broke by a Shot from the Enemy . . Hind ... One.
"32 pound Cap Square Broke . . . . One.

"The above render'd Eight Guns unfit for Action till repaired. Powder fired in the Action Barrls. & pds. . . . Ninty-nine, & ten pds.

(Sign'd)   "JNO. SMYTH, Gunr."

Copy of the Carpenter's Report of the Damages.

" The Report of the Damages done to His Majesty's ship *Grafton* Charles Holmes Esqr. Commander on the 27 July 1756 by engaging with four sail of French Men of War of Louisbourg.

To the Hull of the Ship

" Received Seven Shott between wind and water.

"   Do.   In the Ships Sides Twenty Nine Shott.

"   Do.   In the Counter of the Ship Two Do.

" The Stern laid open, and quarter Gallerys Shott to pieces, the quantity of Glass broke, One Hundred and Ninety Seven Pains.

" The Cistarn of the Chain Pumps part of the Bottom and end entirely Shott away.

" Part of the Supporter of the Catt head shott away and the Round House and Tunnel shot all away.

" Ten Iron Stantions in the West and quarter Shot away with the Mens Hammocks and Twenty Broke.

" The Three Poop Lanthorns Shot to pieces and the Top Light much Damaged.

" Two Cranes of the Gangway Shott to pieces.

" Sundry Dammages done to Ladders, Grating, Boats, &c."

To the Masts of the Ship

" One Large Shott through the Body of the Main Mast Eleven foot from the uper Deck. The Cheek of the Main Mast Shott to pieces about the Middle of the Cheek in length.

" The Foremast One Shott of two Inches & a half Diamiter five Inches in Just above the Collar of the main Stay.

" The Flying Jib Boom One Third in from the outer end the upper part Cut Two Inches in with a Shott.[1]

(Sign'd)   " MELBOURNE WARREN, Carpr."

(Copy)

" *Nottingham* at Sea,
" 28th *July* 1756.

" SIR,—I herewith send you the Boatswain & Carprs. Reports of the Damages Received on board his Majesty's Ship *Nottingham* under my command, yesterday in the Time of Action with four sail of French men of War. I hope the Main topmast will stand till I have an Opportunity of Rigging an other, it being very much Wounded, but I have secur'd him with the Hatch bars and a strong wolding over 'em, the Head of the Main Mast, being shot afore & abaft the Mast, just above the Barrel of the Main Yard, is only what the Carpenter can Repair, without getting out the Mast, so that we shall soon be to rights again.—I am, &c.,

" S. MARSHALL.

" To CHARLES HOLMES ESQR."

---

[1] There is also a long report of damages given by the boatswain—2 full foolscap pages. This has not been copied.

"Dear Sir,—I desire you will immediately send me out any Ship that may be ready to come to Sea to Join me of St. Esprit or between that and Louisburg. I have had an Action with the French Squadron who I have made bear away for their Port. My Main Mast being much Wounded I was afraid could not secure him at Sea but hope I have by fishing him very well and am now going to see if the said Gentlemen have a Mind for any more of it. I would have the Ships Join me as fast as they can get Ready, without waiting for Each Other. After any One ship Joins me I shall Cruize off Louisburg and Scatary agreeable to our Rendezvous. Capn. Hood will give you the Particulars of the Action and of their Force.—I am &c.,

(Sign'd) "Chas. Holmes.

"*Grafton* at Sea
"at Noon Louisburg bore N.E.b.N. 10 or 12 Leagues
"July ye 29th, 1756.
"To Capn. Spry, *Fougueux* by the *Jamaica* Sloop."

D. Captain Hales' Report

"Halifax, *Septem.* the 13th, 1756.

"Sir,—I take the opportunity by Mr. Clewitt to give you some Account of my Expedition to Louisburg and to Assure you how Sorry I am that I could neither get out of that Harbour time Enough to inform you of what it was of the Greatest Consequence for you to know, nor get a Sight of your Squadron when the French thought proper to dismiss me.

"On the Third of August as you may remember I saild from Halifax and on the 5th I arrived at Louisburg where I found *Le Heros* Monr. Beaussier of 74 Guns *L'Illustre*, Montallete 64, *La Serene* Brugnon 36 *L'Alicrone*, Larrigaudiere 30 Guns being the same Ships which you Engaged. *Le Heros* close to which I was moor'd had 22 Shott which I counted in her Larboard Side about a Dozen in Different parts of her Stern. One Shot in her Rudder, Her three Topmasts disabled her Main Main Mast fish'd from top to Bottom, Her shrouds & rigging Cutt to Pieces, and altogether in a Condition which did great Credit to the Grafton, her kill'd and Wounded upon a Comparison of all Accounts Amounted to one Hundred the other Ship and the Frigates had not Sufferd any damage at all that I could learn, these Ships came from Quebec and their Orders to Land a Sum of Money at Louisburg was as they say the Occasion that they did not Engage you the Evening you first Saw them, but I have good reason to think that they put into Louisburg for a Reinforcement of Men, etc. The Reason that they did not renew the Engagement the Next day but run into Harbour was, as an Officer of the *Heros* confess'd to me because that ship was so much disabled. I cannot omit in this Place a Compliment which a French Captain paid you, Mr. Brugnon the Capn. of the *Serene* in a Letter which he sent by me to a French Officer at Halifax has these Express'd Words, Les Englois ont fait des Merveilles leurs Cannon a été Services Comme de la Musqueterie.

"These have arrived at Quebec this Summer the Abovementioned Ships together with *Le Leopard* of 64 Guns the *Concord* and Sauvage Frigates who brought over two Regiments Le Sarre & Rousillon. The three last sailed Seperately for France before my Arrival at Louisburg the four others of your Acquaintance after waiting till the *Heros* was ready (upon which they had work'd incessantly) sailed out of Louisburg Harbour at about 7 o'Clock on Friday Evening 13th August, and I supposed according to Intelligence they had Received from without steer'd a Course all night by which with the assistance of a Fogg in the morning they had the good luck to Escape you. On Saturday the 14th as the True reason for which I was detain'd Ceased the Governour dismissed me and the Instant I got my Letters which was 5 in the afternoon I stood out of the Harbour towards your station we steer'd S.E. some time and then brought too the wind blowing fresh at S.W. on Sunday morning being 12 Leagues to the Eastward of Scatery we stood in for the Land and as it was Clear and we Saw Nothing of your Ships I flatterd my self you had got Sight of and was in pursuit of the French Ships and immagining my Stay could be of no Service I made the Best of my way to Halifax where I arriv'd on Wednesday the 18th there is not at present a Single Ship or Frigate at Quebec or Louisburg that I am sure of and have reason to think that none are Expected.

"By a Calculation which I made by Counting the Officers I have good reason to think there are not above eleven Hundred men at Louisburg 'tis probable they have Spared part of the Garrison to Cannada, they are greatly distress'd there for meat drink and Shoes and I assure you fish dress'd different ways makes up great part of their Entertainments ; what I have farther to Add is with Regard to One Baptisto Dion who is on bd. the *Fougueux* and whose history is as follows, he Came Pilot last Summer to a French Flag of Truce and was detain'd by One of the Admirals as an English Subject and was put on board The Fleet in Quality of a Pilot. Mr. Beaussier the Captain of the *Heros* and Mr. Drucour the Governour of Louisburg have both made Strong remonstrances to Mr. Lawrence about his being detain'd and Mr. Beaussier said he had as much right to detain my Pilot, it is Certain the Man was formerly an Inhabitant of Nova Scotia but it is as Certain that he Abandoned long since his Habitation and that his wife and children are now at Louisburg. If I may be Permitted to give my Opinion I should think it better to Release him for otherwise the French will detain the first person they get into their Hands or do something that will put an End to all Commerce and Understanding between us which an Exchange of Prisoners or other Business renders often Necessary during a war.

. . . .

"Your most obedient Servant,
(Sign'd) "John Hale."

E. Captain Hood's Report

"*Jamaica* at Sea,
"*August* 25th, 1856.

"Sir,—Agreeable to your orders I have had a look at Louisburgh. Falling in to the westward Monday afternoon I stood very near in, then ran close along shore to the Eastward, so that nothing in the Harbour escap'd my Notice, where were only Two Topsail vessels. And as I thought it of some consequence to know where the men of war were gone to, that engag'd you on the 27th past I did my utmost to gett a Fishing Shallop ; and not succeeding with the Sloop, made all the sail I cou'd off the Land just at dusk, and as soon as it was dark stood in again : At 12 sent the Lieutenant in the Pinnace to go & lie under the Land to the Eastward of the Lighthouse, with directions to seize the first he cou'd. In the meantime I stood off and on; and at day light was close in, took up the pinnace & a shallop she had taken with four men, whom I have examin'd seperately, and found to tell the same story. One of the Topsail Vessels in the Harbour is the large storeship, that unloaded at Millidue quite unrigged, & the other a snow from Rochfort. The Men of War sail'd for France fifteen days since, and were join'd at Sea by a Frigate call'd the *Concord*, from St. Ann. There names and force are as follows; The *Hero*, a new ship of 74 guns, the *Illustrious* of 64, the *Perfect* of 36, & *Serene* of 30. Upon my asking how the French came not to engage the English on the 26th they say they went in to put some money on shore, and gett men, and that they press'd a great number that night. I then asked them, whether it was not expected, by the people on shore, that the English wou'd be taken; They reply'd every one made sure of it; and it is allow'd the English behav'd well. They likewise tell me that their Commandant had 26 men kill'd on the Spot, that Fifty died of their wounds in three or four days, and that above a hundred more were wounded: that her Lower masts were so shatter'd, as scarcely to be made serviceable by Fishing to carry her home. Her sides full of shot Holes, and had Nine and Twenty shot between wind and water; many of them thro' and thro'. The other large Ship but little damag'd; and the Frigates came off in the same manner. I have made enquiry about Major Hale, who went with the Flag of Truce. They say he was detain'd, till the men of war were gone, and sail'd next day. . . .

"This is the amount of what I have collected from the French Men (who are inhabitants of Louisburgh) who are now on board the *Jamaica*, and shall be glad to know whether I may be permitted to let them go: I promis'd I would interceed in their behalf with you, if they wou'd tell the Truth; and I believe they have done it, by their agreeing so exactly in what they have said.—I am &c.,

"SAMUEL HOOD.[1]

"TO CHARLES HOLMES ESQR."

[1] Samuel Hood was the future Admiral Viscount Hood.

CHAPTER XII

As English blockades had suspended the normal activities of the people of Isle Royale, it is well, at this point, to measure the degree of success they reached in carrying on the business for which they had settled in Louisbourg and its outports. What else remains of the history of the place is mainly a narrative of military events, of its siege and capture ; implicitly, therefore, of its failure to protect its people, to maintain French influence on this Atlantic seaboard, and to safeguard the sea approaches to Canada.

The manner of carrying on the fisheries has been described in the memoir of 1706 at some length. As its writer, so the present, refers the reader interested in the details of this trade to the Sieur Deny's elaborate description.[1] A rare book[2] has some pages dealing specially with the Cape Breton trade. It may be noted that the Island is spoken of as Cape Breton Island instead of Isle Royale, the same survival of a name in common use, after an official change, which finds a later exemplification, in the continuance to-day of the name of Cape Breton in cases where the correct official designation has been since 1820, Nova Scotia.

The following is a free and somewhat condensed translation of this description of the trade :

Vessels are sent out in three different ways to Cape Breton.

Some go there simply for fishing, and leave about the 15th of February, or, at the latest, in the beginning of March.

Those which go for both fishing and trading leave during April.

The others who go simply for trading alone leave in May or June. These voyages are usually of seven or eight months, and the vessels return to our ports in November and December.

Fishing is carried on at Cape Breton as in the Petit Nord, but the vessels which are sent there are generally only of from 50 to 100 tons and need

[1] Deny's *Description of Acadia*, Champlain Society, p. 257 *et seqq.*

[2] *Remarques sur plusieurs* (?) *branches de commerce et de navigation*, M.DCC.LVII.

consequently only from four to six boats (Chaloupes) which are bought from the people of Cape Breton in barter for fishing gear or merchandise.[1]

The goods sent out are delivered at Louisbourg. The captain lands and remains on shore with his trading stock, while his lieutenant goes fishing with one or more inhabitants, who under a written agreement for a wage, payable in kind, fishes on the ship's account. The captain chooses men skilled in catching and preparing cod. The vessels of 100 tons have ordinarily twenty-five or twenty-six men, sometimes hired at a monthly wage, sometimes on shares. In either case the owner makes them advances.

The captain keeping shop at Louisbourg sells his goods for ready money, that is to say, payable at the end of the fishing season, which ordinarily lasts four months, either in cod at an agreed price, or in Bills of Exchange.

A vessel of 100 tons for this voyage costs usually 24,000 livres : its cargo about 18,000, and the wages and provisions for twenty-five men, about 10,000 livres.

The cargo of a vessel of 100 tons for trading at Cape Breton would consist of salt provisions, fishing implements, ship chandlery, stuffs, boots and shoes, lead, iron, linen, a small quantity of brandy, wine and spirits. The only touch of luxury among the commodities is, that in mentioning shoes (Souliers) for women, the list adds for the most part, coloured ones.[2]

The principal consumption of dried cod is at Marseilles, where the greater part of the vessels discharge.[3] Thence some is sent to Italy. Cadiz and Alicante take from Marseilles nine or ten cargoes, and the balance is distributed to Bordeaux, La Rochelle, Nantes, St. Malo, and Havre.

In fishing for dry and green cod, Granville sends 55 to 60 vessels. The ports between Agon and St. Malo 65 to 80 ; Nantes, Olonne, and neighbouring ports, 55 to 60 vessels.

From St. Malo, Nantes, La Rochelle, Bordeaux, and Bayonne 60 to 80 vessels go to Cape Breton for fishing and trading.

The voyages for dry and green cod, including those to Gaspé and Labrador, employ fifteen or sixteen thousand seamen, and the air of the climate is so healthy that in ordinary seasons there scarcely die ten out of this whole number. With these there are from eighteen hundred to two thousand apprentices.

The same writer devotes a few pages to the fisheries of New England, in which he says that from Boston, Plymouth, Barnstaple, Cape Ann, and Marblehead, are sent out annually 180 vessels of 35 to 40 tons, and from Nova Scotia (Canso) 17 or 18 vessels, and that each of these makes three trips a season, taking from 200 to 250 quintals each voyage.[4] He speaks of the

---

[1] The number of boats seems overstated by the official returns. [2] "Surtout en couleurs."
[3] New England also did a large trade with this port. [4] His estimate is less than that of Douglass'.

illicit trade with foreign ports, and estimates the number of men employed as from seventeen to eighteen hundred.

He concludes his sketch with a panegyric on the people of this industry, and notes the lack of attention to the services of the sailor-fishermen in comparison with that of the soldier. "One will recognize that the latter is useful to the State only in time of war, and nevertheless, that he costs at all times at least 125 livres a year, and that the sailor who serves his country at all times, who even enriches it by his labour and industry, costs the State only when the King makes him serve on his vessels; these men, brought up so to speak among the dangers of the coasts, whom the greatest perils do not amaze, are as nimble in handling vessels, as intrepid in conflicts. Does not this class of men justly deserve a high place among the objects of the State, of which to-day its only rival is a Maritime Power?"

In addition to the fisheries conducted from French ports, there was the shore fishery of Isle Royale carried on by its own people, and occupying the labours of its permanent inhabitants, and the capital of the merchants resident at Louisbourg. Many of these merchants were, judging by such names as Rodriques and Daccarette, originally Basques, and long in the business. The representatives of the Rodriques in 1781 appealed to the Assemblée Nationale for a loan to carry on their business. They recounted in their memoir that they had lost all, first, at the capture of Port Royale in 1710, then at that of Louisbourg in '45 and in '58, wherein their losses were 240,000 l., and, again, at the capture of St. Pierre-Miquelon in 1778. They stated that at Louisbourg they had employed 200 to 300 fishermen.[1] Early in the history of Louisbourg, Normans also came there, although the majority of the names are Basque. Indeed a Widow Onfroy claimed to have begun this trade, in which she was followed by other outfitters of St. Malo. The traveller in France at all times has been struck with the business capacity of the Frenchwoman. The conduct of a fishing business at an outport of Isle Royale is a striking example of this capacity, which was exercised by more than the Malouin bourgeoise. Other women at various times are noted as administering fishing stations, usually established by a deceased husband.[2]

The boat-builders seem to have been Acadians, and it is early noted that scarcely a vessel came out which did not require a mast or spar, the supplying of which gave employment to the habitant. It also led to poaching on British

[1] Their many purchases of vessels from the New Englanders in '49 and '50 would seem to substantiate their statement.

[2] In 1753 at Petit Lorambec, we note four widows. One owned five chaloupes and had twenty-five fishermen. Another, four fishermen. The third owned two chaloupes and had nine fishermen. At Miré, one widow, Marie la Boyne, owned a schooner and grew wheat, corn, and fruit. At Port Dauphin we note another woman owner of property.

territory, for many fine sticks were brought from Pictou, presumably rather for these refittings than for the vessels which were built on the island.[1]

The proximity of Isle Royale to the banks,[2] the excellence of the shore fishing, that is the catch made in open boats, which a more or less fabulous New England statement said was so good that the fish were taken with grapnels, and the skill of the French fisherman made Louisbourg a place of the first rank in this industry. Its annual catch was about 150,000 quintals. How great, relatively, is measured by the fact that in its best days, the Marblehead district caught 120,000 quintals, and that from the establishment of Louisbourg the New England fisheries declined.[3]

The commerce which resulted from these products of the sea was large : some 7000 or 8000 tons of valuable commodities to be transported. In consequence, Louisbourg and its outports had a splendid concourse of vessels during its busy season. Below is tabulated the shipping of Isle Royale for ten normal years, 1733-1743 (1741 being wanting) of its industry.[4] It shows that one year with another 154 vessels visited its ports, principally Louisbourg. Again a comparison shows how important was its trade. Only three ports of the populous, enterprising, and sea-faring British colonies saw more vessels come in from sea than those which visited this outpost in Isle Royale of French commercial enterprise.

[1] A minor industry was the brewing of spruce beer, the valuable antiscorbutic qualities of which made a demand for it not only from merchantmen, but also from men-of-war. Pichon, p. 69, says that the Acadian women chew spruce gum, and that it whitens their teeth and keeps them in good condition. A well-equipped brewery existed in the outskirts of the town.

[2] TABLE SHOWING DISTANCES FROM FISHING PORTS TO THE PRINCIPAL BANKS

	Louisbourg.	Lunenburg, N.S.	Gloucester, Mass.
Virgin Rocks, Grand Banks .	370	574	868
Green Bank	406	410	699
Artimon	91	251	553
Canso	50	170	468
Middle Grounds . . .	83	156	450
Sable Island Bank . . .	150	132	405
Cape North	69	295	589
North Bay	201	328	623
St. Pierre Bank	156	350	651

Prepared by Mr. H. C. Levatte, of Louisbourg.

[3] Marblehead's fleet declined from 120 schooners in 1732 to 70 in 1747 (Douglass, vol. i. p. 302. He states the total catch of B.N.A. as 300,000 in 1747, which seems to include Newfoundland).

[4] Local fishermen and coasters are not included.

[TABLE

Shipping of Isle Royale

Year.	From France.	From Canada.	From French West Indies.	From New England and Acadia.	Total.
1733	70	17	25	46	158
1734	53	31	19	46	149
1735	68	25	16	52	161
1736	60	23	14	35	132
1737	43		15	{ 35 / 5 = Acadia / 30 = English }	99
1738	73	14	15	42	144
1739	56	20	24	49	149
1740	73	19	22	50	164
1741	Wanting				
1742	57	9	24	67	157
1743	58	7	32	78	175

English Colonies (from Douglass)

Place.	Date.	Entries.
Portsmouth	Xmas '47–48	121
Newport	March 25, '47–48	56
,, ...	'48–49	75
New York	Sept. 29, '50	232
Boston	Xmas '47–48	540
Philadelphia	Xmas '47–48	303
Salem and outports		
Marblehead		
Cape Anne	Xmas '47–48	131
Ipswich		
Newbury		

Prévost wrote on January 4, 1753, a letter dealing with the trade of Isle Royale,[1] which supplements the statements just quoted. Fishing, he pointed out, was the base of the commerce with France, the West Indies, and Canada. The shore fishery was carried on by residents, in fishing-boats, which did not go more than four or five leagues off shore. The larger boats ("batteaux") and schooners went to the Scatari, Green, Sable Island, and St. Pierre banks, as well as to those in the gulf, although the home banks are better.

Shore fishing was the easiest, and produced better fish, but the bank fishing

[1] C¹¹, vol. 38.

was preferred as it was easier to get men, and the schooners employed in it could be loaded for French ports in the autumn.

When a quintal of fish would buy a barrel of flour or one of salt, the trade was on a sound basis. Prévost estimated the profits of the merchants at twenty-five or thirty per cent. They obtained six months credit on many French goods, such as those of Montauban and Beauvais, and on sailcloth, and they did a good trade with the French Windward Islands in their schooners. The trade with these islands would be much improved if their merchants were prohibited from sending rum to St. Eustache and the other foreign islands, for if it all came to Louisbourg it would greatly increase the trade of that place. The traffic in New England vessels was an advantage, for the old vessels in which the purchasers came from the southern colonies were not broken up, but were bought by the inhabitants for the coasting trade.

Two causes, therefore, forced Louisbourg into being the entrepôt at which a distribution of commodities from various sources could be carried on. These were the abhorrence of the shipowner for a voyage in ballast or partly laden, the equal abhorrence of the trader for an adverse balance compelling payment in money for his purchases.

More shipping capacity was required to export the fish of Louisbourg than to carry thither the imports of the place. The owners loaded the vessels to their capacity, and this surplus had to find an outlet. Thus Louisbourg became a trading centre, as it were, a clearing-house, where France, Canada, New England, and the West Indies mutually exchanged the commodities their vessels had brought, to avoid making unprofitable the round voyage, which would have unduly enhanced the cost of its fish. The tobacco, rum, and sugar of the West Indies, the cloths of Carcassone, the wines of Provence, sailcloths and linens, came to Louisbourg, far in excess of the possibilities of local use, and were sent out again. The permitted trades with Canada and the French islands could not absorb them, so the thrifty Acadian housewife bought from Louisbourg the few luxuries of her frugal life. The more prosperous New England trader, who supplied Louisbourg with building materials, with food, with planks and oaken staves, thence exported to the sugar islands, took in exchange the commodities of France and the rum-stuff of these islands. The towns of France furnished part at least of the sailcloth for his many vessels engaged in freighting and trade from Newfoundland to the West Indies. Much of this trade was illicit. The meagre returns of the commerce show this clearly. We have for 1740 the number of vesssels and their tonnage, as well as their declared cargoes inwards and outwards. The number of vessels from New England was 39, their aggregate tonnage 1131, their cargoes were :

Inwards.		No.	Value.
Cows		24	@ 50 l.
Bricks, M. . .		58	15
Planks, M. . .		443	30
Sageaux Bus. .		239	3
Indian corn . .		1237	2
Shingles, M. .		446	9
Pork (lbs.) . .		6300	0.5
Pipes (gross) .		316	3
Bureaus and chest of drawers . .		95	60
Rice (cwt.) . .		100	20
Axes		1122	4
Pigs		52	20
Oxen		18	75
Sheep		445	10
Pears and apples, etc. (qts.). .		486	8
Value . .			49,147 l.

Outwards.		No.	Value.
Rum (bbls.). . .		715	@ 65 l.
Molasses (bbls.) .		460	40
Brandy (kegs) .		200	5
Iron (cwt.) . .		48	20
Sailcloth . .		713	1
Cordage . .		23	40
Coal (bbls.) . .		670	3
Iron for anchors (cwt.) .		5	40
Value . .			70,678 l.

Unless the measurement of vessels has materially changed it seems obvious that neither inward nor outward was an adequate lading declared. Incidentally one may note the higher state of New England industry. The surplus of their fields and their handicrafts were exported. Isle Royale returned to her the products of other places with the exception of the trifling shipment of coal. The advantages of her superb situation for the fisheries, the skill and enterprise with which her people prosecuted them, were minimized by her unfortunate position as regards the sparsity of her population, the uncertainty and high cost of its sustenance.

Much of this trade was done with Louisbourg, much of it through Canso, where so important a merchant of Boston as Faneuil[1] had a resident partner. The trade was known to the authorities, both English and French.

This intercourse had a further development. The French bought the fish of the New Englanders. The intercourse for this trading begun before the war, continued at Martengo, the first harbour to the westward of Canso, where both met and exchanged their commodities untroubled by officials. It has been interpreted that this meant that the superior enterprise of the New England man enabled him to catch fish cheaper than the French.[2] A sounder view would seem to be that through Louisbourg was the easiest channel for him to get the French commodities the British provinces required, and that he found that the

---

[1] See p. 399.   [2] *Weeden*, p. 596.

Louisbourg merchant could dispose of his fish to better advantage than he had found as the result of his shipments to Toulon and Marseilles.[1]

In the commercial interest of France and England is found the cause of complacency with which their Governments looked on this illicit trade. The merchants of these countries were continually in a position to point out that an outlet for home manufactures and other products would be lessened if the trade were checked, so that nothing was done in this direction. It was not the peculiar offence of the colonist. The impulses of commerce are ever towards expansion and to profits. The predominant share of outfitters in the mother country in these trades, the greater ease with which, as compared with the colonist, their influence could be brought to bear on the official, so frequently a sharer in mercantile ventures, made it easy to ignore laws which checked profitable trade. The influence of the City was potent in Westminster and Whitehall. When the Ohio Company embroiled France and England, its English shareholders prevailed on the Ministry to take a firm position, with a promptness which would have been wanting had its only shareholders been Virginian planters and merchants. A seizure of a contraband trader in Isle Royale touched the interests not only of the Louisbourg agent, but of his principal in Bordeaux, Bayonne, or Marseilles, and he, like his London confrère, had means of bringing influences to bear on Ministers, which led to the discouragement of too zealous administrators. These influences, creditable or the reverse, were backed by the fact that French industry or French commerce in a particular case would be hurt.[2] The concrete prevailed over the general theory, with peculiar ease, as the theory was unsound.

This line of argument is supported by the fact that where interests of the French merchant came into conflict with those of the colonist the latter suffered. Raudot, it may be said again, with remarkable prescience saw that if Isle Royale was to really flourish, it should have free trade with New England. Costebelle, an experienced administrator, after a little experience at Louisbourg, saw the necessity of this, and recommended it to the Regency (April 19, 1717) ; but he adds with bitterness :

" He is persuaded that the merchants of France will always strenuously oppose it, being aware that the restriction (on foreign trade) will leave them always able to keep under their yoke like slaves the inhabitants of the colonies, whom they will sustain and support only in as much as their labours contribute to the profit of the commerce " (of France).

In this he was right, for the threat of the French merchants to send no vessels to Isle Royale, if this were permitted, ended the matter. Had it been

---

[1] This New England trade with these ports was, nevertheless, very important (*Weeden*, p. 659). On these trades as well as that of Isle Royale he quotes Bollan, 118-120 (Mass. Arch. 14, p. 560, and 22, p. 21).

[2] See Appendix on illicit trading.

proposed later when the illicit trade with New England was in full operation, their view would have been different; but by 1727 the question was no longer open. In that year the Government of Louis XV. had committed itself to prohibition of foreign trade.

Again Bigot, who was an accomplished official, and understood the value of making no troublesome suggestions to an easy-going Minister, wished Isle Royale cod to take the place of Irish beef in the sugar islands. He spoke of it as only possible if it were not detrimental to the interests of the merchants of the kingdom.

The comparisons which had been made between the economic conditions of New England and Canada, not only in English, but by Charlevoix and other French writers, the assumption that in industries connected with the sea the English always had a marked superiority, make the conclusions as to the economic importance of Louisbourg surprising. We find that it was a source of wealth to France, that it surpassed the colonies of England engaged in the same trade, and that the most important in which the northern colonies of both France and England were engaged.

The facts as to the trade on which this opinion is based are given later in this work. There is also abundant evidence that English and colonial observers were fully alive to a progress which excited their admiration, envy, and fear.

Shirley's estimate is that the fisheries were worth annually a million sterling.[1] A French writer says that the whole value of the fishing of New England is worth £138,000.[2] This is confirmed by an English writer who says that in 1759 the French had nine hundred ships, and that the English trade was declining. Auchmuty, the first to get in print with a proposal to capture Isle Royale, says its fisheries were worth £2,000,000, confirmed again by a " Gentleman of a Large Trade in the City of London" (London, 1746), who says French trade is increasing, English diminishing. The English fleet outnumbered the French in 1700 five to one, and now was less than the French, and he confirms or repeats Shirley's estimate of its value as a million. The writer adds with wisdom that Fleury contributed to this result by promoting competition with England, and made " war upon this Kingdom by all the arts of peace." " An Accurate Description of Cape Breton," 1758, speaks of Raudot's scheme for its settlement as " a beautiful and well-digested project," and confirms the other opinions of its value. " A Letter to the Right Hon. W. P." (Exon., 1758) says that if things had gone on as they had been, the French " would have beat us out of the Trade of Europe." " The Advantages of the Definite Treaty " (London, 1749) says that had the French not been molested, in a few years they would have totally ruined British foreign trade ; " as it was, they had in a manner beat us out of our

---

[1] C.O. 5/900, f. 212, and Appendix. [2] *Hist. et commerce des colonies angloises*, Paris, 1755.

Levant Trade, our Fishing Trade, and our Sugar Trade"; and "A Letter from a Gentleman in London to his Friend in the Country" (London, 1748), in a eulogy of Cape Breton, says, "in no part of the world is the cod fishing carried on with better success."

Every chapter of Weeden which deals with the fisheries speaks of their fundamental importance. Douglass (vol. i. p. 6) says:

> "The French had already the better of us in the fishery trade, and in a few years more would have supplied all the markets of Europe, and, by underselling, entirely excluded us from the cod fishery, which is more beneficial and easier wrought than the Spanish mines of Mexico and Peru."

This the writers of the Memorials to Pontchartrain, 1706–9, foresaw. The alarmed pamphleteer in 1746, about the same time as Douglass wrote the above, says:

> "In that Piece the Author having observed that the *English* Nation is too apt to have a mean Opinion of the Trade and Navigation of its Rivals, especially the *French*, and was not convinced of its Mistake, 'till the Incidents of the present War, the numerous *French Fleets*, and large Prizes Open'd our Eyes; he proceeds to shew the Steps by which the *French Commerce* and *Colonies*, from being inferior to ours, have risen to a dangerous Superiority over us, in less than half a Century.
>
> "For this Purpose a Council of Commerce was established in the Year 1700. . . .
>
> "Since this Establishment, and in Consequence of the Memorials presented by them to the Royal Council, containing Propositions for Regulations and Remedies in Trade, being thoroughly executed, 'the Trade of *France* has been extended to the *Levant*, the *North Africa*, *North America*, the *South Seas*, and to the *East* and *West Indies*, even so far as to make more than double the Value in Sugar, Indigo, Ginger, and Cotton, in their *West India Islands* than what is now made by the *English*, who before that Time exceeded the *French* in this Branch of Trade abundantly.'
>
> "In the Article of Sugar they are increased from 30,000 to 120,000 Hogsheads *English* in a Year (*i.e.* as 3 to 12 or 1 to 4). Two Thirds of which are shipped to *Holland*, *Hamburgh*, *Spain* and other foreign Markets.
>
> "In the same Time the *English* have encreased from about 45,000 to no more than 70,000 Hogsheads, *i.e.* as 9 to 14, not near double, 'of which they now send but little to foreign Markets, altho' they had formerly the best Share of that Trade, and even *supplied* France *with Sugars*.' And moreover the *French* have already engrossed the Indigo Trade from the *English*, and have greatly encreased in the Fisheries, and Beaver and other Fur Trade in *North America*, since their Settlement of *Cape Breton*, which they have fortified at a vast Expence;—and it is from this last mentioned Trade, and their Fisheries, that they find a Vent for most of their Molasses and Rum that the *English* do not take off their Hands.
>
> "These Advantages gain'd by the *French* are conspicuous from the immense Sums which 'They drew *annually* from other Countries, *and which enable them to maintain powerful Armies, and afford such plentiful Subsidies and Pensions to several Powers and*

People in Europe: From hence they build their Ships of War, and maintain Seamen to supply them.

"It is computed that they draw from two to three Millions of Pounds Sterling per *annum* from foreign Countries, in return only for Sugar, Indigo, Coffee, Ginger, Beaver manufactured into Hats, Salt-Fish and other American Products, and near one Million more from *Great Britain* and *Ireland* only, in *Wool* and *Cash*, in return for Cambricks, Tea, Brandy and Wine, and thereby *fight us in Trade, as well as at War, with our own Weapons*. But it is to be hoped that the Measures lately taken by the *British* Legislature to prevent the Importation of foreign Cambricks and Tea, and the taking and *keeping* of *Cape Breton*, will be attended with considerable national Advantages." [1]

The opinions of London pamphleteers were confirmed by the soldier on the ground, Amherst's instructions to Whitmore, August 28, 1758 :

"I would have the settlements in the different parts of the island absolutely destroyed, it may be done in a quiet way, but pray let them be entirely demolished, & for these reasons, that in the flourishing state this island was growing to many years wd not have passed before the inhabitants wd. have been sufficient to have defended it." [2]

Further and conclusive testimony is borne to the soundness of the trade of Louisbourg, by the fact that it was always on a specie basis. Its commerce never suffered from paper money, as did that of the British colonies and Quebec. The expression that Louisbourg was a clearing-house is further justified by a statement of Prévost to the effect that the New England traders could pass there Spanish gold and silver which was not current in the French West Indies.

This consensus of opinion,[3] in addition to the returns of the trade, shows that Isle Royale had completely justified the memorialists who had urged its establishment. Nor was this trade—in value, say, three million livres a year—brought into being at an excessive price. Roughly speaking, for to analyze the figures contained in returns would require an expert accountant ; the outlay of the Government, including the cost of the fortifications, which was yearly about 130,000 l., was, say, ten per cent of the trade. In other words, had a private Company taken up Isle Royale, as was proposed before its settlement, and carried on its business, had such a thing been possible, even spending as lavishly on administration and defence as the King, it would have been a not unprofitable venture. There has been much exaggeration as to the outlay on the fortifications. Contemporary and later writers have spoken lightly of millions. The accounts do not indicate any large total. The

---

[1] "Two Letters concerning some further Advantages and Improvements that may seem necessary to be made on the taking and keeping of Cape Breton" (London, 1746). It quotes "State of the British and French Trade to Africa and America considered," London, 1745.   [2] C.O. 5/53, Amherst to Whitmore, Aug. 28, 1758.

[3] I have found no other view expressed by any writer of the period.

memoir on this subject[1] given to the King in 1743, makes the total about 3,500,000 l., a larger amount than seems justified by the returns of the Treasurer.[2]

Isle Royale was not the only fishing establishment, but it was most important ; as an entrepôt, it as fully served its purpose as the economic principles of the age permitted. The course of the narrative has indicated that the unfavourable conditions at Louisbourg were not peculiar to that place, for those of Canso and Annapolis Royal were as bad as under the French régime. The British Government was as deaf to the appeals of its local officials, and as late in taking action, as was Maurepas. Newfoundland had a population of 4000 in 1713 and 6000 in 1755. Canso remained about stationary throughout this period, so that the progress of Isle Royale compares well with that of the two British settlements nearest to it, not only geographically, but in the pursuits of their people. The fisherman justified himself commercially at Isle Royale. His rulers made no gains in Europe to counterbalance the injuries to the commonwealth resulting from their neglect to safeguard his industry. When the victories of peace come to be as highly esteemed as those of war, the French historian, who then writes of the colonial development of his country under the Bourbon kings, will have more pride than our contemporaries in writing of Isle Royale. He can then point out that the American colonies of his country were lost, by her rival, beaten in the arts of peaceful development, wresting them with a strong hand from the government of his ancestors incapable in the last resort to force of defending possessions so valuable.

After this digression, it seems desirable to touch on the human side of life in the little town before narrating the culminating incident of its history.

The increase in its garrison overcrowded it, and pushed settlements of others than farmers out into the environs.[3]

Under ordinary circumstances such increase of the population would have raised prices. When the effect of a heightened demand was increased, through a diminished supply, the aggravation of the economic position was extreme. Important sources of supply were cut off by the embargo on exportation from the British Colonies, the active efforts of Cornwallis to stop any supply from Nova Scotia, and the captures of vessels by the blockading fleets.

---

[1] C11, L.R. vol. 26, f. 219.

[2] There are two sources of information on this subject, besides occasional references in the general correspondence, Arch. Col. Amerique du Nord Isle Royale, vols. 8 and 11, and Arch. Marine G, vols. 52, 53, and 54 ; the latter gives a short annual statement from 1733, of various statistics about the colony.

[3] Chassin de Thierry, Senior Captain of the garrison, lived about five miles from town on the Miré Road (*Derniers Jours, etc.* p. 215).

It was at best of times a community with little money ; military salaries were low, as were those of other officials.[1]

This involved a meagre life, occasionally relieved by a place at the table of the more fortunate.   Drucour recounts the following incident in a letter to Surlaville :[2] " Mme. de la Boularderie has just dined here ; we drank your health, and she told us you made her so merry that she saw eight candles instead of one ; we did not carry things as far."

Johnstone was delighted to have permission to embark ten or twelve days before the vessel sailed on a voyage to France, " in order to repair the bad fare which I had during a year at Louisbourg, which ordinarily consisted during the winter solely of cod-fish and hog's lard, and during the summer, fresh fish, bad salt rancid butter, and bad oil." [3]

Captain Hale wrote after being in Louisbourg with a flag of truce in 1756 :

" I assure you fish dressed in various ways makes up a great part of their entertainment " (Ad. Des. 1, 481).

M. Joubert writes in January, 1757 :

" Il n'y a rien de nouveau ycy depuis mes dernières ; nous sommes tous réduits à la sapinette (spruce beer) . . ." [4]

The cuisine of Louisbourg had other resources than cod : Johnstone's servant,

"an excellent Jack of all trades, expert for furnishing my table, bringing generally eight or ten dozen of trouts, in two hours' fishing with the line, the streams in the neighbourhood being very full of fish." [5]

The prevalence of gambling circumscribed the opportunities of the poorest of the officers for going into society.   Des Bourbes writes :

" I am a useless member of a society where there is nothing but gambling, I am not in demand as I do not wish to play, and cannot do so.   I go out only to pay my respects, and find gaming tables everywhere ; I watch the players for a second or two ; I sit in an armchair out of decency and this politeness on my part is most boring . . ." [6]

Johnstone found :

". . . the society of the ladies of the place very amiable, but having always cards in their hands, my avocations would not permit of me daily to make one of their parties . . ." [7]

---

[1] Captains, 1080 l. ; lieutenant, 720 l. ; enseigne en pied, 480 l. ; enseigne en second, 360 l.   So hard was the position of the junior officers that after 1754 a bonus of 6000 l. annually was divided among the lieutenants and ensigns.   The Governor's salary was 9000 l., with a bonus of 6000 l.   Surlaville says the Governor's position in salary, bonus, and allowance was worth 19,800 l., and that the nominal salary of the Commissaire-Ordonnateur of 2400 l. was raised in the same way to 6000 l.   Compared with similar positions to-day these emoluments were not inconsiderable, but in all the subaltern positions the pay was small, and was eked out by frugality or commercial ventures.

[2] See *Derniers Jours*, etc. p. 128.   [3] *Memoirs of the Chevalier Johnstone*, vol. ii. p. 172.
[4] *Derniers Jours*, etc. p. 213.   [5] *Memoirs*, etc. vol. ii. p. 179.
[6] *Derniers Jours*, etc. p. 182.   [7] *Memoirs*, etc. vol. ii. p. 178.

Both he and Des Bourbes speak with thankfulness of a taste for study which lightened the dreariness of their narrow life. Others had less innocent pastimes. Duels were not infrequent, and we have one instance of the misery caused by jealousy in the suicide of the unfortunate Montalembert. He was driven to distraction by the liaison of his wife with one of the officers of Bourgogne, whom even at the time of her marriage she preferred to the elderly husband chosen by her mother.[1]

The rivalries and jealousies between different factions in the service were many. Few towns could have had more. There was the common one of antagonism between the *gens de l'épée* and the *gens de la plume*, the military and civil orders of the administration, mitigated in this case by the ascendency Prévost had gained over Drucour.

There was the antagonism not only between the army and the navy, but also between naval officers serving afloat and on shore. The old Companies officers had grievances against those of the Companies raised in 1749. All these were on indifferent or hostile terms with the officers of Canada, who were occasionally transferred from Beauséjour to Louisbourg; while Artois and Bourgogne aroused in the breasts of the ordinary garrison those feelings which it seems the fate of regular troops of all countries to excite among their colonial fellows ; while all of them were agreed in thinking the honours paid to Franquet were excessive.

At Louisbourg this jealousy produced its evil effects; Du Caubet, an officer of the Louisbourg garrison, was detached for service at Beauséjour. There he met the Langis brothers, officers of Canada, and a quarrel broke out. It reached, at Louisbourg, where they had both returned, its fatal end. One evening Du Caubet was found in his quarters dead from many barbarous wounds. It was an open secret that the elder Langis was the instigator of the deed. An inquiry was held, but led to nothing, and Langis escaped punishment. Pichon looked on this as significant, for he says, " The colonial officer would like to do as much to the last of the French officers." [2]

It was Prévost, however, who drew down on himself the most universal dislike. Such was the fate of the Intendant or his equivalent the Commissaire-Ordonnateur in most colonies, unless he were a man of rare tact and judgment. This Prévost was not. Neither Des Herbiers nor Raymond approved of him, but on the other hand he succeeded in making himself indispensable to Drucour. On one side there are incidents to show that Prévost was a man of independence. He refused, for example, to assist in

---

[1] See *Derniers Jours, etc.* pp. 149, 214.

[2] " L'Officier colon voudroit en faire autant au dernier des officiers de France " (*Derniers Jours, etc.* p. 131).

carrying out the categorical orders of La Jonquière to seize English vessels in the Port of Louisbourg ; and his correspondence with the Minister is that of a man of parts.

On the other hand, there are incidents which show that he was small and vindictive, perhaps to a greater extent than might be expected from any man of low birth and unattractive manners, occupying a position which gave him power to retaliate for the annoyances and indignities inflicted on him by his social superiors. He tells himself of the humiliations to which he was subjected on his official visit to De Bauffremont's ship. De Bauffremont was absent, but his officers were of the same opinion as their commander, who "always treated him (Prévost) as the last of miscreants." The officers of the colonial troops, as well as those of Artois and Bourgogne, also sent him to Coventry and refused his invitations.

Johnstone relates one striking instance of his insubordination :

"When the English fleet appeared before Louisbourg in 1757, all the troops marched out upon the instant to man the intrenchments . . . in order to oppose their landing, and . . . our surgeon-general having given M. St. Julien a recipe for a sling, some spirits, and other things necessary for dressing wounds. Prévost replied to M. St. Julien, commandant by seniority of all our troops, that 'there was nothing at all in the King's magazines, that if the English forced our entrenchments, it would fall to them to take care of our wounded, and if we repulsed them, they would have to look after them.' M. St. Julien reported immediately the affair with his complaints to M. Bois de la Motte, who at the instant landed at nine o'clock at night, proceeded directly to Prévost's house, and having threatened to set it on fire, and to send him back to France, if everything which the store contained was not ready by the next day, in the morning, all was furnished, to the great disappointment of this inhuman monster, who wished from his hatred to all the officers, to make these brave people perish for want of assistance, and he wept through rage."[1]

Nevertheless, he managed to have some friends, partly owing to the chance of his having married on February 14, 1745, a very attractive demoiselle Marie Thérèse Carrerot, the daughter of one of the principal merchants of the place. The power of conferring benefits gave him some allies and associates. Their sentiments find expression in a madrigal, the joint efforts of the Père Alexis of the Frères de la Charité, and M. Beaudeduit, one of the Conseil Supérieur. The poem was presented to him at an entertainment in his house, and goes as follows :

> A la paix toujours tranquille
> Prévost donne un sûre asile.
> Qu'il est doux de vivre sous ces loix !
> Les plaisirs renaissent à sa voix.

---

[1] See *Memoirs of the Chevalier Johnstone*, vol. ii. p. 181, *note*.

Prévost veut tout obéir ;
La paix vient, le trouble fuit ;
Sous luy l'on voit la justice
Triompher de l'artifice.[1]

The most striking figure in Louisbourg at this time, even by standards other than that of official position, was the Chevalier de Drucour, its Governor, a younger son of a noble Norman family, who entered the service in 1719. His career was successful; while still a lieutenant he was appointed Lieutenant of the Gardes de la Marine (Midshipmen) at Brest, and later Commandant of that corps, a responsible position, for which he was selected without personal solicitation, on account of his wisdom and good conduct. In discharging the social duties of this position by entertaining the young noblemen under his charge, he exhausted not only his salary and income, but seriously cut into his patrimony, which he completely exhausted in the expenses incident to taking up the Governorship of Louisbourg. He further involved his affairs by obtaining advances from his brother, the Baron de Drucour, and the expenses of his administration left him penniless. It is obvious from this conduct of his affairs that Drucour was one of those nobles who preferred to maintain the dignity of any position to which his sovereign had called him, rather than exercise a reasonable regard for his private interests. He even did this with a liberality which seems unnecessary, for in rearranging the canteens he abandoned to the Majors of the place that share of the profits which had been the perquisite of every preceding Governor.[2]

In the arrangements he made, he went contrary to the opinion of the Company officers, but neither this nor any other of his acts gave rise to any criticism excepting that Prévost had gained an undue ascendency over him, and that his judgment of men was not discriminating. No one writes of him except in praise, and his good sense and firmness are more than once spoken of. The one personal letter we have from his hand is that of a pleasant and capable writer, who speaks of his difficulties without discouragement or vexation.

Madame Drucour, a daughter of the Courserac family which had given many officers to the French navy, did her part in making his régime popular. She was a woman of intelligence, gracious towards every one, and succeeded in making Government House extremely attractive.

Later events show that, in addition, she was a woman of rare heroism and

[1] His *États de Service* shows that, notwithstanding the dislike of his associates, he had the confidence of successive Ministers, and received promotions. It also shows the hardships to which an officer was exposed in the Colonial Service in those days. It was not until 1763 that there was any effective examination of his conduct. In consequence of the rial of de la Borde, treasurer of l'Isle Royale, Prévost, by order of April 18, was arrested, and taken to the Bastille Marine B, vol. 117). On the 10th April 1764 he was set at liberty, but was never again to be employed in any osition of confidence (Marine B, vol. 120).

[2] The right to sell to the troops brought in about 3000 l. to the Governor (Papiers Surlaville).

a devoted wife. It may be noted, in passing, that the first and last Governors of Louisbourg both married widows, were splendidly mated, and left them in extreme poverty. Madame de Drucour was the widow of a Savigny. She received a pension of 1000 l., but died only a few weeks after her husband, about the time, October 1763, it was granted. In granting the pension, Drucour's character was recognised. He "s'étoit comporté dans cette place avec la plus grande désintéressement et la plus grande probité." The authorities therefore believed him when he wrote in 1757 :

"J'aurai l'exemple d'un seul gouverneur qui aura mangé son bien au lieu de l'augmenter."[1]

Drucour's government was a time of continuous trial. In the first few months he was embarrassed by the multitude of promises which Raymond had made before leaving. But these embarrassments and the ordinary trials of the head of a community, with such clashing interests as that of Louisbourg, were trifling compared with the difficulties which confronted him in the succeeding years. He had no control over the fortifications, the condition of which was unsatisfactory, owing to the lack of activity of Franquet, and the sufficient supply of men, materials, and money for their repair. The finances were not in his charge, and part of the inadequate supply of funds was stolen by La Borde, the Treasurer.

The garrison was too small. He pointed out the necessity for its increase, proposing that the companies be increased to 70 men each, and eight more added ; he emphasised the advantage of this course by pointing out that the colonial troops of 104 officers and 2446 men, the force he proposed for the establishment, would cost annually 166,325 l., whereas 164 officers and 1050 men of regular troops, like those of Artois and Bourgogne, would require an annual expenditure of 250,109 l.

But more insistent than the necessity of making the place effective as the guard of French supremacy in America, were the claims of subsistence for its garrison and its people. Each year the port was blockaded, each year its supplies were curtailed, and in 1757, after a winter in which not a family had an ounce of flour in the house, a winter so protracted that there remained eighteen inches of snow on the ground on the 12th of May, there was cause for the greatest anxiety. In June a vessel arrived which relieved the tension, but it was not until January 6, although Du Bois de la Motte had left all the spare provisions from his ships, that they felt assured of sufficient food for the winter. Doloboratz arrived with a cargo of provisions from France on that date, far later than had been thought possible to navigate these seas (Johnstone). The people and the garrison believed during the greater part

[1] A.N. Marine C¹, vol. 489.

of this time that the Royal storehouses contained provisions for two years, a tribute to the firmness and tact of Drucour and Prévost. It is equally to Drucour's praise that during the blockade of Holburne he had kept in touch with Halifax. His scouts, notably Gautier, haunted the outskirts of the English settlement, occasionally making captures, sometimes bringing with them a willing deserter, at other times returning empty-handed. This information he passed on, and, in addition, he promised the Government that he would destroy the new buildings at Halifax if provisions arrived by the middle of November. They did not arrive, and the project fell through. In this discouraging condition, but undismayed, Drucour awaited an attack which he knew was inevitable.[1]

[1] Le Loutre's Indians, who flocked to l'Ile Royale after the fall of Beauséjour, where they had been so bountifully supplied, were a source of trouble, and an additional drain on the inadequate store of provisions at Drucour's disposal. He speaks several times of their misery. He intended to use them and the Acadians in the foray against Halifax. Boishébert had been in command of this force (280 men) which had remained in Port Toulouse all summer.

CHAPTER XIII

THE war had been, so far, barren of results satisfactory to the English people. It had yielded only a succession of failures or defeats. Pitt described the operations of 1757 as "the last inactive and unhappy Campaign," and prepared "for the most vigorous and extensive Efforts to avert by the Blessing of God on His Arms, the Dangers impending in North America."[1]

On the same day he wrote to Loudon :

"My Lord, I am with concern to acquaint Your Lordship that the King has judged proper that Your Lordship should return to England."[2]

Loudon was superseded by Abercromby, to whom Pitt addressed a long, masterly and lucid statement of his plans for 1758.[3]

The reduction of Louisbourg was their first objective, and lavish preparations were made for its success. Engineers were ordered to Halifax to prepare siege material, and in his first letter to Abercromby Pitt said that the supplies gathered for Loudon were to be cared for and held in readiness. Troops and ships were to be concentrated at Halifax, so that the siege of Louisbourg might begin as early in the year "as the Twentieth of April, if the season should happen to permit.[4] Abercromby was to apply himself to other operations.

Fourteen thousand troops, the greater part regulars, were provided, and a General officer appointed for the command. Colonel Jeffrey Amherst, then serving in Germany, was selected and promoted to the rank of Major-General.[5] Amherst's brigadiers were Whitmore, Lawrence, and Wolfe. Boscawen was given command of the fleet, which was a force of twenty-three ships of the line, from which Boscawen had to provide convoys for the transports.[6] Hardy, Boscawen's second in command, had preceded him to take up the blockade of Louisbourg with eight ships of the line and two frigates. He arrived at Halifax on March 19, and left there on April 5 ; but the first time the French

---

[1] Dec. 30, 1757. Pitt to Governors of the Northern Colonies (Kimball, vol. i. p. 136 from C.O. 5/212).
[2] Kimball, vol. i. p. 143 from C.O. 5/212.   [3] Kimball, vol. i. p. 143 from C.O. 5/212.
[4] Orders were given to rendezvous at Halifax, not later than April 12.
[5] 600 Rangers were to be sent, but the number of Regulars was not to fall below that planned, Dec. 30, 1757.
[6] His Instructions are in Ad. O. and I., vol. 80.

note his appearance so close to the town that his force could be counted was on April 28, although early in the month his ships had been sighted off Scatari. The safe arrival of French ships, hereafter stated, shows that his blockade, like most, was not effective. He sent into Halifax, however, as captures the *Diane*, 22, a frigate "full of Provisions, Cloathing and Arms," and four other provision ships.

Boscawen's voyage was extremely slow. He was clear of the Channel on February 24, but did not arrive in Halifax until May 12.[1]

The forces had not all arrived, and Amherst was still at sea. Boscawen and Whitmore had received instructions for preliminary steps to be taken in the event of such delay as had occurred. They were to land on Cape Breton, either at Gabarus Bay or at Mira.[2] But before this could be attempted, preparations were complete. The fleet and forces straggled into Halifax a month behind Pitt's appointed time.

The account of an eye-witness,[3] who regretted not to have been appointed to serve on the expedition, gives a livelier account of these days in Halifax than a transcript of diverse official documents.

"On Board the 'Ludlow Castle' at Sea,
May 30th, 1758.

"My Dear Lord— . . . In my letter to your Lordship from Boston dated in March I informed you of what was at that time transacting on this Continent and of my motives for proceeding to Halifax, and I cannot say that I repent of the Voyage I made ; I must own I was a good deal mortified that my situation obliged me to quit a service I was so deeply interested in, and in which some intimate friends of mine have so great a share ; both my gratitude to General Abercromby in appointing me his Aid de Camp, and obedience to your Lordship's intentions, that I should serve with him, soon determined what part to take.

"*April 23rd.*—I imbarked with General Lawrence, his Battalion and Frazers at Boston.

"*28th.*—We arrived at Halifax where we found that from the 15th to that day the *Prince Frederick* and *Juno*, Transports with Amherst's Regiments on board, and some Ordinance Store Ships, had arrived from England. The *Prince Frederick* had lost her masts in a gale of Wind, and had replaced them from the *Le Arc en Ceil* [*sic*] of 50 Guns—which lay at Halifax. One transport had sprung a leak at Sea, was lost, but the Troops saved. We found the Royal 40th, 45th and 47th Regiments that wintered at Halifax, employed in making Fascines and Gabiens, etc., and 90 Carpenters that had been sent from New England employed under the direction of Colonel Basteed, in making six Block Houses of Squared Timber, upon the upper part of which a Platform is made for small Cannon, with a Parapet

---

[1] Wolfe gives, in a letter to Lord George Sackville, an account of the voyage (Ninth Report, Hist. MSS. Com. p. 74).

[2] C.O. 5/213. In the preparation of these instructions to his commanders, Pitt had before him a communication from Brigadier Waldo, second in command to Pepperrell in the siege of 1745. Waldo recommended the attack, actually carried out by Amherst. The document is to be found in R.O. Secret and Miscellaneous Papers, 1756-61, and has been reprinted in *Can. Archives Reports*, 1886.

[3] James Cunningham on Abercromby's staff, letter to Lord Sackville.

Musquet proof, and underneath Musquetry may likewise be used through loop holes. The Timbers are marked, and the edifice may be constructed in a few hours. They will answer the end Ridouts for the protection of the Camp. They were likewise employed in making a sort of Sling Cart, with wheels Eight Feet high, of a great breadth to transport Cannon over Marshy Ground, this at Mr. Boscawen's request. The Troops remained on board the Transports and were extremely healthy.

"At this time General Hopson was Ignorant of his destination, and Continued to command. It was determined to send to Boston for fifty Horses and fourty Yoke of Oxen to adjust [sic] in drawing Artillery Horses, etc., at the Siege.

"*March* 19th.—Sir Charles Hardy arrived in the *Captain* from England, and found the Squadron that had Wintered at Halifax in great forwardness.

"*April* 5th.—Sir Charles sailed to cruize off Louisburg with the following ships. *Northumberland* 74 *Summerset* 70 *Terrible* 74/ *Orford* 70/ *Deffence* 60/ *Captain* 64/ *Kingston* 60/ *Southerland* 50/ and one Frigate. Sir Charles sent into Halifax Four Provision Ships taken off Louisburg.

"30th.—He sent in a French Frigate of 22 guns, called the *Diana*. She sailed from Rochfort in Company with the *Prudent* of 70 Guns and another Frigate that are supposed to have got into Louisburg.

"*May* 2nd.—She was full of Provisions, Cloathing and Arms.

"The *Juno* Frigate sailed to join Sir Charles Squadron, and the same day the *Trent* Frigate that had been separated ten days from Mr. Boscawen's Fleet off the Island of Barmudas, arrived.

"8th.—A Fleet was seen to the Eastward of the Harbour.

"9th.—Admiral Boscawen arrived with the following Ships. *Namur* 90/ *Princess Emelia* 80/ *Royal William* 84/ *Burford* 70/ *Pembroke* 60/ *Lancaster* 68/ *Prince of Orange* 60/ *Bedford* 64/ *Nottingham* 60/ *Shannon* Frigate, *Etna* and *Tylo* Fire Ships.

"The same day arrived the 35th/ 48th/ and Monckton's Battn. of R. As/ under Convoy of a 20 Gun Ship from Philadelphia.

"The whole Fleet immediately on their arrival begun to take in Water and clean—the ships all healthy, except the *Pembroke* and *Devonshire*.

"12th.—Arrived Captain Rouse in the *Sutherland* of 50 Guns from the Squadron off Louisburg. Sir Charles says in a letter of the 8th of May, that after a Storm of Snow which Continued thirty-six hours, upon its clearing up, he perceived several Ships within him, near to the Harbour, to which he gave chase, but they escaped him. Soon after he stood into the Harbour, and perceived Seven Ships at Anchore, three of which he imagined were of war. In Chaberouse Bay they perceived the enemy throwing up an Intrenchment.

"13th.—Sailed the *Beaver* to Piscatua for Masts. Sir Charles's Squadron seems to have Cruized off Louisburg as Early as the Season would permit. The cold was extremely severe, and the Ice floating very troublesome. They saw a French ship catched in it, which they could not reach, & some of his Squadron at times stuck fast.[1]

"14th.—Sailed the *Squirrell* and on the 14th the *Scarborough* to join the Fleet.

"16th.—Arrived Commodore Durrell from New York, with the *Devonshire* of 66 Guns, the *Ludlow Castle* of 40, and three Frigates, with Brigadier General Whitmore the 17th/ and 22nd/ Regiments, all the Artillery and Stores intended for the Siege of Louisburg last

---

[1] The *Magnifique*; see p. 244.

year, except some Howitzers kept by General Abercromby Three Companys of Artillery, Thirty-two empty Transports and Victuallers. Those empty Transports were provided at home for the Troops to be imbarked at New York, but General Abercromby that no time might be lost had imbarked his Troops from different places ordering them to proceed to the place of Randesvouse in Separate divisions. And when your Lordship considers, that the orders for this Imbarkation did not reach General Abercromby before the 11th March, Great dispatch must have been used, to mark [sic] the Troops from these Cantonments about Albany and elsewhere, to have them imbarked, and the last of them at the place of randes-vouse by the 16th of May. All the Transports from the Continent are Victualled for four months. They will find full employment for the empty Transports to carry Fascines, etc.

" 17th.—Arrived the *Centurion* of 60 Guns from Plymouth, and informed us that General Amherst was to Imbark in the *Dublin* which was to replace the *Invincible*, want of canvass prevented the *Centurion* from proceeding with Admiral Boscawen from Plymouth. The same day arrived the *York* Man-of-War of 64 Guns, and Anstruther's Regiment which are sickly. The *York* in her passage ran foul of the *America*, lost her head, and carried away the Masts of the *America*.

" 20th.—*Royal William* and *Prince Frederick* sailed to join Sir Charles Hardy's Squadron. The same day the Massachusetts Province Ship, 20 Guns, brought in three Prizes, two of which were bound to Louisburg with provisions.

" 21st.—Brigadier Lawrence received a letter from Admiral Boscawen, acquainting him that he should be ready to sail on the 23rd May, no objection occurring it was determined, but calm thick weather and Contrary winds prevented them.

" A Body of Rangers were formed consisting of 1100 from Detachments of the several Corps and 500 were sent from New England, all under the Command of Captain Scott of the 70th Regiment, who has been accustomed to that service. Their Clothes are cut short, & they have exchanged their heavy Arms, for the light fusils of the Additional Companies of Frasers that are left at Halifax. This body of Troops will be of excellent service in protecting There Camp from the Insults of the Indians. The Company of Carpenters consisting of 90 men will be extremely useful as they have been accustomed to the drawing of Masts.

" During the recess there stay at Halifax afforded them, the Generals did not fail to accustom the Troops to what they were soon to encounter. Some Military operations were dayly carried on. They frequently landed in the boats of the Transports and practised in the Woods, the different Manuvres they were likely to act on the Island of Cape Breton. In all these operations you may imagine that Gen. Wolfe was remarkably active. The Scene afforded Scope for his Military Genius. We found it possible to land 3500 Men in the Boats belonging to Transports, and when the Boats from the Men of War assisted, 5000 Men could be landed.

" To facilitate the landing at Chaberus Bay the following Scheme was that they seemed inclined to put in execution, and which the following scetch of the Coast will explain. It was proposed to detach Brigadier-Genl. Wolfe with the 15th/ 48th/ Fraser's Battn. of Highlanders & 1100 Rangers, to perfect a landing at Miray Bay, 15 miles from Chaberus Bay, and to force his march thro' the Woods along the road, against whatever might oppose him, making short marches in case of opposition, & securing his Camp every night in the best manner.

"Colonel Monckton to be detached, to perfect a landing with two Battalions at Grand Lorem Beek, and to secure his small force with an Intrenchment.

"The rest of the force under cover of the Cannon of the Ships, to land at Chaberus Bay, but I suppose they will delay making that attempt, should any formidable force oppose them, untill the other two Bodys of Troops can co-operate, in making a diversion in their favour.

"Your Lordship doubtless knows that General Whitmore was directed from Home to Command in Nova Scotia, & to detach General Lawrence, in case General Amherst did not arrive in time, to proceed in the operations of the Siege.

"28th.—The wind coming fair in the night, the Admiral made the Signal to unmore at daylight, at seven she weighed, and the whole Fleet were under Sail at Eight O'clock, little Wind, including the whole they amounted to 180 Sail. The *Pembroke* having 200 Men sick, the *Devonshire* sickly. The *L'Arc en Ceil* whose Masts were taken to refit the *Prince Frederick* were left at Halifax with orders to join the Fleet when in a proper condition, from hence you will find that Mr. Boscawen sailed from Halifax with Twenty-one Sail of the line, & fourteen Frigates. I mean when he joins Sir Charles, his Fleet will amount to that number. He was fortunate in meeting with a fair Wind, & clear Weather for three Days together, which must have afforded them an opportunity of surveying the Coast, & making their disposition.

"The inclosed return will show you the effective strength of the Troops on the expedition, & those left at Nova Scotia, & I dare say that you must approve of General Abercromby's doing everything in his power, to forward the service, in many things at the expence of that he is himself to Conduct.

"It is impossible for me to express to your Lordship, the harmony, Spirit, and confidence, that reigns universally thro' the Army and Navy. I parted with my friends General Lawrence, Gen. Wolfe and the Admiral on board the *Namur* when they were under Sail, and I cannot say but that I earnestly wished that I had been destined for that service. I imbarked on board the *Ludlow Castle* of 40 Guns with General Hopson, we cleared the Harbour before the Fleet. We met the *Dublin*, and saw her join the Fleet. I suppose that General Amherst was on board. I esteem myself unfortunate in not meeting him before my departure, as he possibly might have dispatches for General Abercromby.

"As the Enemy will certainly exert the whole Regular Canadian and Indian Force of Canada against General Abercromby so soon as they are at a certainty of our design against Louisburg, I cannot persuade myself that he will be able to act offensively against the enemy unless a diversion is immediately made up the River St. Lawrence, which may oblige the Enemy to divide their force. I had several opportunities of urging this point to Admiral Boscawen, and he desired me to inform General Abercromby that he proposed sending some Men of War and Troops up the River St. Lawrence to make a diversion the moment that he was persuaded that he could spare them. We all have the utmost confidence in Admiral Boscawen's zeal and activity in the service and when we heard that he was to command the Fleet we assured ourselves that the Campaign would be vigorous & Active. The unanimity that presides at Home seems to defuse itself abroad, whereas of late we have been a divided and distrustful people. A successful Campaign will I hope give Peace to America. Without it I fear the Country will be exhausted and provisions for the supply of a large Army must grow scarce from so many hands being employed in the Field.

. . . .

"Capt. Boyer who lately got a £10,000 Ticket has promised me to deliver this letter to your Lordship, he is a particular friend of mine.—I am, my dear Lord, Your faithful servant,   JAS. CUNINGHAME."[1]

Wolfe, who landed at Halifax from the *Princess Amelia* on May 8, was eager and dissatisfied. He thought the troops were too few, as deaths, wounds, sickness, and a necessary garrison would take up three thousand men, and suggested reinforcements. He spoke well of the Highland regiments, both officers and men, then beginning their glorious service in the British Army. "The Highlanders are very useful serviceable soldiers, and commanded by the most manly corps of officers I ever saw.[2] The Rangers he described as "little better than *la canaille*."[3]

He had a poor opinion of the Americans as soldiers.

"The Americans are in general the dirtiest, most contemptible cowardly dogs that you can conceive. There is no depending upon 'em in action. They fall down dead in their own dirt and desert by battalions, officers and all. Such rascals as those are rather an incumbrance than any real strength to an army."[4]

But these strictures were but little more severe than those he wrote about the regulars, who, like the Rangers, as the event proved, so willingly and successfully followed his leadership. Of their spirit he had no doubt, but otherwise they fell far below his standard. "Too much money and too much rum necessarily affect the discipline of an army." "I believe no nation ever paid so many bad soldiers at so high a rate."

The siege supplies were inadequate in important respects ; the muskets were in poor condition.

"We ought to have had a dozen of the largest sort (Howitzers) for this business. I am told too, that his Excellency had a great mind to keep the tools, in which case there was an end of the siege of Louisbourg altogether, and I believe it will now be found that we have not one pick axe too many.

"Our Cloaths, our arms and accoutrements, nay even our shoes and stockings, are all improper for this country. . . . The army is undone and ruin'd by the constant use of salt meat and rum . . . so your lordship may rest assured that the enterprize of Louisbourg will cost a multitude of men."[5]

Although Wolfe was dissatisfied with the forces gathered at Halifax, Pitt had nevertheless placed at the disposal of the commanders a powerful armament.

---

[1] I owe the full text of this letter and the map, not reproduced, to the kindness of Colonel Stopford Sackville of Drayton House. A few lines of it are quoted in Ninth Report Hist. MSS. Com. p. 75.

[2] Ninth Report Hist. MSS. Com. p. 74.   [3] *Ibid.*   [4] *Ibid.* p. 77.

[5] The above quotations are all from Wolfe's letters to Lord Sackville (Ninth Report Hist. MSS. Com. pp. 74 to 77).

On the naval side it was made up of 23 men-of-war and 16 smaller vessels, mounting 1842 guns, and carrying crews of 14,005 men.

The land forces consisted of 13,142 men and officers.   Lord Ligonier had responded to the call of Pitt, in a lavish supply of munitions of war.

Detailed statements of the forces and supplies are printed later, in which will also be found the quantities used, which show that Wolfe's fears were groundless ; as well as for purposes of comparison, the resources in men and ships of the French.

On Monday, May 29, the advance was begun.[1]   At dawn the signal to unmoor was given from the *Namur*.   At nine the fleet was under way, and saluted with seventeen guns by the little citadel, was passing out of the harbour. The breeze was so light at 10.30 that the ships' boats towed them out, and by the afternoon they were still off Cape Sambro.   Even at the last it was augmented. The vessels carrying Bragg's, and some detachments from the Bay of Fundy and the new settlement of Lunenburg, joined the fleet and continued with it. The *Dublin* came in from sea, transferred Amherst to the *Namur*, and went on into the harbour, as her crew was sickly.[2]

With varying but not unfavourable weather, the fleet tacked along the coast of Nova Scotia and Cape Breton.   When the weather cleared, on Friday, June 2, Boscawen saw Louisbourg, and with light airs came slowly to his chosen anchorage in Gabarus Bay, which he reached about four that afternoon.   He was followed that evening and the next day by the rest of the fleet.   As they passed in, Amherst and his men saw rise above the circumvallation the slender spires of the principal buildings, and beyond them the slenderer masts of the ships in the harbour.

The position taken by Boscawen was dangerous.   His principal ships were anchored about the middle of Gabarus Bay, six miles from the entrance of Louisbourg harbour, and little over two from the shallow water at the head of the bay.[3]   As happens yearly at this season, there was much fog, and the prevailing winds were easterly, so that ships leaving the harbour could have run down on the anchored enemy crowded in a bay with a lee shore close aboard. On Sunday, Boscawen's account of conditions is as follows :

" At 4 A.M. it was little wind with a thick haze, the *Kennington* and *Halifax* still continue firing.   At 5 the breeze began to freshen and it came on foggy. . . . At 8 the gale increased, got down topgallant yards and the Sheat Anchor over the side, and at noon

[1] The time in naval records of the period was from noon to noon. Thus Boscawen says " at 4.30 A.M., Sunday, May 28," where Gordon says " Monday, May 29."   May 28 is, in the former case, from Sunday at noon to noon on the Monday, 29th.   The dates in the text follow the reckoning of landsmen.

[2] The *Grammont* was dispatched to reconnoitre Gabarus Bay, and discover the best landing-place ; the *Kennington* and a transport arrived from sea.   The number of transports reported by Boscawen is 127.

[3] Their position is indicated on the map, p. 243, from data furnished by the chief Hydrographer of the Navy.

struck yards and topmasts." Although the weather fell lighter in the afternoon, it was not until 5 the next morning that they "got up topmasts and Yards."

The *Kennington* and other frigates, with the sloop *Halifax*, ranged on shore close to the French batteries with which they were engaged, had to be towed by the ship's boats into deeper water. The *Trent* took the ground, but was got off with a damaged rudder. "It looked," says Gordon, "as if many vessels would go ashore and many suffered the loss of anchor and cables."

It would appear that the disposition of the British fleet was the least favourable for defence. Its first line, the frigates, were dragging ashore under the fire of the batteries, while the battleships, to leeward of the transports, were dismantled, and incapable of speedily protecting these ships on which were the troops and warlike stores. The conditions were most favourable for attack. Fog at times hung over all to obscure movements of the French, who had a wind favouring them, strong enough to produce disorder among the British, but, as it was not so heavy as to prevent the working of the fleet's boats, it was favourable to the manœuvring of the French ships. The easterly winds were against any assistance coming from Hardy and his ships. Everything was prepared for a disaster, which would have stood out in naval annals with Quiberon and La Hogue, had the French grasped the overwhelming value, at critical moments, of an aggressive defence.[1]

The French defence, instead of being greater than that of 1757, in face of the greater forces arrayed against Louisbourg, was weaker. The supply of money in the treasury of France was low, and was engaged for the land war in Germany. The British captures of her men-of-war and her merchantmen had diminished the number of seamen. The appalling mortality of the autumn and winter, through plague brought back to Brest by Du Bois de la Motte's fleet, had further reduced the forces available for manning the ships.[2] Insubordination and desertion, the results of ill-treatment, lowered the quality of those who embarked. So few were the men, that La Clue was nearly a year recruiting for the six ships under his command.[3] So bad was their quality that Le Chevalier de Mirabeau refused command of a squadron, giving his reasons to the Minister in these outspoken words :

"My life, Sir, and not my honour, belongs to the King. They have broken pledges to the sailors in an unheard of manner. Not paying these wretches is a cruelty, palliated here (Toulon) by necessity without doubt, but marked by incidents which make one shudder when they happen before one's eyes. . . . Du Quesnel's men failed him before the enemy; I cannot, nor do I wish to expose myself to the same hazard."[4]

[1] This condition is further dealt with in Chap. XV.

[2] See Chap. XV.   [3] La Cour-Gayet, p. 179.   [4] La Cour-Gayet, p. 282.

With such crews La Clue left Toulon, November 8, to repeat, if possible, the voyage to St. Domingo and Louisbourg which De Beauffremont had so successfully made in the spring.   Admiral Osborne held for England the Straits of Gibraltar, and forced La Clue to take refuge in Carthagena, where he was joined in January by some ships under De Motheux, which brought his strength up to thirteen vessels.   Preparations to strengthen Louisbourg, notwithstanding this delay, were continued by the French.   Du Quesnel, lately Governor-General of Canada, by drawing on men recently returned from a cruise, was able to sail from Toulon in command of the *Foudroyant*, 80, one of the finest ships of the French Navy, and peculiarly endeared to that service as she had been La Galissonière's flagship at Minorca.   She was accompanied by the *Orphée*, 64, and two smaller vessels.   In sight of La Clue, Du Quesnel engaged the English ships off Carthagena on the 28th of February.   The *Orphée* fell at once, and after a combat carried on by the *Monmouth*, 70, with unabated pertinacity, after the death of her captain, Du Quesnel struck to the smaller ship.[1]   La Clue had to return to Toulon, for the superior forces of the British, with Gibraltar as its base, blocked the passage to the Atlantic.

The strengthening of Louisbourg from the Mediterranean being thus rendered impossible, efforts were made elsewhere, and the intendants of the naval dépôts on the Atlantic were ordered to hasten the dispatch of ships for Isle Royale.   The *Magnifique* left Brest early in March, and arrived in the drift ice off Louisbourg on the 31st of that month.   She hung there with appalling sufferings of her crew.   One hundred and twenty of her men died, twelve from cold in one night.   On another, the ship was unworkable from a " silver thaw." Villeon, her commander, abandoned the voyage, and with only thirty men, including officers, fit for duty, arrived back on May 5, at Corunna.[2]   Another vessel never got away from the French coast : the *Raisonable*, 64, commanded by the Prince de Montbazon, was overpowered and captured just after leaving Brest for Louisbourg.[3]   The *Prudent*, 64, commanded by the Marquis des Gouttes,[4] arrived at Louisbourg on March 24, and on the 28th Beaussier brought into port his squadron consisting of :

L'Entreprenant, 74 (Beaussier).	*Le Capricieux*, 64 (De Tourville).
Le Bienfaisant, 64 (Courserac).	*Le Célèbre*, 64 (De Marolle).
La Comète, 74 (Lorgeril).	

The two first named were fully armed ; the other three were *en flute*, that is, serving as freighters and transports.   They brought provisions, and a battalion of Volontaires Etrangers under D'Anthonay.[5]   The supplies brought by these

---

[1] Corbett gives a brief and picturesque account of this action and its significance to the two services, vol. i. 259.
[2] Marine, B⁴, 80.   [3] La Cour-Gayet, p. 311.   [4] See Appendix.   [5] See Appendix.

vessels and others[1] placed Drucour in a position to carry on his defence without further anxiety about munitions or supplies.[2]

The Court was anxious to supplement Drucour by officers of experience in warfare. Blenac de Courbon[3] was transferred from his position as Commandant at Brest to Louisbourg with the grade of Commander of its sea and land forces.[4] He set sail on the *Formidable* on May 11, found Louisbourg blocked, and returned to Brest on June 27.[5] His appointment was made on April 10, so that there was no haste displayed in his setting out, while his report to the Minister, that he was " exceedingly happy to bring back to a good port the ship which had been entrusted to me," [6] would indicate a lack of energy which made his absence no great loss to the defence. On March 30, De la Houlière was appointed to command the land forces, and arrived in Louisbourg by the *Bizarre* on the 30th of May. The troops were assembled and his position proclaimed on June 1.[7] On the same day there came to the town an officer of the *Dragon*, and the adjutant of Cambis, with the welcome news that Duchaffault had arrived at Port Dauphin. His force consisted of six vessels; only two of them and a frigate had then arrived, but these had on board a battalion of Cambis as a reinforcement for the garrison. An officer was sent with instructions for Duchaffault to land this regiment, and to come with his ships to Louisbourg as soon as possible.

The sight of Boscawen's fleet was no surprise to Drucour and his officers. Indians had come with the news that they had seen the fleet off Fourchu. His vigilance was fully awake. He had, as early as the 28th of April, manned the entrenchments along the shores which Du Bois de la Motte had planned and erected in 1757 against Loudon's threatened attack. In consultation with Franquet, he had visited the shore and agreed on the sites at Pointe Blanche and Pointe Plate for cannon (May 1 and 3), and forthwith proceeded to prepare for their emplacement (May 5), while on the eastern side of the harbour he established posts of 100 men, afterwards increased to 250, drawn in part from the fleet, at L'Anse à Gautier, the most practicable landing near the lighthouse, as well as at the Lorembecs.

The garrisons of Port Toulouse and Port Dauphin were brought in on the 7th, and Drucour for the first time this spring had authentic news, but

---

[1] The *Apollo*, April 15 ; *Le Chèvre*, April 24 ; *La Fidèle*, frigate, May 10 ; three merchant vessels on May 19–27 ; the frigates *Bizarre* and *Aréthuse* on May 30, the former *en flute*.

[2] He says that Louisbourg was fully provisioned for a year for the first time since 1735 (Drucour's Journal).

[3] See Appendix.   [4] I.R. B, 107.

[5] Marine, B⁴, vol. 80.   [6] Waddington, *Guerre de Sept Ans*, vol. ii. p. 336.

[7] Fo. further details of De la Houlière's interesting career see Appendix. De la Houlière had seen much service, had taken part in nine sieges, and had been since 1735 King's Lieutenant at Salces, near Perpignan.

not later than early April, that the ships which had wintered in Halifax were refitting.[1]

Various bands of Indians and Acadians came in, and the younger Villejouin brought ninety Acadians from L'Isle St. Jean, who were sent to a camp at Gabarus Bay. In expectation of harassing the besiegers by these irregulars and Indians, two dépôts of provisions were made on the Miré. A battery was even erected at Port Dauphin and abattis and other siege material prepared. The troops in the entrenchments were relieved weekly, but, before the month had ended, the chapel of the spacious hospital had to be turned into a ward, to accommodate the men who had fallen ill from exposure to the fog and rain. A council of the captains of the ships of the navy was held on the 15th of May, to concert measures for the defence of the port. It was decided to prepare fire-ships, and an armed chaloupe, and to range the men-of-war in positions most favourable for the defence of the port. The larger ships lay in their new positions in a crescent between the Royal Battery and the Bastion de la Grave.

Those of the men-of-war which had arrived *en flûte*, had mounted their guns, but were otherwise inactive. An English frigate more than once came along past the town and penetrated, with her boats out, taking soundings, into the very bottom of Gabarus Bay ; she lay at anchor another night, only two cannon-shot off Pointe Blanche; and although in the former case no supporting ships were within four or five leagues, no attempt was made to attack her. Drucour notes with admiration the daring of her commander.

A few words will describe the site of the impending conflict. The shores of Gabarus Bay slope upwards from beaches and rocky points to a considerable height, which is reached at about a mile distant from the water. This tract, except where the morass or moorland extends to the shore, or the rocky ledges rise in bare shoulders, is covered with forest or scrub growth. The farthest point to the westward, which the French guarded by seventy troops under the younger Villejouin, was the Montagne au Diable, from which a footpath led to the Miré road, giving by it access to the town. About 4000 yards nearer was L'Anse à la Coromandière, which French and English strategists alike had picked out as a vulnerable point. It was, therefore, the object of attack, but also the place where were made the most elaborate preparations for defence. The distance between its headlands is about 660 yards, but on neither of these points did it seem possible to land. Midway on the arc of its shore is a rocky point, and on either side of it a beautiful sandy beach, from which the cliff rises abruptly about 15 or 20 feet from high water. Along this higher land the trenches were strengthened by an abattis of trees felled with their tops outward, thickly strewn along the beach below. So thickly were they planted that they

---

[1] Eleven Indians brought back 7 prisoners and 16 scalps in a schooner they had captured.

appeared as a natural grove.   A little brook runs into the sea close to the eastern point of the cove.   This point is a shoulder of land high enough to hide from the shores of the cove all the coast and sea to the eastward.   This disadvantage of the position had been foreseen in the defences made in 1757. A *nid de pie* or watch-tower had been erected on or near this ridge, from which could be seen the whole range of the shore towards the town, say about four miles ; and during the time in 1757 that a descent by the English was possible had been occupied by a detachment.[1]   It was now left unoccupied.   Pointe Platte and Pointe Blanche were strongly entrenched and guarded.   The stretches of coast between these defences was most difficult to land on, and, by the more sanguine of the defenders, thought inaccessible.   Tourville, perhaps the most accurate of the observers of events in Louisbourg, however, took a less hopeful view.   He walked forth one day, the 7th, to inspect the defences at these nearer posts, and was satisfied with them, and knew Coromandière was good ; but, while the coast was rock strewn, the intervals between the defences were great, and he believed there was danger of an unexpected landing.[2]

The gale of Sunday subsided, and Monday was a day of calm and thick fog, so that both sides were ignorant of what the other was doing.   The French heard the sounds of hammering without knowing its cause, the carpenters of the fleet working at the *Trent's* rudder.   While the fog continued Wolfe reconnoitred the shore to see if a landing was practicable.   Boscawen, possibly not to have to depend on the decision of a marine question by an impetuous soldier, sent Commodore Durell on the same mission, but there was no difference of opinion between the sea and land officers.   They agreed that a landing could not be made.

As was known to Amherst, the French were strengthening their defences. An 8-inch mortar was mounted on the 5th on a small hillock between Pointe Platte and the Coromandière, and fired that day until the fog came down.[3]   The same day the encouraging news came in that eleven companies of Cambis had arrived at Miré, and that De Chaffault had worked out of Port Dauphin with the remaining six on his ships, and lay under Cibou Islands, at the mouth of that harbour, in the most advantageous position, to sail with the first fair wind for Louisbourg.[4]

Details of men from their ships in the harbour were engaged in hauling a 24-lb. cannon to its position at the battery of the Coromandière, an arduous task, delayed by the nature of the ground and the breaking of its carriage.

Although the Bay of Gabarus was occupied by the enemy, in whose sight

---

[1] Johnstone says he served there.   [2] " Je croy qu'il a lieu de craindre à cet égard " (Journal of the *Capricieux*). [3] Lartigue, in a note on his map, says a battery should have been placed at this point, but Drucour's account is confirmed by the Anon. Jl.   [4] Ten arrived in Louisbourg the next day, the other on the 7th.

they performed the feat, two boats' crews of Basque fishermen, volunteers for the service, carried two heavy cannon to Pointe Blanche ; where they were at once mounted.[1]

The disposition of the regular troops in the field was finally :

	Cannon.	Swivels.	Mortars.	Men.
At Coromandière under St. Julhien, Col. of Artois	{1 of 24 / 4 ,, 6}	6	...	1000
Pte. Platte. Marin, Col. of Bourgogne	{4 ,, 6}	6	1	930
Pte. Blanche. D'Anthonay, Col. of V.E.	{1 ,, 24 / 6 ,, 6}	...	...	350
Cape Noir	2 ,, 24	...	...	75
				2355

On the eastern side of the port :

The Lighthouse	{3 ,, 18}			
Anses à Gautier	{4 ,, 6}	...	...	350
Grand Lorembec	{3 ,, 18}			
And detachments of 50 soldiers each at La Montagne du Diable and Petit Lorembec, at the west and east of the fortified entrenchments	}	...	...	100
				2805

In addition there were the militia, Acadians, and Indians, making the total force over 3000.[2]

While these preparations for defence were being carried on the plans of the besiegers were modified by fresh discoveries of local conditions. The landing-force was to be divided in three parts : Whitmore's, the white division, was to form the right wing ; Lawrence's, the blue, the left ; and Wolfe was to lead a body of Highlanders, Light Infantry, and Irregulars. Amherst's general orders of the 3rd indicate that his purpose was to attack at three places, at White and Flat Points, and Wolfe's force[3] further to the west. A heavy surf prevented an attempt being made that day ; and it was, moreover, discovered that the water off White Point would not allow the frigates to approach that point near enough to have their fire cover effectively the landing troops of the right division. A modification of the first plan was made in the orders of the 4th.

Amherst determined to have the white division, Whitmore's, distract the enemy's attention at White Point, and then to follow Lawrence's division, the

---

[1] Drucour's Jl. 7th.

[2] There is no great discrepancy between this list and the number of guns taken as given by Gordon, p. 116.

[3] It was, after a landing, to join that of Lawrence.

blue, which was to land on the shore opposite their station, Flat Point, or to follow the Grenadiers. The reconnaissances along the shore had obviously failed to give Amherst and his staff any adequate idea of the French strength, for these orders state that :

"The General, not to lose a moment of time, has thought proper to order that an attack be made upon the little Intrenchments within the Fresh Water Cove with four companies of Grenadiers. That no Body, regulars or irregulars, may dare stand before them. These detachments are to be commanded by Brigadier General Wolfe. . . . The Army is to land and attack the French in three different Bodies and at three different places, all the Grenadiers and detachments of the right Wing land upon the right in the bay within White Point, the Light Infantry, Irregulars, and Highlanders are to land in the Fresh Water Cove in order to take the Enemy in the flank and rear, and cut some of them off from the Town. The Highlanders, Light Infantry, and Irregulars, are to Rendezvous to the right of the Island lying before the Fresh Water Cove to be ready to run in the cove when the Signal is given."

It seems probable that Amherst's Fresh-Water Cove was at the outlet of the stream which falls into the sea near Flat Point. Here is an islet only about a furlong from the shore to the right of which might advantageously be placed the supports of the four companies which were to effect the landing. From this point they could best "take the enemy in flank and rear," and cut some of them off from the town. If Fresh-Water Cove was the same place as Coromandière, the supports of the four companies were to rendezvous at an islet six or seven times as far from the shore as the one at Flat Point, and the position, if the landing were effected, the least favourable for cutting the enemy off from the town. The operation would have been a pursuit, as in the event it was, not an intersection of a line of retreat. Moreover, if Fresh-Water Cove was the same as Coromandière, as it was in the usage of the navy,[1] it would be absurd to assemble the force for an; attack on it, at the most distant part of the line, "the right of the right attack." But if there be doubt as to Amherst's intentions on different days, it is clear that attempts to effect a landing were being made.

On the 6th, a day which opened with south-west wind and fog, Boscawen signalled to prepare to land, in an interval when the weather showed signs of clearing. The boats were sent to the ships, and by eight the troops were in them, under the immediate supervision of Lawrence and Wolfe. Boscawen and Amherst went later to order the disembarkation, but it fell calm, the fog came down with heavy rains, and, following a rising breeze, "a large swell tumbled in from the sea." The men, after rowing in shore and finding it

---

[1] Boscawen's Jl. speaks of Cormorant, and Captain Jacobs of Fresh-Water Cove, referring to the same place (Captains' logs, 499).

impossible to land, were recalled and ordered back to the ships, Amherst "first acquainting them with the reason for so doing." With the knowledge fresh in his mind of the irritation in subordinate officers, and. the rank and file, over the faint-hearted attack on Rochefort, the previous year, Amherst doubtless did not wish to damp the ardour of his force by an appearance of a lack of enterprise.

Wednesday, the 7th, the weather was clear, but the surf was still high, though operations at sea could be carried on, and Wolfe spent the early morning in sounding at the head of the bay. Bragg's regiment, which were still in the small vessels in which they had come from the Bay of Fundy, were detached, under convoy of the frigate *Juno*, to make a feint on the lighthouse point and L'Anse à Gautier. This had little effect, for the French recognized it as being not serious. Hoping that the next day would bring better weather, Boscawen gave orders to the captains to have their boats at the transports at midnight, and that profound silence should be observed. Amherst again, on the 7th, issued general orders. The boats of the right were to assemble at the transport *Violet*, to which they were to be guided by three lights hung on the seaward side at the water's edge. The left wing, under Lawrence, assembled at the *St. George*, which hung out two lights ; and Wolfe with the Grenadier Companies, the Highlanders, Light Infantry, under Major Scott, picked marksmen from all the regiments, and colonial irregulars, was to be in readiness at the *Neptune*, distinguished by a single lantern. After midnight no other lights were to be shown on the transports, and the men were cautioned to prevent the accidental discharge of a musket, as the General's intention was to surprise the French as well as attack them. He asked for the care and vigilance of the officers of the transports, and expressed his confidence in the good disposition of the troops, and added that should the Admiral and General decide to alarm the enemy earlier, the troops were to take no notice.

Although the fire from the French positions, well maintained between the 4th and 7th, indicated that they were stronger than Amherst had thought, it did not alter his later dispositions,[1] and the attack was arranged for in this order :

The right wing directed against Pointe Blanche :

Brigadier Whitmore

Colonel Burton	and	Colonel Foster
Regiments 1st Royals		48 Webb's
47 Laselles'		58 Anstruther's
2nd Batt. Americans		17 Forbes'

Bragg's, which should have formed part of this brigade, was detached to make a feint to the eastward to distract the enemy.

[1] The fog lifting on the 7th disclosed to some degree these positions to the British (Gordon Jl. 7).

The left wing directed against Pointe Platte :

Brigadier-General Lawrence

Colonel Wilmot		Colonel Handfield
22nd Whitmore's	and	35 Otway's
3rd Batt. Americans		40 Hopson's
45 Warburton's		15 Amherst's.

The 63 Fraser's were detached from this brigade to form part of

The Left Attack

Brigadier Wolfe
Colonels Murray and Fletcher
The Grenadier Companies of the 15th, 22nd, 17th, and 1st Regiments
The Irregulars and Light Infantry
The 63 Fraser's Regiment and the Grenadier Companies of the 40th, 47th, 45th, 35th, 58th, and the 2nd and 3rd battalions of the 60th and 48th Regiments in the order named.

The right wing took up its position behind its supporting frigates, the *Sutherland* and *Squirrel*; the left were, until the decisive moment, to be drawn up behind the *Gramont*, *Diana*, and *Shannon*; while the left attack was supported by the *Kennington* frigate and the *Halifax* snow, which were close in shore at the Coromandière, to which the frigate has since given her name.[1]

Nothing but success was counted on. The troops were to take in their pockets bread and cheese for two days, and leave their blankets to follow after a landing had been secured.

Thursday, June 8, Durell rowed along the shore unmolested by the French, and came back to report that there was not so heavy a surf as to prevent landing, at least in Coromandière. The French batteries began firing at the nearer ships, and their troops were mustered in the entrenchments. The frigates fired briskly on them for about a quarter of an hour. It being then light, the watchers from the ramparts of the town, drawn there by the heavy firing giving poignancy to their anxiety, saw three to four hundred boats row in divisions from between the sheltering ships. The attack they thought was being delivered on the eastern points. In a little time, before these boats had reached the shore, they were seen to turn towards the Coromandière. As Wolfe's force, the weakest of the three in numbers, but made up of picked men, rowed into the cove, "the enemy," says Amherst, "acted very wisely, did not throw away a shot until the boats were close in shore," and then poured in on them so deadly a fire, as the soldiers in the trenches were provided with spare loaded muskets, that

---

[1] The *Kennington*, Captain Jacobs, had taken up her position on the 3rd (Captains' Logs, No. 499). As they were being damaged by the fire from the shore, she and the other frigate were ordered by Boscawen to warp further off on the 4th (Boscawen's Journal). On the morning of the 8th, she took her position within a musket-shot of the shore (Captains' Logs, No. 499).

landing was impossible. It looked as if Wolfe's first experience in command was to be a disastrous failure, for, notwithstanding his eagerness and the courage of his men, his advance was decisively checked. He gave the signal to retreat, and his boats turned to the open. In Amherst's orders, the officers in charge were cautioned to "avoid huddling together and running into a lump." Three boats on the right of Wolfe's force drifted or rowed towards the east and there found themselves sheltered by the ridge from the fire of St. Julhien's men. Just at its foot is still a little space of sand among the rocks of the shore. They effected a landing on it. Wolfe saw the movement, or was advised of it by one of them, and turned again to the point. The repulse had not chilled the ardour of his men. A sergeant in one of the boats, as they rowed into the first attack, stood up in his boat and cried out, " Who would not go to Hell, to hear such music for half an hour ? " [1] A shorter time was given him, for he was shot dead as he stood ; but there were many among the soldiery as reckless of consequences. Some of the boats, when they reached the rocky shore, were dashed to pieces or stove in by collision. The men, Wolfe among them, leaped into the water. Those who kept their feet waded ashore, those who fell were drowned or crushed by the heaving boats. Some of them had taken regular formation on the higher ground before the other brigades reached the shore. St. Julhien, his outlook obscured by the smoke of his own fire and that of the frigates, was busy serving his guns at an enemy which he thought was still in the boats in front of his position. The distance was too great for Marin at Flat Point to know what was taking place. Some skirmishing between irregulars and Wolfe's men occurred.[2] When St. Julhien was advised of the landing, he hesitated, lost time, and, instead of a brilliant attacked delivered by him, on a handful of men with wet muskets, what took place was an attack of his flank and rear by an enemy pouring over the ridge. His troops, which had been in the trenches in bad weather, some for a week, others for a fortnight, were in no condition to stand such an onslaught.[3] They broke and fled towards the town, pursued by Wolfe and the light troops. So rapid was the advance that it was only by travelling with seven-league boots, " à pas de géant," that Marin's men were not cut off in their retreat from Flat Point. The French rallied for a little above the Barachois, but were there in danger of being surrounded by the two forces in which the British advanced. The pursuit was only ended by a cannonade from the walls, which marked for Amherst the point at which he could safely put his advanced camps. The artillery and stores at Coromandière and Flat Point fell into the English hands. D'Anthonay held his ground at White Point until he received orders to retire,

---

[1] Hamilton MSS.   [2] "Our troops killed and scalped an Indian Sachem the day we landed" (Wolfe to Sackville).
[3] " Ye Rangers Started them first, they Ran and Hollow'd and fired on behind them and they left their Brest work " (Knap, p. 8).

and then came in, after destroying his material.[1] It was after four when the attack began, it was six when Boscawen landed, and at about eight the French troops were under the protection of the guns of the town. So short a time had this decisive event taken, but little more than twice as long as leisurely and unmolested pedestrians would take to land and go over the same broken ground.[2]

The young officers who turned the tide were Lieutenants Hopkins and Brown and Ensign Grant of the 35th Regiment.[3] Their exploit may well have been one of the foundations for the tradition as to the luck of the British Army. Wolfe's attack was a direct frontal one on an impregnable position. Had St. Julhien allowed his enemy to land and become entangled in the abattis, the appalling disaster which befell at Ticonderoga[4] the equally gallant troops of Abercomby would have been anticipated at the Coromandière. Had a corporal's guard been on the ridge, the first boats might have been beaten off. Had Wolfe been no quicker to act than at least one of his fellow-brigadiers,[5] or had St. Julhien been as quick as Wolfe, success would have continued with the French. Neither Wolfe nor Amherst mention the incident ; we know of it through private accounts both French and English.

The three young officers leading Highlanders, says Hamilton, the light infantry, says Gordon, struck a new note in the Seven Years' War. Vacillation and an excess of caution had marked its conduct, but later its most brilliant exploits were in the form which they first gave, accomplishing the impracticable. Perchance to them had filtered down the opinion of Wolfe, " The greatness of an object should come into consideration as opposed to the impediments that lie in the way." Its spirit surely informed their action. Wolfe, himself, but followed their example at Quebec ; and like them, Lambart " by attempting a place where

---

[1] He did not spike his guns.

[2] After much hesitation I have adopted this version of the sequence of these events. It follows Amherst's account in so far as the main attack, being intended against the Coromandière. There are, however, difficulties in accepting this view. If the attacks of the main brigades were not to be serious, why did Whitmore come under fire ? (Anon. Journal). If it was the well-ordered operation which appears in Amherst's account, it is difficult to explain Wolfe's view of the event, except by attributing to him a talent for exaggeration quite phenomenal. That opinion was, " Our landing was next to miraculous. . . . I wouldn't recommend the Bay of Gabarouse for a descent, especially as we managed it " (Wolfe to Sackville, Hist. MSS. Com. Ninth Report, p. 76).

The losses at the landing were :—

British Regulars :—Killed 3 officers, Captain Baillie and Lieut. Cuthbert of Fraser's. Lieut. Nicholson of Amherst's, 4 sergeants, 1 corporal, and 38 men. Of these only 8 were shot, the others were drowned. Wounded : 5 lieuts., 2 sergeants, 1 corporal, and 51 men.

Rangers :—1 ensign and 3 men killed, 1 wounded and 1 missing. They took 4 French officers and about 70 men prisoners, 17 guns, 2 mortars, and 14 swivels, with supplies and stores of all kinds.

The French loss is stated by Drucour as 114, including deserters from the Volontaires Etrangers. Three officers were wounded.

[3] For the meagre details I have been able to find about these officers, see end of Chapter.

[4] July 8, 1758. See Parkman, *Montcalm and Wolfe*, chap. xx., and his App. G.

[5] " Whitmore is a poor, old, sleepy man " (Wolfe to Sackville, Ninth Report Hist. MSS. Com. p. 76).

the mounting of the rocks was just possible" won a foothold at Belle Isle.[1] True it may be that had there been above the rocks of Coromandière a post in the "magpies' nest," had a more vigilant officer than Vergor held the outpost at L'Anse à Foulon, had the force under the gallant De Ste. Croix been larger, failure and not success had befallen the British arms on these decisive occasions, but greatly daring, and promptly succoured, they all won, through unexpected ways, the crucial foothold.

APPENDICES

A. MEMO. *re* LIEUTENANTS HOPKINS AND BROWN, AND ENSIGN GRANT

It is impossible to say with any certainty who these three were. An examination of the records of the time reveal one Lieut. Hopkins, 3 Lieuts. Grant, and no less than 6 Lieuts. Brown, all serving in America at the time of the siege of Louisbourg, and probably all serving at the siege itself.

Hopkins.—Among the "Commissions granted by the Earl of Loudoun during his command in America."[2]

Thomas Hopkins is appointed a Lieutenant in the 48th (Webb's) *vice* Gordon, pd., on the 6th June 1757. A Return of killed and wounded, sent in Amherst's dispatch of 27 July 1758, includes the name of "Lt. Hopkins, of Webb's," among the wounded.[3] Presumably he resigned in America, as among the Commissions granted by Amherst in America we read, "Jno. Clarke, Lt., 48th *vice* Hopkins, resd., 8 Mar. 1759." The Army List for 1759 (War Office copy) also has Hopkin's name crossed out and a MS. addition—"Res. —John Clarke, 8 Mar. '59." This appears to be the only Lieut. Hopkins who served at the siege of Louisbourg.[4]

Grant.—*John Grant* was appointed Lieutenant to the 58th (Anstruther's) 28 January 1758.[3] He appears to have been the only lieutenant of the name at Louisbourg at the actual time of the surrender, but among the "Commissions granted by Amherst at the camp at Louisbourg" appear commissions to[5]

Allan Grant, as Lieutenant of the Royal Americans, 2d Batt., *vice* Hart, killed, 28 July 1758; and

Alexander Grant, as Lieutenant of the Royal Americans, 3d. Batt., *vice* Longsdon, dead, 23 August 1758.

Brown.—The Army Lists of 1758 and 1759 give the following :—

22d (Whitmore's)	Lt. *Henry Brown*	25 Oct. 1756.
28th (Bragg's)	Lt. *Frans. Brown*	9 April 1756.
35th (Otway's)	Lt. *Thomas Brown*	16 Feb. 1756.
60th (Amherst's)	Lt. *John Brown*	9 Feb. 1756.

---

[1] In 1760 (see Corbett, vol. ii. pp. 160-167, for an account of this event, in which we read the names of places familiar to us in the pages of Dumas).

[2] (W.O. 25/25 Commission Books 1757-60), C.O. 5/53.

[3] W.O. 25/25.

[4] Army List, 1759.

[5] W.O. 25/25.

In addition to these, the E. of Loudon in America granted a commission to Lieut. *William Brown* of the 60th *vice* Ridge, pd. 13 Dec. 1756;[1] and Amherst at the camp at Louisbourg granted a Lieutenant's commission to *William Browne* of the 35th (Otway's) *vice* Thomas Comeford, killed 31 July 1758. A "Lt. Brown of Otway's" is included among the wounded in Amherst's Return of killed and wounded at Louisbourg. This was probably the above-named Lt. Thomas Brown, as William Browne was only an ensign until July 31, four days later than the date of the return.

LIEUTENANTS BROWN[2]

Henry Brown, 25 Oct. 1756, Lieut. (Disappears in 1761.)[3]

Francis Brown, 9 April 1756, Lieut. (In the Army List for 1763 there is *written* against his name, "Francis Brown 28 Mar. '63." After this his name disappears, so that is probably the date of his death, or may be retirement).[4]

Thomas Brown, 16 Feb. 1756, Lieut. (Disappears in 1761.)[5]

John Brown, 9 Feb. 1756, Lieut., 15 Sept. 1760, Capt. (Disappears in 1764, but reappears in 1765 as):—14 Jan. 1764, Capt.; Army Rank, 15 Sept. 1760; 22 Sept. 1775, Major; 14 June 1777, Retired.[6]

William Brown, 13 Dec. 1756, Ensign; 31 Oct. 1759, Lieut. (Disappears 1769.) [Too late.]

ENSIGNS GRANT[7]

Allan Grant,[8] 1 Feb. 1756, Ensign; 28 July 1758, Lieut; 7 Oct. 1763, Regt. Rank. (Continued in Army Lists until 1772, when his name is crossed out and a Ml. note written against it. "David Alexandre Grant, 11 May '72." He does not appear later.)

Alexander Grant,[9] 2 Feb. 1756, Ensign; 23 Aug. 1758, Lieut. (Crossed out in the Army List of 1760 and marked "dd.")

Commissions were granted at the camp at Louisburgh to:—

Allan Grant, Rl. Americans, 2d Battn., as Lieut. *vice* Hart, killed, 2d July 1758.

Alexander Grant, Rl. Americans, 2d Battn., as Lieut. *vice* Longsdon, dead, 23 Aug. 1758.

By referring to Amherst's account in Gordon's Journal it will be seen that the boats on the eastward of Wolfe's attack contained officers and men of the 1st, of the Irregulars, Fraser's, the 35th and 48th regiments, and next to the last named, the 60th. The head of the flotilla having actually got into the cove, the boats most likely to get beyond the sheltering front were those to the rear. I therefore hazard the opinion that these officers were Thomas Brown of the 35th (Otway's), Thomas Hopkins of the 48th (Webb's), and one or other of the Grants in the 60th, for it does not seem probable that a boat of the 58th, in which John Grant was Lieutenant, would have got from the extreme left of the detachment to its extreme right.

---

[1] W.O. 25/25. [2] Army Lists. [3] 22nd Regiment, Whitmore's.
[4] 28th Bragg's. [5] 35th Otway's. [6] 60th Amherst's.
[7] Army Lists and Commission Books. [8] 60th Regiment. [9] 60th Regiment.

B. Various Accounts of the Landing

Boscawen's Journal

Thursday, 8th June 1758.

At Midnight sent all the boats with proper Officers in them to assist in landing the troops. The Generals went with them, attended by their Aide de Camps. The Commodore with Captains Buckle, Lindsay, Balfour and Goostree went likewise to assist in the Disembarkation. By the Dawn of the Day all the Troops were in the Boats and ranged in their proper Divisions. The Enemy upon observing of this motion, began to throw Shells amongst the Frigates and Transports. The *Kennington* and *Halifax* ran close into Cormorant Cove, and at 4 I saw the Boats rowing towards the Shore with the Troops and at the Sun's rising the *Kennington* and *Halifax* began to fire upon the Enemy to cover the Landing, which was followed by the *Sutherland*, and rest of the Frigates placed in Shore. About 5 o'clock the Enemy began a very smart Fire at the Boats with both Cannon, Swivels and Small Arms, which continued about 15 minutes, when it ceas'd, part of the Troops having Landed and driven the Enemy out of their Entrenchments.

Gordon's Journal

When the Fire from the Ships was thought Sufficient the Signal was made for the Grenadiers to row into the Cove which they accordingly did. The Enemy began a very hot fire of Musketry and Swivels, from their Entrenchments, and the same with Grape from their Batteries in Flank. After standing this some time still making for the shore, a small body of Light Infantry Commanded by Lieutenants Hopkins and Brown and Ensign Grant of the 35th Regiment seeing a convenient place on the right of the Cove that is free from the Enemy's Fire, the Surge being equally or more violent than in the Cove, made for it and getting ashore, were soon followed by the Whole; came upon the Flank and back of the Enemy drove them, and Brigadier Wolfe, with a small body, pursued them within Cannonade of the Town.

The right and Left Wings landed afterwards and were followed by the second Embarkation. The Line was formed and marched nearer the Town, laid out the Encampment for the Army, every Corps taking up their own ground.

Amherst's Journal

On the 8th The Troops were in the Boats before the break of Day, in three Divisions according to the Plan annexed, and Comodore Durell having viewed the boats by order of the Admiral and given me his opinion that the Troops might land, without danger from the Surf, in the bay on our left the *Kennington* and *Halifax* now began the fire upon the left followed by the *Grammont*, *Diana*, and *Shannon* Frigates in the Centre and the *Sutherland* and *Squirrell* upon the right, when the fire had continued about a quarter of an Hour, the Boats upon the left rowed into the Shore under the Command of General Wolfe, whose Detachment was composed of the four Eldest Companys of Grenadiers, followed by the light Infantry (a Corps of 550 men chosen as Marksmen from the different Regiments, serve as Irregulars and are commanded by Major Scott, who was Major of Brigade) and

Companys of Rangers, supported by the Highland Regiment, and those by the Eight remaining Companys of Grenadier.

The Division on the right under the Command of Br. Genl. Whitmore consisted of the Royal, Lascelles, Monckton, Forbes, Anstruther and Webb, and rowed to our right by the White Point as if intending to force a landing there.

The Centre Division under the command of Br. Genl. Lawrence was formed of Amherst's, Hopson's, Otway's, Whitmore's Lawrence's and Warburton's, and made at the same time a Shew of landing at the fresh water Cove : this drew the Enemy's attention to every part and prevented their Troops posted along the Coast from Joining those on their right.

The Enemy acted very wisely, did not throw away a Shot till the Boats were near in shore, and then directed the whole fire of their Cannon and Musketry upon them : the Surf was so great that a place could hardly be found, to get a boat on shore ; notwithstanding the fire of the Enemy and the Violence of the Surf, Brigadier Wolfe pursued his point, and landed just at their left of the Cove, took post, attacked the enemy, and forced them to retreat. Many Boats overset, several broke to Pieces, and all the Men jumped into the water to get on shore.

As soon as the left Division was landed the first Detachment of the Centre rowed at a proper time to the left and followed, then the remainder of the Centre division as fast as the boats could fetch them from the Ships, and the right Division followed the Centre in like manner.

It took a great deal of time to land the Troops, the enemy's retreat, or rather flight, was through the roughest and worst ground I ever saw, and the pursuit ended with a canonading from all the town which was so far of use, that it pointed out how near I could encamp to invest it, on which the Regiments marched to their ground, and lay on their Arms. The Wind increased, and we could not get anything on shore.

<hr />

Anon. Journal (Brit. Mus. Add. MSS. 11,813, f. 82-88).

The morning very Clear, Little wind and Surge. The Troops Rendezvoused according to order at ½ past 3 o'clock in the morning. Our Bomb Ketch then Began to Exchange shells with the Enemy at 4 o'clock our Frigates and Sloops Cannonaded furiously. ½ past 4 the Left wing rowed close in with the shore, in Fresh Water Cove, the Enemy kept so brisk a fire from their Entrenchments and from three Batterys with Grape shot that our troops were order'd to retreat and Land to ye Right of ye Cove, which they perfected with Great Difficulty, One Boat in which were Twenty Grenadiers and an officer was stove, and Every one Drowned. The African Rangers[1] under the Command of Major Scott, were the first that Landed. Fifty of these repulsed above a hundred French, who were coming to oppose the landing of our men, the Difficulty of Landing at this place was such that they thought the Devil himself would not have attempted it.

<hr />

An Authentic Account, June 8.

About 4 this morning under cover of the Ship's Guns, the Boats with a *Division* of the Troops, after a general Rendezvous near *White Point*, made an Attempt of landing

<hr />

[1] An obvious mistake for "American."

to the Left at *Kennington Cove* with 600 Light Infantry. The whole Battalion of *Highlanders*, and 4 Companies of Grenadiers, under the Command of *Brigadier General Wolfe*; while a Feint of landing was made to the Right towards *White Point* conducted by Brigadier General Whitmore; and the Brigades in the centre were commanded by Brigadier General *Laurence*, who made a Shew at *Fresh-Water Cove*, the move to distract the Enemy's Attention, and to divide their Force.

The *Left* Wing finding the Shore at *Kennington Cove* impregnable, withdrew with some loss from the warm fire of two *Batteries* discharging Grape and round Shot upon them in Flank; while several *Swivels*, and small Arms almost without number showered on them from the Lines, that were about 15 feet above the Level of the Boats.

As the Enemy had for some *Years* been preparing against such a probable attempt; they had now been some Days in Expectation of our Visit: They had accordingly posted 3000 Regulars, Irregulars, and a few of the native *Indians*, in all the probable places of the landing, behind a very strong *Breast-work* fortified at proper Distances with several pieces of *Cannon*, besides *Swivels* of an extraordinary Calibre, mounted on very strong perpendicular Stocks of Wood, driven deep into the Ground: They had also prepared for flanking, by erecting *Redans* mounted with Cannon in the most advantageous Situations— Nothing of the Kind has perhaps been seen more complete than these *Fortifications*.

Besides, all the approaches to the *Front lines* were rendered so extremely difficult by the *Trees* they had laid very thick together upon the Shore round all the *Cove*, with their Branches lying towards the sea, for the Distances of 20 in some, and of 30 Yards in other places, between the Lines and the Water's Edge; that, had our people not been exposed to such a *Fire* from the Enemy, the bare attempt of possessing these Lines, would have been like that of travelling towards them through a *wild Forest*, from the interwoven Branches of one Tree to those of another with incredible Fatigue and endless Labour.

Nor, was this Stratagem possible to be suspected at any great Distance, as the Place had the Appearance of one continued *Green* of little scattered Branches of Fir. And, but very few of the Guns on their Lines were to be distinguished out of the Reach of their Metal, the rest were artfully concealed from our View with *Spruce-Branches* until the Boats advanced towards the Shore, with the Resolution of *forcing* the Works—The latent Destruction was then *unmasked*, by the removal of the *Spruce-Branches* and the adventurous Spectators were soon convinced, those works were not *capable* of being forced by numbers much superior to theirs. The Enemy *depended* much on their Strength here, which perhaps occasioned them to be somewhat *premature* in their exertion of it. For, before our Boats came near the water's edge, they began with great alertness to play their Batteries, and to fire *red hot* Balls, besides a continual Discharge of their small Arms among them. The consequence had been much more fatal to our People, few if any of whom would have escaped, had the enemy timed their fire with more Judgment, by permitting the Boats to have actually landed their men on that narrow Shoal beach, taking no other notice of them until they had been all in their Power, than they had done before of the Fire from our *Frigates*, and of some *Boats* that had been with Commodore *Durell* to reconnoitre the Shore, before any of the Troops had put off from the Transports.

Exasperated, not discouraged, at this Repulse from the Enemy's irristible Fire, the

---

[1] *Authentic Account, etc.,* June 8.

troops of that *Wing*, drew off with all convenient expedition towards the *Centre*, determined to rush on Shore wherever they saw any Probability of Success, whatever Loss they might sustain. Soon after this the Lieutenants *Browne* and Hopkins, with Ensign *Grant* and about 100 of the Light Infantry happily gained the Shore over almost impracticable Rocks and Steeps to the Right of the *Cove*. Upon which Brigadier *Wolfe* directed the Remainder of this Command to push on Shore as soon as possible, and as well as they could—which heightened their eager Impatience so much, that the *Light Infantry, Highlanders* and *Grenadiers* intermixed, rushed forward with impetuous Emulation, without Regard to any previous Orders, and piqued themselves mightily which Boat could be most dexterous and active in getting first on Shore. In this manner, though all the while exposed to the Fire of a Battery of *three Guns*, that sometimes raked, sometimes flanked their Boats very furiously, and of small arms within 20 yards of them, they were all expeditiously landed with little loss, besides about 22 Grenadiers, who were unfortunately drowned by having their Boats stove in the Bold Attempt.

Among the foremost of these parties was Brigadier *Wolfe*, who jumped out of his Boat into the Surf to get to the Shore, and was readily followed by numbers of the Troops amidst a most obstinate Fire of the Enemy. Soon after landed Brigadier *Lawrence*, and was followed by the rest of the Brigades with all possible expedition. After him in a little time Brigadier *Whitmore*, and the Division of the Right Wing, gained the Shore, amidst a continual Charge of Shot and Shells, from the Enemy's Lines, several of the latter reaching also as far as the Brigades in the Centre. And last of all landed the Commander in Chief. Major-General Amherst in the Rear, full of the highest Satisfaction from seeing the Resolution, Bravery and Success of the Troops on surmounting *Difficulties* and despising Dangers.

The Lieutenant of Warburton's ("Valbetone"), who died at Louisbourg after the siege, who was in the division which attacked the Sandy Cove (Coromandière), "said to me that their landing on the left of the Cove was made by chance, that they had not believed this place possible for landing, that three boats had sought there refuge from our fire (s'y étaient jettées pour éviter notre feu), and that they had signalled the others to come on" (avaient fait signal aux autres d'advancer).—(Poilly's Journal.)

Princess Amelia.—Captain's Log. No. 736. Captn. John Bray.

June 8, 1758.—Sent boats "to assist landing Coll. : Fraizer Grenadiers first & then what other Troops that remained not Landed a Cutter with a Mate to Land the Rangers at sun rising the *Sutherland* & all the Frigates began a Cannonading the Enemy's Batteries & Breast Works the Boats with the Troops at the same time begun to Approach the shore the Enemy suffer'd them to Come within pistol shot of the shore before they began to fire and then begun to fire with Great Guns & small arms excessively hot which continued 14 minutes, but some Boats getting into some Rocks a little to the Eastward of the Bay Landed about 40 Rangers which Clamber'd up them & got into a small wood which Flank'd the Enemy's Breastworks, which when perceived by them on receiving their Fire quitted their Battery & Breastworks & took to the woods with the utmost Precipitation in the Battery & Breastwork were upwards of 1100 men, the Landing then became

General they now and then firing single musquets out of the woods at the Boats." They 5 killed & 10 wounded.

FRENCH ACCOUNTS

Three barges of this division to avoid our fire, rushed (ce sont jetté) behind a head Cap called Cap Rouge, which encloses the left of this Cove (Coromandière). On this head they had built a "nid de pie," where unhappily there was no detachment for what reason I know not. These barges found here a nook or two where they landed their men, and the third went to seek the others.—(Anon. Journal.)

This division (Wolfe's) thus shattered (Rompie) sought to retire beyond our fire. Their right sheltered themselves by the rocks which ended our entrenchments unmolested (Comme ils Voulurent). Seeing that they were not observed they tried to land among the rocks, and did it so diligently that they had already put a considerable number of men on shore before they were seen.—(Poilly.)

The W.S.W. winds drove the smoke of the cannon on shore, and in this they were favorable to the enemy, nevertheless of the first boats which entered the Coromandière there were a score destroyed by our artillery. One noticed that the others curved toward the second division with the exception of five or six which through fear or through a knowledge of the ground went into the cove Nid de Pie twelve or fourteen yards across in sand surrounded by steep rocks situated between the Coromandière after Sandy Cove and Flat Point, a place where there had been last year a detachment of twenty-five or thirty men, and this year none. Thus the first barges landed troops without opposition and the first success drew on the others.—(Drucour.)

Capricieux.—At four o'clock in the morning, a little before the enemies made a general attack in Gabarus, all (of them) who appeared before the entrenchments were driven back, but the second line of the forces which had attacked the Coromandière seeing the first repulsed drew off to the left, and having found a ravine got on shore there, some boats of the first line followed them.

Jeuly 8 à 4 heures du matin un peu avant les enemies ont fait une ataque générale dans Gabarus, tout ce qui s'est présenté devant les retranchements a été repoussé, mais la seconde ligne de troupes de débarquement qui avoient ataqué la Coromandière voyant la première repoussée a filé sur la gauche, et ayant trouvé un ravin y a mis pied à terre, quelques barges de la l^tre ort suivis.—(Tourville of the *Capricieux*.)

They advanced their barges towards two large bays. . . . The English maintained their attack a long time without being further advanced than the loss of a great number of men, and without being able to force the retrenchments. A struggling barge that in appearance had been repulsed from the bays discovered a small creek, where two boats could enter at the same time. This creek was on the left of the regiment of Artois, and through negligence was left without a guard, although it was so surely comprehended in the general plan of defense the year before that in the summer of 1757 I was posted there with a detachment. . . . This barge gave a signal to the others to follow, and at last they all slipped away from the two bays (Coromandière and Flat Point) without being remarked by the French in their retrenchments until several thousand of English soldiers had been landed and drawn up in battle array, having cut off the regiment of Artois from the rest of our troops.—Johnstone (Que. Lit. and Hist. Soc.).

LIST OF ENGLISH FLEET, 1758

Rate.	Ships.	No. of Guns.	No. of Men.	Commanders.	Lieutenants.	Sailed from England.	Disposition.
2nd	Namur . .	90	780	Hon. Adl. Boscawen Matw. Buckle	Phil. Afflick	15 . 2 . 1758 from Portsmouth ; 23d from Plymouth	In No. America under the commd. of the Honble. Adl. Boscawen.
2	Royal William .	84	765	Sir Chas. Hardy Thos. Evans	Wm. Dumaresq	Do.	
3	Prs. Amelia .	80	665	Commre. Durell John Bray	Wm. Hall	Do.	
3	Dublin . .	74	600	G. B. Rodney	Jams. Worth	16 . 3 . 1758	
3	Terrible . .	74	600	Rd. Collins	Wm. Chads	16 . 4 . 1757	In No. America under the command of Vice - Adl. Holbourne.
3	Northumberland	70	520	Rt. Hble. Ld. Colville	Edwd. Thornborough	16 . 4 . 1757	
3	Orford . .	70	520	Rd. Spry	Ridgwl. Sheward	16 . 4 . 1757	
3	Somerset . .	70	520	Edwd. Hughes	Robt. Mortimer	12 . 7 . 1757	Gone to No. America.
3	Vanguard .	70	520	Robt. Swanton	Humphy. Rawlins	8 . 4 . 1758	...
3	Burford . .	66	520	Jas. Gambier	Thos. Pemble	23 . 2 . 1758	Gone to No. America under the commd. of Honble. Adl. Boscawen.
3	Lancaster .	66	520	Hble. G. Edgcumbe	Thos. Barker	23 . 2 . 1758	
3	Devonshire .	66	520	Wm. Gordon	Salkd. Jno. Proctor	29 . 6 . 1757	
3	Captain . .	64	480	John Amherst	Saml. Spendlove	20 . 1 . 1758	
3	Bedford . .	64	480	Thorpe Fowke	Lews. Davies	23 . 2 . 1758	
3	Gr. Frederick .	64	480	Robt. Man	Jno. Gordon	29 . 1 . 1758	
4	Defiance . .	60	400	Patk. Baird	Heny. Phillips	2 . 5 . 1757	
4	Pembroke .	60	420	Jno. Simcoe	Geo. Allan	23 . 2 . 1757	
4	York . .	60	480	Hugh Pigot	Thos. Fitzherbert	30 . 1 . 1758	
4	Kingston . .	60	400	Wm. Parry	Wm. Cock	16 . 4 . 1757	In No. America under the command of Honble. Adl. Boscawen.
4	Pr. of Orange .	60	400	Jno. Fergusson	Jno. Jarden	23 . 3 . 1758	
4	Nottingham .	60	400	Saml. Marshall	Wm. Bunyan	23 . 2 . 1758	
4	Sutherland .	50	350	Capt. Rous	Isah. Hay	6 . 4 . 1756 from Cork	
4	Centurion . .	50	350	Wm. Mantell	Jno. Barnsley	16 . 4 . 1757	
5	Juno . .	32	220	Jno. Vaughan	Chas. Wood	29 . 1 . 1758	
5	Diana . .	32	220	Alexr. Schomberg	Jos. Norwood	14 . 1 . 1758	...
6	Boreas . .	28	200	Hble. Rt. Boyle	Jno. Bernard	21 . 1 . 1758	...
6	Trent . .	28	200	Jno. Lindsay	Patk. Calder	23 . 2 . 1758	...
6	Shannon . .	28	200	Chas. Medows	Jno. Mann	23 . 2 . 1758	...
6	Portmabon .	24	160	Paul H. Ourry	Thos. Piercy	23 . 12 . 1754	...
6	Hind . .	24	160	Robt. Bond	Thos. Ellis	25 . 1 . 1758	...
6	Scarborough .	20	160	Robt. Routh	Robt. Carpenter	24 . 9 . 1757	...
6	Squirrel . .	20	160	Jno. Wheelock	Crean Percival	15 . 1 . 1758	...
6	Kennington .	20	160	Maxm. Jacobs	Lewis Gordon	23 . 2 . 1758	...
Frig.	Gramont . .	18	125	Jno. Stott	Petr. Baskerville	15 . 2 . 1758	...
Slo.	Hunter . .	10.14	110	Jno. Laforey	Jno. Sharpe	25 . 1 . 1758	...
Slo.	Hawke . .	10.14	110	Robt. Hathorne	Wm. Denne	16 . 4 . 1757	...
Fires Vessel	Lightning .	8.6	45	Wm. Goostrey	Hy. Ashington	23 . 2 . 1758	...
Fires Vessel	Altna . .	8.6	45	Geo. Balfour	Wm. Bloom	23 . 2 . 1758	...
Armed Vessel	Tagloe . .	...	40	Davd. Pryce	...	25 . 1 . 1758	...

Eighteen of these Captains had served as recently as 1757 in American waters.

LIST OF THE LAND FORCES IN 1758

Commanding Officers on the Expedition against the Fortress of Louisbourg

Major-General JEFFRY AMHERST, Commander-in-Chief of His Majesty's Forces.

Brigadier-General EDWARD WHITMORE. | Brigadier-General CHARLES LAWRENCE. | Brigadier-General JAMES WOLFE.

Train of Artillery commanded by Colonel GEORGE WILLIAMSON.

Chief Engineer—Colonel JOHN HENRY BASTIDE.

Rangers commanded by Lt.-Colonel SCOTT.

No.	Name.	Regiment. Modern Name.	Battalions.	Colonels.	Lt.-Colonels.	Majors.	Captains.	Lieutenants.	Ensigns.	Chaplains.	Adjutants.	Qr.-Masters.	Surgeons.	Surgeons' Mates.	Sergeants.	Drummers.	Rank and File (Actual).
1	Royals	Royal Scots (Lothian Regt.)	2nd		1	1	7	20	9	1	1	1	1	2	38	18	854
15	Amherst's	East Yorkshire Regt.		1	1	1	8	18	9	1	1	1	1	2	35	19	763
17	Forbes	Leicestershire Regt.			1	1	7	10	10		1	1	1	1	29	20	660
22	Whitmore's	Cheshire Regt.		1	1	1	8	17	9	1	1	1	1	2	37	20	910
28	Bragg's	1st Batt. Gloucester Regt.			1		7	9	8		1	1	1	1	30	20	627
35	Otway's	Royal Sussex Regt. (1st Batt.)			1		5	12	8		1	1	1	2	20	14	566
40	Hopson's	Prince of Wales' Volunteers (South Lancashire Regt.)			1	1	7	16	5		1	1	1	1	30	16	550
45	Warburton's	1st Batt. Sherwood Foresters (Derbyshire Regt.)			1		6	17	6		1	1	1	2	38	19	864
47	Lascelles	Loyal North Lancashire Regt. (Wolfe's Own)			1		5	15	6	1	1	1	1	2	38	18	857
48	Webb's	1st Batt. Northamptonshire Regt.			1	1	7	16	9	1	1	1	1	1	38	20	932
58	Anstruther's	2nd Batt. Northamptonshire Regt.	2nd		1		8	8	8		1	1	1	1	26	15	615
60	Monckton's	King's Royal Rifle Corps	3rd	1	1	1	6	20	7	1	1	1	1	2	39	20	925
60	Lawrence's	King's Royal Rifle Corps	2nd	1	1	1	6	16	7		1	1	1	2	35	17	814
78	Frazer's	The Seaforth Highlanders		1	1	1	10	22	10	1	1	1	1	2	43	22	1,084
...	Effective total	...		4	11	10	97	216	1c6	6	13	14	14	23	476	258	11,021

To these were added—Train of Artillery 267

                Rangers 499

Making a total of rank and file 11,787

And others 1,355

                                         13,142

The forces intended for the expedition were: 14,815. (C.O. 5/212.) There is a slight discrepancy between Gordon's and Cunningham's accounts of the numbers. The above follows Gordon (*Journal N.S. Hist. Soc.* vol. v.).

MUNITIONS OF WAR.

	Supplied.	Expended.
Canon	88	13
Mortars	52	1
Howitzers . . .	6	8
Shot	45,861	14,630
Shells and carcasses . .	41,962	3390
Grenades	4000	...
Powder bbls. . . .	4888	1493
Sand-bags . . .	115,000	39,500
Cartridges . . .	53,513	30,230
Musket	726,756	750,000
Fuzes	45,261	14,119

It may be noted that only in musket cartridges was the supply short. In other things only about one-third of the supply was used. The above statistics are from Gordon's *Journal.*

No such accurate figures are available for the French forces in Louisbourg. They seem to have been :

SHIPS.

	Guns.	Men.
Prudent	74	680
Entreprenant . . .	74	680
Capricieux	64	440
Célèbre !	64	440
Bienfaisant . . .	64	440
Apollo	50	350 [1]
Aréthuse	36	270
Fidèle	36	270
Chèvre	16	150
Biche	16	150
	494	3870

LAND FORCES (FRENCH).

Artois	520
Bourgogne	520
Cambis	680
Volontaires Etrangers	680
Compagnies Détachées	1000
Gunners	120
	3520

There was an overwhelming superiority on the side of the attack, demonstrating the value of fortifications, which in this case were neither well placed nor substantial.

[1] The complement of the four smaller ships have been estimated.

CHAPTER XIV

THERE was great caution displayed by the British leaders in carrying out their careful preparations. The site of the camp was the same as in 1745. It was now strongly entrenched. Blockhouses or other protective works were erected : three on the west side, another to the north, and a fifth on the Miré road, beyond which was placed the camp of the Rangers. These works were to protect the army from the attacks of the Indians and irregulars, and to prevent such disturbance as had befallen other British commanders in American warfare. Similar works, three in number, were placed on the other side of the camp, to guard against operations from the town, and to make secure a way to the site of the batteries for its bombardment.

Louisbourg was open to attack from both land and sea ; on the latter side, success involved the destruction of the Island Battery, and the men-of-war in the port. It may be recalled that Warren strongly expressed the opinion that it would be madness, even when there were no ships in the port, to attempt to force a passage past the Island Battery. It follows that, until this battery and the French ships were reduced to defensive inefficiency, the function of Boscawen's fleet was that of an adjunct to the land forces.[2]

When, however, a way into the port was made clear, or, by a desperate *coup de main*, it was forced, the town, scantily protected on this side, was doomed, without one shot having been fired against its walls. Equally, a destruction of its land defences would place the men-of-war in the harbour in a *cul-de-sac* between the guns of the conquered town, the batteries which had reduced it, and the hostile fleet waiting at the harbour mouth. It is obvious that carrying on, together, both attacks, would expedite the fall of the fortress, but the only means of attack on the ships, and the Island Battery, was by artillery on the Lighthouse Point. The reports of Hardy's frigates, and the result of a night expedition sent on June 2 to discover the enemy's strength to the eastward, gave Amherst reason to believe that the landing-places were then occupied, and that

---

[1] Attention is directed to the large map of the siege operations.
[2] For its great importance see *Logs of the Fleet*, Wood, Champlain Society.

to some degree, on a landing on that side, the attack on the Coromandière would have to be repeated.

Not only was there this operation to face, but when hostilities actually began, there were five men-of-war and one frigate in the port to supplement the land defences of the French. These ships of the line mounted twice as many guns as the shore batteries. Their crews, if fully manned,[1] equalled three-quarters of the troops and militia. Their mobility added greatly to their powers of offence. Boscawen's and Hardy's ships kept them, it is true, in the harbour, but it afforded safe anchorage for the largest of them within four or five hundred yards of the places on the shore where any effective batteries could be erected. The power of the ships to impede the siege operations was fully recognized by the British,[2] but that power of the fleet was minimized by the independence of its commodore. The regulations of his service made necessary the Governor's permission for him to leave port. He had to consult with Drucour, but in other respects he disposed of his ships at his discretion.

The weather continued bad,[3] and there was great delay in landing materials. It was the 16th before a moderate reserve of twelve days' provisions was landed, and no heavy artillery had yet been put on shore. On the 11th some 6-lb. guns were landed ; on the 18th the first 24-lb. gun ; as late as the 3rd of July we find in Boscawen's journal that they were still landing stores, so that it was a month before all the materials and guns were transferred from the ships and transports to various points on the shore.

These preliminary works of encampment and defence seemed so important to Amherst that he did not, until the 17th, personally look over the ground. He, then, accompanied by Bastide and McKellar, chief and second engineers, and Williamson, in command of the artillery, rode out toward the citadel.[4] The tone of Amherst's remarks indicates that he was not entirely in accord with Bastide, who, Amherst says, "was determined in his opinion of making approaches by the Green Hill, and confining the destruction of the ships in the harbour to the Lighthouse Point and the batteries on the side."[5]

In the meantime operations had been begun under the command of Wolfe. The first deserters, a sergeant and four men of the Volontaires Etrangers, came in on the 10th, and with false information as to the spirit of their regiment, told the truth in informing Amherst that the detachments to the eastward had been called in, and the Grand and the Lighthouse Batteries destroyed. This

---

1 There was, however, much sickness among their men, and in some cases at least they were below their full omplement.

2 "The opinion of most people here, sea and land, who had a terrible notion of their broadsides " (Wolfe Hist. MSS. om. ix. p. 76).   3 See logs of ships for weather conditions.

4 The ground was familiar from 1745 to Bastide, who since then had served at Port Mahon.

5 Amherst to Pitt, June 23, C.O. 5/53.

determined the place at which to begin. Four hundred Rangers, as an advanced guard, started at two in the morning of June 12. Wolfe, with his force, 1220 men drawn from all the regiments, and four grenadier companies,[1] in light marching order,[2] set out at five.

The weather favoured them. They marched round the harbour in a fog so thick that they could not see the men-of-war, although they were so near that they " heard very plain the noise they made on Board in the course of their duty." Unseen and unheard by the ships, they escaped cannonade, and by the late afternoon had visited Lorembec and made two encampments, one under Major Ross at the head of the North East Harbour, and another, the main camp, under Wolfe by the Lighthouse.[3] They found in the French camps the tents still standing, the cannon useless, and a considerable quantity of tools. They opened the entrenchments so that the artillery, which was being sent by sea to the camp, could be landed. While these things were being done, the Rangers returned to the main camp. It was found when the Island Battery opened fire on them the next morning (13th) that it reached Wolfe's camp which was, therefore, moved back to a place of more security, and the work of making roads to the sites selected for batteries was vigorously pushed on. Wolfe was now, for the first time, in command. His orders show the vigour of his actions, the care he took not only of the health but of the comfort of his men, his judiciousness not only in equalizing duties but in the rewards of rum and fresh fish he gave to those who had worked hard. Their tone inspired his men, and his reputation for fearlessness and activity soon spread from this detachment, not only throughout the army but even to the French.

The latter had been busy on their side with results which made a greater show than those of the English. The latest landed companies of Cambis arrived in the town on the 8th. Duchaffault was warned, by an express overland, not to attempt to gain Louisbourg. Hardy had taken his position, on the 10th, close to the harbour-mouth to prevent any vessels slipping out, but the *Bizarre* to Quebec, and the *Comète* carrying news to France, successfully eluded him. The *Echo*, which sailed on the 13th was, however, pursued and captured.

Drucour's forces and materials were complete. It was his duty with them to save the town, or at worst to delay its capture to the latest possible day. He had made the repulse of landing the vital element of his defence ; when it failed he felt the town was lost.

Those of Otway's, Hopson's, Lascelles', and Warburton's.   [2] " The officers must be content with soldiers' tents."
[3] A few shot were fired on them from the Island Battery.

" This unfortunate occurrence which we had hoped to overcome, casts dismay and sorrow over all our spirits, with every reason, for it decides the loss of the colony ; the fortifications are bad, the walls are in ruins and fall down of themselves, the outer defences consist only in a single covered way which, like the main works, is open and enfiladed throughout its length ; everything predicts a speedy surrender. What a loss to the State after the enormous expenses made by the King for Isle Royale since 1755 ! "

" Cet évènement malheureux qu'on espéroit surmonter jette de la consternation et de la tristesse dans tous les esprits, avec d'autant plus de fondement qu'il décide de la perte de la colonie, le corps de la place est mauvais, les murs sont en ruines qui tombent d'eux-mêmes, les fortifications extérieures ne consistent que dans un simple chemin couvert qui est donné et enfilé de partout ainsi que le corps de la place, tout annonce une rédition prochaine. Quelle perte pour l'Etat après les dépenses immenses que le Roy a faites pour l'Isle Royale depuis 1755 ! "

At five the next morning (9th) a council was held at the Governor's house. Its members were the officers of the place, of the Battalions, and of the principal ships. Des Gouttes, the Commodore, demanded permission to take his ships out of the port as they were of little use. He said that his action was founded on the repeated demands of his Captains, made to him in writing.[1] Des Houlières and Prévost were the only land officers who, at the council, sided with Des Gouttes and his Captains. The result of the council was that the ships were to remain and hold the harbour against Boscawen.[2] Most of the opinions were like Drucour's, that the place was doomed. D'Anthonay alone said that, notwithstanding its bad condition it might be saved.[3]

With such a spirit the defence began, but while hopeless, the efforts of the French did not lack vigour. Five companies of Rangers were formed from the townspeople. The demolition of buildings and of the limekiln near the Dauphin Gate was carried on, skirmishes took place, and three officers, the seniors of whom were the two Villejouins, were sent with a dozen soldiers and seventy Acadians to the Miré, to join sixty Acadians who had arrived there from Isle St. Jean. They had orders to remain in the woods and harass the enemy. A sally of three hundred men was made on the 13th, which, although repulsed, did some damage. After false alarms on the night of the 14th, based on a report that the enemy was marching in three columns on the town, Vauquelin anchored the frigate *Aréthuse* broadside to the Barachois to rake the enemy should it appear within range.[4] In this position she

---

[1] Tourville, of the *Capricieux*, says that Des Gouttes asked for their opinions at a preliminary meeting, in writing and at once, " par écrit et précipitamment."

[2] There can be no question of the soundness of this view. The Island Battery was made almost useless by the 25th of June. Had Des Gouttes and his ships gone out, Boscawen would have come in and destroyed the town at once. It was approved at headquarters. A.N. B, vol. 107.

[3] These letters are at the end of Drucour's Journal, A.N. Am., du N., vol. 10, Prise de Louisbourg.

[4] His position is marked by an anchor on Plan I.

commanded, through a depression in the land, a wide extent of the ground
over which any advance against the town had to be made.

Further efforts at defence were completed by work on the walls, the
establishment of shelters to prevent the raking of them, the necessity for
which had been pointed out by Drucour, and much of the powder was
removed from the citadel to the ice-house and limekilns outside the eastern
walls. These buildings were protected by hogsheads of tobacco "that was
in great plenty in Louisbourg, from the English prizes, brought there by the
French privateers (Johnstone)." [1]

Wolfe continued work at his roads and batteries, being supplied with
guns and materials, by sea, in boats and lighters. These were protected by
a frigate and sloop, which were attacked by an armed chaloupe, with two
24-lb. guns, which did not interrupt the work, although it caused some damage
to the nearest frigate (14th). The work was pushed on, but it was not until the
night of the 19th-20th that fire was opened. The reputation of the French
army made the besiegers act with caution. Sentinels were posted to overlook
the harbour. The troops were cautioned against surprise. Although Wolfe
stated in his orders that he thought an attack was scarcely possible, when he
was ready to open fire, a plan of defence against a boat attack had been
perfected. A strong detachment was moved out from the main camp, the
Rangers occupied the ground between it and Ross's post, at the head of the
North East Harbour, and a system of signals and bonfires was arranged,
not only to give warning, but to deceive the enemy as to the strength of the
position. The fire of Wolfe's batteries was brisk, and as briskly returned by
the Island Battery and ships. Ross's post was strengthened by guns on the
shore, Wolfe's at the Lighthouse was added to, and under fire from the ships
a new battery was begun at the head of the harbour (June 23). They were
too distant from each other to do damage, and two new batteries were later
erected, which, firing over the Grand Battery, reached the shipping. Wolfe's
works had now covered much more than half way round the harbour from
the Lighthouse. Its batteries kept up a fire on the island, which on the 25th
seemed much shattered. The besiegers surmised rightly, from its firing only
shells after four on that afternoon, that its guns pointed towards the active
enemy were disabled, so the British fire on it was reduced to an occasional
shell for the purpose of retarding the work of reconstruction.

The battery at Rochefort Point was used to supply its place, and the
men-of-war fired constantly, but with little effect. The engineers of the town
did their best to make repairs to these most important guns on the island.

[1] So large was this quantity that notwithstanding its free use as protection for the men-of-war and buildings, after the
capitulation Amherst sold a part of what was found in the town for £1500. Amherst to Pitt, Aug. 30.

A sally was made from the town on the 1st of July, and the troops advanced towards the Grand Battery. The engagement was kept up for two hours. Then the French gave ground rapidly, and retreated to the shelter of the outposts, while Wolfe's force, which pursued them closely, had to retire under a heavy fire from the ships and the town. This gave him the advantage of fighting over ground he had already, June 30, intended to occupy. "When the cannon and mortars are placed in battery, the Brigadier proposes to carry one Establishment nearer to the Town, and to take possession of two Eminences not far from the West Gate." [1]

At dusk, July 1, he took possession of the mound he had coveted, and the next day, under heavy fire, his men at this advanced post skirmished with the French from cover, and succeeded in making the redoubt practicable, and carrying on other works, so that on the 5th, a battery of five guns and two mortars opened from this new position.

Their fire was damaging to the town and the ships. It raked the walls, rising from the Dauphin Gate to the Citadel, and demolished the Cavalier at the Dauphin Bastion, which gratified one of Wolfe's many personal animosities.

"You know I hold Mr. Knowles in the utmost contempt as an officer, and an engineer and a citizen. He built a useless cavalier upon the Dauphin Bastion which fell to my share to demolish, and we did it effectively in a few hours." [2]

The new battery damaged the town and the shipping with a fire to which, on account of the elevation, the latter could not successfully reply. The position also enabled Wolfe to send out a detachment every night, to hold the French pickets on the town side of the bridge over the Barachois. As up to this time these were the only operations which had produced the slightest effect against the defence, it is not to be wondered at that Wolfe's celerity became famous. None knew where or when he was to be found, but certain they were that "wherever he goes he carries with him a mortar in one pocket and a 24-pounder in the other." [3]

For the first four weeks events had not gone badly with the French. The Island Battery, it is true, had been destroyed, but the men-of-war amply protected the harbour. Not a gun, until the last few days, had been fired against the main works, and for a longer period the French were in doubt as to the place, in their defences, where the serious attack would be delivered. The elaborate approaches of the enemy were impeded by the fire of the *Aréthuse*,

---

[1] Wolfe's Orders, June 30.

[2] Hist. MSS. Com. ix. p. 76. Knowles, as Governor of Louisbourg, built this work in 1746.

[3] An Authentic Account, June 30. The writer attributes this saying to the "Garrison," which I take to mean the French.

until shells and grenades, from a battery erected for the purpose, drove her on July 6 from her position. Even in the camp of the enemy the French condition was not regarded as hopeless. Deserters came into the town with more or less accurate information as to the strength, the movements, and the projects of the force they had left (June 25 and 30). The troops were doing well. Their pickets held the ground beyond the outer works, and engaged in constant skirmishes with the outposts of the enemy. Sorties were made, siege material was brought in or destroyed, and the English harassed in their operations. In this desultory warfare, the soldiery was helped by the town militia, under command of volunteer officers of the garrison, and Daccarette, a merchant of the place.[1]

But in other respects Drucour's position was less satisfactory. The elaborate preparations of Amherst to protect his camp indicated how effective would have been a force of irregulars, particularly in the early days before his redoubts and entrenchments were completed. The Indians and Acadians did nothing, however, but capture wandering sailors, and rush, at intervals, a sentinel on outpost duty. News had come in on the 23rd, that Boishébert, the most famous of Indian leaders, had arrived at Port Toulouse, and from him and his forces much was expected. The Minister had sent to Drucour the Cross of St. Louis, to present to Boishébert, as a reward for his distinguished services, but he was a dreary and astonishing failure. He who, as a lad, had performed amazing feats of endurance and leadership, had driven back the New England forces at the St. John River, was useless at Louisbourg.

Further embarrassments were caused by the action of the Abbé Maillard and his Indians.

"We counted on that in all security (supplies of powder, ball and provisions sent to the Miré River for the use of the irregulars). But the Abbé Maillard, Missionary Priest to the Indians in this Island and Head of the Missions, who was in town the day the English landed at Gabarus, having departed hence on the evening of the same day, out of precaution and care for his person, took with him for greater safety all the Indians who were here at the time; and presumably he left Louisbourg in the firm belief that within a few days it would fall into the power of the English. At least we must piously think so, because of his conduct, for being accurately informed where the munitions and stores were placed, the Indians who accompanied him, with great care, took away the one and the other. His care should have been to prevent their doing so by his exhortations, the supreme power of a Missionary to the Indians, but once again we assume that he truly believed the colony was lost, nevertheless the number of years during which the King

---

[1] The elder Daccarette, Michel, was long settled in Louisbourg. His son, also Michel, was born there in 1730, married a daughter of La Borde, the treasurer of the colony, and was more likely at twenty-eight to be the leader of the irregulars than his father. The latter was a man of substance and exemplary life, although he had embroiled himself with the Church by marrying his deceased wife's sister, a marriage which was rehabilitated by the Bishop of Quebec under authority of a Bull of Pope Clement XII. Two of his daughters married officers, La Vallière and Denis.

has given him a stipend, the favours he has received from him in the form of a pension founded on a benefice, and those conferred on him by the head of the colony, should have been powerful enough to give him the thought that this store, in spite of his opinion, might be of use to his Majesty's service. However this may be, everything was carried off, and the Missionary, with foresight for himself, thought rather of securing abundant provision for his escort, than of the good of the state, and these are the reasons why it has been necessary to re-establish the stores and to have them sent by sea at infinite risk.[1]

"The conduct of the Missionary is remarkable; not only should he have made every effort to prevent the stores being taken away, but, moreover, ought he not to have remained in the town? His staying would have meant the Indians remaining also, and they numbered about sixty.[2]

The effects of the incapacity of these irregulars were negative. The attitude of Des Gouttes and his captains seriously weakened Drucour's defence, and caused him the gravest concern. Throughout his own restrained account, in the tone of his letters to Des Gouttes, in the comments he makes on events as they pass, one feels the serious situation. There breathe through his words the emotions of a man strong enough to be patient under the depression of fighting without hope, and yet not of the uncommon force which can impose his purpose on the unwilling and the backward.

The view of the possibilities of the ships, already stated (p. 265), is not merely retrospective. Drucour says about the evacuation of the ships:

"If it is carried out, it would have been as well, had they (the ships) not been here. Instead of that, such splendid floating batteries should have been in constant motion so as to prevent the besiegers establishing their batteries around the harbour and opposite the place."[3]

English and French accounts agree that the ships kept up a brisk fire;[4] it was not effective at any time, and decreased, while that of Wolfe's batteries became more damaging as they gained positions of greater vantage. When the attack was begun the ships ranged in a crescent between the Batterie de la Grave and the Royal Battery. A night's fire from the lighthouse made them move nearer the town. A few days later they came nearer in, and finally on the 2nd of July they took positions so close to the town that in it fell shells which overpassed them.

"The vessels L'Entreprenant and the Célèbre have again approached so near the quay that both of them have risen about eight to ten inches higher at low tide, the Prudent is so near the angle of the batterie de la Grave that she is touching ground also."

They were in water so shallow that three of them were aground. Des Gouttes renewed his request to leave; proposed once to remain himself and

---

[1] This was accomplished by one Paris, a pilot of the town.   [2] Drucour's Journal, July 1.
[3] Drucour's Journal, July 1.   [4] Marolles says he fired 3500 shot from the Célèbre.

defend the port, and let Beaussier's four ships sail; gave orders, without Drucour's consent, to the captains of the *Célèbre* and the *Entreprenant* to sail at the first favourable opportunity; and gave only the assistance of a midshipman in securing the blocking of the entrance of the port.[1] He also prepared for the worst by arranging with his captains a signal on the display of which they should scuttle their ships.

The climax of his unwillingness and incapacity was reached on the 1st of July. Then the captains held with Des Gouttes a council, at which they discussed the evacuation of the ships, and in consequence Des Gouttes gave each of them a formal order to disembark their crews, leaving on board only a guard of twenty-five to thirty men.

Prévost got wind of this before any one in the town. He hastened to Drucour, with whom he found at the moment Des Gouttes, Beaussier of the *Entreprenant*, and Marolles of the *Célèbre*. Prévost addressed the Governor: "Have you asked, Sir, that the crews of the squadron should all land to-day in the town to reinforce your garrison?" The Governor, surprised, answered that the idea had not as yet occurred to him; then M. Prévost showed how prejudicial it would be to the King's service and to the safety of the place that these five vessels should be abandoned, and recalling to the memory of these gentlemen to whom the King entrusted their ships, his regulations of 1689, he asked whether they had received up to the present other losses than the death of two officers, a midshipman, two sailors, and a cabin-boy. He represented that with a guard of twenty-five to thirty men in each, of which the enemy might be informed through deserters, he (the enemy) would arrive with barges and carry them off in the night, and that then the King's own ships would destroy and reduce his town.

"That rather than abandon them they should be used to destroy the deadly works formed by the enemy and still being formed around the harbour and in the environs of the place. All these reasons decided the officers to return on board their ships.

"Some remarks should be made on this so extraordinary conduct, first of all, that this evacuation of the ships was founded on a written statement (procès verbal) of these gentlemen made in a council on board the *Prudent*, which written statement Monsieur Beaussier refused to sign to-day mid-day, though he was the moving power in the affair, for the reason that he held in his hand before signing, M. Des Gouttes' order.

"In the second place that it was probably stipulated in the written statement that the evacuation of the ships should only be executed as a result of the Governor's request in order to have the crews as reinforcements to the garrison and to make sorties on the besiegers. There is a reason to believe that such are the terms of the written statement, since in Monsieur Des Gouttes' order to each vessel the crews are to be so employed;

---

[1] Four ships were sunk on the 28th and 29th of June, the *Apollon*, *Fidèle*, *Chèvre*, and the *Ville de Saint Malo*, and, on the 30th of June, another.

however, the Governor did not only not make the request, but he did not know that he was involved in the affair." [1]

The return to the ships was temporary, for a request to Des Gouttes for 150 men to assist in the work of the defence was taken as what must seem a pretext to land the crews. Those of the *Capricieux* and the *Bienfaisant* were sent on shore on the 4th, although, on the 6th, Tourville,[2] for whom no work was found on shore, took his crew back on board to fire on Wolfe's new batteries. The crews of the other three ships were withdrawn on the 6th. The orders were in the following form :

COPY OF A LETTER FOUND IN A DROWNED MAN'S POCKET AT LOREMBEC

"In the evening of the 27th of June the English bombarded the Squadron, and the *Capricieux* received a small shell on her Forecastle, which notwithstanding every obstacle it mett with, went thro' both decks a lower deck beam, and bursting, sett her on fire, which was with much difficulty extinguished. As the Danger of the Squadron becomes each Day more evident by the increase of the Enemy's Bomb Batteries, I went immediately to consult the Governor upon the necessary measure to be taken to prevent the ships being blown up, and we determined to bring them as close to the town as we could and to moor them with 4 anchors each, so as to bring Broadsides to bear as much as possible on the passage ; also that their powder should be landed, some few rounds excepted ; that they should put on shore as much of their Provisions as would subsist their Complement in case they should be totally evacuated with a reserve of 6 weeks for each ship ; that they should each raise Tents in such places as the Governors should appoint for the looping the seamen to be landed for the service of the Garrison : These articles having been well thought and agreed on with the Consent of Mr. Drucour, it is ordered that Mons. Beaussier de l'Isle Capitaine de vaisseau du Roy, Commdnt. of the *Entreprenant*, shall conform thereto and cause the above orders to be put in execution with all the vigilance & exactness he is capable of." [3]

It seems probable that the drowned man was one of the executive officers, to whom a copy of Des Gouttes' letter was given officially.

This happened while the ships were seaworthy, and practically undamaged by the fire against them, for there is mentioned in the Journals that up to this time only one shell had struck the *Prudent*, on the 29th. The casualties were trifling : from the 19th of June to the 6th of July, two officers, a midshipman, and seven men were all that were killed on these ships.[4]

If these actions of Des Gouttes neither raised the indignation of Drucour

---

[1] Drucour's Journal, July 2.
[2] So, Drucour. Tourville does not mention this, though his journal reads as if he were daily on his ship after this date.
[3] Bell MSS.
[4] The number of men put ashore : *Prudent*, 330 ; *Entreprenant*, 500 ; *Célèbre, Capricieux, Bienfaisant*, 660. Total, 1490.

high enough to take action against such incapacity, nor even adequately to express it in his account of these events, others were not so reticent.

"To-day, the fourth of July, the vessels have just confirmed the idea which their unceasing bad manœuvres had given to all. Can it ever be believed that five pieces of artillery, placed on an eminence, at less than a quarter of a league from the shore, could have obliged M. Desgouttes and his Captains to abandon their ships, leaving in each one a guard with two officers, which were to be relieved every four and twenty hours? This, however, is the result of the council of war these gentlemen have held and dared even to execute, leaving shamefully their vessels in front of five cannon while they had three hundred to defend them with. . . . If these commanders are treated according to the regulations, I believe their heads are in the greatest danger."

"Aujourd'hui, quatrième de Juillet, les vaisseaux viennent de confirmer l'idée que les mauvaises manœuvres qu'ils n'ont cessé de faire, avoient donné d'eux à tout le monde. Croira-on jamais que cinq pièces de canon placées à un petit quart de lieue de la mer, sur une montagne, ayent pu obliger Monsieur Dégoute [sic] et les capitaines de ses vaisseaux de les abandonner ; ne laissant dans chaque, qu'une garde avec deux officiers, qu'on devoit relever toutes les vingt et quatre heures : c'est cependant le résultat du conseil que ces messieurs ont tenu, et qu'ils ont bien osé exécuter, abandonnant honteusement leurs vaisseaux, devant cinq pièces de canon, tandis qu'ils en avoient trois cent quarante, pour les défendre. . . . Si l'on traite tous ces capitaines selon l'ordonnance, je crois leurs têtes fort hazardées." [1]

Johnstone confirms this :—"It is true that all of them (the land forces) had the most sovereign contempt for the sea officers of the French squadron, which contempt their dastardly and base conduct justly merited." [2]

There was the sharpest of contrasts between the effectiveness of the ships of the line and that of the *Aréthuse*, a frigate of thirty-six guns, commanded by Vauquelin. The land officers had nothing but praise for him. When he proposed to Drucour, now that he could no longer impede the English attack, that he should escape through their fleet and carry dispatches to France, Des Gouttes, present at the interview, gave his opinion that Vauquelin might still be useful at Louisbourg. To which Vauquelin replied : "Yes, by God, if you will give me one of your men-of-war of the line that are laid up doing nothing, you will see that I will do much more yet than I have done hitherto with the frigate." [3]

After the first days of July, Drucour's defence was weakened while the vigour of the attack increased. The advantages of Wolfe's new position have been pointed out. The first batteries brought into action were one of six guns, another of two mortars, specially directed against the *Aréthuse*. This

[1] Arch. Nat. B⁴, vol. 80, f. 82.

[2] Quebec Lit. and Hist. Soc. 2nd Series. Tourville says Des Gouttes' view was that seeing the ships could not silence Wolfe's batteries, it would save life to employ their crews on shore, to which Drucour consented (July 3). Tourville received orders at 11 P.M. He saw to his anchors and landed his crew.

[3] MS. relatifs à la Nouvelle, France, vol. 3, p. 480. See Appendix for biographical details on Vauquelin.

made her position untenable, and on the 6th she withdrew. The testimony as to the result of her guns is unanimous. She had, although under-manned, seriously impeded the advances of the besiegers.[1] An elaborate and costly epaulement " about a quarter of a mile long, nine feet high and sixteen feet broad," had been erected to protect the workers from her fire. When she was driven away work was carried on more rapidly, so that by the 10th Wolfe had completed a line of batteries from behind the Grand Battery to the slopes above the Barachois. His admirers, contrasting his activity with the slowness of the other Commanders, hoped that the most startling proof possible of his superiority as a leader might be given :

". . . he is very Alert, Lives as his soldiers and Acts with such Vigour that it is Expected by many that he will make a Breach at ye West Gate in a few days and Desire the Generals on ye Right to walk in."[2]

Notwithstanding the protection given to the French ships by cables, tobacco, and other materials, they were pierced by the nearer guns and began to suffer.

On the 6th, the city was damaged from the shells thrown into it. The besiegers took as marks the spires of the principal buildings. One shell fell in the courtyard of the citadel, another in the ditch, and just before the fire slackened for the night, another exploded in the crowded hospital, killing the surgeon of the Volontaires Etrangers, and dangerously wounding two of the Frères de la Charité. Drucour, the next morning, sent a letter to Amherst proposing to set apart a place for the sick and wounded, which would not be fired on. An answer was not returned until the evening, as Amherst sent for Boscawen before replying. It was to the effect, as there seemed no place within the town where they might be secure, that under certain somewhat stringent conditions the sick should be placed on Battery Island, on one of the French men-of-war detached from the fleet, and anchored in the upper part of the harbour, or placed among Boscawen's fleet outside. Drucour felt that he could not accept this offer. The buildings which might have been used on Battery Island were in ruins, and to detach a ship, as an hospital, would apparently weaken their naval force. His own view was that the ship was useless as she was, but that this could not be thought possible by the English commanders. So the civilians, nearly four thousand in number, the soldiers off duty, the sick and the wounded, as well as the combatants, all in a town, the area of which was about 600 yards in one direction, and about 400 across, had to undergo the fire of the besiegers from the lighthouse, which reached

---

[1] Vauquelin kept a man at the masthead to give directions to his gunners.
[2] An account of the expedition, etc., B.M. Add. MSS. 11,813.

as far as the citadel, and from Wolfe's new batteries. In two days, the 6th and 7th, 125 or 130 shells and 60 or 70 shot had fallen in the town. The purpose of the enemy seemed in the early days of the bombardment rather to destroy the buildings of the town than its defence.[1]

This communication was not the first which had passed between the commanders. No summons to surrender had been sent, but early in the siege, choosing a way which would give most information to the messenger bearing a flag of truce, says the observant Tourville, Amherst sent a polite note to the Governor, and a present of two pineapples to Madame Drucour. An equally polite note was returned, and Drucour again displayed his lavishness by sending back some bottles of champagne (June 17 and 18). This promptly brought back again more pineapples, one at least of which was not good (Tourville). The present in return included some fresh butter, which indicates that the ordinary activities of life in the town had not been entirely suspended. Inquiries and replies as to the missing officers taken prisoners at the landing had been exchanged ; effects had been sent to them ; and never, said one diarist, was war carried on with more courtesy.

During a truce many officers talked together.

" The Sieur Joubert, Captain of a Company of Volunteers while the drummer was in camp, was visited at the Barachois, by an English lady, whom he thinks is his cousin, three officers introduced her to him, they offered him refreshment, he thanked them and made the same offer ; the lady asked for permission to pick a salad, this was accorded her " (Anon., July 6–7).[2]

The slowness with which the town was invested surprised the French. They thought the army was deficient in good troops, as so long a time was spent in fortifying their camp and making roads. " The sluggishness (indolence) of the English General in approaching the city makes me think he expects reinforcements." This was the opinion of Tourville on June 22. The engineer, Poilly, ten days later speaks of the slowness of their approach as exhibiting a prudence beyond bounds (" Nous fait montrer d'une prudence plus que mesurée ").

These are indications that this was owing to divided counsels. There was obviously a difference of opinion between Amherst and Bastide later than that on the 17th. Amherst again writes on the 24th :[3] " Colonel Bastide remained

---

[1] As Amherst gave orders on July 22 to fire at the fortifications rather than the buildings, it is probable that this view of the French is correct.

[2] Joubert's relationship with the English lady must have been through some European connection. He was one of the French officers who came to Isle Royale in 1750, after service in the regiments of Picardie and Grassin. He served in the old war in Bohemia, Bavaria, in the Rhine, and in Flanders ; received many wounds ; carried a ball from Raucoux, which could not be extracted, and at Langenfield was galloped over by the enemy's cavalry. He, some thought, should have commanded the irregulars instead of Boishébert. He served in the Windward Islands as Major in 1760, and was made Governor of Marie Galante in 1763.

[3] Letter of July 6, C.O. 5/55.

fixed in his opinion of advancing by Green Hill." The first work was pushed in this direction until about the 14th of July, when batteries were traced out on the shore, between Cap Noir, still in the French possession, and the English redoubt which had been begun on the 1st. It would, therefore, appear that the elaborate epaulement, to cover the depression which was open to the *Aréthuse*, was not necessary ; nor were the trenches in the vicinity, for the attack was not made by Green Hill. Even if there had not been a change of plan, work, which in any case must have been slow, was drawn out by the adoption of European methods in road-making. "Instead of laying hurdles and fascines on the surface of this swamp the sod had been pared away injudiciously, which caused a miserable waste of time and materials." Boscawen's cart[1] was not apparently used, nor were sledges such as colonists employed to bring up their heavy guns in 1745. The expedients possible to those familiar with the country were not suggested, for smallpox ravaged the New England carpenters, the loss of whom Amherst regrets.[2]

Notwithstanding delays, the advance was steady, and no position once gained was afterwards lost. On the 9th, a sortie in force was made from the town to check the English advance on the right. Seven hundred and twenty-four men, under the command of Marin, Lieut.-Col. of Bourgogne, divided into two parties, left the town about midnight and advanced along the shore, They surprised the advance post of the English, who were asleep or careless, carried this with the bayonet, and followed the fugitives to the second line, where they found a detachment drawn up to receive their charge. The English broke under it, and left Marin in possession.

The workmen he brought with him, began to demolish the entrenchment. The alarm was now a general one, supports came up from a detachment of the 15th near at hand, daylight was near, and Marin accomplished little in the way of destruction, but led his forces back to the town in good order, bringing with him two officers and twenty-eight grenadiers as prisoners. The accounts of this sortie differ.[3]

---

[1] Wolfe's orders mention on the 7th "a machine lately provided for that purpose," *i.e.* drawing guns from the Miré road to his battery.

[2] "Colonel Messervy and his son both died this day, and of his company of carpenters of 108 men, all but 16 in the smallpox, who are nurses to the sick, this particularly unlucky at this time" (Amherst to Pitt, June 28, C.O. 5/53). Knap says the Colonel's son, John, was buried on June 29.

[3] It was stated that a good many of the French had been drinking. The French loss was 50/60 men and 2 officers. It seems certain that time was lost, and although all nocturnal movements are difficult, the alarm was the sooner spread to the British supports by the French having fired on the retreating foe, instead of having pursued them with the bayonet. Drucour's account is the most favourable to Marin and his men. Amherst admits that his men were taken by surprise, but claims that the result was not important.

The casualties in this sortie on the English side were, Lord Dundonald killed ; a Lieutenant of the 17th and Capt. Bontein of the Engineers taken ; 4 men killed, 12 missing, and 17 wounded (Amherst).

The French loss was 50 or 60 men killed, and 2 officers (Drucour). Other figures are given in different journals.

Lord Dundonald, the 7th Earl, was born at Paisley in 1729, served in the Scots regiment in the service of Holland

The French tried to check the main attack. Small guns were erected at
Cap Noir, and new cannon brought into position on the Queen's Bastion. The
range was so long that their fire could not be effective. The condition of the
walls was so bad that Poilly said that the fire of their own cannon would make
in their own walls a breach for the English ; but to his superiors the need of
replying, even ineffectively, to the attack seemed so urgent, that he was as one
crying in the wilderness. The progress of the besiegers, which was satisfactory
to them, and discouraging to Drucour, was still that of the left attack. New
batteries were established, and bombs were thrown into the town, some days
numbering as many as a hundred and twenty or thirty. The enemy carried
stores from the eastern shore of the harbour to the Royal Battery unmolested by
the ships. Their supineness made Drucour fear it would suggest to the
English a project for cutting them out.[1] Fire was reopened on the Island
Battery, and its wretched garrison had to seek shelter among the rocks, unable
to defend themselves. On the night of the 15th the *Aréthuse*, having been
repaired, slipped out of the harbour, was seen by the watchers of the Lighthouse,
who gave signals to Hardy's fleet, which unsuccessfully pursued her.

Wolfe's account of this episode is worth quoting, as an illustration of the
power of the point of view. After saying that he had often been in much pain
for Hardy's squadron in the rough weather it encountered, he goes on : "a
frigate found means to get out and is gone to Europe *chargé de fanfaronnades*. I
had the satisfaction of putting two or three haut-vitzer shells into his stern, and
to shatter him a little with some of your lordship's 24 pound shot, before he
retreated, and I much question whether he will hold out the voyage." [2]
When one knows that Vauquelin had impeded the progress of the siege for at
least a fortnight, that Wolfe had erected a mortar battery for the purpose of
dislodging him, that Vauquelin was a gallant man and a skilful sailor, Wolfe's
reference to his escape shows a less generous spirit than that of Boscawen.[3]

The French, uninspired by any success of moment, disheartened by the
ineffectiveness of the ships, and by the prompt restoration of the damage their
guns inflicted on the works of the British, toiled on at a task which was
patently hopeless. The discouragement shows at length in Drucour's Journal.
On the 13th he writes :

"The garrison becomes weaker from day to day, the ordinary fate of that of a besieged
town, but this is an uncommon and special plight, it has no secure shelter for rest, so here

---

returned to Scotland, and, after 1753, joined the 17th Regiment, and with it went to America in 1757, wintered there,
and was Captain of the Grenadier Company of Forbes at the time of his death. (From notes for a history of the
Cochrane family by Mrs. Parker).

[1] July 12.

[2] Hist. MSS. Com. ix. This was as bad a prophecy as Wolfe's at Halifax. The *Aréthuse* made an extraordinarily
rapid voyage, notwithstanding her condition.   [3] See Chap. XV.

the soldier who is on duty by day passes the night in the open, on the ramparts or in the covered way. He is overcome with weariness, nevertheless always shows good will which delights, but he cannot hold out. We estimate to-day a diminution of a quarter of the troops compared with the day of the landing."

His weariness shows in this, for on the next page of his Journal he states the loss, which is one-third.[1]

A further step was made in advance on the 16th. Towards evening the French picket at the Barachois bridge was driven in. In the night, a body of troops massed just beyond it, rushed the position, entrenched themselves, and held the ground against a belated fire from the ramparts. This gave them a position about 200 yds. from the Dauphin Gate, which they held under the heavy fire of the walls. The trenches were extended, preparations for a new battery were made,[2] although the loss in officers and men was heavy. The spur was silenced, the Cavalier damaged, and the fire from the ships was much slackened. From the 19th of June, when fire from the Lighthouse began, to the 16th of July, Wolfe had extended batteries from the former point to ever closer quarters, and his men were at the latter time holding a position within 250 yards of the walls. The forces he had at his disposal were not great, apparently never more than 2000 men. Amherst had apparently overruled Bastide. The main attack was erecting batteries which had not yet fired a gun, the nearest of which was more than three times as far away from the walls as Wolfe's advanced position. When the first of the batteries of the main attack were ready, a day or two later, their fire was directed against the Queen's Bastion and the southern side of the Citadel, from which it was separated by ground most difficult for troops to cross. Therefore, even if a breach had been made in that part of the walls, it would have been practically useless for assault. The fire of cannon and musketry from the walls was very hot. Officers and men in the trenches constantly fell before it,[3] and it was vigorously returned from the batteries above the Barachois. These mounted 16 guns and 2 mortars.[4] The French heard the enemy at work, fired on them, and longed for

---

[1] On the 13th muster was :

Artois	.	.	.	.	.	.	250
Bourgogne	.	.	.	.	.	.	300
Cambise	.	.	.	.	.	.	300
Volontaires Etrangers	.	.	.	.	300
Colony	.	.	.	.	.	.	400
Grenadiers	.	.	.	.	.	.	200
Militia	.	.	.	.	.	.	300
Battery Island	.	.	.	.	.	150
							2200

Out of 3080 on June 8.

[2] A battery of heavy guns on the 17th.

The loss in killed and wounded up to the 12th :

			Officers.	Soldiers.	
Artois	.	.	.	7	27	
Bourgogne	.	.	.	6	55	
Cambise	.	.	.	1	6	
Volontaires Etrangers	.	4	17	
Colony Troops	.	.	4	51	
Civilians	.	.			26
			22	156	26

[3] "18 officers and men killed in trenches in 48 hours."

[4] Drucour says 4 mortars.

a ship in the position of the *Aréthuse* from which the enemy in their trenches would have been uncovered down to their shoes. The ships remained as they were, firing occasionally, but with direction so bad that on the 18th their grape fell among their own men in the covered way. Cartridges began to be scarce, also balls for their 24-lb. guns. Iron scraps were used in the mortars, English shot were picked up and fired back. Houses had to be torn down for wood to repair fortifications, and such work had to be carried on under a fire which swept not only the defences, but the streets of the town. The work of repairs and the fire of the town were kept up with spirit. A lieutenant, and a handful of men of the Volontaires Etrangers, seized an outpost in front of the trenches, and held it all the afternoon of the 19th, until at nightfall they were given orders to come in—a gallant feat, but, like all that the garrison had done, of no avail. Amherst had not only his army, but the crews of the ships to draw on. As the fire drew nearer, and became more accurate, it the more incommoded the town. It was concentrated on the Citadel between eleven and two, when the whole garrison assembled there for dinner.

Des Gouttes was being roused from his torpor as far as to make a promise. He had arranged for the *Bienfaisant* and another ship to move out so that they could fire on the advance works, to prepare for and support a sortie of 1500 men in the early hours of the 21st. He failed to keep his word for that night, but promised again for the 22nd. In the early afternoon of the 21st, a shot struck the poop of the *Célèbre*, which set off some cartridges stored there. The fire caught her mizzen mast, and the score of men on board were unable to check it. She swung so that sparks from her caught aft on the *Entreprenant*. While her men were working at this blaze, fire had been smouldering on her bowsprit. It broke out freely in a quarter of an hour, and she in turn set fire to the *Capricieux*, unable to move. The *Prudent* escaped, for she was to windward, the *Bienfaisant* by swinging on her cable. The enemy poured their heaviest fire on the ships, and on the boats plying between them and the town. The French speak quite calmly of this as an ordinary incident in warfare. It impressed more deeply some of the enemy. Gordon says, "in short, to humanity tho' an enemy, the scene was very shocking." Hamilton saw both sides of such occurrences and thus comments on them in his Journal :

"About 1 A.M. (?) as I was patroling the heights in the neighborhood of the Camp overlooking the Town and harbour, I perceived a thick column of smoke and presently a great explosion announced some fatal accident, this proceeded from the accident, as I afterwards heard, of a shot from one of our batteries firing the powder magazine on board one of the French ships of war in the harbour. I was soon joined by some stragglers, among others our Chaplain, who highly enjoyed the scene, confounded the French &c. On our return to camp a great smoke arose from that part of the encampment where our Regiment lay.—

Oh, Lord, cried an officer, I am afraid our hospital is on fire, what will become of those poor fellows, lame and wounded. The sober divine exclaimed, I am afraid that idle rascal, my Cook, has set the hut on fire and my piece of beef will be burnt to ashes. It was not in effect so bad as either."

The horror of the conflagration was increased by the loaded guns of the ships, as they became hot, going off and taking effect on the other ships, on the boats, and town. The ships made a prodigious blaze all night, and finally drifted with the tide to the Barachois shore, where they lay with their guns and iron-work tumbled into their holds.[1] As their flames died down, there must have sunk with them the hopes of the most optimistic of the defenders. The sortie was abandoned, nothing more could be done with exhausted troops than repair works, which before the siege began were known to be faulty in plan and hopelessly bad in condition, and to keep up a fire from their crumbling walls on an enemy with resources so superior that its advance could not be checked by any effort the defenders had made. This was done with spirit. The defection of the navy spurred the garrison to greater efforts and a stalwart endurance. Nor do we find any record of pressure to surrender brought on them by the non-combatants; indeed, Madame Drucour daily walked the ramparts, and fired three cannons to encourage the troops.

Thus far the storm which they had endured had been heavy. It now became a tempest. The batteries now on the 22nd playing against the town were :

Gun Batteries.	Weight of Metal.	Mortar Batteries.	Size of Shell.
Left attack, Wolfe's: 1 of 7	32 and 24		
1 „ 6	32 and 24		
1 „ 5	24 and 12		
1 „ 2	32		
1 „ 2	24	1 of 2	13 inches.
1 „ 2	12	1 „ 2	8 „
Right attack: 1 „ 8	24	1 „ 3	13 and 10 „
1 „ 5	24	1 „ 4	8 „
Total . 8 „ 37		4 „ 11	

In addition there were great numbers of coehorns, royals, etc.,[2] which during the day were added to by the erection of an advanced battery of four guns, and a mortar battery, which almost drove out the French from the covered way.

About seven that morning a large shell fell in the barracks to the north of the belfry in the building, which closed, on the town side, the parade ground of the Citadel. It was thought to have done no damage, but about half an hour later a brisk fire broke out in the roof. The efforts made to stop it were

[1] Forty-seven guns were afterwards recovered.   [2] Gordon, p. 139.

unsuccessful, and all except the Governor's apartments at its southern end was destroyed. The English during this fire, which lasted five or six hours, showered bombs and ball with the greatest activity into this area; nevertheless all the workmen of the garrison and the ship's carpenters gathered there and worked with uncommon courage and energy. Without both these parties the fire would have made greater progress. There was a sad and moving sight during this time.

"The few casemates are placed in the inner part of the citadel, in them were shut in the ladies and some of the women of the town, and one was kept for wounded officers. There was every reason to fear that the fire would reach the protection which had been placed in front of these casemates, and by the direction of the wind the smoke might stifle the women shut up in them, so that all the women and a great number of little children came out, running to and fro, not knowing where to go in the midst of bombs and balls falling on every side, and among them several wounded officers brought out on stretchers, with no safe place to put them" (Drucour).

"All the above-mentioned batteries played extremely smart the whole time it lasted" (Gordon).

The six-gun battery fired 600 balls that day, although three of the guns were dismounted by the fire from the walls, and remounted again. Three times in this wretched day did the wooden barracks in the Queen's Bastion, "as inflammable as a pack of matches," catch fire, and three times they were extinguished. All night long bombs, some of them charged with combustibles, were hurled into the town, and at daylight it was worse. The siege at length was conducted with fury. The works were suffering on the left and right, and while shells passed over their heads the soldiers in the covered way and in the trenches exchanged a continued fire of musketry. In the evening the barracks were set on fire beyond control. Little help was sent in the first hour, and later, only by pulling down the neighbouring huts and a favouring wind, was the fire prevented from spreading to the town. The next day, the 24th, there was no abatement in the bombardment. Deserters who came in to the camp said the townspeople had entreated the Governor to capitulate, and this inspired the artillerymen in the trenches with the hope that the end was near. The Dauphin defences were down, the gunners were driven from the artillery of the Citadel, but they managed to serve a few guns, the fire of which seemed to Drucour more like the minute guns at a funeral than a defence (" Qu'il ressemble plutôt à des honneurs funéraires qu'à une deffense ").

Part of the English fire was directed against the walls, to make a breach, but the destruction of the town was the main object of the British, it seemed to Drucour (" Il paroît aussi que leur intention n'est pas encore à battre sérieusement en brèche, mais auparavent de tuer du monde et d'incendier la ville "). Fire now seemed concentrated on the hospital and the houses near it, all filled with wounded.[1] The breaching began seriously on the 25th. Franquet alone, of those who inspected it, thought its result did not yet make an assault practicable. The town was no longer defensible, and scaling ladders were ready in the trenches. The British had seen great pieces of the wall fall into the moat after every successful shot, and meantime the fire of the bombs, as many as 300 in a night, was continued, so that there was not a house in the town which was uninjured. There were only five cannon to reply to this bombardment—two on the wall between the Dauphin Bastion and the Citadel, and three on its northern flank.

The condition of the town was desperate, but the two battered ships were still in the harbour, and to some degree effective, or with possibilities of effectiveness. No precautions had, however, been taken to afford them the extra protection needed after the burning of the others. They were now to fall, and with them the last hope of protracting the siege.

The entrances of the harbour had been reconnoitred by Boscawen's orders, and the report of Balfour, Captain of the *Etna* fire-ship, being favourable, Boscawen determined to give the navy more special work than supplementing the forces on shore. During the morning of July 25, the larger boats, pinnaces, and barges of both squadrons were manned and armed. Those from the ships in Gabarus Bay went down to Sir Charles Hardy's station off the harbour mouth in small detachments, in order not to attract the attention of the town. The boats were divided in two divisions ; the command of one was given to Balfour of the *Etna*, and of the other to John Laforey, Commander of the *Hunter*.[2]

The night was thick, and the expedition entered the harbour undiscovered. The division under Laforey was directed against the *Prudent*, which was anchored near the Batterie de la Grave, resting on the ground. The men on board, with the exception of the sentinels, were below decks ; the highest officers were ensigns. The sentinel hailed a boat. A voice from it replied in French that it was from the town, and coming on board. An officer mounted to the deck, saw all clear, called over the side, " Monté [*sic*] cinq ou six hommes." Before the French bluejacket suspected anything, there were two hundred men in possession of the deck. The officers were taken, guards placed on the hatchways, twenty English prisoners released, combustibles placed in the gun-room and at the foot of the masts, ignited, the sentries withdrawn, and the English made off to the north. The few shots that were fired aroused the town. Drucour hurried to the battery, and directed a fire of cannon and musketry on the ships. Within half an hour the midshipmen and the men, some sixty or seventy in number,

---

[1] Parkman has admirably paraphrased Drucour's account of the effect of this fire on the wounded and their attendants.

[2] John Laforey was the descendant of a French Huguenot family settled in England in the reign of William III. In 1748 he became a lieutenant, was with Holburne in 1757, at Quebec in 1758, was made a Baronet in 1789, Admiral of the Blue in 1795, and died in 1796.

came ashore. The capture of the *Bienfaisant* was as expeditiously made. A short conflict took place. Seven of the assailants were killed, nine were wounded, before she was carried. Then she was towed by the boats of the squadron to the head of the harbour, and the port lay open to the British. The anonymous officer of the garrison comments thus on this disastrous event : [1]

"One is at first surprised to see two great ships letting themselves be taken by little boats, but one's astonishment diminishes when one knows that the officers and the crew (équipage) kept themselves hidden in the hold of the ships for fear of blows, that they had only a few men on deck to give warning. I do not undertake to say that all the ships did the same, but this is certain (mais ce qu'il a de sûr) that most of them acted in the same way. It is claimed (on prétend) that a naval officer is dishonoured when he hides himself a moment in the hold. On this principle what should one think of these gentlemen who were so long hidden there ?   The officers on guard on the *Prudent* and their midshipmen were quartered in the boatswain's storeroom (la fosse aux lions) where they were so safe and comfortable (si en sûreté et si tranquilles) that the English were already masters of the ship before they knew anything about it, that there was only one officer got on deck before the English had placed sentinels on the hatchways. The others only came out when they were told to come up and surrender."

The service of the naval officers on shore was equally condemned. Poilly says :

"Our batteries entrusted to the naval officers were entirely abandoned, there was in them not even a lighted match (linstock) in readiness. We have received no help from this essential part of our forces. Their reasoning is as hard-hearted as their conduct. I should erase the word. It (their conduct) merits a greater scorn."

When daylight came the bombardment was resumed. A new battery erected by volunteers, under Gordon, as was the one before this, was brought into play. The senior officers of the town inspected the fortifications, from which only three guns could play on the enemy, and met in council. Franquet held that the breaches were not yet practicable, and after hours of discussion it was decided to ask for a truce, in which terms of capitulation might be discussed. While this was going on, Boscawen was composing a letter to Drucour, directing him to surrender at discretion, acquainting him that he would this night be attacked by sea and land.

"I went on shore and communicated this Letter to Major General Amherst, who approved of it, and was Sealing the said Letter when a Letter was brought to Us from Monsr. de Drucour, offering to Capitulate." [2]

Loppinot, who, in the glory of a new position and a new uniform, had been rowed in from the *Tigre*, on June 29, 1749, to arrange the preliminaries of the return of Louisbourg to the French, was now, July 26, 1758, worn with the siege, conducted to the tent of Amherst, to tender Drucour's offer of capitulation. The reply of the victors was, that Drucour and his garrison, as a preliminary to a capitulation, must yield themselves prisoners at discretion, than which no surrender is more humiliating, and that only an hour would be given for their decision.[1] Drucour and his council were horrified at such hard terms. D'Anthonay was sent out to endeavour to obtain better. Whitmore, who commanded in the trenches, refused to let D'Anthonay pass beyond, and would send no message from him to Amherst. The council resolved to stand the storming. While D'Anthonay was in the enemy's lines, the engineers were assembled to arrange some interior entrenchment in case of the place being carried by assault. As, in the defence of Gabarus, no rendezvous for the detachment had been arranged, so now no provision for failure had been made, and this new problem had to be faced on the spur of the moment. Franquet was in favour of the Princess Bastion, but it was pointed out to him that it would not hold 150 men, and a place was required for the whole garrison. The Brouillan Bastion on the Eastern walls was proposed, and visited, while there they were surrounded by so great a crowd of the townspeople that they could do nothing. D'Anthonay returned from the enemy's lines, unsuccessful, and Loppinot set forth with a letter to say that the town would submit to assault rather than accept the terms offered. Then Prévost presented a memoir to the council. It pointed out the hardships to the people, the discouragement to colonization, the difference between soldiers whose professional duty it was to face horrors, and civilians forced to undergo such terrors as awaited them. His view prevailed. D'Anthonay and Du Vivier overtook Loppinot with powers to capitulate. The news spread through the town. With whatever joy it may have been received by the populace, and the sick and wounded, it enraged and humiliated the troops. The attitude of the officers verged on sedition ("il y eut un mouvement violent parmi Les Officiers de la Garnison qui tendoit à la sédition"). Drucour was blamed for not surrendering two days earlier, when they could have obtained the honours of war, or for surrendering now when they could have held out for two days more. The men of Cambis, in rage, broke their muskets and burned their colours.[2] The capitulation was signed, the barriers to the Dauphin Gate were cleared, the bridge repaired. The vaulted roof of its gate rang the next morning to the tread of the advanced guard of the victors, the grenadier companies of the Royals, Hopson's, and Amherst's. At noon, the garrison laid down its arms. It had been "good, brave, and patient," and felt the humiliation to which its men were subjected.

The terms were hard; even Wolfe admitted this; but the taking of

---

[1] The term was softened to prisoners of war.   [2] Johnstone and Poilly.

Louisbourg was the first important success in a war which had begun with Boscawen's high-handed action in 1755. He and Amherst determined to make the most of it, and bring back to Britain not only a long-deferred victory, but a striking one.

Such was the course of events in this siege. The summing up of its salient features seems necessary to make clearer, than the foregoing narrative, the causes which produced this result. At first sight it appears that the overwhelming superiority of the British in men and material made the result a foregone conclusion. Careful reading of the documents leads to a modification of this opinion. While the fortifications were bad in design and condition, the resistance made by their defenders indicates that had they been seconded by the men-of-war with anything like the fervour of which Vauquelin displayed in fighting his frigate, the difficulties of the British would have been greatly increased.[1]

As the defection of the fleet was not sporadic, although the annals of the French Navy has perhaps no darker page than this, the next chapter deals with this subject at length. There was a fine spirit in the rank and file on both sides. There was on the British the stupendous advantage, rarely enjoyed, of complete harmony between the sea and the land commanders. Boscawen was on shore every day when it was possible to land. His men were drawn on to supplement the land forces, and the handiness and the celerity of the sailors seems to have been marked.[2] Whatever were the difficulties of the French, and they were many, it must be evident that no commanding officer on that side displayed the dash, the keenness, the military science of Wolfe, any more than that these qualities were shown by any other officer of high rank on his own side. Amherst stands as a shadow in the background, Whitmore and Lawrence seem to have done nothing but routine duty. Wolfe was the moving spirit of the attack. The table on p. 281 shows how many batteries he had erected, with his small force, compared with the two the right attack had brought into action up to that time, and that table does not include three other batteries, the usefulness of which was then overpast. It was, however, his leap into the surf among his men, his appreciation of their good actions, his tireless activity, that made a spirit almost invincible among the British. Had there been a Wolfe in command of the French, there had been a battle of the Titans. Harsh as are his comments on many of his associates, unlovely as were some aspects of his character, Wolfe was a great leader, and to his presence at Louisbourg the result was largely due. The comments of the diarists indicate that there were in the place men who chafed at what was done, even more at what was left undone, just as a year

---

[1] Wolfe's opinion was: "that, to defend the Isle Royale it is necessary to have a body of four or five thousand men in readiness to march against whatever force of the enemy attempts to land. In short, there must be an army to defend the island. . . . We must not trust to the place or to any of those batteries now constructed" (Hist. MSS. Com. ix. p. 76).

[2] The quickness with which they erected batteries was noticed.

before Wolfe had been indignant with the incapacity and slowness at Rochefort. It must be admitted that the task at Louisbourg was difficult. Two-thirds of its whole force was required for manning the defences. Their troops had no secure resting-place, and were soon exhausted. The most difficult expeditions to manage are night attacks, and these required a *moral* which could not be expected from tired men, and yet these sallies were the most effective means of checking the advance. Much of the cannon fire from the walls did far more damage to the walls themselves than to the works of the besiegers. It was exhaustion again which prevented the French from utilizing the mortars they had, against the batteries, after they had once mounted them to protect the harbour. The difficulties which oppressed and overwhelmed Drucour were such as his character ill-fitted him to cope with. The tact, the high-mindedness, the generosity, which made him an admirable head of a naval school, were not the qualities best fitted for the rough work he had to do in Isle Royale. He naturally had no experience in land warfare. He had, indeed, mostly held a shore appointment ; and the engineer, and commandant of the troops, were both dull, and one a cripple. The quality of Drucour's mind, which makes one respect his memory, is his scrupulous fairness. He was Governor ; his reputation was at stake. He states every case fairly, he blames little, he emphasizes every good action, he minimizes every failure in his account of the siege. Rare and worthy of respect as is such a character, it must be admitted that it is not the temper of which successful commanders are made.

The townspeople merit great praise. We have only the evidence of a deserter to show that they were eager for capitulation before the assault was inevitable and imminent. Daccarette's company, made up of the principal merchants, when the attack was so far advanced that they could no longer skirmish outside, took charge of the battery in the southern flank of the citadel, and served its guns with a brilliancy which surprised and delighted an observer ("ils ont surpris et charmé"). Others of the bourgeoisie worked with the garrison in other batteries, undaunted by danger, and displayed the calmness of veterans ("avec autant de tranquillité que l'homme du monde le plus aguerri "[1]).

Louisbourg was in extremities when Drucour surrendered.

" Indeed when our ships came into the Harbour, there was hardly any part of it, which had not the appearance of Distress and Desolation, and presented to our View frequent Pieces of Wrecks, and Remnants of Destruction—Five or Six Ships *sunk* in one Place with their Mast-Heads peeping out of the Water—the Stranded Hull of *Le Prudent* on the muddy shoal of the other Side, burned down to the Water's Edge, with a great deal of her Iron and Guns staring us in the Face—Buoys of slipped Anchors *bobbing* very thick upon the Surface of the Water in the Channel towards the Town—a number of small Craft and

[1] Poilly.

Boats towards that Shore, some entirely under Water, others with part of their Masts standing *out of* it; besides the *stranded* Hulls, Irons, and Guns of the three Ships burned on the 21st upon the Mud towards the Barrassoy—and in the N.E. Harbour little else to be seen but Masts, Yards and Rigging *floating up and down*, and Pieces of burned Masts, Bowsprits, etc. driven to the Water's Edge, and some parts of the shore edged with *Tobacco Leaves* out of some of the ships that had been destroyed—the whole a dismal Scene of total Destruction." [1]

If this were the appearance of the harbour with the advantages of its effacing waters, the imagination can picture more vividly, than any written page can convey, the condition of the town. There was great outlay of materials in reaching the final conclusion of the siege. The loss of life was not, however, great : 195 of the British killed, and 363 wounded ; on the French side, according to De la Houlière, between 700 and 800 killed and wounded. [2]

A compilation of the troops on the eve of hostilities makes the total 3520. The French loss, therefore, was 411.

	Officers.	Soldiers fit for Duty.	Sick and Wounded.	Total.
24 Companies and 2 of Artillery .	76	746	195	1017
Artois, 2nd Batt. . . .	32	407	27	466
Bourgogne, 2nd Batt. . .	30	353	31	414
Cambis, 2nd Batt. . . .	38	466	104	608
Volontaires Etrangers . . .	38	402	86	526
Total Garrison	214	2374	443	3031
Sea officers and seamen . .	135	1124	1347	2606
	349	3498	1790	5637

Great stores of artillery and munitions of war fell, by the terms of the capitulation, as spoils of war.

Hardy entered the harbour on the 30th. Boscawen came in on August 1. The town was occupied. Arrangements were completed for the embarkation of the French troops and to clear the entrance of the harbour. [3]

The news of this victory, the first important one of the war, was received with great rejoicings, when Captains Edgecumbe and Amherst, on behalf of Boscawen and the General, arrived on the 18th of August. Comparisons were drawn between the attitude of the people when they heard of the fall of Port Mahon and that with which they exulted over this success. Addresses were sent

[1] An Authentic Account.   [2] To Minister, Aug. 6.

[3] Cambis and Artois and some seamen on the *Burford* ; Bourgogne and Vol. Etrangers and some seamen on the *Kingston* ; the Companies on the *Northumberland* ; the Naval Officers on the *Dublin* ; Drucour, his lady and retinue, and forty officers on the *Terrible*. These ships sailed about Aug. 14/15. The other prisoners and inhabitants were embarked as rapidly as possible. Some of them were fortunate enough to go directly to France for exchange, among them Des Gouttes, who did not deserve this good fortune.

to the King from the Universities and the principal towns of the kingdom. The colours taken were deposited in St. Paul's. (These have disappeared.)

"HISTORICAL CHRONICLE, *Sept.* 1758 [1]

Wednesday, 6.

"*Whitehall.* The king having been pleased to order the colours taken at *Louisbourg,* which were lately brought to the palace at *Kensington,* to be deposited in the cathedral church of *St. Paul*; proper detachments of horse and foot grenadiers were ordered to parade at *Kensington* at ten o'clock, and marched before his Majesty in the following order :

"A serjeant, and twelve horse grenadiers.

"A field officer, and officers in proportion.

"A detachment of fourscore of the horse grenadier guards.

"Then eighty of the life guards, with officers in proportion, with their standard, kettle drums and trumpets.

"Then a serjeant and twelve grenadiers of the foot guards.

"Then eleven serjeants of the foot guards carrying the eleven *French* colours, advanced.

"Then the four companies of Grenadiers of the foot guards closed the march.

"In this manner they proceeded from *Kensington,* through *Hyde Park,* the *Green Park,* into *St. James's Park,* and through the Stable yard *St. James's,* into *Pall Mall,* and so on to the west gate of *St. Paul's,* where the colours were received by the dean and chapter, attended by the choir ; about which time the guns at the Tower and in *St. James's Park* were fired.

"These colours are put up near the west door of the cathedral, as a lasting memorial of the success of his majesty's arms, in the reduction of the important fortress of *Louisbourg,* the islands of *Cape Breton* and *St. John.*"—*London Gazette.*

When Boscawen returned, the rejoicings broke out again. He received an address when he took his seat in the Commons, and an address was also sent out to Amherst, conveying the thanks of Parliament for their achievement.

The rejoicings in the colonies were no less widespread. All grasped the significance of the victory.[2]

Drucour had saved Canada for the year. It had been decided by Amherst and Boscawen that it was too late to go up the St. Lawrence. While they were engaged in removing the army into the town, and sending away the prisoners, the news came to them, August 1, of the defeat of Abercromby at Ticonderoga. It determined Amherst to hasten to his assistance. British troops were sent to Halifax on the 15th ; Amherst himself sailed to Boston on the 30th, and landed there on September 13. Meantime, expeditions were sent out to the Bay of Fundy, to Isle St. Jean, under Lord Rollo of the 22nd Regiment, and to Gaspé and other French settlements on the Gulf, under Wolfe.[3] The last was, like

---

[1] *Gentleman's Magazine,* 1758, vol. 28, p. 447.

[2] *The Last Siege of Louisbourg,* C. Ochiltree MacDonald, London, Cassell & Co., contains many interesting details of these rejoicings.

[3] See Appendix for an account of this expedition from the unpublished Bell MSS. lent me by Dr. A. G. Doughty.

Spry's in 1757, a pillaging of unarmed people, which excited the disgust of Wolfe ; that to Isle St. Jean resulted in the deportation to France of 3540 people. This number added materially to the task of providing transport, so that it is not until the end of September that Boscawen's journal ceases to include items as to the sailings of transports. Boscawen left on October 1, and reached the Channel a month later, and Durell, promoted to be a Rear-Admiral, took charge of the fleet left in these waters. The garrison left in Louisbourg consisted of Whitmore's, Bragg's, Hopson's, and Warburton's, under command of Whitmore. The salient point in the letter in which Amherst encloses Whitmore's appointment as Governor, is Amherst's opinion of the island : [1]

" I would have the settlements in the different parts of the island absolutely destroyed, it may be done in a quiet way, but pray let them be entirely demolished, & for these reasons, that in the flourishing state it is growing to, many years wd. not have passed before the inhabitants wd. have been sufficient to have defended it." [2]

The next year, 1759, Louisbourg was the base from which sailed the expedition against Quebec. It gathered there in May, and sailed for the St. Lawrence on the 6th of June.

The possibility of its being given back to France was before all. Pitt, however, unshaken in his determination to break the maritime power of France, and to make it impossible for her to prosecute the fisheries, decided to make the return of Isle Royale to France, if it should be given back again by diplomacy, a barren one. He wrote to Amherst :—

"WHITEHALL, *February 9th*, 1760.

"SIR, I am commanded by His Majesty to acquaint you, that after the most serious and mature Deliberation being had, whether It be expedient to maintain, at so great an Expence, the Fortress at Louisburg, together with a Numerous Garrison there. The King is come to a Resolution, that the said Fortress, together with all the works, and Defences of the Harbour, be most effectually and most entirely demolished ; And I am in consequence thereof, to signify to you His Majesty's Pleasure, that you do as expediously as the Season will permit, take the most timely and effectual Care, that all the Fortifications of the Town of Louisburg, together with all the Works, and Defences whatever, belonging either to the said Place, or to the Port, and Harbour, thereof, be forthwith totally demolished, and razed, and all the Materials so thoroughly destroyed, as that no use may, hereafter, be ever made of the same. You are not, however, to demolish the Houses of the Town farther than shall be found necessary towards the full and entire Execution of the Orders for totally destroying all, and every, the Fortifications thereof ; And in the Demolition of all works, You will particularly have an Eye to render, as far as possible, the Port, and Harbour, of Louisburg, as incommodious, and as near impracticable, as may be. [3]

---

[1] Aug. 28, C.O. 5/53.

[2] Whitmore, as far as is shown in any documents I have seen, does not seem to have carried out these orders.

[3] On the same date he confirmed these instructions to Whitmore (C.O. 5/214). The Hon. John Byron, grandfather of the poet, was sent to Louisbourg in 1760, with a small squadron, to assist in this work.

Amherst dispatched these orders to Whitmore by Captain De Ruvyne, a Captain of Miners, April 21, 1760.[1] The view of the town shows that the intention that the final state, " which is not to have the least appearance remaining of having had any works about it," was not entirely realized.

The people of Louisbourg who returned to France were wards of the State. The Louisbourg companies were kept together for some time. Some of the officers were given commissions in similar regiments in the southern colonies of France ; all of them received pensions or were provided for. Dangeac and the Baron de l'Espérance became Governors of St. Pierre and Miquelon, Joubert of Marie Galante, and Villejouin of the island of Désirade. Many of the families received pensions. An effort was made to have many of them emigrate to Cayenne,[2] but they feared the tropics, and asked to be allowed to remain in France. The Minister had his troubles with them. De la Boularderie was given a pension on the condition that he would not come near the Court. The Henriau family for many years received a pension as Acadians to which they were not entitled. Their daughter Sophie, moreover, was not eligible although born in Isle Royale, as she was singing in the Chorus of the Opera.[3] But much of the correspondence which deals with these people consists in replies to letters from Tours, Loches, Tonnay Chàrente, and other provincial towns, asking for increases of pensions for survivors. They carried with them to France the robustness given them in the colony. Madame Costebelle did not die until 1779, and her pension began in 1720.[4] Madame De la Perelle lived until 1784. The law made by the Assemblée Nationale when, in 1791, it was setting in order the affairs of France, shows that there were still a goodly number of people drawing pensions.[5]

Madame Eurry De la Perelle, to whom reference has just been made, came to Louisbourg when it was founded, a young woman of twenty. Her husband was the first officer who died in the new settlement. She lived there until the second capture ; her three sons were officers in the troops. She did not die for twenty-four years after the demolition of the town, all of the fortunes of which passed before her eyes. That the life of a town should fall so far short of that of one of its people suggests the instability of the unimportant. Yet against this one background, with this unity of space and time, developed events which displayed the genius administrative, economic, military, of two peoples. The two score and six years of Louisbourg's existence show forth causes and consequences as clearly as the colonial history of two centuries.

---

[1] Notwithstanding delays the work was completed November 1760. The last mine was sprung on the 8th (Gibson Clough's Journal).

[2] Forant's legacy was applied to the missions of that colony. [3] B, vol. 164, 1778.

[4] B, vol. 165. [5] See Appendix.

APPENDIX A

An Account of the Guns, Mortars, Shot, and Shell found in the Town of Louisbourg.

In Ordnance mounted on Standing Carriages with Beds and Coins.								Brass Mortars with Beds.				Iron Mortars with Beds.				Round Shot.					Grape Shot.					Case Shot.	Double-headed Shot.			Shells.					Return of Muskets, Accoutrements, Powder, Musket Cartridges and Balls.			
36-Pounders.	24-Pounders.	18-Pounders.	12-Pounders.	8-Pounders.	6-Pounders.	4-Pounders.	Total.	12¼ Inches.	9 Inches.	6⅔ Inches.	Total.	12¾ Inches.	11 Inches.	9 Inches.	Total.	36-Pounders.	24-Pounders.	12-Pounders.	6-Pounders.	Total.	36-Pounders.	24-Pounders.	12-Pounders.	6-Pounders.	Total.	24-Pounders.	24-Pounders.	12-Pounders.	Total.	13 Inches.	10 Inches.	8 Inches.	6 Inches.	Total.	Muskets with Accoutrements.	Powder (Whole Barrels).	Musket Cartridges.	Musket Balls (Tons).
38	97	23	16	10	28	6	218	3	1	3	7	6	4	1	11	1607	1658	4000	2336	9601	139	134	330	130	733	33	243	153	398	850	38	138	27	1053	7500	600	80,000	13

Return of Lead, Iron, Entrenching Tools, etc.

Lead Pig.	Lead Sheets.	Iron of all Sorts.	Wheel-barrows.	Shovels (Wood).	Shovels (Iron).	Pickaxes.	Large Iron Crows.	Small Iron Crows.	Iron Wedges.	Hand Mauls.	Masons' Trowels.	Hammers.	Adzes.	Pin Mauls.
7 tons	5 tons.	6 tons.	600	760	900	822	22	12	42	18	36	36	18	12

Those last two returns are according to those sent home by General Amherst, but more was expected to be found.

For comparison is added the guns captured at Quebec. In large cannon Louisbourg was much superior.

(C.O. 5/51). An Account of the Guns, Mortars, Ammunition & arms, etc., found in the City of Quebeck upon its surrender to H.M.'s troops the 18th September 1759. Vizt.—

Brass Ordnance	6-Pounders	1
	4 ,,	3
	2 ,,	2
	36-Pounders	10
	24 ,,	45
	18 ,,	18
	12 ,,	13
Iron Ordnance	8 ,,	43
	6 ,,	66
	4 ,,	30
	3 ,,	7
	2 ,,	3
Brass Mortars	13-inch	1
,, Howitzers	8 ,,	3
	13-inch	9
Iron Mortars	10 ,,	1
	8 ,,	3
	7 ,,	2
Brass Petards		2
	13-inch	770
	10 ,,	150
	8 ,,	} 90
	6 ,,	

with a considerable quantity of powder, ball, small arms & intrenching tools, etc., the number of which cannot at present be ascertained.

WILLIAM SALTONSTALL
Commissary Artillery.

CHAPTER XV

THE ineffectiveness of the French Navy in connection with the military events which occurred at Louisbourg is striking. These events were of such a character that the action of naval forces, as it seems to be in all conjoint operations, was of paramount importance. The French recognized these crises. Even at a time when their naval forces were lowest, they did their best to send a strong force to protect or recover Louisbourg. The fleet of D'Anville in 1746 was an Armada, that of Du Bois de la Motte in 1757 was superior to Holburne's. Had the plans of the Minister not miscarried, the naval force for the defence in 1758 would have been less inferior to the fleet led by Boscawen to the attack on the position which held secure the French dominions in America.

In these major operations nothing was accomplished adequate to the resources placed at the disposal of the French commanders. The inaction of Meschin in 1744, the disastrous lack of judgment of Maisonfort in 1745, the betrayal of Beaussier de l'Isle by his supporting ships in the conflict with the *Grafton* and *Nottingham*, less critical episodes, show the same inertia, slackness, or incompetence.

This condition, if we, the English-speaking, are not to fall back to the absurd point of view of the boys' book of adventure or the naval novel, demands explanation.

The condition is summed up, from the practical standpoint, in the statement of a gallant French officer,[1] Coëtnempren de Kersaint, who fell in the Homeric fight at Quiberon. He wrote to the Minister in 1755 :

"The *Deffenseur* (a new 74) distinguished herself in our meeting with the English by sailing qualities superior to those of our other two ships. 'Tis a merit, my lord, in the heart-rending necessity in which we find ourselves for so long a time, to fly at sea before the English, or to be overwhelmed by their numbers."[2]

The general state of the French navy in the years we have been dealing with is shortly stated as a gradual decline. At the beginning of the eighteenth century it consisted

---

[1] "The best sailor that we had " (A French Account of Quiberon, Brit. Mus. Add. MSS. 35,898).
[2] Arch. Nat. Marine, B⁴, vol. 68.

of 281 vessels, while that of England at the death of William III., in 1702, had 271 vessels.

	In 1751	Effective.	Building.
England had	. . . .	116	21
France had	. . . . .	38	22

In 1755 the forces were as follows, but it must be noted that the French included ships building, the English effective vessels :

Guns.	110	100	90	80	74	72	70	64	60	54	50	Smaller.
English .	1	5	13	8	5	0	29	0	39	3	28	112
French .	0	0	0	6	21	1	4	31	2	0	6	32

Seventy-one French ships mounted, therefore, 4790 guns, while 131 English ships mounted 8722 guns, not far from double the French strength.[1]

This was the deplorable weakness of the French at a time when a vast colonial empire was at stake, the prize of naval strength. The extent of that empire is measured by the fact, that not only off the coasts of Canada and among the West Indian Islands, but along the shores of India, thundered the broadsides which gave that empire to England.

After the influence of Louvois overpowered that of Colbert in the councils of the Great Louis, European conquests alone appealed to the absolute Monarch. Under the Regent and the young Louis XV., the policy of the Cardinal-Ministers, Du Bois and Fleury, the one anxious to placate England, the other for peace, was to neglect the navy lest they should alarm and give offence to their only rival in overseas expansion. The consequences of that neglect were to some slight extent enhanced by the personal qualities of Maurepas, from 1723 to 1749, in full control of the navy.[2]

Maurepas knew the necessity to France of a strong navy. His memoir[3] states most ably this necessity. He, as a Minister, was the prototype of her Prime Ministers from his time to the Revolution. They knew that things were wrong, but were incapable of setting them right. A government, like an individual, exhausted by excess, retains insight into what should be done, long after the power to execute has failed. Maurepas accepted the trifle given for the navy and expended it judiciously. He was unwilling by a vigorous protest against a fatal parsimony to imperil the power, the patronage, the perquisites of a splendid position.[4]

---

[1] Entinck, vol. i. p. 119.

[2] St. Simon speaks of "commoners born in the purple" ("Bourgeois porphyrogénètes"). To no family does this expression apply more justly than to the Phelypeaux, Counts of Pontchartrain and Maurepas, who succeeded each other as Secretaries of State from 1610 to 1755 (La Cour-Gayet, p. 86).   [3] Arch. Marine, G⁴.

[4] It is gratifying to quote in support of this view the latest work touching on Maurepas. The Marquis de Ségur, *Au Couchant de la Monarchie*, Paris, 1910, p. 50, says, "Il discernait nettement le bien, il le désirait de bonne foi ; le courage lui manquait pour le réaliser." Jos. Yorke, son of Lord Hardwick, wrote to his brother-in-law Anson from

This great office he lost through an inability to restrain a facile and mordant pen. Its play, directed against Madame de Pompadour, sent him into exile until 1774. Then the accident of a broken spur gave time for palace intrigue to divert the messenger from the road to Machault, at Arnouville. Maurepas, with age added to his other weaknesses, was recalled from his domain of Pontchartrain, to the more splendid position of Prime Minister of Louis XVI.

The lack of the French Navy was in the numbers of ships, not in their quality. The models on which its vessels were built were surpassingly excellent.[1] They were apparently well handled, although one admirable British officer, quoted below, thinks, "our officers are better seamen." The accuracy with which various squadrons joined each other, the greater celerity with which the French fleets crossed the Atlantic as compared with the English against which they were acting, and the remarkable instances of certain voyages show that there must have been some very good navigators among the French commanders of the mid-century. Vauquelin, for example, escaped from Louisbourg on July 15 with his little frigate patched up after the bombardment of the English batteries, and with only sixty men fit for service. He drove her across the Atlantic at such a rate that, after attempting to get into Bayonne, he was able on the 2nd of August to write from St. Andero of the plight of Louisbourg.[2]

"The clever concentration of the French was drawing to a head.[3] All these ships got through, and in remarkably quick time. Boscawen had been more than a month out when they started, and was still struggling with baffling winds somewhere between the Canaries and Bermuda, with seven more weeks before him. Yet Beaussier reached Louisbourg by the end of the month, nearly a fortnight before Boscawen made Halifax. Beaussier actually made the passage (from Brest to Louisbourg) in twenty-four days, April 4 to 28, a feat not consoling to British seamanship. Boscawen made Madeira, the Canaries, the Bermudas, and the Isle of Sable. Rodney took seventy-two days, and Hardy two months."[4]

Drucour, however, acknowledges the superiority of the British in handling vessels in port. After recounting, that there were 33 vessels of war, including frigates, together with 80 or 90 transports, brought into Louisbourg after the capitulation, he goes on, "all these vessels are ranged in an admirable way in this roadstead, where the French last year scarcely found space enough for 25 vessels and frigates."[5]

Warren, an active, capable officer, wrote to his friend and superior, George Anson :

Paris, March 8, 1749 : "The Marine of France don't seem to get up so fast as some people fancied it would, though I believe Msr. de Maurepas does all he can to put it on a good footing again, and he is allowed to be capable, indefategable and to have it much at heart " (B.M. Add. MSS. 15,957, f. 338).

[1] Warren said the *Vigilant*, a sixty-four, was larger than an English eighty (Feb. 14, 1745/6, Ad. Des. 1/480).

[2] Arch. Nat. Marine, B⁴, vol. 80, f. 285.

[3] Corbett, vol. i. p. 168.   [4] Vol. i. p. 316.   [5] Drucour's Journal, Aug. 9, 1758.

" I am greatly pleas'd to hear it has been propos'd with a Prospect of Success to Augment the Number of men, and weight of Metall, in all the different classes of our ships, to putt them upon a Parr with those of the French. When that is the Case, there will no excuse be left for ill behaviour ; and I dare say upon all occasions when no Extraordinary or unforeseen accident shall Intervene, our Ships, and people, will give a good account of their Enemys of equal Force, when and wherever they meet. For I cant help thinking, we have this advantage of them that our Officers are better Seamen than theirs, and I hope as valiant, and our Men in general more Robust, and Stronger, and never were thought to want courage, tho' they have very little virtue of any other kind." [1]

This letter does not convey the impression that Warren felt any overwhelming sense of English superiority, unit for unit, over the French. [2]

His view is borne out by the fact that the French preferred boarding and close combat to cannonading, which implies a confidence in their crews. [3]

These considerations point to the conclusion that, in general, the French lacked in numbers of ships, rather than in the quality of the ships themselves, or their armament, or the way in which they were placed to give the best results. There are many instances of heroic courage. Maisonfort, in the trap in which he allowed himself to be caught, fought the *Vigilant* gallantly against an overwhelming force. In 1755, *L'Espérance*, an old tub, with only 22 guns mounted, fallen behind the fleet of Du Bois de la Motte, on its way back to France, was overtaken by the *Orford*, 70 guns. The Vicomte de Bouville, her commander, twice drove off the English ship. In the third attack the *Orford* was reinforced by the *Buckingham*, also of 70 guns, and the *Espérance* was surrendered in such a state that she had to be sunk, and the *Orford* had to hasten to Plymouth for repairs. Anson and Warren won a great victory over La Jonquière off Cape Finisterre, on May 14, 1747. The French fleet had 384 guns, the English 938, yet so sanguinary was the conflict that nearly 800 were killed on the French ships. [4]

But while disparity in numbers accounts for many English naval victories, it does not affect the conditions at Louisbourg, where twice the superiority was with the French. The efficiency of a navy depends, in a peculiar degree, on the temper and professional attainments of its officers of all ranks, because to all of them, above the subaltern grades, some important degree of independence is left from time to time. It is difficult to picture, for land forces, circumstances

---

[1] Warren to Anson, April 2, 1745, Brit. Mus. Add. MSS. 15,957.

[2] How badly things were managed in the British Navy, only a few years before he wrote, is seen in the opening chapter of Anson's voyage.

[3] " For the reason that M. de Beaussier had determined to board, having a crew superior in numbers and quality to those of the English, who prefer always cannon fire (" la manière de se battre au canon ") to that of boarding, which with them rarely succeeded against the French " (Du Fresne du Motel to Surlaville, *Derniers Jours*, p. 193).

[4] Prévost gives an account of the losses, written from the *Devonshire* entering Plymouth. The staff and garrison of Louisbourg, which had been sent back to France, were being returned to Canada on La Jonquière's fleet.

in which so young an officer as the officer of the watch, on a battleship, would have dependent on his immediate action the safety of so many men, the preservation of so potent an engine of war.   The work of a Foreign Secretary is hampered to the slightest degree by the mediocrity of his clerks ; so it is with other Departments of State.   But in a fleet, until new orders are received, the captain is in absolute command of his ship.   General orders are of necessity vague in many points, so that even to the commander of the smallest vessel there is left scope for their interpretation, a chance for initiative, and in unforeseen contingencies, nowhere more likely to arise than on the sea, opportunities for independent action.   It is on account of the scope the necessities of the service give them, that in a navy the *moral* of its officers of all grades, and the standards of performance to which they are held by their superiors, are of the most vital importance.   We have to look into the internal administration of the French Navy, and the effect on its personnel of that administration, to find explanations of conditions fully accounted for neither by numerical inferiority nor the character of the unit.

One of these explanations is closely connected, however, with relative strength of opposing navies.   The most serious consequence of inferiority was not the difficulties it created for the staff trying to dispose of it to the best advantage, but its effect on the sea officers.   This can be illustrated from the world of business.   The merchant, with abundant capital which is constantly earning ample profits, will take more risks than any competitor other than one who is on the verge of bankruptcy, ready to risk all on a desperate venture. England was in the position of the former.   France was not yet in the straits of the bankrupt.   Her naval policy was similar to that of the man who fears bankruptcy and struggles to avoid it by husbanding resources, the inadequacy of which he clearly recognizes.   Instructions, even when relations with England were strained, were pacific, to avoid the enemy's ships, and not to fight unless required by the honour of the flag.   Thus, the native hue of resolution in her commanders seems often sicklied o'er by the thought that imperilling his ships was of vastly more consequence to his service than a similar risk in the enemy's fleet.   To be exact, this consequence to the French, in 1755, was as one to one hundred and three ; to the English, as one to two hundred and forty-three. Clear proof that great gains were probable, would condone a miscarriage in the view of superiors with the ampler resources at their disposal.   The relative weakness of the French sea forces, therefore, not only dictated a cautious policy to its staff, but benumbed the energy of those who were carrying it out.   From this point of view, the prudent course for the French captain was to preserve his ship, for the English to risk his with any fair prospect of success.

The cautious temper which these inadequate resources would induce, was confirmed and heightened by the ineffective discipline of the French Navy. Those amiable qualities of Maurepas, which preserved for him, throughout his exile, a host of friends, made him a poor head for such a service as a navy. His ordinary attitude, however disappointing might be the result, was that the officer had presumably done his best. There are many bulky folio volumes,[1] dealing with the personnel of the French Navy, covering his administration and those of his ephemeral successors. They give the origin and the family connections of the officers and notes on their character. It is the rarest thing to find in these records any evidence of discipline for ineffectiveness.

Maisonfort was never given a sea command after his error contributed so largely to the fall of Louisbourg in 1745. He, however, received pensions in due course, which could not greatly "encourager les autres."[2] The two commanders who failed to support Beaussier de l'Isle were acquitted by an easy board of inquiry,[3] aided by the magnanimity of Beaussier. One of them forthwith committed suicide; the other not only retained his position, but was promoted to the command of a larger ship, which was sunk with all her crew at Quiberon.

The most striking instance of accepting a poor performance when opportunities were given for an effective one, was in the case of Du Bois de la Motte. A skilful junction of three squadrons at Louisbourg, which there came under his flag, gave him command of a fine fleet. He passed the summer in making defensive works, while the inferior fleet of Holburne blockaded the port. A tempest in September, which did little damage to his ships, so shattered the enemy's fleet that it was a fine feat of seamanship, even after refitting at Halifax, to bring it home across the Atlantic. Du Bois, instead of issuing out and crushing Holburne, remained inactive in Louisbourg. His instructions were reasonably explicit. After recounting the forces to be placed at his disposal, the document goes on :

"His Majesty has chosen the Count Dubois de la Motte to take command of all these vessels and frigates, and the proofs he has given at all times of his zeal, of his skill and of his experience, makes His Majesty hope that he will fill to his satisfaction this high office, which is one of the most important which can arise in the navy in the present war.

"Its purpose is to foil (faire échouer) the projects which the enemy have made against Louisbourg or Quebec, and perhaps even against both projects for the execution of which they have made efforts which they will not likely be in a state to repeat if they do not succeed this year. . . . If the junction of the men of war of His Majesty can be made at Louisbourg, there is ground for believing not only that the enemy will not venture to undertake anything against Louisbourg or Quebec, but even that Count Dubois de

---

[1] Marine, C¹.   [2] Arch. Nat. Marine, C¹, vol. 167.
[3] It was headed by the Cte. du Guay, who was the mouthpiece for the noble officers in their protest the next year against the promotion of "officiers bleus" (La C.-G. p. 225).

la Motte will find himself able to attack *them with advantage.* . . . His first object must be to assure the safety of the places which the enemy may wish to attack or threaten. . . . He can render a great service without question if he can prevent them succeeding in their projects by making useless their efforts. Not only the best means of securing the failure of their plans *will be to destroy their fleet and transports,* but the advantages of an engagement (combat) will be moreover of great importance for the glory of His Majesty's arms, for the honour of His Navy, and for promoting a peace. . . . With such forces he should have superiority over the enemies. Every reason makes His Majesty wish that he (Du Bois) should profit by his superiority."

So far, these instructions show a grasp of the conditions and their possibilities. They are so stated as to be stimulating to an officer eager to distinguish himself, or even adequately to carry out his orders, but they go on as follows :

" His Majesty, however, does not positively order him to attack the enemy. Assured as is His Majesty of his zeal, his valour and his prudence, His Majesty can only refer in this manner to what he believes ought to be done in this regard, *without too greatly risking the forces committed to his care, the safe keeping of which so vitally affects the Navy.*" [1]

Here is the loophole for the cautious, so commonly was it taken advantage of, that Du Bois returned home feeling that he had done well. He asked that he should be given the baton of a Marshal of France, or appointed Vice-Admiral of France. The first seemed too great a step. There were difficulties in the way of the second, but he was given a pension of 12,000 l. until he was made Vice-Admiral, which grade he reached in 1762. [2] While he accomplished the principal purposes of the expedition, the failure to do his utmost again suggests, in the effect on the service, a comparison with Byng. [3]

The chance which Du Bois de la Motte let slip seemed in England one fraught with the greatest possibilities—

". . . but it seems much to be feared that the French may have come out of Louisbourg, and picked up our almost wrecked ships. . . . Such is the lamentable end of that more boasted than well planned, and as ill-conducted as unfortunate American Expedition, which was to have restored this country ; and here I suppose concludes all the schemes, if there were any, upon which part of this fleet was ordered to winter in America. God grant us a tolerable peace if possible before we are more undone, for *to go on* is sure not possible" (Brit. Mus. Add. MSS. 35,376, f. 143. This letter was written from the Admiralty, Oct. 31, 1757).

These are not the views of an irresponsible pamphleteer or a re-echoing of the opposition to the Government. They were written by Lady Anson, wife of the First Lord of the Admiralty, daughter of Lord Hardwicke, the Vice-Chancellor, than whom no one could be closer to the Ministry.

---

[1] Arch. Marine, B⁴, vol. 76.   No italics in the original.   [2] Arch. Nat. Marine, B⁴ and C¹, 165, 166.
[3] The sweeping condemnation of Admiral Matthews and his captains in 1744 is an earlier example of the severity in the English service.

In justice to Du Bois de la Motte, it should be said that his force was seriously weakened by sickness; on his return to Brest, November 23, he disembarked 4000 sick, which spread typhus and scurvy in the town, so that not only the crew died, but over 10,000 of the inhabitants of the seaport were victims of the contagion which his squadron brought back.[1] The *Inflexible* states that 2000 sailors died, and that they brought back more than 2400 sick.[2] Du Revest, commander of the *Hector*, died at Brest, December 31.[3]

Des Gouttes again lost a chance for a dashing exploit. He, with his command of six ships of the line and frigates, was blockaded in Louisbourg by Boscawen's twenty-two ships of the line. Unless they all could escape through the blockade, a most improbable performance, they were bound, as the event proved, to be "burnt, sunk, or destroyed." Loss being thus most probable, there was little additional risk in taking an active course. When an easterly gale sprang up on the 5th of June it found Boscawen's principal ships either dispersed or at anchor well down in Gabarus Bay, that is on the lee shore, and encumbered by scores of transports mostly to windward of them. The possibilities of the situation are stated by an eye-witness:

"It is well to note that if the commander of the squadron which is in our port had wished he might have immortalised himself, but that glory which is gained by danger to life is not that which this officer seeks. He has proved this in many circumstances. The hostile fleet was well down, as I have said, in the bay, by winds favourable to him (Des Gouttes), and by a fog, which would have hidden his movements from the enemy, he might have driven in to the fleet and with his six vessels destroyed it entirely. The worst would have been to lose his ships. . . . They could have beached them and saved themselves on shore under the fire of our entrenchments. This manœuvre was easy. I have heard it said by sea officers, M. de Brunion (Brugnon), a man whose zeal equals his capacity, wished to do this with his ship, the *Bizarre*. They gave to his project the name of the vessel he commanded, and the commander . . . looked on what he did not dare to undertake, as an ill-considered and impossible project."[4]

The bitterness of Poilly is surpassed by that of another writer, an officer of the garrison, on the events discreditable to the navy, in the later days of the siege. He to disguise his identity wrote his version in capitals, but, as it is preserved among official documents,[5] it must have fallen under the eyes of those in authority. There was no question of the naval commanders having "risked their heads."[6] Des Gouttes continued in the service unscathed, and retired from it in 1764 with high rank of (Chef d'Escadre) Rear-Admiral.

These instances show that no high standard of performance was demanded from officers, not only under Maurepas, but his transient successors. Equally

[1] La Cour-Gayet, p. 360.   [2] *Canadian Archives*, 1906.
[3] *Etat sommaire*, p. 178.   [4] Poilly.
[5] Arch. Nat. Marine, B⁴, vol. 80, f. 82.   [6] This officer is quoted in Chap. XIV. pp. 274 and 284.

one fails to find the converse of this, recognition and reward of brilliant and effective services. The records show for the most part a series of jogging, monotonous advancements from step to step, appointments given by seniority rather than capacity. It was not until Choiseul took charge of the French Navy, that some degree of the same life reanimated a dormant and discouraged service which Pitt instilled earlier into the forces of England.

Seniority counted for too much. Meschin,[1] on whose action hung, in 1744, the fate of Acadia, had commanded the *Semslack*, from which the first settlers of Isle Royale landed in 1713. Du Bois de la Motte[2] was an excellent officer. The disposition of his ships on the voyage and in Louisbourg seems to a layman admirable, but he was seventy-four. A Schomberg, whose leadership at eighty inspired confidence in a nation, is the rarest of commanders. Retirement at a ripe age with a pension was sure of attainment to any one who did not disgrace himself. The incentive of prompt reward was lacking. Boscawen inquired, when he landed, about Vauquelin. When he heard that it was the captain of a little frigate who had handled his vessel so brilliantly, he said that if Vauquelin were in his command he would recommend him for captain of a ship of the line. It would have been difficult for the French officers to whom he said it to find a similar instance in their own service. His remark might well have been made in the presence of one of his own captains, whose recent promotion was a proof that Boscawen's disposition was that of the Lords of the Admiralty.

On the New Year's Day, 1758, the *Adventure*, Captain Bray, lay at anchor in Dungeness Roads, and saw a snow reach in. They engaged. By good seamanship and great personal bravery, Captain Bray and his pilot passed his mizzen topsail sheet and a hawser round the Frenchman's bow-sprit and made it fast to his capstan, and then after an hour's sharp fighting, the privateer, hailing from Dunkirk, surrendered. Before the January number of the *Grand Magazine* had gone to press it was able to announce that from the fifth rate, *Adventure*, 44 guns and 250 men, Bray had been promoted to the third rate, *Princess Amelia*, 64 guns and 600 men, in which he joined Boscawen's fleet. The capture of a privateer mounting 14 nine-pounders by a ship of 44 guns was insignificant. The great reward was given for good seamanship and personal courage.[3]

---

[1] He entered the service in 1683, and completed in all fifty-nine years.

[2] Entered the service in 1698. He had, therefore, served fifty-nine years when he was placed in command of this fleet.

[3] Four promotions were made in Louisbourg in consequence of the boat expedition. Balfour was given command of the *Bienfaisant*, which was repaired and sent to England; Laforey was made captain of the *Echo*. Affleck and Bickerton, senior lieutenants of the *Namur*, took command of the *Ætna* and *Hunter*, vacated by these promotions (Boscawen to Pitt, July 28, 1758). In 1745 also, Douglas, who, in command of the *Mermaid*, had been instrumental in the capture of the *Vigilant*, was promoted to her immediately after he towed her safely to Gabarus.

Another characteristic of the French service, which one naturally contrasts with the system of its rival, was that the former was aristocratic. The young noble who entered as garde-marine was clothed in scarlet and gold lace. He found himself not only among his social equals, but in very many cases among his kinsmen, or others of naval families allied in the service to his own. In his list of the fleet sent out to America in 1757, La Cour-Gayet[1] gives biographical details of the twenty captains. Twelve belonged to naval families. The influence of these social conditions would tend to give a high sense of personal dignity insistent on personal rights ; to some extent, a feeling of superiority to drudgery, and hostility, or at least coldness to the outsider among them,[2] and, it is not to be doubted, the disadvantages as well as the extraordinary advantages which one naturally looks for in a body of men united not only by *esprit de corps*, but by social equality and the ties of blood.

There were, owing to relaxation of the conditions as to noble birth, some officers who were from a lower social stratum. They were not well received in the service. Beaussier de l'Isle was a son of the Port Captain of Toulon, and it was hinted that his supporting captains hung back in the engagement already referred to, to embarrass and discredit one who was an outsider in their own service. He rose to a high rank in the service (Chef d'Escadre), but the *officiers bleus*, who came in from outside, rarely were as fortunate. Vauquelin, a ship-master of Dieppe, whose services, not only at Louisbourg but at Quebec, were so extraordinarily brilliant, never rose to a higher command than that of a king's freight-ship (*flûte*), although he remained in the service until 1772.[3]

Rosier was said to be the son of an important merchant of Bordeaux. The brilliant defence which will shortly be recounted, gained for him a lieutenancy, and after some years the rank of a captain of a fire-ship, which seemed to be the highest rank he reached before his death in 1769.

The relations between Anson, one of the most brilliant and distinguished naval men of his time, and Warren, whose social origin was relatively humble, were probably not exceptional in the English service. I have found in French documents no evidence that it would have been possible in that service for an

---

[1] P. 508.

[2] " It is incredible the magnificence of the table on board the French men-of-war, served with all the elegance that it is possible to do on land, which the captains of English vessels would never be able to imitate, for as soon as they receive orders to sail with the first favourable wind, of which they render an account to the Admiralty, which they do daily in all the ports of England, they are not allowed to remain longer, as the French ships are obliged to do, sometimes during three weeks, to wait for provisions on the table ; and the English captains are often sufficiently unfortunate as to be obliged to content themselves with salt beef and bacon like the sailors, with this difference, that the captains have the choice of the pieces. It is true that the Commissioners of the Admiralty take great care that the provisions of the ships should be of good quality, well-conditioned and in good case " (*Memoirs of the Chevalier Johnstone*, vol. ii. p. 174, note). The gossip of the New England camp had it that Maisonfort's service of plate was worth £5000.

[3] Arch. Nat. Marine, C¹, vol. 174, f. 1656.

officer of Warren's origin to write to his superior as freely as Warren wrote to
Anson ten days before their crowning victory over La Jonquière.

"*April* 23, 1747.

" Dear Sir : I am glad you have alter'd your Line of Battle for I observed it as you did
yesterday weak in the Center, where tis most probable ye Enemy (should wee be so happy
to meet them) will be strongest.   You see Sir how necessary 'tis to Exercise fleet.   'Tis
pretty difficult to keep a good Line close by the Wind—and I think when you next
please to Exercise the Fleet in separate Divisions, and a Breast, The Lines should be
form'd at a distance one Division to windward of the others as you shall judge proper, and
the Windward one, to go down on the Leeward, in order of Battle, so near as you wou'd
have them Engage an Enemy you'l pardon my taking this Lyberty." [1]

The momentous consequence to the French Navy of this difficulty of
entrance to others than those to the manner born, was that it lost the services
of many who had a taste for the sea, a capacity for command, and a desire to
serve in the fleets of their country.   Scores of men rose to high rank in the
English service who entered it as ordinary seamen or as volunteers.   This was
the case of Warren, and of many others.   The flag of an admiral was in the
kit-bag of the English sailor, generations earlier than the staff of a marshal was
placed, by Napoleon, in the knapsack of the French soldier.   The tradition in
one English family is, that the talk of an admiral, who, through the breaking
down of his carriage, took shelter in a clergyman's house, led the two sons to
run away to sea.   Two peerages ultimately rewarded the success of their careers. [2]
There is found an explanation of the prodigious exploits of French privateers [3]
during this period, in what well may be a fact, that many of them were
commanded by men who, had the fleets of France been as open as those of
England, would have fought on her King's ships as valiantly as they made
conquests of the British mercantile marine.   The magazines of the period give
lists of captures on both sides, and the bravery of the privateersmen and the
commanders of armed merchantmen, the skill with which they handled their
vessels, show the large numbers of men who might have been available for
service in the French Navy, had that service been made attractive to them.

The following is the narrative of a voyage printed in full, as a condensation
cannot give, as well as the main actor's own words, the impression of capacity,
modesty, and courage it conveys.

" Narrative of the engagement between the *Robuste* of Bordeaux, Captain Jean Joseph
Rosier, freighted by the King for Quebec, and armed with 6 eight-pounders and 18 six-

[1] B.M. Add. MSS. 15,957, f. 172.

[2] The captain of the *Jamaica*, whose skilful manœuvres in search of information off Louisbourg harbour are
recounted, was one of these boys (Ad. Des. 1/481).

[3] The privateer *Machault*, which Bray captured, apparently did not hesitate to engage a man-of-war of 44 guns.
The latter only avoided being raked by very skilful manœuvring.

pounders, with a crew all told of 77, and 150 soldiers of the regiment of Volontaires Étrangers, and an English frigate of 30 guns in a tier and a half ('dans une batterie et demie').

"The 13th April 1757, on my voyage towards Quebec, in latitude 44° 55', and longitude (of Paris) 5' 35", at daybreak I saw a vessel on my lee, pointing northwards, the wind W.N.W., carrying her four principal sails, her mizzen and mizzen-top sails without topgallant masts.

"She changed her course to my wake and gave chase. I set her down as a merchantman obliged to approach in tacking. Her greater speed gave her the advantage of coming at noon as near as the gunshot of a twelve-pounder. I then watched her and saw she was a frigate with a tier and a half of guns, crowded with people, and extraordinarily high out of water. Not being able to withdraw, and thinking it useless to parley, I clewed up my lower sails to wait for him. When he stood across my course, I showed him my colours, and, as customary, fired a shot. He broke out his, with all his broadside. Then the engagement began and was most sanguinary, always side by side up to 7 o'clock, when our common disorder compelled us to draw off to set things to rights. I had my main and main top-sail yards broken, my mizzen and fore top-sail yards brought down, all my sails in tatters and useless. I had in this attack 18 instantly killed and 42 wounded, several mortally, and several cannon-shot ('à fleur d'eau') between wind and water.

"Our plight seemed so sorry that after making an inspection of my ship I decided, with my staff, that we should turn back on account of the impossibility of making repairs at sea. In consequence I set my course for Perthuis, or the River of Bordeaux ; the wind being favourable, I proceeded all day and the next night under easy sail.

"About noon on the 15th my look-out saw a vessel about four leagues to leeward, which was manœuvring to come up with me. My few sails did not permit me to avoid him ; he was within a long cannon-shot at 6 o'clock in the evening. He showed a white flag and fired a shot ; not perceiving that he showed any special sign of need, I kept on my course. I took his bearings at sunset, and thought he was in my wake, and the flares and rockets which he was throwing out made me think he was in chase. At nine he was within earshot, and hailed me. I answered him. He said to me in a compassionate tone, 'Poor prisoner, I advise you to strike and not to make any resistance ; I will give you good terms.' His exhortation was followed by his broadside in my stern, where I was exposed, his sails giving him this advantage over me. In consequence I handled my ship so that it was broadside to him. Then the battle became general from stem to stern, and was more savage though less fatal than the former one. I had in this attack, which finished at one o'clock in the morning, my main and mizzen top-masts smashed, and my sails more destroyed than the former ones, 5 men killed and 11 wounded. My adversary, drawing off, favoured me in making repairs, which I did at once. I refitted my mizzen and foretop-gallant yards, these being the only ones I could trim to keep on my course, which I did.

"At daybreak my enemy, which had watched me all night, manœuvred to rejoin me, which he accomplished at 11 o'clock. I recognized him as the same frigate with which I had my first affair. I counted his guns, which were fifteen on each side, and some of my officers assured me that they had seen cannon on his forecastle and quarter-decks. The engagement began anew and did not stop until 6 o'clock, when he hailed and I answered. He said to me, 'Yield, gentlemen, yield, you will be treated as you deserve. We will give you good terms. We are a frigate of the English King's, so be undisturbed.' Thereupon he hoisted a square flag at his foretop. I answered, not being able to hoist a square flag like him, as I had no mast standing, that I was flattered to have intercourse with my equals, that I had still powder and shot, that I regretted extremely that I had no canvas to show him a course contrary which he would compel me to take, and, moreover, that he had only now to do his duty, and I would keep on doing mine. I gave him three Vive le Roi, my broadside of guns and musketry, at which we kept steadily until half-past seven. My enemy, as crippled as I was, was pumping out water at all his scuppers and steered with galley sweeps. I gathered that his rudder was useless, and at the same moment discovered that mine was also damaged. I had it repaired at once. In vain then would either have yielded to the other. Our condition allowed us only to think of ourselves. The night which followed put us out of sight of each other.

"I worked hard to effect repairs. At daybreak I saw a ship ahead coming toward us. We came together at ten, and I made him out as a privateer of 16 guns and several swivels, with a large crew. He began the fight, but drew off at the end of an hour, setting his lower sails and making a following wind, satisfied with our response and our gunnery. In these two last attacks we had 3 killed and 8 wounded. At noon I sighted the land at Oleron. At eight that evening I cast anchor a league from Chassiron.

"My situation is most pitiable. I have standing my mizzen, and that without its top-mast, and my bowsprit, not a working bit of rigging from stem to stern. At least fifty shot above the water-line and a prodigious number in the hull. I think that on one side and the other there were fired 3000 shot, and we fired 15,000 rounds of musketry, which I have verified by counting the remaining cartridges. I have had 29 soldiers and seamen killed and 61 wounded.

"M. Diaparraguerre, my chief officer, received a ball in the right thigh in the first fight and is dangerously wounded. This accident greatly alarmed me, knowing his worth.

"M. Charriolle et Du Salier, my two lieutenants, bore themselves with all imaginable bravery. The latter, who was wounded in the right shoulder in the first fight, was found faithfully at his post in the three following, and behaved himself with distinction. M. Bière, second lieutenant, was also wounded in the first fight in the right thigh, and is unfit for service.

"MM. the officers of my passengers, the Volontaires Étrangers, distinguished themselves. In particular M. de St. Rome, the Captain, who threw into the sea a fire-pot, which fell into the midst of twenty men, and never ceased rallying his men, and by his worthy example making their volleys effective.

"M. de Gagnereau, his lieutenant, does not merit less praise, and although wounded by a splinter in the arm, was always at his post.

"M. de Coussade, whom the Court had sent as a passenger, has died from his wounds. He bore himself with distinction.

"The soldiers, slack at first, afterwards displayed an intrepid bravery, and I know not how to give them praise enough.

"I was also excited to make a most vigorous defence, not being ignorant of the importance of my cargo to the King's service. ROSIER."[1]

The sense of responsibility for a few hundred tons of stores for Quebec which animated so desperate a defence, indicated a temper of mind which would not be uncommon among such men. The vividness of impressions of one in a novel position enhances greatly the sense of the importance of its duties. The incident gives rise to the thought that had the resources of Des Gouttes been at the disposal of Vauquelin, Rosier, or Brugnon, there would have been found at Louisbourg as many of the militant righteous as would have saved the city.

In support of this view it may be pointed out that there was not a great difference in motive between the privateersmen and the merchant captain on the one hand, and the naval officer on the other, in times when every merchantman was armed, when regulations regarding naval prize money and letters of marque were issued at the beginning of every war. Prize money was an important factor in the career of the naval officer, while the privateer was not devoid of patriotism. In a crucial case, the former would be expected to sacrifice gain for the honour of the flag, a lower standard would suffice for the man whose voyage was primarily for booty. The order of the motives might, however, be reversed, without necessarily any material change in their normal power. The richness of the fleets of the French East India Company, the extent of French commerce revealed in the War of the Austrian Succession, whetted the appetite of the British naval officer. Warren, a portionless Irish lad, through his captures on his long term on the North American station and at Louisbourg, had the reputation of being very rich.[2] There are many

---

[1] Arch. Nat. Marine, B⁴, vol. 76, f. 377. Guebriant, Intendant at Bordeaux, transmitted this account to the Minister with his approval, and recommended a bonus to them all, as they had lost everything.

This account is so interesting, and displays on the part of this French merchant captain such a vigorous fighting quality, not always found in commanders of the King's ships, that a search has been made for a verification of his statements. A search through the Admirals' list-book showed that no frigate of the size of his adversary was in a position to have taken part in this fight, nor were there any sidelights found in the Admiralty papers, nor did the best of current news, namely, the Magazines or the *London Gazette*, give any trace of this encounter. The *London Chronicle*, however, prints the following account, which shows that the vessel with which the *Robuste* was engaged was an English privateer :

"*Bristol, May 7th.*—By a letter received from an officer on board the *Cæsar* privateer, brought by a Spanish vessel arrived at Plymouth, we have an account that besides taking two prizes (viz. the *Black Prince* from Bordeaux for Cape Breton, a snow of about 180 tons, laden with 1200 barrels of flour, 25 tuns of wine, etc., and the *Jolie Pontac*, of about 120 tons, bound from Bordeaux to Mississippi, laden with flour and wine) they had an engagement with a French frigate of 36 guns, the 13th, 15th, and 16th ult., which was very obstinate and continued seven hours the last day ; and when the *Cæsar* left her she looked like a wreck, having lost all her masts and rigging. The *Cæsar* had but a corporal of the marines killed and 22 men wounded. During the engagement she fired 8000 musket and 700 cannon shot, besides an incredible number of Largin and Partridge shot, and three 30 Hand Grandes (?) out of the tops, which did great execution. This account was dated April 25th, in Lat. 45,00, Long. 4,50, at which time the *Cæsar* was in sight of two sail to windward, supposed to be part of a fleet from Bordeaux, two of them of 30 guns each, 9 and 12 pounders, which she had seen for seven days, and hoped to meet with some English Men of War or Privateers to assist her."

[2] His correspondence with Anson refers more than once to the investment of his prize money. It may be noted

fair mansions built, with some remote suggestion of a flagship in their architecture, by retired and enriched naval commanders. The dignity of more than one peerage is maintained by the investment of the prize money of those on whom they were conferred for naval victories. These possibilities were ever present to the naval commander. Warren proved his zeal in not murmuring in leaving the rich hunting-grounds of the West Indies for the barren seas off Isle Royale.[1]   When Boscawen was in the fogs off Newfoundland, uncertain of his position, he writes to his wife :

"I own I was in hopes never to have seen America again, but now I earnestly wish for it, not but that I think of home, and for amusement this morning, drawn a house after Lady Essex's plan, sure I am you will like it, and if we have a war, it is hard if I dont get enough to build and maintain it."[2]

Land officers were interested in privateering. General Whitmore had a privateer schooner, while Governor of Louisbourg.[3]

There were other examples, differing from these, in which the desire for prize money was pushed to undue lengths. West Indian merchants complained that men-of-war captured in the old war French and Spanish merchantmen, instead of ridding those seas of the many privateers which were destroying English commerce. A more striking instance was that of Rodney, who was bringing out Amherst to the armament which was awaiting him at Halifax. Rodney lost over a fortnight in securing a very rich prize he made off Brest.[4] Such keenness led to a lack of decency in carrying out captures. The officers of the *Alcide* and *Lys* complained bitterly of being ill treated, and robbed of personal effects.[5]

Don Antonio d'Ulloa, a Spanish scientist, had the misfortune to be a passenger on the *Notre Dame de la Déliverance*, when she was captured in

---

that he wrote to Anson in 1747 (19th May), saying that if an accident befell him he must "leave his wife and pretty Babes to the mercy of his King and Country," as his private affairs were very unsettled (B.M. Add. MSS. 15,957).

[1] "I cou'd have pitch'd upon none attended with a prospect of greater uneasyness, and less personal advantage, I mean where Booty is esteem'd so, which I hope will never be so with me" (Warren to Anson, April 2, 1745, B.M. Add. MSS. 15,957, f. 152).

[2] *Torbav* at sea, May 25, 1755, Falmouth papers. Boscawen's tombstone states that he

DIED OF A FEVER
ON THE 10TH OF JANUARY IN THE YEAR 1761,
THE 50TH OF HIS AGE,
AT HATCHLANDS PARK, IN SURREY,
A SEAT HE HAD JUST FINISHED AT THE
EXPENSE OF THE ENEMIES OF HIS COUNTRY.   Etc.

[3] Clough's Jl. 11 Oct. 1759.

[4] "Considering that he was engaged in the special duty of carrying to the seat of war the belated commander-in-chief of the main operation of the campaign, the incident will hardly commend itself as a precedent to modern judgment" (Corbett, vol. 1, p. 315).   [5] Arch. Nat. Marine, B⁴, vol. 68, f. 267, and Pichon MSS., Halifax.

1745 off Louisbourg. He says that they were stripped naked before the crew, from apprentice to Captain, and searched in the most humiliating manner possible, so that not a penny might escape, and most astonishing of all, that in this search the English captains themselves took a foremost part. It was obviously professional, for one of these captains turned over to the Spaniards for their use a house in Louisbourg, of which he had taken possession and did not require, as he remained on board his ship.[1]

The French naval officer also knew the charm of prize money and of gain. The documents the writer has searched deal little with their success. It was far less than the English. The motive, however, seems as potent, and the official encouragement in prize money was as great. A contemporary attributes the lack of zeal among them to three causes : they remain too long idle in port, they look to their profession as a means of enriching themselves, and often their share of goods for trade (*la petite pacotille*) which they have on board is their only fortune.[2]

These explanations, illustrated for the sake of local colour, with incidents connected with Isle Royale, may be summarised in saying that a neglected service[3] was opposed to one high in favour with its court and country. One which was starved in money, men and equipment, had to meet in conflict another on which were lavished the resources of a country constantly growing in wealth. The commanders of one were drawn from a single class, of the other, from a whole nation. Officers, whose experience led them to expect defeat, were opposed to others flushed with victory, or desirous of emulating the exploits of their colleagues ; those knowing that neither victory nor defeat made a vital difference in their careers ; these, assured of all the rewards of success, speedy professional advancement, rank, wealth and glory.

That period during which Louisbourg existed covers, save for a score of earlier years, that in which these striking changes in the two services were brought about. Up to a certain point the strength and morale of the French navy, if not superior, was at least not inferior to that of England. Her colonies, and still more, the vast territories brought under her sphere of influence by the energy and intrepidity of her explorers, was the vastest the

---

[1] D'Ulloa, *Voyage Historique*, vol. 2, book 111, p. 116.

[2] Surlaville, *Derniers Jours*, p. 273. All commerce was forbidden to officers of the Navy, 13 March 1717, Isambart Recueuil, xxi. p. 139.

There were rumours afloat not only in Isle Royale, but also in France, that Vauquelin had carried in his *Aréthuse* a valuable cargo when he escaped from Louisbourg. One of the New England carpenters, Knap, says it was thought "she had much Riches on board." This was the gossip of a camp. The Minister wrote to Vauquelin (October 26, B, vol. 108), asking him if he brought any cargo and for whom, which would point to some suspicion that this might be the case. I have not found Vauquelin's reply. The implication seems to be that he was acting for some one else. An "officer bleu" would be careful to obey the regulations.

[3] The *Almanach Royal* gives a little more than a page to the Navy.

world had ever seen. The advantages to France of this Colonial Empire were enormous. It was not until after that Empire was broken up that the growth of her maritime commerce ceased to compare favourably with that of the greatest of her rivals. The turning point seems to have been reached in 1692, when at the end of May the combined fleets of England and Holland in overwhelming force destroyed the fleet of Tourville at La Hogue. The exiled James saw in it only another disappointment; the English ministry, a proof that their fleet could be depended on ; the English people, a passing of the fear of invasion. Louis XIV., at the height of his glory, with the inviolate fortress of Namur at his feet, saw in this naval disaster only " the burning of a few ships." The perspective of time enables us to see that from it, and the subsequent neglect of the French Navy, ensued consequences, which were not written on the page of history until the signing of the Treaty of Paris in 1763. The revival of France's navy about this time, and the essential aid it gave to the revolted colonies of America, led to a loss to England, which seemed for generations greater, as far as America is concerned, than that of Canada, and proves how an earlier revival might have avoided disaster to France.

Facile generalisations about the special aptitudes of one people for successful colonisation, and pre-eminence in the arts which are based on sea-faring, do not bear examination. History shows that such pre-eminence passed in distant centuries from one people to another about the shores of the Mediterranean. An Italian town, now without sea trade, once gave to the world a code of maritime law based on the practice of its merchant adventurers. Spain and Portugal were each in their turn foremost. Later, at a time when exploration for England was most successfully conducted by foreigners hired by her Tudor monarchs, native-born Frenchmen were establishing for their kings claims to the possession of vast and fertile spaces. Holland once stood in the forefront in maritime adventure. For a long time England has held this position, but it is to be remembered that, three score years since, the marine of her most splendid offshoot, the American Union, was, in quality at least, becoming the most formidable of her rivals. If more northern nations may not succeed England in the front rank it is for reasons which were understood close on two centuries ago. These periods of expansion have been for each people most glorious and fruitful. Conquering on the sea, and the struggle with its dangers, have always produced an energy and a breadth of outlook which have invigorated every activity of the corporate life of these nations. If one would seek light for the future from the lessons of the past, it is found in the page of La Cour-Gayet on which he says, the imperial crown of overseas possessions rests on three supports—colonies, a mercantile marine, and an adequate navy. The history of all ages makes clear that the latter cannot be neglected.

It was not through ignorance of the supremacy of sea power that France fell from her pre-eminence as a colonial power. Maurepas shows a firm grasp of this doctrine. Even Desenclaves, a priest in Acadia, implies a knowledge of it in writing ; "What good is Louisbourg? It would be good if France were as strong at sea as England." A Monsieur Du Plestay wrote in 1759 :

"France under Henri IV. and since has had no other object in its wars than to lessen the power of the House of Austria, which it suspected of aspiring to a universal monarchy. We have nothing more to fear on that side, but we are about to suffer the same disadvantage (on va tomber dans le même inconvénient) in allowing England to usurp the sovereignty of the sea, which is at least as dangerous as the other, in this respect, that she increases her riches and prevents France enjoying hers, as you prove in the present war, and with her money produced by commerce, she excites against you enemies on land, who put it out of your power to use against them the resources, which otherwise ought to have been the case " (I.R. vol. 38).

Indeed, the doctrine was never more succinctly stated than by a French poet of the period :

"Le trident de Neptune, c'est le sceptre du Monde."

INDEX

EDITOR'S NOTE

It is regretted that some of the entries in the index refer to appendices printed in the first edition; these have unfortunately had to be omitted from this new edition and the Editor apologizes for any inconvenience this may cause readers.

INDEX

INDEX

THE END